Radon's Deadly Daughters

Radon's Deadly Daughters

Science, Environmental Policy, and the Politics of Risk

Michael R. Edelstein
and
William J. Makofske

ROWMAN & LITTLEFIELD PUBLISHERS, INC.
Lanham • Boulder • New York • London

ROWMAN & LITTLEFIELD PUBLISHERS, INC.

Published in the United States of America
by Rowman & Littlefield Publishers, Inc.
4720 Boston Way, Lanham, Maryland 20706

12 Hid's Copse Road
Cumnor Hill, Oxford OX2 9JJ, England

British Cataloging in Publication Information Available

Library of Congress Cataloging-in-Publication Data

Edelstein, Michael R.
    Radon's deadly daughters :   science, environmental policy, and the politics of
risk / Michael R. Edelstein and William J. Makofske.
      P.   cm.
    Includes Bibliographical references and index.
    ISBN 0-8476-8333-8 (cloth: alk. paper). — ISBN 0-8476-8334-6
(pbk.: alk. paper)
      1. Atmospheric radon—Government poicy—United States.   2. Environmental
policy—United States.   I. Makofske, William J.   II. Title.
QC913.2.R3E35 1998   96-35148
363.17'99—dc20   CIP

ISBN 0–8476–8333–8 (cloth : alk. paper)
ISBN 0–8476–8334–6 (pbk. : alk. paper)

Printed in the United States of America

⊖™ The paper used in this publication meets the minimum requirements of American
National Standard for Information Sciences—Permanence of Paper for Printed Library
Materials, ANSI Z39.48—I984.

To the memory of our parents:
Nathan M. and Evelyn Edelstein
Harold A. and Amelia Makofske

Edelstein and Makofske, *Radon's Deadly Daughters* — Errata

Page x: *caption 9.6 should read:*
Selected messages from the 1986 *Citizen's Guide to Radon*

caption 9.7 should read:
Key risk communications findings

caption 9.8 should read:
Risk from radon compared to commonly feared risks

Page 3: *first paragraph, last two sentences, should read:*
She trusted his judgment; Stanley purchased the house and moved in.
His wife and sons, including a newborn, followed shortly.

Page 17: *second paragraph, line 1, should read:*
Kay's later ability to regain control was directly related to her success
as an activist

Page 37: *line 4 should read:*
the fuel cycle, both mining and extraction of uranium ores and

Page 115: *note 1 should read:*
1. Figure 5.2 shows the lognormal findings of both the LBL study
(in white) and the Cohen study (in black). For values less than 8 pCi/l,
the studies are identical. Differences appear for values greater than
8 pCi/l and are shown on the right axis. The two studies diverged at
higher radon levels. Projections for single family homes with annual
radon concentrations greater than 4 pCi/l were 7 percent (four million
homes) for LBL and 6 percent for Cohen; for homes exceeding
8 pCi/l, 1–3 percent for LBL and only 1 percent for Cohen; and for
homes with radon values above 20 pCi/l, 0.1–0.2 percent for the LBL
study and only 0.02 percent for the Cohen study, barely discernible
in the figure.

Page 200: *second paragraph, last three sentences, should read:*
The subsequent initial EPA informational approach reflected a strategy
for combating panic by educating the public to clearly rate their risk
and then easily but effectively respond to the threat. But when public
panic proved not to be in evidence, an escalating change of strategy
was demanded in order to address EPA's new challenge, indifference
toward radon. Let's examine the program's transformation toward a
focus on public apathy.

Contents

Figures

Tables

Preface

At the breakfast table, staring at the hateful words "deadly radon gas," I couldn't help thinking of all the delicious breakfasts of bacon and eggs and buttered toast I had sacrificed for a claim on the golden years. . . . But they hadn't told me of the deadly radon gas. Deceived and embittered, I seized the newspaper, bit into the deadly radon gas story and ate it. It was like eating fiber.
—Russell Baker

Radon's Deadly Daughters looks at the convergence of two very different realities—the invisibly small and the observably large. In the first, an unseen drama continually unfolds around us at the atomic and subatomic level where atoms change their nature through a radioactive decay chain. Not only are events at this scale impossible to detect by normal human senses, but the time frame through the decay chain changes dramatically as well. Uranium-238, the ultimate parent of many lighter radioactive atoms, was placed on Earth billions of years ago when gravitational forces caused the planet to coalesce. Its half-life, the time it takes for a given amount of uranium-238 to decay to half its value, is at a cosmological time scale of 4.5 billion years. Over time, the resulting lighter radioactive atoms (called progeny or daughters) continued to decay to their daughters, until a daughter product of human significance, radium-226 with its own half-life of sixteen hundred years, was created. When radium, in turn, gives birth to the inert radioactive gas radon, with a half-life of four days, the drama suddenly speeds up. Radon-222 decays to its immediate daughters polonium-218, lead-214, bismuth-214, and polonium-214, all with short half-lives measured in minutes to fractions of a second. It is this cluster of radioactive atoms that is commonly and collectively referred to as radon's daughters. Before they reach a relatively long-lived form of lead (lead-210), the short half-lives of these progeny result in the quick emission of a series of alpha, beta, and gamma particles. It is at this point that this subatomic world begins to have a direct influence on humans.

Radon gas, escaping from the earth, forms part of our atmosphere, providing background radiation. Surprisingly perhaps, radon levels can build up in homes, and radon's daughters, breathed into our lungs, can decay allowing hazardous alpha particles to bombard our lung tissue. While it is impossible for humans to sense this bombardment, over a period of decades, the microscopic world connects with human reality, in the form of observable damage to lung tissue—lung cancer. But how clearly is this process understood, marked as hazardous, and subject to detection and control? To answer these questions, we must shift from the invisible linkage between the subatomic world and cancerous consequences to a different focal plane: the complex scientific, social, and political response of our society to this environmental hazard. It is this second drama that is the main subject of *Radon's Deadly Daughters.*

As students of the chemical and radioactive hazards that have been introduced to the world by human actions, the authors were struck early on by the potential of geologic radon as a litmus test for how we approach the task of understanding, addressing, and accepting environmental hazards. One of us, an environmental psychologist, had been investigating the social and psychological dynamics of community contamination and the dynamics of decision making regarding environmental hazards since the late 1970s. The other, a nuclear physicist, had long reflected on the issues of radiation and health. Both of us had become community activists. Radon caught up with us when, within a matter of months of the issue's emergence, the region where we live and work was geologically linked to the original radon hot spot more than a hundred miles away in Pennsylvania. When our health officials in New York State dismissed the significance of this newly publicized threat even as, in New Jersey, where we work, officials perceived a major risk, we were first confronted by the radon issue's duplicity. On one face, this Janus wears a benign smile. It is a natural, chronic, god-given gas that has been with life through all of evolution, no more dangerous than many common acts of daily life. The other profile, however, is considerably darker. Here is an inert radioactive gas that, freely moving about through earth and mortar cracks, brings the threat of lung cancer to our living rooms. Which face is the real radon? Is radon merely "background radiation," an ambient feature of the natural world? Or is its place in the foreground, among the priorities of an era of environmental awareness?

Our response to the enigma took several forms. On one hand, through a nonprofit community organization, we undertook to organize a radon testing cooperative that, in providing low-cost radon tests to interested people, would amass a database capable of confirming or disproving that significant levels of radon were common in local homes. That project would serve some one thousand people at a time when there were few radon services, proving that more than a quarter of the buildings in our county exceeded the EPA/CDC guidance for radon. At the same time, we organized perhaps the first national conference on radon, held in May 8–10, 1986, at Ramapo College of New Jersey. The conference and the resulting book (Makofske and Edelstein, 1988) explored the full breadth of the radon issue, setting forth the elements of an interdisciplinary evaluation of the issue. We now knew enough to begin the quest that ends here.

But what are the right questions about any environmental hazard? From a personal perspective, we might ask: Is it real—do I believe this invisible hazard exists? Whom will it affect? How bad are the consequences? Is it likely enough to demand my attention? Is there a way of making it visible? Is there anything I can do to avoid it? Are there other concerns that I have that are even more imminent, more important, and more urgent? Do I have the resources to deal with the problem, and how should I spend them? How much of a chance should I take? Meanwhile our social selves are forced to ask a different set of risk questions. Whose fault is it? Whose responsibility is it to address the hazard? Who has been victimized and in what way(s)? What assistance do victims require? What is the best way to detect the threat? Are there affordable remedies? Are there boundaries around the threat and, if so, what are they? What resources are needed to address the hazard? Are we willing and able to make those resources available? Are there other demands on those resources that are higher priority? Can we delegate others to respond? How much of the risk is it acceptable to tolerate? What do we define as safe?

These questions underlie our evaluation of all environmental risks and thus form one basis for environmental policy. While radon illuminates this general arena, it particularly sheds light upon certain questions—such as how we think differently about natural hazards than we do about human-caused ones, which issues are people's private responsibility to resolve and which belong to the larger society, and which concerns loom large in people's fears and which wither away with the press of real life? In a society that has magnified the impact of environmental hazards as personal threats, we remain selective, compartmentalized, inconsistent, and naive—not all risks get the same attention. In part 1 of this volume, we explore how geologic radon moved from the periphery of environmental issues to the center. Chapter 1 takes us to the events that forced the issue center stage. Chapter 2 questions why the importance of the issue had not earlier been recognized. Chapter 3 explores the policy response once issue recognition had occurred.

Central to the radon issue are questions about the use of science in policy. How do we accumulate knowledge about the hazard so that our beliefs about it correspond to fact? In part 2, we show that radon policy and understanding are more swayed by historical myths about the hazard than by a rational practice of science. Each area of science invites its own critical query. Thus, in chapter 4, we ask how much proof is required to be confident that a cause (radon) and effect (lung cancer) are related. In chapter 5, we query how we determine what the boundaries of the hazard are. Chapter 6 examines whether the methods we use to identify the hazard are valid and reliable. And, in chapter 7, we ask how we can come to understand the hazard's behavior well enough to tame it.

But to portray environmental policy as a response solely to the science of risk assessment and risk management is to ignore the politics of risk. We must additionally include in our framework the manner by which environmental policy has been constrained and shaped by the political realities of its time. Part 3 places the radon issue into its milieu, the era of Reaganomics. That the geologic radon issue blossomed during this harsh environmental season suggests that the issue had adaptive characterisitics that fit the political setting. In exploring the dimensions of radon policy, we are thus able to observe radon as a test case of the Reagan administration's approach to environmental policy, an approach that lingers on through the current neo-Reaganomic era. The tenets of Reaganomics, much like the myths of radon science, serve as a convenient framework for our analysis. Chapter 8 explores the ability of the marketplace to meet the demand for radon services. Chapter 9 ponders the role of the individual as a consumer of radon risk. Chapter 10 questions whether a nonregulatory approach to radon has been sufficient. And chapter 11 examines the effort to decentralize environmental policy from the federal to the state and local levels.

Finally, having grown up under these constraints, might not the radon response represent a hardy new species of environmental policy that is perhaps a more adaptive and resilient form of government response than the increasingly out-of-favor and much-criticized regulatory approach? In part 4, chapter 12, we return to such broad questions facing science, environmental policy, and the politics of risk. What are the limits and liabilities, but also the lessons and innovations, that have occurred around the natural radon issue? Are there models here for a next generation of environmental policy?

Acknowledgments

The almost nine-year journey that has resulted in *Deadly Daughters* could not have been undertaken without the help of many others. This acknowledgment only scratches the surface. We conducted scores of interviews with key informants who generously gave of their time, knowledge, and personal experience. We particularly acknowledge Stanley Watras, Kay Jones, and Kathy Varady and their families for their hospitality and willingness to take time to share the early radon story.

We received guidance from many in the radon field, as well, and gratefully acknowledge the support and help that allowed us to understand the radon issue from many perspectives. Harvey Sachs suggested we write this book and was generous in sharing his knowledge. Terry Brennan, radon mitigator par excellence, was often a warm and musical companion on our early radon travels. There have been many renditions of the Radon Blues, beginning with Mike on kazoo and Terry on guitar, but later often involving Bill's guitarist son Adam. Bill benefited by his close association with Terry, Bill Broadhead, and the other members of the fantastic New York SEO radon training team. Richard Guimond of EPA and many staff from the radon program have been generous in their assistance, particularly Steve Page, Joe Gearo, the late Dan Egan, Ann Fisher, Mike Mardis, Jed Harrison, Susan MacMullin, Kirk Maconaughey, Dennis Wagner, Anita Schmidt, Jennifer Keller, Elizabeth Zanoviak, David Rowson, Mary Smith, Elissa Feldman, Marcia Carpentier, and Laraine Kohler. Susan Rose of DOE and her colleagues Tony Nero and Rich Sextro were also of great help, as were the late Assistant Surgeon General Vernon Houk, Tom Gerusky of the DER, Gerald Nicholls of the DEP, Karim Rimawi of the New York DOH, Linda Gunderson of the USGS, Senator Frank Lautenberg and his staff member Rich Erdman, Michael Nuess and his colleagues at the Washington Energy Extension Service, Paul Locke of the Environmental Law Institute, and Radon Professionals Art Scott, Harvey Greenberg, and Joe Norton.

Ramapo College of New Jersey and the Ramapo College Foundation provided various forms of support, including travel money and a sabbatical for Mike and assistance for our 1986 radon conference and in preparing the subsequent edited book. Many of our Ramapo colleagues and students have helped along the way, most notably our secretaries Sherri Cox and Diana Alspach and librarian Pamela Dong. The Goshen Library also deserves thanks for its support.

Our colleagues at Orange Environment, Inc., also deserve mention, particularly Liana Hoodes for her management of OE's radon testing and assistance program and Margaret (Gretchen) Gibbs for her collaborations with Mike in studying radon-related behaviors and beliefs.

Allan Mazur of Syracuse University assisted us in many ways and gave very helpful comments on an earlier version of the manuscript, as did Kristin Shrader-Frechette of the University of South Florida. Their insight was invaluable.

Mike's son Joel, the computer wizard, assisted with some figures and helped develop the cover concept. And our wives, Debby and Mary, both academics as well, were usually understanding when we became absorbed in radon to the exclusion of all else.

And last but not least, Dean Birkenkamp, our editor at Rowman & Littlefield, has been all that one could ever hope for in an editor—friend, guide, and trouble-shooter. Julie Kirsch has been an enormous help with production.

For all of those named above, and for many others, thank you.

Part I

The Recognition of Radon Risk

Chapter 1

Victims of a New Threat

Not until Stanley Watras literally sounded the alarm in 1984 did radon become a household word.
—Richard Guimond
The systems they're installing aren't working. I'm dealing with something that is invisible, it's silent, and it's a killer. I don't understand it and I'm terrified.
—Kay Jones

A House on Indian Lane

It was just another job transfer in January 1984 that brought Stanley Watras to the unassuming suburban house in Colebrookdale Township, Pennsylvania, nearby Boyertown.[1] Stanley, a construction engineer for Bechtel Corporation, was being sent to work at the new Limerick nuclear power plant in nearby Pottstown. Because his wife, Diane, was pregnant with their second son, Stanley had been forced to find the house by himself. It had been a difficult search, given the inflated housing market of the greater Philadelphia area. But then a realtor had brought him to Indian Lane. Stanley was drawn to the rural feeling, the rolling hills, and the uncrowded layout of the houses. He and Diane had moved frequently, but this new area reminded him of their current home in Bloomsburg, Pennsylvania. He fell in love with the split level on two acres, completing a detailed drawing before driving home to show Diane. She trusted his judgment; purchased the house and Stanley moved in. His wife and sons, including a newborn, followed shortly.

That first year in their new home was a hectic one. Stanley averaged twenty to thirty hours a week in overtime. Additional pressures on the quiet, reclusive engineer came from two traumatic events. Stanley lost his father and was forced to put his mother into a nursing home hours distant. With Stanley gone so much, Diane spent much of her time traveling north to see their old friends in Bloomsburg or south to visit their relatives in Delaware.

During her pregnancies, Diane had made Stanley, a heavy smoker, go outside to light up, even on the coldest nights. The same level of concern did not surround the possibility that the Watras household might be exposed to radiation. As someone who worked with radioactivity on a daily basis, Stanley was confident in his ability to limit his own exposure. Diane trusted him to protect their family, as well. They did not worry about the possibility that Stanley might become contaminated at work. As a result, they were both shocked by the events of December 1984.

An Alarm Heard 'Round the Nation

With the Limerick Unit 1 plant just started up, the weekend of December 2 commenced radiation monitoring activities. At that time, Stanley worked largely in the uncompleted Limerick Unit 2, but on weekends he was to enter Unit 1 to do maintenance tasks. Coming out of Unit 1 at 9:30 A.M. that first day of monitoring, he tripped the radiation alarm. As Stanley recalled it, "the buzzer started buzzing and the big red display lighted up" (Smay, 1985, 76) indicating "that it was my whole body that was contaminated, from the tip of my toes to the top of my head" (Manegold, 1985, A01). Monitoring revealed that his shirt was so highly contaminated that health officials at the plant confiscated it. In the lingo of radiation workers, he had become "crapped up." This, however, did not prove to be an isolated occurrence, for Stanley would spend much of that month working in his T-shirt. He had to enter Unit 1 several times a week, each visit resulting in a four- to five-hour period of delay while he took decontamination showers or sat around waiting for enough radioactive decay to occur that he could legally be allowed to exit. Not only was Stanley frustrated to be sitting around for half days doing nothing, but he was perplexed as well. The areas where he worked were not likely sources for the elements of lead, bismuth, and polonium detectable on his clothing.

Meanwhile, at home, Diane was becoming concerned. At her prodding, Stanley threw one set of contaminated clothing into the garbage. He began leaving his work clothes in the garage, dressing there in the morning and disrobing there after work. Initially he felt that Diane was overreacting to the situation, but as he mulled over his contamination, he began to take it more seriously. Gradually it dawned on Stanley that he must be getting the exposure outside of work—possibly at the house on Indian Lane! By December 13, he told Diane that he now thought that the radiation was originating at home.

Stanley had been taught to carefully trace his steps so as to identify possible points of contamination. On December 14, he arose, took a shower, got dressed, grabbed his lunch, and upon arriving at work, he told his supervisor that he would see him in five minutes or five hours. He entered Unit 1, picked up a radiation dosimetry device and identification, went through the turnstiles, dropped some documents off, swung around, and went right out the exit portal. Red lights blazed and alarms sounded. The detection devices indicated a "zone 1-11" exposure, meaning that his entire body was hot. When the health physicists arrived, they acknowledged the routine of this occurrence with a "Not you again." But for Stanley, this was not just another repetitious event. He now knew that the radiation was coming from his home, and he was worried about his family. Stanley was so visibly disturbed that his demand that the plant send a team to inspect his house for radioactivity was granted even though the senior health physicist, Dick Dubiel, was skeptical that anything significant would be found.

A few days later Stanley drove from Limerick to Colebrookdale with three coworkers who were sent to examine his house. There was a lot of joking; the coworkers did not expect to find much. But the joking ceased when one of them carried a Geiger counter into the house and it began chirping at more than ten times the expected frequency. Gauges on some of their instruments registered off the scale. Presence of high gamma radiation was evident. An air sample taken back to the lab was so radioactive that it had to be diluted in order for the equipment to be able to read it. Stanley's three coworkers were also personally crapped up, as was their car and equipment. With almost ten years experience working at nuclear power plants, the significance of the visit was apparent to Stanley.

Back at work, Dubiel set up a conference call for himself and Stanley with Maggie Reilly of the Pennsylvania Department of Environmental Resources (DER). Stanley could not get to the phone, however, because he had set off the portal monitors. He would have had to go through full decontamination were it not for Dubiel's efforts to wave red tape. When he finally reached the phone, Reilly and Dubiel informed Stanley that his home evidenced radon gas at the unheard of level of contamination of 22 working levels.

It is necessary to digress for a moment to define some terms. Radon measurements are expressed in picocuries per liter (pCi/l) and radon daughter measurements are given in working levels (WL). These units may be looked at simply as concentrations, the number of radon or daughter atoms in a liter of air, or equivalently, as activities, a measure of the rate at which radon or daughter atoms are decaying in a liter of air. For example, 1 pCi/l means a concentration of 18,000 radon atoms in a liter of air, or an activity of 2.2 radon atoms decaying a minute per liter of air. The WL, representing radon daughters, reflects the risk of lung damage. The two measures can be crudely equated; in houses 1 WL is typically equivalent to 200 pCi/l. Thus, 22 WL is the equivalent of 4,400 pCi/l. In order to express the cumulative exposure to radon daughters, the measure "working level months" (or WLM) is frequently used. The WLM is a product of the average rate of exposure in working levels and the number of 170-hour working months of exposure. By reference to occupational standards for radon then in place, what Reilly and Dubiel were telling Watras was that for every 42.5 hours spent in their home, he and his family were equaling the maximum worker exposure per year.

Stanley initially refused to accept this unbelievable news, challenging the calibration of the test instruments, but neither Reilly nor Dubiel budged. Reilly cited the authoritative NCRP (National Council on Radiation Protection) report on uranium miner exposures regarding the risks of lung cancer associated with radon daughter exposure. All that Stanley could think about was that his sons and wife were home so much more than he. What would happen to them? He asked Dubiel to repeat the tests in order to be certain.

Air samples taken on December 21, 1984, in the Watras home indicated 9 Working Levels (WL) in the bedroom, 14 WL in the living room, and 22 WL in the basement. After DER staff retested the home on December 26 with nineteen different tests, they returned to their car and tested themselves to find that their clothes were highly contaminated. The car was contaminated as well. On January 2, 1985, DER personnel returned to pick up an alpha-track detector (a type of radon detection device) left in the home during the prior week.

It was a snowy Saturday afternoon three days later. The Watrases had planned a weekend escape from their new uncertainty over radon to visit friends in Bloomsburg. However, as they packed their car, DER officials pulled into their driveway. They bore a letter from DER secretary Nicholas DeBenedictis which read in part, "I urge you to leave your residence immediately and find alternative safe shelter." When Diane asked them how soon the DER wanted them to move, she was told "Now" (Strecklow, 1985f, B01). Stanley and Diane methodically began packing away their Christmas decorations. They readied most of their belongings to be decontaminated for relocation. After church that Sunday, they moved into the nearest Holiday Inn, where they stayed for six weeks before they relocated to a rented house. As they left home for the Holiday Inn, Diane recalled "I remember thinking we'd never live in the house again" (Smay, 1985, 76). In April, Philadelphia Electric Company (PECO), owners of the Limerick plant, announced that they would fix the Watras house as a demonstration project in radon mitigation. In mid-July, more than six months after their evacuation, the Watrases were able to return to the house on Indian Lane, where they remain to this day.

Events at the Watras house had not gone unnoticed by neighbors or the larger public. Initially, the DER attempted to protect the Watrases' identity, even as they conducted tests in the area and confirmed that severe radon contamination had been discovered. However, it was not long before reporters searching for the "hot" house found the building. Neighbors were queried at length. Staking out the Watras house, reporters encountered Stanley and Diane as they returned to pick up the mail or their belongings. Before long, the Watrases were known worldwide as victims of a strange new environmental threat, radon gas.[2] Further testing revealed that the Watrases were not alone in their predicament, that many other homes in the surrounding area were affected, and that naturally occurring radon gas exposure might be a widespread phenomenon. From the standpoint of both public concern and institutional response, the radon issue was born.

Victims of a New Environmental Contamination

Having discovered that their homes were places of danger due to invisible radioactive gas, the Watrases and their neighbors found themselves in a situation parallel to that of the residents of other contaminated communities. Since Love Canal, a significant new reality of modern life has become apparent for such victims of environmental contamination (see Edelstein, 1988a). Although not human-caused, geologic radon appeared to have all the trappings of Love Canal in terms of its potential to victimize affected residents within a bounded area. While ostensibly no one was responsible for causing the hazard, there still were complex issues of responsibility for identifying and remedying the risk that compounded the meaning of an uncertain yet serious health threat. The key elements of victimization due to environmental contamination were certainly evident in Colebrookdale Township, although they took different forms for different victims. While by its nature, victimization disables, disempowers, and debilitates, many victims find ways to regain at least some lost control over their lives. In the Colebrookdale Township case, we find two very different paths toward such empowerment, one indicated by the grassroots advocacy of two of the Watrases' neighbors and the other by Stanley Watras' professional/ expert response to radon.

Radon Victimization As a Stimulus for Community Organization

Contamination victims are often isolated from the normal sources of social support assumed to be there in the time of need. Friends, coworkers, and family are unlikely to understand a sudden change of circumstance based upon an unknown and ill-understood environmental cause. They may be unsympathetic, ridiculing, and blaming. Even if supportive, there may be little that they can offer by way of help. Victims look beyond these social networks, turning to specialized government agencies for information, assistance, and support. However, officials playing catch-up themselves to understand an issue may seem more concerned with laws, regulations, scientific proof, competing priorities, budgets, and caution in setting precedents than in directly addressing victims' concerns. Scientific uncertainty may compound the overall social uncertainty that victims confront. The net result is often their dependency upon officials and experts, needed to address problems beyond the victims' own resources and competencies. In contrast to a previous sense that one could manage life's challenges reasonably well, victims are left with a profound sense of disability. Particularly where victims are spatially bounded by the contaminant, such disabling frequently gives way to an effort of victims to band together in order to gain a source of support, power, and trusted information (Edelstein, 1988). We see just this scenario of mobilization when we examine two of the Watrases' Colebrookdale Township neighbors, the Joneses and the Varadys.

Life in a "Hot" House

Just across Indian Lane from the Watrases, Kay Jones and her husband Rich enjoyed a panoramic view of the surrounding valley from "Radon Hill." Six years earlier, they had been drawn to the privacy of the countryside in Cole-brookdale Township, near their home community of Boyertown. Located in a former peach orchard, with a creek for fishing and also a woods, their three acres afforded enough land for their two daughters and son to run and play. Their neighbors were close, but not too close.

Following the American Dream, the Joneses' resources and aspirations were focused on the home. The ranch house answered their dreams. It served as a place to raise children and to establish family unity. It was a place that generated warmth. The entire family saved money so that improvements on the property could be made. They installed a woodstove in the basement as a way to save money, and Kay often slept down there to keep it going all night. Rich did most of the work on the house himself. Their first goal, to pave the driveway so that the kids could ride their bicycles there, was achieved after the initial year. After the third year, enough had been saved that concrete for a patio could be poured. Another improvement involved finishing the basement to create a rec-reation room. All of the Joneses shared the excitement that these improvements generated.

Heading into 1985, the Joneses were not overly concerned about environmental hazards. They had found no reason to question the serenity that surrounded them. Even the accident at the nearby Three Mile Island plant had not unnerved them. Like his neighbor Stanley Watras, Rich worked at the Limerick Nuclear Power plant. He was similarly no stranger to the potential dangers of radiation. But, despite the Joneses' general familiarity with nuclear hazards, residential radon gas was something they had never even heard of before the Watrases' discovery.

In December 1984, as the Watrases, PECO, and the DER sought to confirm the levels of radon found in the Watras home, presumably no one else knew what was happening. Nevertheless, vague rumors circulated in the neighborhood. Kay recalled that her first inkling that anything was happening came from a comment made by one of her children during dinner in late December that someone on the school bus had said that "there is a house in this neighborhood that glows." Kay laughed about it with the rest of the family. Then, on that New Year's Eve, the Joneses were playing "spoons" with some neighbors in their basement. One neighbor said that he was going to make whoever got the spoon go and stand in front of "the irradiated house." However, the neighbor didn't know the whereabouts of the house. Following their return to school in January,

Kay's children brought home more news. They pointed to the Watras house and said, "They made the people who lived there move out" (in actuality, the Watrases had not as yet been told to leave their home). Glancing across the street, Kay recalled that she had recently seen strange men there holding scientific-looking equipment. But, until now, she hadn't thought much about it.

On Saturday, January 5, immediately after the DER personnel delivered the letter telling the Watrases to move out, Stanley Watras stood outside packing his car while the environmental officials knocked on the doors of neighboring houses, telling people about the problem in the area, and offering them free tests. Kay was taking down her Christmas tree when four Department of Environmental Resources staff appeared at her door. As they entered, their Geiger counter went wild. A few days later, the DER reported to her with the outcome of air tests taken from her basement. Her initial levels were measured at 0.8 WL (although a longer-term alpha track would find an even higher level of 2.32 WL). The officials wanted Kay to discontinue using the basement, including the laundry and recreation rooms. She was not to allow children to play or even visit downstairs. Windows in the house were to be left open.

Coping with the News of Exposure

There followed from this discovery a period of limbo for the Jones family. Kay recalled that her acceptance of the radon threat was gradual, following four stages of evolution.[3]

First Stage—Initial Denial. For Kay, "the first stage was when I thought that if I pretended it wasn't here, it would go away." During this stage, Kay refused to forgo her basement chores. She continued to do her laundry, load the woodstove, and keep the room clean. In doing this, Kay rationalized that, if she had been sleeping downstairs for years in order to feed the woodstove, "my coming down here to do a wash wouldn't put the final peg in my coffin." As she recalled, "I went down there. I couldn't see anything. How could anything be going on here that I couldn't see, hear, or feel? My first reaction was 'It's not here. They made a mistake.' Someone can't just come into your home and say that you can't go into your basement! This could happen to others, but it couldn't happen to me."

When a DER official caught her in the basement, Kay confronted the official, and, puffing a cigarette in her face, Kay catharted, "You know lady, I'm sorry I ever let you into my home. You know lady, I've lived here for nine years. You're telling me not to do a wash, not to heat my home. Do you want to start paying my bills for oil heat, the laundry, and everything else?"

Although Kay personally challenged the DER's restrictions, she actively played gatekeeper to her children, keeping them out of the basement. But, in doing so, she did not initially portray the basement as a place of danger. Rather, "when the kids asked why they couldn't play down the basement, I told them 'let's make these people (from the DER) happy and not go down there'." In contrast, Rich understood and admitted the danger, refusing to go downstairs at all for the next three months. He dealt with the loss of the basement recreation area by abandoning his work on the house, instead spending his time at home sitting in front of the television playing video games.

Second Stage—Self-pity. The persistence of the DER officials eventually convinced Kay that the radon risk was to be taken seriously: "I realized that the state was not going away." But, in accepting the problem, she was forced to ask "'why me?' I felt sorry for myself." In this needy stage, Kay and Rich turned to the state to clarify the risk and to help them address it. This dependence upon the state for aid resulted in disappointment and caused anger.

Third Stage—Anger. The shift from dependence to anger directed at state officials was precipitated by the DER's handling of a February 1985 public meeting in the wake of publicity about the Watrases' evacuation. Facing four hundred anxious residents at the meeting, state officials were equivocal about the radon risk in the community. Furthermore, they declined to disclose information about the Watrases at the family's request. Kay recalled that residents whose houses had been tested for radon were advised by the DER to keep the findings secret. As a result, people did not know what their neighbors had found. Those with high radon counts, such as the Joneses, were thus isolated with their fears. "Each of us was thinking that we would be the next to have to leave. Where would we go? What would we do? We were grasping at straws to try to compare ourselves to Watras."

As Kay recalls the meeting, the audience demanded to know whether there was a problem or not. A DER official tried to dispel panic by stating that little was known about the problem and minimizing its significance. Thus reassured, many members of the audience left the hall believing that radon was a nonissue. But, Kay and Rich were in a different situation. They already knew that they had an extreme radon level in their home. Additionally, they had talked earlier to the guest speaker for the evening, Tel Tappan, the radon mitigator who was working on the Watras house. They believed that he disagreed with what the DER officials were saying. When he was finally able to speak, at 9:45 P.M., Tappan stressed the risk of lung cancer associated with radon exposure while showing slides of the radon-affected neighborhoods in Montclair, New Jersey, and Grand Junction, Colorado. However, by this point, the bulk of the community had left, having made up their minds not to worry excessively about radon. By the next DER meeting, attendance had dropped to fifty. Boyertown had been split into a major group of radon disbelievers and a smaller group of believers. Kay blamed the DER's handling of this first public meeting for what she viewed as a subsequent denial of radon by the Boyertown community at large.[4]

Fourth Stage—Fear. Kay now found herself confused by mixed messages. On one hand, the DER continued to remind her to stay out of her basement, a warning that fit with Tel Tappan's views on the severity of the threat. But she also believed that the DER had played down the urgency of the radon problem at the public meeting. She realized that she needed an independent opinion to resolve the ambiguity. She tracked down Robert Yuenke, an attorney with the Environmental Defense Fund who had been deeply involved in the mine tailings radon issue in Colorado. Yuenke at first found Kay's report of extraordinary radon levels in her home to be unbelievable, but ultimately spent two hours educating her about the perils of radon and "scaring the tar out of me." Kay now shared Rich's fear. Her concern was no longer merely to force government to fix a problem with their house; the issue had been refocused as a dire health threat for the entire family.

Yuenke also spoke with Kathy Varady, a neighbor of Kay's, whose house tested at 2.12 WL. Kay had met Kathy, a mother of four, while going door to door collecting signatures on a petition demanding that the government remediate the neighborhood. Kathy recalled her conversation with Yuenke vividly.

> His reaction was incredible. "My God lady, you can't be living in that house. Do you realize what that your children's bedrooms measure the same level at which they shut down uranium mines! And young children spend most of their time sleeping! I don't want to tell you what to do, but I wouldn't spend one more hour—one more minute—in your house." This was the first time that I ever felt fear—the first time I ever felt fear and anger at the same time. Why was he telling me this and nobody else was? Prior to this there was no fear attached to our radon levels. No one knew what it signified. It's natural; what can it do to you?

The DER subsequently offered a crude interpretation of their radon levels by equating the Varadys' exposure to smoking twenty-two packs of cigarettes per day. For Kathy, "This was a real slap in my face because neither of us smoke, yet the environment that we put our children in was far worse than if we did smoke around them." Also underscoring the risk for Kathy was the time that moon-suited workers came to test a nearby house. "We were sitting here eating dinner, and they were protecting their workers. . . . It did not make sense. . . . We were the ones living, breathing and sleeping in this."

Final Stage—Activism. Spurred by fear for their families, anger at government, and encouragement from Yuenke, their husbands, and the local press, in April 1985 Kay and Kathy formed a grassroots organization that they called "PAR"—Pennsylvanians Against Radon. At first, PAR served as a source of emotional support and education about radon. But over time, PAR began to lobby and to inform state and federal legislators about the issue. PAR also offered support and outreach to radon victims, initially throughout Pennsylvania, and then across the country. By the summer of 1987, the group had 150 members. Their goal was to get government assistance comparable to that received by the Watrases for other families with high radon levels. Kathy explained, "After they fixed the Watras house, they would have dropped the whole thing. When the Watras house was fixed, the state brought them a big certificate. All the television stations carried the message that 'The radon problem is over.' More than one hundred families in Pennsylvania were sitting with over 1 WL, a level at which you have a 50 percent chance of cancer. It was as though, if you weren't the hottest home, you didn't matter." On the national level, PAR argued that further inequity was evident in the restrained manner with which the EPA addressed the Pennsylvanians' natural radon problem compared to the human-caused radon problem in Montclair, New Jersey. There, residents were evacuated who had radon levels of less than 1 WL. And when PAR asked why Colebrookdale families had not been relocated to trailers, as were victims of floods, they were told that had been considered, but there were not enough trailers available.

In pushing for a more inclusive radon program, Kathy and Kay were forced to grow beyond their prior roles as mothers and housewives. In this sense they modeled themselves after Lois Gibbs, the former head of the Love Canal Homeowners Association, who made the transformation from housewife to national citizens' leader. Kathy recalled, "I was shy. I was a private person. I wasn't opinionated. I never heard of our congressman, let alone called him up to tell him I didn't like what he was doing." Yet, it was her first conversation with her congressman Gus Yatron that she believed had converted him into an ally.

When Yatron telephoned Kathy from the House floor, he was stung by PAR's public criticism over his alleged failure to deliver government radon assistance. "He said, 'I have feelings too you know.' I said that your feelings are probably nowhere near the feelings that I have. When I got off the phone I was shaking." But Kathy felt that the conversation had made the congressman realize that he had been blinded by the Watrases' high levels into thinking that other families were not at comparable risk. She noted that families like the Joneses and Varadys with somewhat lower radon levels actually had more exposure because they had lived in their homes longer. To help Kay and Kathy get this point across in Washington, Yatron invited them to join Watras in testifying before Congress in October 1985.[5]

Meanwhile, state senator Michael O'Pake took Kay and Kathy to Washington to meet with officials from EPA. Kathy recalls being intimidated. She and Kathy were surrounded by fifteen EPA staff who sat listening and taking detailed notes of everything they said. "For two-and-one-half hours they said nothing, they just wrote." The PAR activists had felt hopelessly dependent upon EPA. Now they realized that in fact there was a two-way dependency. As Kathy recalled, "Things were happening in our homes that they were never exposed to, so the government needed us like we needed them." Similarly, as *the* radon activists, others needed them, as well. Kathy remembered, "The phone would ring from 7 A.M. to 9 P.M.—everybody and anybody would call—media people with the 'solution,' people calling to say 'this is serious but if you say I talked to you,

I'll deny it.' We got reports anonymously in the mail to make public. That upset us because who would believe two housewives?"

Kay and Kathy's anger drove their persistence. They knew they were succeeding when they called people they had never spoken to and the people knew who they were. But even as they started to have an effect externally, the pressure of their effort began to extract a cost at home.

Family Impacts

Kay's newfound activism profoundly changed daily life in the Jones household, becoming a major source of stress to which her family was forced to adjust. Rich was acutely aware of the risk and fully supported Kay's activism. But, particularly at the onset, it was unsettling for her three children who now found her preoccupied and emotional. As the radon issue intruded directly into their family life, the children claimed that Kay took her radon frustrations out on them, as Kay's eldest daughter, Sherri, recalled. "It's hard. If she's not on the phone, she has somebody here talking to her. She is moody some days—crying, mad. I sometimes go over to our neighbors to get away. I leave her alone to figure her problems out."

Kay gradually began to manage these family disturbances, spending compensatory time with the children and limiting her time on the phone. Kay also attempted to explain her preoccupation to the kids. "It's been a big adjustment. I tell my children that I'm doing it for other children. 'We were fortunate to have someone come and fix our home and make it safe for us. When I go away, I try to help other boys and girls with radon problems.' My son understands, but he's not happy about my leaving." This communication drew Kay even closer to her children, particularly to Sherri, whom she came to use as a sounding board. Sherri grew to empathize with the plight of families calling her mom for advice and to serve as a general source of strength for her mother.

In 1996 Kathy reflected back on how the radon issue had impacted her family. "This changed all of us. My daughter became very vocal. I know where she is coming from. She was only four then. Now she is sixteen. She goes around fighting for her rights. That's me at that time, but not me before that time. They made me into that kind of person. They made her totally different than she would have been too. It changed the whole family unit. We stayed together as a family. But I could see this pulling a family apart."

Life during Mitigation

The identification of the radon problems in Colebrookdale initially presented a "mitigatory gap," where there was no practicable way to address the contamination that had been discovered. In an effort to address this gap, the DER's Tom Gerusky told PAR of two avenues that were being pursued (Lewis, 1985,

B01). First, he reported that EPA had lined up a volunteer contractor to do remedial work as research for a book he wanted to write. Also, DER was pursuing an arrangement with a vocational technical school in Berks County that would train students to do the repairs. Kay's response to this latter idea was blunt, "Do they really think I'd let an eleventh or twelfth grader come into my home and work on a radon problem? I don't trust the local contractors to do this, why would I trust students?" PAR continued to push vocally for government action on remediation.

Meanwhile, as an outgrowth of his conversations with Stanley Watras, Congressman Gus Yatron had investigated options for assisting in remediation of the community. In the Superfund legislation, he found an important tool, the potential for authorizing an experimental remediation. It was just such government assistance that PAR was loudly demanding. The experimental remediation effort would allow EPA to create a laboratory for identifying methods to fix high radon homes without creating a precedent in which government would take responsibility for an expensive effort viewed as a private problem. The result was the "eighteen-home study," the first of a number of EPA radon mitigation experiments, announced in April 1985. Initially, EPA chose only twelve homes for this study, including the Watrases' and the Joneses'. Subsequently, the Watrases were removed from the study after PECO announced on April 16, 1985, that they would undertake a $40,000 study of the Watras house as part of their residential energy conservation program (Strecklow, 1985b).

The Varadys were shocked to receive a rejection letter from the initial study, even though their house was one of twelve homes at that time identified as being over 1 WL. In despair, they examined their options. They explored paying for mitigation, but the only estimate they could get was for $14,000, far beyond their means. They reluctantly considered moving. But finally, EPA added them to the study for reasons that Kathy saw as political. "They wanted to keep us quiet."

The Joneses were confident from the onset that radon could be removed from their home. In fact, influenced by misleading information made available early on by the DER, they initially thought that it was a do-it-yourself venture— one more task around the house for Rich to carry out. However, it soon became evident that this was not the case. With the eighteen-home study, their mitigation was tackled by Art Scott, whose firm, American Atcom, had received the EPA contract to conduct the research. And research it was. Scott experimented in their home with different systems over time, seeing what effect each variation had on the viability of their residential air. As different techniques were tried, the Joneses' radon levels swung wildly. At one point, a counterproductive sub-slab depressurization system sent levels upward as high as 15.688 WL. The Joneses' basement was littered with the skeletons of failed radon technology.

There was a psychological cost to this experimentation. As Scott proceeded, Kay lost her confidence that her home could be made safe. She became demoralized. She also felt hassled as she was forced to participate in experiments that required periodic changes in window openings. Officials intruded three times a day to take measurements. Yet, nothing seemed to work. As Kay tells it, "By Christmas last year [1985], I felt that there was no way that our home could ever be made safe. They tried all these different systems, and it kept getting worse." Beyond these problems, Scott had also found that the well water used by the family was another significant source of radon, requiring construction of an experimental water mitigation system. With each relapse, Kay's confidence in the safety of her house was returned to zero.

Finally, it appeared that the house was cured. With the home showing levels of radon approaching the 4 pCi/l guidance, EPA decided that it was time to celebrate success. On her part, Kay wanted to use the occasion to call attention to how shoddy the work had been done (Strecklow, 1985c). The press was invited to the Joneses' house to view the remediation at a time when U.S. Senator Arlen Specter would be in the neighborhood and could attend. Kay prepared refreshments for her guests. While waiting for the senator's arrival, William Belanger of EPA turned on a "real time radon monitor." As Kay recalled, "The numbers kept going around and around. He got whiter and whiter." The house was hardly low in radon. News reports claimed that the levels had topped the Watrases' for the highest ever recorded in a residence (Heine, 1985; Strecklow, 1985c). Kay recalls that she nearly fainted. There were several culprits for the high levels. According to Kay, Scott later determined that the Jenn-aire ventilating stove top that she had used in preparing food for the celebration had caused the surge in radon levels. Apparently the EPA had a different theory, blaming the high levels on Kay's having opened a window in her first floor bathroom, which created a vacuum in the house, causing soil gas to be drawn into the basement. Jones said she had been instructed by the DER to open the window whenever someone took a shower because the water supply contained radon. As a result, the window was open nearly every day. Kay commented to the press (Strecklow, 1985c, B01), "We were told by the DER that by ventilating we would alleviate the problem. Well, we ventilated, and look what it did. To me it proves that the average homeowner cannot deal with the situation themselves." While Bellinger had halved the radon levels within two hours and returned them to normal by the end of the day, Kay's confidence had been damaged; "I really thought I had a handle on this. . . . it threw me for a loop" (Heine, 1985, 8).

The Varadys felt similar uncertainty as to whether their mitigation system was working. As Kathy's husband, John, recalled, Art Scott had originally used a low-cost mitigation design that had been suggested by EPA. Scott openly expressed his lack of faith in the system. Around Thanksgiving, he visited the Varadys to give them "bad news." Not only was their system not working, but EPA had no intention of trying other approaches on their house. Scott told them that he felt awful "leaving you like this." With the windows open for ventilation during a cold, windy period, Kathy called EPA to ask what she should do with her family. And, at a news conference, she confronted EPA's Margo Oge with her predicament. The next week, Scott was back, this time to install a system he thought would work. But, John feared that the system might be overpowered by winter winds and fail. For the Varadys, running their fan "twenty-four hours a day" had become a necessity of life. More than a decade later, Kathy reports that she still listens for the sound of the fan every time she goes downstairs.

Lifescape Changes

The radon incident introduced many daily hassles for the Joneses and the Varadys. Their lifestyles were altered in very definite ways—including their lost use of the basement, the constant intrusion of radon workers, and the diminished amount of time that the family spent together. But, perhaps of even greater significance, the radon incident fundamentally changed the lifescape—their basic assumptions about the safety and security of their world (see Edelstein, 1988a).

A Changed View of Health

Reflecting the high probabilities of cancer associated with their exposures, Kathy expressed worries for her children's health similar to those frequently heard from victims of environmental exposures. "I get upset sometimes when I hear the children discuss what is going on in the future and you wonder if they have a future. They were all babies in this house. There's a lot of cancer in my family. Their odds aren't too great." Kay's thoughts dwelt on the fact that before the radon discovery, her children's toys had been kept in their basement recreation room "domain." She frequently hid her real emotions, camouflaging her fear in the guise of anger. "I've been told that there is an 85 percent chance of one of my kids getting lung cancer by the age of twenty-one. But I don't think about it. I can't. But it comes into my mind. Last month, I saw the kids playing out back with a kite, and it popped into my mind, and I got emotional. I was in Pottstown with the kids shopping and the three kids were in the car playing around and suddenly my tears erupted."

Did the children share this shift in perception? Kay wished her children did not know as much about radon as they do, but the children essentially lived in a radon subculture. They could not help but know something about what was going on. Sherri voiced her consequent fears. "I'm scared about what is going to happen when I grow up. Will I die of cancer or not? I think about it a lot." In 1996, Kathy still feels guilty over exposing her children to the risk. She suspects that her oldest daughter's college interest in premedicine with a focus on oncology is not just a coincidence.

A Loss of Control

The inability to protect her children was experienced by Kay as a loss of control.

> I felt like I was losing control with radon. I didn't know what I had exposed my children to. When they were babies, instead of letting them go out, I'd have them go into the basement to play. It would have been safer letting them be exposed to diseases outside. These three children are our responsibility. I couldn't live with myself [if they got cancer]. What did we expose these kids to these eight years? What damage has already been done by the eight years that we lived in the basement? I don't know that I want to know.

Kay's later ability to regain control was directly to her success as an activist in being able to move along the remediation of her home and in her ability to protect her children from additional hazards, for example, declining dental X-rays for her children. As she explained, "I'm trying to control what happens now. My control is getting a little better because I feel better about it now; my home is fixed and now I try to concentrate on preventative measures. I've heard that when people stop smoking after ten years, they get better. Are we now able to alleviate the damage done by giving the kids radon exposure in the basement?"

Inversion of Home

Before the discovery of radon, Sherri Jones recalled that the kids hung out in the basement, site of the family television. But now their place was off limits; her father was even afraid to visit the basement, and her mother ran only brief errands there. Accompanying the new perception of danger was a virtual inversion of feeling about home. Home was no longer a place of well-being but rather one of threat. Kay reported that many radon victims she spoke with "have lost their enthusiasm about their homes. It just does something to you. There are a lot of feelings here."

Once the Joneses accepted that their house was contaminated by radon, its previous importance as a place that reflected their efforts and aspirations was shattered. Not only didn't they want to continue putting more and more resources into a home that had suddenly lost its "value," but, additionally, Kay noted that with the remediation of the basement, "eight years of accomplishment were ripped out in one weekend." In particular, Rich's ties to the house were severed. "We had to do it because of the children. We lost everything we worked for. It was hard on my husband. I like to say 'this is life.' He says, 'I'm getting older. I'm not going backwards.' He has lost the greatest amount of enthusiasm for the house. He would say, 'pack it up.'" The Varadys expressed the effect on their feelings about home even more bluntly. "We used to check the woodstove twenty times before we left home. After we found out about radon, we didn't care if the house burned down. The house was really once our sense of pride, but we lost it."

A dilemma created by the inversion of home is that, even as one no longer wants to be in the affected building, it is insurmountably difficult to leave. During the uncertain period of remediation, the Joneses were torn between two competing elements of self-interest—their lifetime investment in their home and their concern for their children's health. As Kay recalled: "My husband and I worked twenty years to get into this house. Do you run a risk with your children's lives or get into a car with the clothes on your back and start over? We can't afford an apartment, a mortgage and the money for remediation! There is the added guilt for the homeowner of exposing your children to this." The Joneses, already in their early forties, did not feel like they were ready to start over again elsewhere.

Uncertainty and the lack of trust in mitigation added to the inversion of home. Around the interior perimeter of the Joneses' basement, channel drains had been attached to two fans. For Kay and her family, the hum of these fans signaled security because the sound indicated that the radon was being removed. Yet, there remained a concern that a house that has been mitigated for radon still holds the potential to relapse to its formerly high levels. Human error might additionally contribute to renewed exposure, as well. For example, on one of the first author's visits to the Jones' house, Kay busily opened windows in the basement, explaining that she had closed them the night before because it was muggy, but had forgotten to put the fans on. When she awoke and realized her mistake, she had become "panicky and paranoid" over the likelihood that radon levels had risen. And, even if all systems worked, Kay wondered if the basement would ever be safe for the children to again occupy.

Not only did inversion of home affect the victims' psychological feelings for their homes, but the public nature of the contamination caused environmental stigma, resulting in financial inversion, as well (Edelstein, 1988a, 1991). Kay claimed that Stanley, Kathy, or she "could not give our houses away even if we wanted to. We're labeled." In fact, when she and Rich had attempted to sell their home, fully disclosing the problems, not one person had come to look at it.

A Changed View of the Environment

Victims of contamination commonly experience a changed perception of the environment, now seen as a source of unseen and unseeable danger. Not only was their home now a place of danger, but the setting, the place the Joneses had chosen to live because of the accessibility and security of its natural features for their children, had turned on them. The lovely view framed by their picture window was the culprit in this Stephen King plot; an environment whose malignant forces had been loosed. Knowing the ugly secret of "Radon Hill" could not help but change their relationship to place. No longer a benign backdrop for their lives, place now demanded respect and precaution. And the known hazards of their place stood in stark contrast to potential invisible hazards of other places. Elsewhere, they would be ignorant of these risks and thus helpless to protect their families. Thus, a further factor in the Joneses' reluctance to leave their home was the uncertainty over what radon problems they might find in a new location. On Indian Lane they at least felt that they had a handle on the problems. When one of Kay's children was asked to sleep over at a friend's house, where radon had also been found, a condition of the visit was that the sliding glass door be kept open to ventilate radon in the room where the children slept. Thus, they became bound to the known dangers of place.

Loss of Trust

Contamination events frequently alter the trust held for government. Even when not responsible for causing the problem, government may be held accountable first for not preventing the problem and then for not effectively addressing it. Kay and Kathy viewed the DER with distrust for both these reasons. They cited DER's knowledge of excessive radon before 90 percent of the homes in their area had been built, the result of a study of uranium potential. As Kay noted, "I was a red dot on the 1978 map. But they never told me. They let me expose my children. I feel they should have warned me. I harbor deep grudges." Furthering the blame was their belief that the inaction had resulted from a cover-up of the radon problem by DER.

Politicians at the state and federal levels were also generally a disappointment to PAR, whose leaders criticized congresspeople, even from states facing a major radon problem, who failed to support pioneer radon legislation because of its cost, yet who spared nothing on behalf of their pet causes. And, despite their good working relationships with officials at both EPA and the DER, Kay voiced their anger that so many important responsibilities were left to PAR. "The Reagan administration says that our radon situation is as deadly as Chernobyl, but nobody is doing anything about it. I'm not able to give the homeowners an agency to talk to for stress. I talk to them. Am I telling them the right thing? Am I making it worse? All I can do is tell them what I go through. I still get angry." This cynicism for government was shared by Kay's daughter, Sherri.

A key focus of their distrust was the lack of openness they found in government. Kathy recalls key decisions happening behind closed doors, without their input or knowledge. They would only learn of some decisions because of anonymously leaked documents or phone tips. "It was almost like espionage." The two PAR leaders were certain, at times, that their phones were tapped. They felt "totally paranoid" and sometimes feared for their safety. Government officials, they believed, deliberately lied to them and tried to sabotage their efforts. They felt that EPA staff had the primary role of minimizing agency damage. Sometimes Kay would be given different information than Kathy by the same source, as if there was an effort to drive a wedge between them. One time, after Kay received a last-minute call that a scheduled television appearance was canceled, she stayed home. In fact, the show was not canceled, and the station later claimed none of their employees had phoned. Another time, after weeks of intense yet unsuccessful effort to talk to the governor, a key state news conference was timed for the exact day that Kathy and Kay were away in Washington giving statements before a congressional committee. The governor announced a new radon loan program, Kathy charged, "when he knew we were testifying and would not be there to badger him."

However, government was hardly the sole target for distrust. Colebrookdale residents were subjected to exploitive businesspeople seeking to take advantage of their plight. A "cancer-insurance" salesperson told Kathy, "You don't see a fire burning on the hill and wait." And a vacuum-cleaner salesperson told Kay that a congressman had sent him to remove the dust particles from her home.

Generally, distrust of others resulted from a more subtle situation. Contamination victims are frequently isolated by the events that follow the discovery of their exposure. They quickly find that friends and relatives who might be supportive in normal life situations lack any understanding of what they are going through. Others are even less sympathetic. It is common to hear the complaint, "Outsiders just don't understand." Besides being unhelpful, outsiders often engage in blaming the victims. And the more that the contamination victims act to call attention to their plight, by appearing in the media, speaking at meetings, and otherwise demanding action, the more they are likely to be blamed. Stigma surrounding the "contaminated" victims is easily spread to the community. Those who disbelieve the threat may still fear a loss of values for their homes and of image for their community. Victims, particularly activists, are blamed. Often, understanding and support is found only among those sharing belief in the threat.

These issues were mirrored in Kay Jones' experience. Kay had many old friends in the Boyertown area and even in her development. Given the neighborhood's many children, it was not difficult to meet other neighbors. Overall, the neighborhood was friendly and relaxed. However, after the radon issue emerged, even many of her childhood friends appeared to be unsupportive. Some felt her efforts to promote the radon issue would damage their own property values. Now she realized that these "weren't good friends after all." Thus, the radon issue fundamentally tested and altered Kay's social relationships. "I'd get angry at my friends. This wasn't me. I couldn't wait to get back to Boyertown and now there is bitterness and almost hatred. Why aren't they here to help us?"

Then there was the ostracism from the larger community. As a result of her activism, Kay was singled out by her fellow townspeople. The result was her loss of comfort in her own community. "I find it hard to accept others' attitudes. My husband doesn't care what they think. I'd like to get out. I don't handle it well when I go into town and people say 'you're the lady from Radon Hills' or 'Who you talking to this week?' They don't like that I'm keeping this alive."

Ironically, nonnatives of the Boyertown area were more likely to join PAR and to work with Kay and Kathy than were their fellow residents. Isolated in their own activism, Kay described how she and Kathy formed a two-person support group. "Kathy and I are really the only ones. If it had not been for her, I would have broken, especially over Christmas. We talk daily. We share. Each of us is there to keep the other going. Lois Gibbs at Love Canal had a lot of people behind her. She had residents who were dealing with the immediate health effects. We are not talking about that here. There are only two of us. She wasn't knocked down as many times."

Environmental Stigma

It is not surprising that the Colebrookdale houses were stigmatized by the radon issue (Edelstein, 1988, 1991). And the blaming of the activists reflected the combined threat of the radon issue to both personal and community interests. In becoming activists, the Joneses had anticipated and accepted the risk that their property values would be harmed. Their decision stood in stark contrast to that made by many PAR members who, though they might come to meetings to hear speakers, remained publicly silent for fear of real estate problems.

But it was Kay and Kathy who, as activists, attracted further blame for deliberately generating publicity, through which they extended the risk of environmental stigma to others. Philip Shabecoff, the *New York Times* environmental reporter whose coverage made radon into a national issue, once joked to Kathy that radon was the first story he had ever covered that he could not take a picture of. Yet, it was Shabecoff's writing that gave radon the "surrogate" visibility it needed to cause environmental stigma. With the help of PAR, the radioactive threat in Colebrookdale Township became a much-publicized story.

A key factor in environmental stigma is the "bounding of the problem," where tangible geographic boundaries are thought to surround the contamination. Those inside the boundaries are affected, those outside are not. An important characteristic of the Colebrookdale Township radon event was that it suggested that a cluster of homes was defined, even if not all homes within the cluster were affected. The common image of this boundary was suggested by the *Pottstown Mercury* when it ran a cartoon that dubbed Kay and Kathy's area "Radon Hill." Kay described in detail the way that area residents had accepted that the problem was bounded to her immediate neighborhood, even though houses elsewhere around Boyertown also had high radon levels. "If you go into a Boyertown restaurant and talk to people randomly, you'll be told that the radon problem is up on the hill. 'That's their problem up there.' There was a sidewalk sale in Boyertown last week. There were trolley rides. I was going to take the children on them. It's a good thing we didn't. But Kathy took the same ride. They were talking about the scenic orchards of Colebrookdale Township. As they were coming up Funk Road, the driver said 'better known lately as Radon Hills.'"

Because it is the marked or bounded area, rather than the affected area, which is subjected to stigma, Kay was describing a deliberate effort to create perceptual boundaries showing that the problem is "there" not "here." Ironically, even while Boyertown residents viewed the problem as belonging to "Radon Hills," in the national media, the affected area was often inaccurately described as Boyertown, rather than Colebrookdale Township. Nearby Boyertown thus also acquired the stigma. It was not surprising, therefore, that the radon issue was viewed as a direct threat to the image of Boyertown, with its strong collective identity as the host of the American Legion baseball championships. Evidencing its strong tradition of civic spirit was an all-out effort to build a new stadium with voluntary labor and local donations. Yet, although local businesses generously underwrote local sports activities, none assisted with the thousands of dollars of photocopying PAR required.

Back to Normal?

It is not clear whether victims of high radon levels can ever return to their previous life assumptions. In the Joneses' case, their life amid mitigation experiments hardly approached normalcy. Yet, as the radon levels began to stay low, over time, Kay seemed to regain a sense of control over the problem that allowed her to reassess the prudence of staying in their home. "I'm feeling safer now. There was a time when I did not feel that this was a safe house. Maybe because I talked to people, I was here when they did the testing. I'm fairly confident." These comments came in midsummer. Kay's confidence cautiously excluded colder weather. The mitigation in her home had not yet been tested under closed-house conditions during the higher radon-emitting winter months. However, Kay was also optimistic that in the long term her home would regain its economic value.

> Right now there is a problem selling homes. However, somewhere down the road, one, or two or three years, as this becomes nationwide, I think it will be more accepted. People will understand it. They will be aware that it is a national issue. Right now there is too much adverse publicity. People see it as a Stanley Watras, Kay Jones, or Kathy Varady problem. People in Boyertown don't admit that there is a problem. People who are having their houses tested don't want there to be an Arix [Tel Tappan's radon mitigation

company] or government car in the driveway. People know these things through gossip. Just as with asbestos, down the road there are things that one can do. Right now, this has damaged the value of our home, but it will come back with time and education. Time heals all wounds. We're probably sitting in a lot safer home than a lot of people.

While both the Joneses and the Varadys have remained in their homes as of the publication of this volume, the period of radon action has diminished for them. Their homes are long mitigated, as are those of others in Colebrookdale Township. The radon issue matured around them, moving past the phase of government intervention when their advocacy was necessary. And, in their private lives, radon finally took back seat to other life concerns. Neither actively monitors for radon, nor apparently have they acted to update the systems that drove down their initial astounding radon levels. Dreaded lung cancers have not materialized. Children have grown and gone to college. But, while radon has receded as a dominating issue in life, Kathy recently noted that it only takes a television report or a newspaper article (or a call from a book author) to bring back "all that stuff. It never goes that far away from you. This is something that a part of you will not let go of."

Stanley Watras' Expert/Professional Response to Radon Victimization

The victimization of Stanley Watras and his family incorporates similar challenges from living with the radon issue to those experienced by Kay Jones and Kathy Varady, with the added turmoil due to the periods of radon discovery and of subsequent relocation faced by the Watrases. Indeed, the Watrases themselves divided their experience into these three periods (Strecklow, 1985f).

The Period of Discovery

Nearly a month passed between the time that Stanley Watras first tripped the alarms at Limerick and the final confirmation that his home was unlivable. This was a period of suspended reality, as baffling and upsetting new developments occurred for Stanley, first at the Limerick plant, and then at home. The couple described this period as the worst in their lives (Strecklow, 1985f).

For Stanley Watras, the discovery of radon in his home contradicted his pride in his ability to work with radiation on a daily basis while avoiding exposure for himself and his family.

I was taught good concepts on how to deal with radiation. I'm involved with it daily. It's part of my job, something that I choose to do. To be honest with you, it added excitement for me. To know that you have an analytical problem that you know you will have to solve quickly because the longer you are in there, the more exposure you get. You go in, you observe, you leave, you do drawings, and then you go back in and rectify the situation. You know the safeguards. You know the source. You know where there are higher levels and how close you can get. You know what you are dealing with. You are not dealing with being blind. You know your exposure rates and how to extrapolate them.

All of this confidence and competence in working with radiation was of little initial benefit in these new circumstances. Generally, the situation was as novel and unexpected for Stanley as it was for the larger society introduced to residential radon through his discovery. Diane was previously certain that Stanley would never put his family at risk from radiation; she commented, "that's why it was such a shock when this happened." As efforts to confirm the levels in their home continued, Stanley and Diane spent much of their time on the phone seeking advice from government officials, health experts, and private consultants. They were continually met by disbelief when they reported their levels, despite the fact that those results had been confirmed by government officials. And as they sought answers to their questions, Stanley told a reporter (Strecklow, 1985f), "The common answer was, 'I don't know.' Is there any way to fix the house? 'I don't know.' Are we medically hurt? 'I don't know.' Is another day here going to harm us? 'I don't know.'" Diane summed up their efforts, "The more we looked for answers, the more confused we got." The pressure was so great that normally reserved Stanley broke into tears in front of his coworkers.

The Watrases also had to deal with all the emotional issues churned up by their new circumstances. During the Christmas holiday, they faced many emotions, perhaps the most poignant being the guilt they felt for having exposed their two sons to this uncertain yet seemingly huge risk (Strecklow, 1985f). They did not know whether it was safe to continue living in their home, what their options were for addressing the threat, and where they would go even if they decided to leave.

Confronting Forced Relocation

The choice of whether to stay or leave was taken from Stanley and Diane on that snowy Saturday in January when, in Stanley's words, the DER "threw us out of the house." What are the things that loom large when one is confronted by the message to leave the place where one has invested time, money, and feelings? Clearly, forced relocation is a traumatic experience. Stunned, yet needing to act, Stanley and Diane methodically took down the Christmas tree, reflecting their fear that the tree might catch fire and the house burn down if they were gone a long time. As they packed through the next day, the Watrases thought that they would never be moving back. They were about to become dislocated—virtual refugees due to this novel threat.

Lacking any other options, the family moved into the local Holiday Inn. In a newspaper interview (Strecklow, 1985f, B01), Diane recalled what it was like raising her family in this environment. "The first week was kind of like a vacation for the boys. They thought it was great. The second week, it began to feel more a drag. By the fourth week, I was ready to pull my hair out. With two kids and a dog living in a hotel." Facing the need for a more permanent temporary situation, the Watrases went hunting for a house to rent. They had difficulty because they did not want to sign a long lease that would obligate them should they be able to return home. By the fifth week, they had located a suitable duplex and moved in.

During this period, the pious and private family had sought to avoid notoriety. They had asked the DER to keep their identity secret. However, the story quickly spread, and they had to cope with the burden of becoming public figures. Other prior pressures continued during this period. Work was demanding for Stanley. And he invested considerable time and emotion to the task of serving as his mother's guardian. Suffering from Alzheimer's disease, in the wake of her husband's death, she had been placed in a residential setting in Delaware. Stanley traveled back and forth until her death in April 1985.

The impacts of the relocation period were greatly complicated by the fact that the Watrases had two young children. The hasty evacuation had been particularly troubling for their older boy, Michael, then three-and-one-half years old. Michael was upset by not being able to sleep in his own room, in his own house. Furthermore, he had to leave his toys behind; if he wanted something, his parents would have to fetch it and decontaminate it before he could play with it. He missed being able to have his birthday party at home. Besides, his parents were highly stressed and completely absorbed in addressing the crisis in which they suddenly had found themselves. And the tensions of the cramped life in the motel room had affected the child. Michael's teachers noticed changes in his behavior at school. He was less outgoing and expressive. In an effort to explain to him what was happening without attempting to describe radon, his parents told him that their house was broken and his toys were broken. It would take a lot of time to fix everything. It was not until after his return home, when he was four, that Michael finally started to ask about radon. In their 1987 interview with the first author, Stanley recalled, "Last year, out of the blue, he asked us, 'Why did you buy a house with radon?' We told him we didn't know the radon was here. He then said, 'when I get older, I'm going to buy a house with no radon because I don't want to have to move out.' He decided never to move again. He equates moving with radon. Talk about a guilt trip!" The younger son, two-year-old Christopher, was also impacted by the disruptions of this period. In retrospect, Stanley suggested in 1997 that he was perhaps the most severely affected of the two boys.

Beyond all of the other worries of this period, relocation presented the Watrases with severe financial pressures. Neither the government nor PECO was compensating them for their added expenses. So, on top of all of the other stresses, they had to come up with money for both their house mortgage and their rent. Reflecting back on just how hard it was to pull through this period, Stanley finds it instructive that none of his neighbors relocated during remediation; none had to face this additional burden during an otherwise trying time.

On April 20, 1985, the Limerick plant announced that it would fix Stanley's house.[6] At that time, the Watrases were slated for inclusion in the EPA eighteen-home study. Over the next two months, the Arix Corporation of Grand Junction, Colorado tackled their house. Between April 22 and June 11, Arix installed a passive radon reduction system. The concrete basement floor was replaced, a radon barrier and underground ventilation system was installed, and the exterior basement walls were sealed. The final bill was $32,670, $11,000 over the original estimate. Stanley told a reporter (Strecklow, 1985e, A01) that he felt uneasy about taking "a handout. I still feel I should have paid for it myself."

In June Arix issued a report claiming the project was "very successful" (Strecklow, 1985e, A01). Radon levels had been dropped "by a factor of approximately 1500" to less than 2 pCi/l. It was "safe to assume" that levels would stay that low. Although there was no guarantee that the system would work, the Watrases returned home in July 1985. But their ordeal was in no way over.

Adjusting to the Return to Radon's Birthplace

Back at home, the Watrases could not return to normal life. News media called continually, as did people concerned for their own homes and seeking information about radon. They dealt with government officials. They even got calls from an astrologer from Atlanta, Stanley told a reporter (Strecklow, 1985f, B01). "She wanted to know our sign to see if we have radon in our stars." Much as the Joneses and Varadys, the Watrases faced major intrusions into their lifestyle and lifescape.

Concerns over Health. Even assuming that their house was now perfectly safe, the Watrases had already been exposed to an extraordinary level of radiation. As the bombarding media continually reminded them, their possible exposure during their year in the house prior to relocation:

- was sixteen times greater than occupational standards for radon exposure in uranium mines and more than one hundred times the allowed uranium miner exposure
- was more than two hundred thousand times higher than the acceptable level for ambient exposures from nuclear power plants

- was six hundred and seventy five times the EPA guidance for radon
- was equal in risk to exposure from 455,000 chest X-rays
- was equal in risk to smoking some fifty thousand packs of cigarettes
- amounted to nearly a one hundred percent resulting lung cancer risk.

This informational assault almost created a certainty from the plethora of uncertainties the Watrases faced. Not afforded the early period of denial that Kay Jones reported, Stanley and Diane went through a period of questioning "Why me" (AP, 1988, 18). As they thought about their children, they were filled with feelings of fear and guilt. Stanley told the *Philadelphia Inquirer*'s Steve Strecklow, "You name an emotion and we have had it. Anger? Definitely. Hurt? Definitely. Sorrow, crying? Every emotion you name, we have had." He and Diane blamed themselves for putting their children at risk, for the fact that their youngest child had spent "80 percent of his life in a radioactive cloud." And, in the same interview, Diane described their situation as follows, "We just have to live each day as it is and pray that God won't let our children have any problems from this. I would pray that one of us would get it, rather than my children" (Strecklow, 1985f, B01). Similarly, Stanley told the first author "I assume the worst but pray for the best and that ten years from now I'll be able to say that it wasn't so bad."

Trust in Their Home. Once mitigation occurred, the Watrases were not afforded a very prolonged sense of confidence in the renewed safety of their home. Only a month after their return home, weekly monitoring by Arix revealed a steady climb in radon levels. This first breach in the mitigation was traced to an exhaust fan that Stanley had installed to replace a broken dehumidifier. While disconnecting the fan allowed results to drop, by October, radon levels had surged toward one hundred times the EPA guideline. This rude awakening dashed any hope that the Watrases had that their home had been truly fixed, bringing back all the upset that they had just started to get over. Underscoring their renewed uncertainty was the comment of an Arix health physicist, "Right at this time we're really not sure what is the cause of it. We're planning on doing some more work. . . . It's a growing process. Everyone learns, of course. And I do believe that if we can't, you know, reduce the levels to below (the EPA guideline), we can reduce them drastically from what they were" (Strecklow, 1985e, A01; see also f).[7]

As with Art Scott's experimentation on the Jones and Varady homes, here we see the virtual disabling of the Watrases, as their home was manipulated by others who only had a rough idea of how to bring radon exposures into line. His powerlessness in the face of this uncertainty must have been torturous for Stanley Watras. Strecklow describes him at the family dining room, his fist clenched, demanding "We need more research. We need something definite" (1985f, B01).

Stanley and Diane soon learned that their radon levels varied with weather conditions, time of day, and the use of house systems. The Watrases began to conduct their own experiments, studying the radon impacts of using their furnace and fireplace and, because of the radon in their water, with how to cleanse themselves. They tried variations of taking showers with the fan on or off and the bathroom door opened and closed before adopting a regimen of what Stanley described as the military shower. "You get wet, turn off the shower, suds and then rinse." The Watrases also had to manage the kitchen carefully. They found that just boiling water "crapped up" their kitchen unless the water was first stored for several days to allow for radioactive decay. Often, they bought drinking water. Food was cooked in canned vegetable stock, not in water. The kitchen vent hood filters needed to be changed periodically to prevent them from becoming too "hot." In the laundry room, the window had to be cracked open whenever the dryer was used to control negative pressure. Initially their feedback came from long-term tests, which did not alert them of surging radon levels quickly enough to prevent exposure. After Stanley brought home a new continuous testing device that provided current information on the performance of their mitigation systems, they were able to regain a sense of comfort in their home. As Stanley explained to the *Inquirer*'s Strecklow, "Before I could never get a result back quick enough to know if I had done something wrong and I was hurting my children worse" (1988, B01). Stanley was so taken with the instrument, aptly named the "At Ease" monitor, that he later became a representative for the manufacturer. In 1997, Stanley reported that they had tested their home every day since.

In fact, like the Jones and Varadys, the Watrases have remained in Colebrookdale Township. But, unlike the others, for the Watrases, their home has become their own laboratory for understanding and minimizing radon exposures. From shortly after their return from radon exile, the Watrases made it clear that they had no intention of ever leaving the house on Indian Lane. They became wedded to their home, in part because they knew how to manage radon levels there, and, in part because they wanted to provide stability for their children.

Another major factor for the Watrases was their deep felt sense of moral responsibility regarding the property. Diane told a reporter shortly after they had begun experiencing problems with their mitigation, "I'd rather walk away from this house, and just leave it . . . than to ever sell this house. If I didn't feel secure here myself, I couldn't do that to somebody else" (Strecklow, 1985f, B01). Indeed, in the wrong hands, theirs was a lethal building. Stanley expounded on this consideration during his 1987 interview with the first author.

> Now we feel a moral obligation to stay here. When I took the position with
> Bechtel [a worldwide nuclear plant contractor], I expected to travel. Now

we feel we couldn't do unto someone else what was done to us. We've done a lot of things here. We know how to keep on top of the radon levels in the house. You almost need to be an engineer to live here. If someone said that they liked the house and wanted to move in, I don't think that the Lord would like it. If we would move away, we would do other people harm by selling the house.

Ten years later, Stanley would report that this was still the family's position. *Regaining a Sense of Control.* As suggested above, the Watrases did not respond to the life in their high radon house by exhibiting helplessness. But unlike the PAR activists who pushed the government to correct the continuing problems in their homes, the Watrases increasingly took matters affecting the radon levels into their own hands, acquiring the tools and competencies to manage the situation themselves.

Similarly, they adopted a proactive and pragmatic view toward the future. From the onset, Stanley and Diane realized that they had to keep an optimistic perspective if they were going to cope with the situation. Stanley told a reporter, "If we're always saying something bad is going to happen, then we are going to go crazy" (Manegold, 1985, A01). Similarly, while Stanley reported in 1988 that he was still wondering daily about his family's health, he added, "There's a fine line between making yourself sick by worrying and having a genuine concern and doing the best you can" (AP, 1988, 18). One of the things that Stanley did was to stop smoking (Strecklow, 1985a).

Likewise, the Watrases were able to rationalize their entire ordeal in terms of its positive implications. Thus, Stanley told the *Philadelphia Inquirer,* "I just thank God that if it was going to be anybody living in that house, it would be me, somebody who could, through their work activities, discover the situation" (Strecklow, 1985a, A01).

The Watrases' desire to provide a normal family environment for their children after the trauma of relocation dictated strict limits on their willingness to allow radon to continue to intrude on their lives. They limited interviews and phone calls in order to make up for the attention that their children had to lose. At the same time, as in their early conversations with the *Philadelphia Inquirer,* they made their story available as a gesture of support for other people facing radon discovery. At that point, they felt they could only offer sympathy rather than concrete information, as Diane explained to Steve Strecklow (1985f, B01). "It would be very nice to be able to say, 'This is what you do if you have a problem. You call this person, you pay this much to get it done.'" In their own quest for a thorough understanding of the hazard that haunted their home, it was precisely this kind of practical approach to solving problems that Stanley and Diane thought was necessary.

Blame and Stigma. The Colebrookdale Township radon issue entailed its share of community conflict. There were concerns about property values. While

PAR's public pressure for action did not always meet with widespread public support, the Watrases also drew blame. Some neighbors even blamed Stanley for causing the radon problem in the first place. He commented during the 1987 interview, "The ultimate accusation was heard a million times: 'This area was okay until you moved in. You work at the powerhouse. You brought it to the neighborhood. Stanley Silkwood!' Elected officials would take me aside when we were alone and ask, 'Did you bring that home from the powerhouse?' People grasped for straws. This was just too far-fetched for them to accept."

The Watrases additionally drew blame for other facets of their experience. There was certainly not much mutual support between PAR and the Watrases. When Stanley refused Kay and Kathy's requests for help, Kathy commented to a reporter, "It's upseting that someone in that position could possibly be doing something more. Everything he does is in the news media. There's no sense in having this much exposure unless you're going to help someone" (Osborn, 1986, 11). And, when Diane approached Kay to offer her emotional support, she was rebuffed. Some neighbors blamed the Watrases for not personally informing their neighbors about the radon problem, a view that the Watrases see as unfair given the DER's notification of the neighborhood immediately following their being asked to relocate. Another murmur in the neighborhood was over all the attention received by the Watras family when they had lived in their house only one year while others had much longer exposures. Stanley dismisses this issue by citing the extraordinarily high levels in his house that gave his family high exposure even if the duration was limited.

The Watrases also encountered environmental stigma, as when reporters were afraid to enter their house and insisted on conducting interviews on the front porch. Stanley blamed the area's stigma on PAR's vocal criticism of the eighteen-home study. He did not agree that real estate sales had been blocked by the stigma, however, citing both realtors who said that the issues never affected realty values and that one high radon home in the neighborhood sold within weeks of being remediated.

Trust in Government. Stanley disagreed from the onset with PAR over the trustworthiness of government. While the PAR activists cited the contradictions in various actions and messages of government, for Stanley, government had handled the radon issue with amazing consistency and clarity. "The DER never downplayed the severity of radon. They kept saying this is a problem. They never downplayed it. It was the opposite. . . . How do you downplay something when you are going door to door to give free tests after they threw us out? If you downplay it, then Stanley Watras would be the only person who knows that radon exists."

Likewise, while PAR continually advocated for government assistance to homeowners, Stanley saw the radon issue as demanding just the kind of new approach to problems that the EPA offered. As he recalled in early 1997, for Stanley, the real grass roots movement around radon was not PAR, but rather the fast growing radon private sector.

By the summer of 1987, PAR had 150 members. By then the radon industry had been created. Government could not do everything. The government set up the industry. The scientific community developed the method to remediate houses for seven to eight hundred dollars. This was well into effect by 1987. PAR may have had 150 members, but what did it do? In 1987 it was saying that government should fix everybody's house. In Pennsylvania alone, 50 percent of the houses are over 4 pCi/l. And the government is going to fix them? Or should government set up the industry and regulate it to assure it is fair? Did PAR want every house in Pennsylvania to be experimented on? Or do you take the hottest house there ever was and experiment and find out about it and create an industry?

A Different Type of Activism

It is evident that Stanley was disdainful of the advocacy approach used by Kay Jones and Kathy Varady. He disagreed strongly with the views of the PAR founders on most points. For him, the stigma and adverse publicity about radon resulted from PAR's "screaming" rather than from the inherent threat of radon itself. He was also not inclined to see himself as a victim, even though he acknowledges that his family suffered severe impacts from the radon events.

That does not mean that the Watrases were not activists, just that they shied away from public confrontation and demonstration. Rather, they sought to influence the issue by using their growing expertise to inform public policy. Stanley recalls that he spent a year briefing Congressman Yatron, helping to set the stage for the eighteen-home study. Stanley prepared an eighty-six-page report on radon that he sent to President Reagan. He served on the DER's radon advisory board. Senator Arlen Specter sought Stanley's input on pending radon legislation. And Stanley gave testimony to Congress in the same hearing as Kay and Kathy.

But it was not until 1989 that the Watrases' involvement with radon reached a defining point. Stanley was a supervising construction engineer at the Limerick nuclear complex. As Limerick neared completion, his employer, the Bechtel Corporation, sought to transfer him to Nebraska. The offer came at a point when housing demand was up; they could have sold their house easily. Here was their chance to escape the house on Indian Lane, and perhaps, the entire radon issue. Instead, Stanley and Diane decided to stay put. Stanley would go into the radon testing and mitigation business full-time (he had been incorporated since 1987). Stanley recalled, "The first day, I walked into the house and said 'Okay, I am now in full time business. How do I get our next meal? We ate a lot of hot dogs in January 1990." That first year, Stanley remediated 50 houses, 70 in the second year, and 160 in the third. Thereafter, he was approaching and then exceeding 300 houses per year. In 1996, he fixed 350 houses, as well as commercial buildings and schools. He is now considered to be one of the largest contractors in Pennsylvania.

In his 1997 interview with the first author, Stanley stressed his devotion to the radon issue. "I have made radon my life's work—seven days a week. Every day I intimately and obsessively talk about doing things about radon. I talk to ten to fifteen people a day about radon. I go to nine or ten houses a day to talk about radon. I test and fix homes. When people talk to me—I call six homes every evening—people ask 'What is radon?'" Ironically, he estimates that few of these people know that it was he who discovered residential radon. Instead of talking about his personal past, he instead approaches his customers like any good contractor, stressing his experience in fixing houses and what he can do for them.

Conclusion

In contrast to their neighbors, radon has continued to be a central focus for the Watrases. Initially "paranoid" about making alterations to the house for fear it might change the way some system functioned, Stanley Watras regained control by using his own experience and engineering competence to understand the dynamics of radon in buildings. Rather than become caught up in the uncertainties over unpredictable health effects, instead the Watrases' energy was put to where they felt they could make a real difference. As a radon professional, Stanley tackled the issue of mitigation with the same thorough introspection that he had originally used to work out the source of his radioactive exposures at the Limerick plant, and later to control his own worst case dwelling. Stanley takes pride in the quality of his work, in the fact that houses are fixed for only seven to eight hundred dollars—a small fraction of what the original remediation of his and other Colebrookdale Township houses cost—and in his observation that people no longer need to be afraid of radon the way he and his neighbors were back in the 1980s. In this climate, he reports that mitigations have become as common as water softeners; it is "now the Yuppie thing to do. 'I have a radon system and you don't.'" Yet, ominously, even though he is one of the largest radon mitigators in his state, he told the first author in January 1997 that he still tests his house daily. "Today I still feel no confidence. I do not feel comfortable in my own house right now. "

Conclusion

The events in Colebrookdale Township thrust the radon issue into the national limelight and subjected a cluster of local residents to the life challenges confronting residents of a contaminated community. Their story, thus, signified to observers in 1985 more than just a warning about geologic radon. It represented, as well, a warning about what happens to the victims of geologic radon. Natural radon was not just an abstract risk after Colebrookdale Township, it was a tangible threat experienced by real people in a real setting. While it was not to prove an accurate predictor of how radon would subsequently affect most other families and communities, the victimization of residents in Colebrookdale Township greatly influenced the shape of the emerging radon issue, as will be seen in the next chapters. Literally and figuratively, the threat of naturally occurring radon had been put on the map.

Notes

1. Research for this chapter involved lengthy focused interviews conducted by Michael Edelstein at the Colebrookdale Township homes of the Watrases on August 7, 1987, the Joneses on June 29, 1986, and August 7, 1987, and the Varadys on June 29, 1986. Additional phone conversations about this chapter were held in September 1996. A further lengthy phone interview was held with Stanley Watras on January 31, 1997. Our appreciation to these families is gratefully given, not only for their time, but particularly for their insight. Except where other sources are noted, it should be assumed that the source for the information in the chapter was drawn from the original interviews conducted in 1986 and 1987 by the first author.

2. Some indication of the extent to which the Watras name was made public was evident in a computer search that netted eighty-seven citations on the first attempt.

3. For examples of media coverage of Kay Jones and Kathy Varady, see Boxall, 1985; Greer, 1985; Osborn, 1986; and Lowry, 1986b.

4. Stanley Watras recalls the meeting quite differently, suggesting a different reason for the departure of much of the audience prior to Tappan's talk and the subsequent split in the community over radon. He blames the confrontational and challenging approach of the activists.

> There was mass hysteria. People were accusing other people. Screaming like two-year-olds. People were sick of the screaming and they walked out. Others followed these people. If people had shut their mouths, Tel would have come on sooner. People who wanted information from the meeting had decided they were not going to get it given all the finger pointing, accusations and screaming.

A fundamental difference is evident here, whereby activists in the mold of Kay and Kathy confront government in an effort to force the truth to come out. Equally concerned and at least as impacted by radon, Stanley was willing to trust the process to reach a point of full disclosure. For him, there was no coverup, just obstruction. Increasingly, while government was the source of anger for the grassroots activists, the activists themselves became an object of anger for Watras and others of his temperament.

5. On his part, Stanley Watras had worked quietly behind the scenes to convince Yatron that other local residents deserved EPA assistance to fix their radon problems. Unlike other politicians, Yatron had been receptive to Watras' calls even before the

news broke. "I went to my elected officials before the news broke and they told me to 'Get away son.' They blew it off. Yatron did not. I worked for a year to inform Gus Yatron. He didn't know anything about it. But he talked about it with others. And he found that there was a provision for the experimental remediation in Superfund. Before it even hit the newspapers, he knew about it. He was not just motivated by reelection or jumping on the bandwagon." It was Yatron's sponsorship of the subsequent eighteen-home-study that Watras credits with the implementation of the program that was initially to fix his own and Kay Jones' house, but eventually served Jones, Varady, and sixteen other families.

6. One source suggests that PECO's generosity to the Watrases may not have been entirely selfless. Thus, Vroman (1988) notes that at the time of the Watras alarm, the Limerick plant was under intense public pressure. Nuclear fuel was on site, but the plant had not as yet gone on line. Antinuclear protesters were at PECO's door. The plant's initial concern that the Watras alarms would fuel the opposition motivated PECO to investigate the source of the radiation. When the trail led away from Limerick to Watrases' house and to natural radon, PECO was relieved to be proved blameless. But they also realized the opportunity to take the public relations initiative by paying for the Watras remediation.

7. Eventually the passive wind-driven turbines atop the Watras house were augmented by in-line centrifugal fans in the attic.

Chapter 2

From Issue Denial to Issue Acceptance

Heads have been buried in the sand for too long. The social implications are horrendous, because what you are saying is that a very large number of houses in the country are unsafe. You're talking about a cleanup here that would make the EPA's toxic waste cleanup program look like chicken feed.
—James Stebbings

The significance of the Watrases' discovery was in forcing acceptance of geologic radon as a residential hazard. But why was such a major hazard unrecognized prior to Watras? As the record reveals, there were ample hints of an "incubating" risk.

Radon Pre-Watras—A Slow Recognition of the Risk

Looking backward, it is possible to trace the first known human illness from radon daughter exposure to late in the sixteenth century, when the physician Agricola documented *bergkrankheit* (mountain sickness), a lung disorder that killed large numbers of miners in the Erz mountains near Schneeberg, Germany, and across the border near Jachymov, Czechoslovakia. It was not until 1879 that two German physicians identified this disease as lung cancer (Cothern, 1987). These deaths were not to be linked with radon for more than thirty years.

With the subsequent discovery of radioactivity and radiation, a period of fascination and unchecked application occurred. Radiation was viewed only as a cure, not a cause of illness. Radiation was widely used for prophylactic or preventative purposes in the first half of the twentieth century (Mazur, 1981). And radon's parent product, radium, received widespread application in the health fields. By the 1930s, more than 100,000 people were treated with radium every year worldwide, receiving the supposedly beneficial health effects of the radioactive emanations (Weart, 1988). Radium was used to kill skin cancers. Radiation pioneer Francis Soddy proposed radioactive gas as a cure for tuberculosis, scourge of the era. Pierre Curie, with his wife the codiscoverer of radium, enthusiastically endorsed the benefits of visiting radon spas, quite popular from the early 1900s through the 1930s and still used in some places. At these "ematorias" or "inhalatorias," people came to take their "cures" for tuberculosis and other ailments by inhaling radon and drinking and bathing in water having naturally high radium and radon counts. Belief in the healthful benefits of "sunshine rays" led to the marketing of patent medicines, elixirs, toothpastes, salves,

35

oils, and other products containing radium or radon. In the United States, over 150,000 radon emanators, devices that employed radium as a source of dissolved radon in water, were sold in 1926 alone. A 1929 listing showed eighty radioactive patent medicines being manufactured in Europe. These medicines promised to cure everything from rheumatism to baldness to old age. Luckily, many of the products were double frauds; they did not contain the radioactive ingredients listed (Cothern, 1987; Weart, 1988; Brenner, 1989). While widespread radon exposure occurred through these cures and products, usage was not subject to physician control, therefore systematic data on the health consequences are unavailable (Mazur, 1981).

Some anecdotal evidence of the possible health consequences of radioactivity did receive considerable publicity: the 1931 death from radiation sickness of a Pittsburgh playboy who for five years daily drank a supposed aphrodisiac called "Radithor" (Weart, 1988) and, in the early 1920s, the death from "jaw rot" (i.e., bone cancer) of female workers at a watch dial factory in New Jersey who had used their lips to maintain a fine point on their brushes while painting luminous dials with radium paint (Brenner, 1989, p. 75; Weart, 1988). Meanwhile, a 1913 study of mortality among Schneeburg uranium miners during the previous thirty-six years identified that 40 percent of the 655 miners who had died were victims of lung cancer. Given the absence of silica in the mines, the culprit was identified as radon and its daughters. A remedy, adequate ventilation, was also identified (Johnson and Dawson, 1994).

The Environmental Policy Cycle

What is notable about these cases is the growth of a popular culture of radon and radioactivity where, even in well-publicized cases, such as the death of the Pittsburgh playboy, government response was limited to shutting down the manufacturer of the specific elixir involved (Weart, 1988). However, no broad review of the safety of the type of medicine was undertaken and the overall public enthusiasm for radioactive cures was undaunted. The point is that it may take a long time before a significant hazard is understood, recognized, and accepted as real. Only then will choices be made from available policy options and the risk be addressed by protective government action. We can illustrate this "environmental policy cycle" (Guimond 1988b) by examining the gradual process of protective policy development evident in the history of radon and the uranium fuel cycle.

Radon and the Uranium Fuel Cycle

With the advent of nuclear weapons during World War II and the subsequent development of the nuclear power industry in the 1950s and 1960s, the societal experience with radiation and radioactivity greatly expanded. Potential hazards were recognized along the entire uranium fuel cycle in the United States, from the initial mining of uranium ores to the eventual effort to deal with radioactive wastes. Protective policy was developed to address the front end of the fuel cycle, both mining and extraction of uranium ores on the front end and the radon contamination caused by uranium mill tailings and radioactive residues from other mining and processing activities. We will examine the development of the environmental policy cycle for both cases.

Case One: Radon in Uranium Mines

The American uranium mining industry developed on a large scale after the cold war began in the late 1940s. The nuclear weapons and commercial nuclear reactor programs set off a uranium "gold rush" in the West and Southwest (Guimond, 1988b). With their intimate knowledge of the land, Native Americans played a significant role in locating uranium sources. Significant deposits were found in the region known as Four Corners, home to the largest concentration of Native Americans remaining in North America (Johnston and Dawson, 1994). By this time, low-cost preventive measures were already being employed in European mines, where lung cancer had been associated with uranium mining since the 1920s. Despite the presence of comparable levels of radon in the U.S. mines, the unregulated American industry chose to take no protective action against worker radon exposure. As a result, the mean working level in Colorado mines in 1950 was 26.5 WL, a level at which a substantial number of the miners were doomed to lung cancer (Pearson, 1980).

Efforts to set permissible levels for miner radon exposure during the 1950s failed for numerous reasons. First, serious uncertainties clouded the issue. The medical establishment at that time had not as yet sorted out what doses of radiation were required to produce adverse health effects or whether smoking was the sole source of lung cancer. The seven-to-thirty year latency period for lung cancer shrouded radon in a veil of what Vyner (1988) calls "medical invisibility." And, wildly fluctuating radon levels invited doubts over the reliability of measurements. A second reason stemmed from the conditions of mines themselves. Many of the mines were small, low budget, unsophisticated operations, employing only a few miners. Within the mines, the threat from an invisible gas paled in contrast to the immediate and serious physical risks faced by miners on a daily basis. A third reason was the stigma attached to miners. Mining was not a high-prestige occupation, and many of the young men were viewed as already putting themselves at risk from smoking and drinking. Also, the miners were ignored because many were Native Americans. In fact, the uranium-mining fatalities that serve as a basis for the estimates of risk from geologic radon occurred heavily among native miners, as Johnston and Dawson (1994, pp. 146–47) note.

An estimated 3,000 Navajo worked, at one point or another, in the approximately 1,200 mines scattered across the Four Corners region. Of the 150 or so Navajo miners who worked at the Shiprock facility, eighteen had died of radiation-induced cancer by 1975, an additional twenty were dead by 1980 of the same disease, and another ninety-five had contracted serious respiratory ailments and cancers. The incidence of miscarriages, cleft palates and other birth defects, bone, reproductive, and gastric cancers, and heart disease deaths have been identified as related health effects of uranium mining and exposure to contaminated environs.

Ironically, mines were able to avoid state mining regulation because most were located on tribal lands. Owners of the highly profitable mines also had strong allies in avoiding federal regulation. The demand for uranium was driven by the cold war nuclear weapons' program and, therefore, justified by national security. The Atomic Energy Commission (AEC) controlled the mines and actively promoted a uranium "gold rush" (Pearson, 1980; Guimond, 1988b; Johnston and Dawson, 1994). As a result, the shroud of government secrecy covered over information about the dangers. Behind the scenes, the AEC and the public health service fought a running battle over miner protection that stretched from 1947 all the way into the 1960s. The AEC joined mine operators in opposing actions such as ventilating the mines as "unnecessary and too expensive." The AEC's medical officers actively discounted the risk and went so far as to prevent influential researchers from speaking out on the issue publicly, particularly in the West. The result was that miners in the Four Corners area of the Southwest were, in the words of one researcher, deliberately "used as guinea pigs and we were essentially watching them die" (Schneider, 1990, p. A1; Hardert, 1993, p. 137).[1]

These issues combined to rob radon of the broad acceptance necessary to allow implementation of protective action. The climate shifted only after substantial evidence of lung cancer deaths in the U.S. uranium industry became available in the late 1950s. Around that time, the health problem also became visible, for example, in the rising number of workman's compensation awards for miner lung-cancer deaths. Identification of this epidemiological pattern, in turn, raised complex questions regarding compensation for slowly developing illness, identification of responsible employers, and the mounting costs to the public from these claims. As the press increasingly reported on the causal connection between radon exposure and lung cancer, public support was generated for strict action. Simultaneously, some of the barriers to regulation were also removed during this period. Of particular importance was the lessened demand for uranium, spurred by the phaseout of government procurement and by a fall in the price of the ore (Pearson, 1980).

In response to the mounting evidence linking lung cancer to radon in mines, by 1968 full recognition of the need for protection for uranium miners was evident. In his State of the Union address that year, President Lyndon Johnson promised that uranium miners who contracted lung cancer would receive worker's compensation benefits. Limits for miner exposure to radon were subsequently promulgated by labor secretary Willard Wurtz, and the need to reduce radon levels in mines was taken up by the surgeon general and the Federal Radiation Council. Uniform standards were implemented in 1971 to lower allowed radon daughter exposure to 12 WLM/yr (roughly 60 pCi/l in a residential environment at 75 percent occupancy or 198 pCi/l in an occupational mine environment) and subsequently to 4 WLM (Pearson, 1980; Guimond, 1988b; Scheberle, 1994).[2]

By the late 1970s, the adequacy of the U.S. standard was challenged when European studies showed a twofold increased risk of lung cancer for miners at 4 WLM (Pearson, 1980). Subsequently, miners' unions petitioned for even stricter standards (Guimond, 1988b). During the protracted fight for worker standards, a nonregulatory guidance for human-caused residential radon exposure was implemented with surprising speed in an effort to address problems associated with mill tailings contamination.

Case Two: Mill Tailings Contaminations

The other obvious connection between the uranium fuel cycle and radon involves the production of uranium wastes from mining and milling. Mill tailings, the piles of contaminated soil left over after mined rock is processed and refined, contain radioactivity from radium, as well as its relatively short half-life daughter products. As radium decays to radon in piles of tailings, the radon can easily escape through the porous sandlike material. As a result, levels of radon nearby as well as considerably downwind or downstream of large tailing piles have been found to be elevated substantially. In addition, radioactive mill tailings themselves have been responsible for significant cases of residential radon exposure (Pohl, 1982).

Use of these sandlike mill tailings for fill and in the construction of homes and schools occurred in places such as Grand Junction, Colorado, and other western communities throughout the 1950s and 1960s. It was not until the mid-1960s that the contamination was discovered through circumstances reminiscent of the serendipitous Watras experience. A state health worker accidentally brought home a film badge that, when later read, revealed a high level of radiation originating in the house (Ford et al., 1974). Two houses in Colorado were evacuated in 1969 due to radon from mill tailings. A 1970 EPA investigation found that radioactive mine tailings had been used as fill in more than six thousand Grand Junction homes and schools, as well as beneath playgrounds and sidewalks. Congressional testimony in 1971 described thousands of contaminated locations, prompting the allocation of five million dollars for remediation. Throughout the next decade, as many as thirty communities in the West were found to have similar problems, including Denver, Colorado, and Butte, Montana. With the Uranium Mill Tailings Control Act in 1978, Congress acknowledged that most of the mill tailings resulted from government weapons production. The Department of Energy (DOE) was ordered to clean up the contaminated buildings; EPA was to develop standards for the disposal of mill tailings and for the clean up effort (Guimond, 1988b; Coyle, 1986; Scheberle, 1994).

Meanwhile, in the late 1960s and early 1970s, EPA had also become involved with the regulation of the fertilizer-producing phosphate mining and milling industry in the state of Florida. Recognizing that radioactive materials were among the contaminants studied, EPA examined homes built on reclaimed phosphate lands. Despite the comparatively low levels of radiation in the soil, they discovered indoor radon levels comparable to those found in houses built atop the western uranium mill tailings. A major radon initiative commenced in Florida (Guimond, 1988b; Coyle, 1986).

Additionally, EPA began to investigate records indicating where in the country industries had historically used radioactive materials. In 1981, an EPA helicopter equipped with sensitive gamma detection equipment flew over a section of Essex County, New Jersey, adjacent to a closed radium reprocessing plant. This was the same factory used early in the century for the painting of instrument dials with a luminescent material refined from uranium ores imported from Colorado and where watch dial painters had developed bone cancer of the jaw. Three distinctly bounded areas of radioactive soil contamination were identified in the area where Montclair, West Orange, and Glen Ridge adjoin, corresponding to the use of radium-contaminated mill tailings taken from the plant for use as fill for residential properties (Wyckoff, 1987; Gordon, 1986).

Subsequently, the federal Centers for Disease Control (CDC) issued a health advisory covering twenty-two homes found to have more than 4 pCi/l of radon—five of which exceeded the allowed occupational exposure. The CDC set 1985 as a target date for the site to be remediated. Federal Superfund money, available for cleaning up human-caused industrial waste problems, was allocated for a pilot program to excavate and remove the soil from beneath twelve homes from which the occupants had been "temporarily" relocated. Excavated soil was placed in drums and stacked in the yards of the empty homes. In Montclair alone, some five thousand 55-gallon drums containing 10,000 cubic yards of contaminated soil filled the yards of four pilot homes. Neighbors remained in the adjacent houses during remediation of these buildings for radon and gamma radiation (Gordon, 1986). During the next four years, strong community opposition prevented the excavated material from being dumped in New Jersey because it was too contaminated, even as national radioactive waste disposal sites refused the material because it was not contaminated enough. Eventually, the soil was taken to Tennessee for blending with highly radioactive wastes that qualified for burial at Hanford, Washington. Meanwhile, hundreds of additional homes were found to have high radon levels due to radium-contaminated soil, but removal of the soil from beneath these buildings was initially rendered unfeasible by the soil disposal problem (see Edelstein, 1991). Agencies were inclined to leave the soil in place and to remediate the houses to reduce radon exposure. However, when citizens in the affected communities rallied on a dramatic scale, a massive program of soil replacement was undertaken under Superfund, with radium removed from some three hundred houses by 1996 and complete removal slated for completion by the year 2000 at a cost of $150 million (Galant, 1996).

As these cases suggest, by the 1980s, the United States had moved beyond regulating occupational exposures to a recognition that radon in homes was also hazardous. The question of health effects due to radon emissions from mill tailings had even forced a tenfold increase in Nuclear Regulatory Commission estimates of health effects from the nuclear fuel cycle during the licensing hearings on the second Three Mile Island nuclear facility (Johnsrud, 1987). Government had become involved with testing, standard setting, and remediation. The rapid movement of mill tailings contamination through the environmental policy cycle did not reflect a recognition of radon as a new problem, but rather the belief that it fit the already-operative regulatory paradigm. These radon problems were approached through a process similar to the Superfund framework used to evaluate and remediate other industrial pollution problems. At the same time, naturally occurring radon was not similarly recognized, accepted and addressed. Because geologic radon did not result from some human-caused pollution source, it lacked the key ingredient necessary to define it as "contamination" and to trigger action.

Missed Signals of a Natural Radon Problem

In focusing on human-caused radon issues to the exclusion of naturally occurring radon, the EPA and DOE overlooked the implications of geologic radon problems in other countries, as well as clear signs of a U.S. geologic radon problem.

Recognition Abroad of a Geologic Radon Problem

Sweden offered the clearest warning of a geologic radon threat. Residential radon exposure was first labeled as a widespread social problem there in the mid-1960s. Originally, the Swedes traced the radon to alum-shale rock used in concrete, but when radon continued to be found in new buildings even after this construction material was banned in 1974, it became clear that the primary radon source was not building materials, but rather radium in the soil. Radon did not emerge as a public concern, however, until the much publicized discovery in 1979 of a cluster of extremely "hot" houses in a central Swedish community, generating eight hundred phone calls to the federal government within one day. Over the next months, real estate values plummeted in areas with known radon problems, a phenomenon referred to by one official as "radon fever." This public concern spurred government action. Research established an epidemiological link between residential radon and lung cancer. The federal government became deeply involved in addressing the crisis and mandating radon-restrictive building codes. By 1980, Sweden had adopted radon standards, which limited new construction to 4 pCi/l, houses undergoing renovation to 10 pCi/l, and existing houses to 22 pCi/l. Local government was made responsible for finding homes with more than about 22 pCi/l exposure. Certification programs were instituted for mitigation and detection companies. Government loans were provided to assist homeowners with remediation. A government radon commission was formed. Eventually, the "radon fever" broke and radon inspection became a routine step during housing transfer. In sum, years before Colebrookdale Township, the Swedes had learned to manage their geologic radon issue (Lautenberg, 1986; Michel, 1987).

Closer to home, the Canadians discovered their natural radon problem in 1975 and began to quietly institute policies for addressing it. In 1976, a study was done of two thousand homes in the northern Ontario uranium mining community of Elliot Lake. About 16 percent of the homes studied were found to be above an action level set at 20 pCi/l, and the source was found to be radon emanating naturally from the soil. A subsequent (1977) fourteen-thousand home survey of nineteen cities in the prairie regions found several cities, including Winnipeg and Regina, with a significant number of houses above 4 pCi/l (Lowry, 1986; Radon Task Force, 1986; Guimond, 1988b). The government kept the results of the Winnipeg study secret until an October 1984 exposé on the CBC television show "The Fifth Estate," just two months before the Watras discovery. Subsequently, the Canadian press kept on the radon story, despite the admonition of a leading government official, "As we say, you can't tame nature; you just have to live with it." But even as they played down radon risk, the government's coverup had made geologic radon into a national scandal (Harrison and Hoberg, 1991, p.19).

Unheeded Warnings at Home

Meanwhile, U.S. officials remained absorbed with their human-caused radon contamination issues, despite clear warnings that a natural radon issue similar to that found in Sweden and Canada threatened the health of U.S. citizens, as well. The signs were everywhere.

Radon in Groundwater

One clue was the presence of radon in groundwater. In 1904, the physicist J. J. Thompson had found that radon could be dissolved in water. Soon afterward, radon was discovered in natural water supplies in both the United States and in Germany. However, it was more than half a century before radon in groundwater caused appreciable concern. In 1957, high radioactivity in groundwater supplies was accidentally discovered in Maine. By 1958, the U.S. Public Health Service and the state of Maine had verified that radon in water was a relatively common occurrence in the granitic mountain environments. While some wells had values of radon as high as a million pCi/l, lower values of 10,000 to 20,000 pCi/l were quite common (Cothern, 1987; Hall, 1988; Hess et al., 1980; Horton, 1985; Smith et al., 1961. Note that 10,000 pCi/l in water is roughly the equivalent of 1 pCi/l in air.).

The NURE Study

Then, in 1957, the NURE (National Uranium Resource Evaluation) study revealed that several areas of the United States had significant uranium deposits. It was not difficult to deduce that homes atop these natural deposits would have radon problems similar to those associated with uranium mill tailings and radioactive building materials. Still, there was no mobilization around geologic radon.

Energy Conservation

The energy crises of the 1970s provided yet another warning of an indoor radon hazard from natural sources. Late in the decade, it was realized that conservation measures might increase indoor air pollution. In fact, the EPA warned that the regulations for residential conservation developed by the Energy Department under the 1978 National Energy Conservation Policy Act would result in ten thousand to twenty thousand additional deaths per year, reflecting estimates of radon's impact. EPA's Deputy Administrator for Radiation Programs, David Rosenbaum, warned that "Radon is by far the highest radiation danger that the American public faces. It's certainly up there with the top dangers EPA deals with. It's easily more serious than Love Canal" (Belkin, 1980, p. 1274; see also Overby, 1986; Hurwitz, 1981; Bowden, 1982).

Given this realization, EPA unsuccessfully tried to convince the DOE to postpone implementing the residential conservation program. However, the DOE disagreed with the magnitude of the problem, arguing that the few thousand deaths that radon might cause would be offset by the benefits of energy use reduction. Despite its concern, EPA did little at that time to implement research on the radon problem or to aggressively combat indoor air pollution (GAO, 1980; see also Belkin, 1980). In contrast, in 1980, the New York State Energy Research and Development Authority began a study of radon levels in a random distribution of New York homes. In 1979, the Bonneville Power Authority became concerned that its weatherization projects might be making radon levels worse and began to develop a program that by 1984 provided free radon monitoring, set an action level of 5 pCi/l, and studied mitigation measures (BPA, 1984).

The Nuclear Debate

Meanwhile, the heated debates of the 1970s and 1980s over nuclear power plant siting made frequent use of the issue of radon as a background source of radioactivity. Mazur notes that the role of radon was polemical, with both proponents and opponents of nuclear power liberally citing radon data to back their positions. For nuclear proponents, the danger from radon in insulated homes was viewed as far more serious than was the danger from nuclear power plants. Furthermore, there was the possibility that the Nuclear Regulatory Commission would deregulate human-caused radiation found to be indistinguishable from the natural background levels created by ambient radon. For nuclear opponents, radon emitted during uranium mining, uranium processing, and power generation bolstered the argument that nuclear power was dangerous. The issue of radon hazard from mill tailings also surfaced in the heated controversy over the dangers from uranium mining in the mountain ranges of northern New Jersey and southern New York in the late 1970s (Mazur, 1987; Johnsrud, 1987). Despite the fact that radon risk was liberally cited during this period because of its significance for nuclear plant siting, no one really took radon seriously, despite the large risk numbers. An early opportunity to recognize natural radon was lost.

Ironically, Johnsrud (1987) suggested that, because of the politically adverse implications of agency research into the dangers of nuclear power, around 1980 EPA was told to focus only upon geologic radon. Subsequently, EPA research in Florida found that excess radon levels were not just due to building atop phosphate-reclaimed lands. By 1984, Florida was sufficiently concerned to promulgate a 4 pCi/l standard for radon in new homes in those counties where mining was prevalent. Meanwhile, in Butte, Montana, it was discovered that indoor radon in some houses did not come from phosphate residues thought to be the culprit, but rather from fractures in rock. Research by the DOE's Lawrence Berkley Laboratory also revealed natural radon as a source (Guimond, 1988b).

The Pennsylvania Discoveries

As early as 1976, rumors of a potential radon problem had circulated in Pennsylvania. Then in 1979, while searching for economically viable uranium deposits, a DER geologist named Robert Smith discovered high levels of background radiation in the Reading Prong. In 1981, a modest amount of publicity focused on the discovery of 55 pCi/l in a $300,000 underground, energy-efficient house in eastern Pennsylvania owned by a physician named Joel Nobel, head of the National Indoor Air Environmental Institute (Higham and Fleishman, 1986; Bowden, 1982; Mazur, 1987). That year, a joint study by Princeton University and Pennsylvania Power and Light Company confirmed the presence of significant levels of residential radon in eastern Pennsylvania, reaching 200 pCi/l, that correlated to soil and bedrock type (Sachs, 1988). Subsequently, the National Indoor Air Environmental Institute, Argonne National Laboratory, and the University of Pittsburgh all began radon research projects in eastern Pennsylvania (Drachler, 1985; Sachs, cited in Makofske and Edelstein, 1988, p. 377).

Ironically, the Argonne National Laboratory study, done with the cooperation of the Pennsylvania Department of Health, had focused upon the Bloomsburg area, where the Watrases lived before their move to Colebrookdale Township. The DOE discovery of a geologic radon problem there grew out of a study of a former radium-dial plant, similar to the facility that caused the widespread contamination in New Jersey. The DOE developed a seven-year, seven million dollar study of radon that, in the winter before the Watras discovery, tested 100 homes in the Bloomsburg area (Strecklow, 1985a). So much information was accumulating on the topic of geologic radon that an entire volume of the journal *Health Physics* (vol. 45, no. 2, August 1983) was devoted to the topic. EPA's radiation specialist in Pennsylvania, Bill Belanger, was sufficiently aware of the problem that, when he built a house in Delaware County in 1983, he tried to make it radon-proof (Goldstein, 1991).

Inaction on Radon

What government response resulted from these early clues about natural radon? In 1975, when EPA had brought indoor air quality issues to the attention of the Department of Energy's predecessor, the Energy Research and Development Administration, EPA was encouraged to investigate. An EPA employee reported that, in fact, just the opposite occurred (Belkin, 1980, p. 1276): "After that, we sat and waited for the results. Funding was reduced to a trickle, and EPA was already up to its ears in Love Canal and acid rain or whatever the pollution of the week was. There was no one there to push this through, so it died of neglect." Another EPA official of the time added that "EPA made a policy decision that the problems of outside ambient air were on top of the list. Indoor air was not" (Belkin, 1980, p. 1276).

Meanwhile, back in Pennsylvania, DER geologist Robert Smith, alarmed by his findings, had told homeowners that their levels of radiation were so severe that the DER would be getting in touch with them. However, the DER failed to follow up (Drachler, 1985). Similarly, Joel Nobel, owner of the underground house, failed to generate government action on geologic radon despite some national media attention (Higham and Fleishman, 1986; Mazur, 1987) and the reported expenditure of some quarter million dollars to promote the issue (Strecklow, 1985a). The Pennsylvania Power and Light data had been analyzed by Harvey Sachs, an outspoken young geographer at Princeton University. Sachs was one of the first to recognize the scope of the naturally occurring radon problem. Along with others, he carried out an unsuccessful campaign to get Pennsylvania to confront the issue (Sachs 1982, 1983). In his communications, Sachs argued that natural radon was a much more serious problem than was radiation from the Three Mile Island accident. But DER officials never responded to Sachs. Leaving Princeton, Sachs continued his research at Nobel's National Indoor Air Environmental Institute, carrying out surveys in eastern Pennsylvania from 1982 to 1984 (Sachs, cited in Makofske and Edelstein, 1988, p. 377; Drachler, 1985). Ironically, Sachs joined the Nobels on national television to promote recognition of the geologic radon threat only two weeks before the Watras discovery forced the very actions that they urged (Mazur, 1987).

Was there a deliberate coverup of the radon issue by the DER, as critics like Sachs charge (Drachler, 1985; Makofske and Edelstein, 1988)? Indeed, DER officials freely admit to knowledge of a geologic radon problem in the Reading Prong prior to Watras. They were planning a study of the Reading Prong in spring 1979, but say that radon "fell through the cracks" due to their preoccupation with the Three Mile Island (TMI) nuclear disaster. But DER officials had not totally forgotten about radon. As their monitoring of TMI wound down in 1984, the agency requested modest funding in its 1985–86 budget for equipment to study natural radon. However, Watras arrived before the equipment did (Gerusky, 1986; 1988; Drachler, 1985; Strecklow, 1985a).

Meanwhile, radon was not making very much progress in Washington either. The EPA had never gotten around to clarifying its policy with regard to natural, as opposed to human-caused, radon contamination. Geologic radon did not readily trigger the emergency conditions that would bring forth assistance from the Federal Emergency Management Agency, which responds to natural disasters.[3] And, yet, it also fell outside of the original Superfund framework, which addressed the need for public response to human-caused industrial contamination, as found at sites such as Love Canal (GAO, 1986; Coyle, 1986). Thus, natural radon did not fit any existing pigeon holes.

Nevertheless, the many clues of a natural radon problem had not gone unnoticed in Washington. Sufficient data existed in the early 1980s to suggest that houses on normal undisturbed land might be at risk from naturally occurring radon, although it was generally thought that exposures from natural radon would be a fraction of that from the human-caused mill tailings exposures (Guimond, 1988b). Based on the Florida experience, EPA's Guimond recalled that "generally, the highest levels we saw in those naturally occurring situations were not as high as the contamination problems. We formulated a belief that levels in natural-occurring houses would be about one-tenth of what we'd seen in houses with contamination problems. And so, while it was of concern to us and we wanted to examine it more, I don't think we felt it was an imminent hazard or a high priority" (Coyle and Drachler, 1986, p. 2).

At EPA, the director of the Office of Radiation Programs proposed a radon program for fiscal year 1982 to begin the task of exploring the issue. However, the prospect of a widespread radon issue emerged at a time when the regulatory and proactive role of government was under siege. Under its new president, Ronald Reagan, American society had begun to question the regulatory paradigm for determining acceptable levels for acting on risk, as well as the active role of government in protecting the environment.

Radon Meets Reagan

The nascent EPA geological radon initiative coincided with the arrival of the Reagan administration. The EPA budget, much as the budgets of all other federal agencies, required approval from the executive branch's Office of Management and Budget (OMB), which was instructed to avoid costly federal involvements. The OMB blocked the proposed radon program, citing fears that if EPA were to find that the radon problem was as serious and widespread as it expected, the program would become extremely costly, a veritable "Superfund for Radon."[4] As a result, EPA's Rich Guimond (1988a) noted, "Radon got lost between 1980 and 1984 due to the new administration—to a degree. Rosenbaum was head of the office of radiation at the time. He believed in radon. He tried to build a radon program. He ran afoul of OMB. He made OMB apprehensive that he would create an extremely expensive monster."

Beyond its extreme sensitivity to regulatory expansion, the Reagan administration was characterized by other ideological stands. There was a strong tendency to favor the marketplace as a mechanism for solving problems, wherein homeowners would be seen as consumers whose needs would be met by private entrepreneurs, not government. For these homeowners, threats such as radon were to be defined as private problems, beyond the scope of government "interference" or responsibility. Cost was accentuated as a determining factor in whether to respond to risk, with extensive research required to substantiate anything but the most blatant threats. Finally, there was a strong emphasis on decentralization of government response, with a tendency to have the federal government yield to states as the primary actors. Thus, beyond the previous barriers to societal recognition and acceptance of geologic radon as a hazard, the predilections of the new administration posed a hard test for geologic radon to meet. However, all these barriers were to fall in December 1994.

The Magic Watras Event—Instant Issue Acceptance

All the flirtation with geologic radon set the stage for what EPA's Richard Guimond later termed "the magic Watras event" (Guimond, 1987, p. 4; see also chapter 1 of this volume). As Guimond recognized, without Watras, there may have been no public recognition and acceptance of the natural radon hazard. The Watrases and some of their neighbors were exposed to levels of radiation far in excess of any other peacetime civilian exposures. Using risk tables developed for radioactive exposures in occupational settings, the risks for the Watras family are dramatic. At 3,200 pCi/l, the Watras family had exposure to radon levels almost fifty times the exposure levels set in 1971 for men working in American uranium mines.[5] In a more vernacular vein, the Watrases exposure while in their house roughly equaled consumption of more than forty packs of cigarettes per day. Neighbors such as the Joneses and Varadys had somewhat lower radon levels, but much longer periods of exposure. The extremity of this contamination found in Colebrookdale Township mobilized the government to act.

Despite the various pre-Watras hints of a national radon problem, in many respects, the Colebrookdale discovery was novel. Relatively little was then known about residential radon, despite the prior mill-tailings cases, and, therefore, government agencies were not prepared to deal with it. Residential radon levels from natural sources had previously been discovered in the 40 pCi/l range, and industrial exposures or contamination due to building materials had on occasion even pushed past 100 pCi/l. Furthermore, mitigation techniques for naturally occurring radon were speculative and experimental, suggesting a potential "mitigatory gap" between the ability to identify the invisible hazard and the ability to remedy it. Initial concerns were focused in the Watrases', Joneses', and Varadys' community. However, evidence of geologic radon beyond Colebrookdale Township quickly accumulated, with discovery of another major hot spot occurring a year later. This time, government was prepared.

Tipped off in 1986 by a resident of the Clinton Knolls subdivision whose commercial radon test revealed 1,000 pCi/l, the New Jersey DEP found a "hot" subdivision of five hundred homes in Clinton. Unlike Colebrookdale Township, local and state health and environmental officials were prepared to act with an extraordinary degree of intergovernmental cooperation. Local residents were consulted. Then a sample of ten carefully selected homes was remediated by mitigator Terry Brennan as part of an EPA demonstration program to identify approaches that could be utilized by other homeowners at their own expense. Given uniform construction within the subdivision, Brennan was able to develop quickly a workable and relatively inexpensive technical fix applicable to the area. Within nine months, all ten demonstration homes had been dropped below 4 pCi/l. EPA provided an additional twenty houses with remediation plans, and New Jersey officials assisted other homeowners to get their homes diagnosed. As a result of this tightly coordinated and well-thought-out program of government support, Clinton residents were reassured that their radon problem was under control.[6] The issue quickly became routinized; it was viewed as a local problem to be detected and, if necessary, fixed by the homeowner. Houses over 20 pCi/l were remediated, and many under that level were fixed as well (see Nulman, 1988; Fisher, 1989). In a rebuttal of the tortured testing of Colebrookdale Township, Clinton demonstrated a strategy for vanquishing radon.

In the face of extreme residential radon levels, there was a strong rationale for federal action. A proposed plan for addressing radon was quickly developed by the Interagency Committee on Indoor Air Quality (CIAQ), jointly chaired by the EPA and DOE (GAO, 1986).[7] However, the nascent federal radon program faced a highly resistant administration. When funding was denied by the Reagan OMB (*[Middletown, N.Y.] Times Herald Record*, 1985a), New Jersey Senator Frank Lautenberg charged OMB with usurping Congress's policy role (Lautenberg, 1988, p. 360). "OMB, which has the responsibility for managing the budget, has invaded the province of the decision-makers by deciding which programs are worth funding and which programs are not worth funding."

The Reagan administration went on to dismantle the CIAQ and silence other radon advocates (Sachs, cited in Makofske and Edelstein, 1988, p. 361). It was almost as if the dramatic extent of the Colebrookdale contamination was counterproductive to the issue's acceptance. A fear was roused that a regulatory program in response to the radon threat would spawn a massive and expensive bureaucracy (Houk, 1989). Faced with this climate, nominee for Deputy Director James Barnes responded during his confirmation hearings four months after the Watras discovery that radon was a low priority (Galen, 1987). As one EPA source noted off the record, the administration feared that EPA action might overcommit the federal government to a threat of unknown dimensions. "The OMB was concerned that the federal government's appropriate role was research and providing information and that the states were better suited to action. They were afraid that we'd scare the hell out of people; that we'd get into it in an aggressive way. They wanted a state partnership."[8]

The administration was not alone in these concerns. The political lessons of the Reagan victory had sensitized Congress to not only the cost, but also the intrusiveness of big government, influencing the entire political spectrum. A case in point was the reticence of Mike Rodemeyer, council to New York Congressman James Scheuer's science and technology subcommittee, to see radon regulated: "Much of the generic concern is not to authorize any new regulatory programs now. There is a great deal of concern whether we want EPA to be indoor air police" (Coyle, 1986, p. 4). Finally, because command and control regulation is extremely inflexible, and does not respond to change, congresspersons were forced to ask whether enough was known to regulate radon, even if they wanted to do so (see Locke, 1993).

How then did radon emerge as the rare environmental risk to receive substantial support during the Reagan and Bush administrations? In part, this success resulted from the shifting significance of radon as a natural hazard. Before the Watras discovery, radon's natural causality had helped to keep it invisible to an environmental movement focused upon human-caused pollution. But for a new president who viewed trees—not industry—as the source of pollution, there could be no better issue than geologic radon, defined as a natural hazard for which no one could be blamed. It was precisely geologic radon's blamelessness that made it an acceptable hazard to receive government attention during the Reagan era. Thus, in contrast to the EPA penchant for regulating, blaming, and fining industrial polluters—the "Superfund" model that pitted the federal government against the very interests represented by President Reagan—radon was defined as a politically safe hazard.

In effect, radon appeared to have a "natural" disinclination to be regulated, as Philip Shabecoff (1986, p. A24) noted in his early coverage of the radon issue.

> The difficulty for government regulators, however, was that radon was not a problem created by human activity. The E.P.A. could not issue a cease-and-desist order to Mother Earth ordering her to stop allowing radon to enter people's homes. . . . But the lack of any villain in the radon problem was also a relief for the agency because it did not have to come up with new "command and control" regulations for industry. Such rules almost inevitably are met with hostility by the Reagan White House and its Office of Management and Budget.

Rick Erdman (1988), an aide to radon program advocate Senator Frank Lautenberg, rationalized that these characteristics of radon might be independent of Reaganomic influences.[9]

> Radon is so unlike any other pollutant. It has no precedent. It affects private houses, is natural, people make their own choice about whether to act, and it does not hurt others if they don't act. Radon fits the Reagan model only because it is a unique problem. It is even different than other indoor air problems, for example, those due to consumer products. The Reagan administration doesn't oppose radon; there is a consensus among concerned people. Because there is no bad guy, it is an easy target.

In an administration seeking to avoid controversial environmental initiatives, what could be less threatening than a contaminant whose presence was no person's fault and could be blamed only on God or nature? As we see in chapter 3, radon's blamelessness was to prove a major policy asset.

Conclusions: The Terms of Radon's Acceptance

Along the roller coaster ride toward a recognition and acceptance of the need for a governmental response to the threat of geologic radon, the Watras discovery stands out as an event that overcame denial, delay, and competing priorities. But importantly, this point of discovery occurred in the political context of Reaganomics. It is not surprising, then, that both of these formative conditions left a clear stamp on policy. In the case of the Watras discovery, our interests are in the central beliefs—or myths—imprinted in Colebrookdale Township. These "myths of Watras" dictated a concern for finding extremely high radon houses and the attendant need for a methodology and testing approach that would support a search for hot radon areas. Also, found here was a belief that the high radon risk was confined largely to hot regions, such as the Reading Prong underlying Colebrookdale Township. Collectively, such myths of the formative period of the geologic radon issue shaped susbsequent government response. Their influence was matched, however, by the influence of Reaganomics, which dictated a focus on minimizing federal involvement and regulation. An additional set of myths were, thus, introduced whereby the radon issue would become decentralized, market driven, and voluntary in form. We see how these various forces interacted in forming radon policy as we next turn to the evolution of the federal radon program.

Notes

1. The uranium mining experience in the United States is a classic instance of environmental injustice and environmental racism. Johnston and Dawson (1994) discuss the difficulty uranium miners had in getting compensation for illnesses (see also LaDuke and Churchill, 1985).

2. The initial standard allowed miner exposure at a rate of 1 WL (working level) for 42.5 hours per week. Because the biological effects of radiation exposure are believed to be cumulative, the WLM (working level month) is the equivalent of 1 WL exposure over a typical work month of 170 hours. Thus, 12 WLM was the maximum allowable exposure of a miner over a year (see Robkin, 1987, for a detailed discussion of radiation units).

3. The Federal Emergency Management Agency (FEMA) was granted a broad mandate under the Disaster Relief Act of 1974 to respond to listed disasters (which did not include radon contamination) and/or to a declaration of emergency by the president. In response to a request from the General Accounting Office (GAO), FEMA issued an opinion that radon exposure could be addressed under the Disaster Relief Act, but it would take a request for assistance from the governor of the affected state and a presidential declaration in order for help to be forthcoming (GAO, 1986).

4. Confirmation of the OMB's role stems from multiple sources, including the authors' interviews with Richard Guimond (1988c), Jim Barnes (1988), and Rick Erdman of Senator Lautenberg's staff (1988). See also Coyle (1986). Galen (1987) reports that within the first six months in office, the Reagan administration deleted the entire proposed fiscal 1982 budget for indoor air pollution, arguing that there was a lack of statutory authority to work on radon.

5. The 1971 miner exposure standards were set at 0.33 WL or 66 pCi/l (4 WLM/ yr). At this exposure level, it has been estimated that perhaps an additional twenty-eight out of one thousand miners would die of lung cancer from their exposure, assuming a standard work week and a twenty-year period of exposure. Not only were the Watrases' levels much higher, but they occupied the house many more hours than reflected in a standard work week. Thus, their exposures were also thought to be higher.

6. The Clinton, like the Colebrookdale, experience is not easily generalizable to other instances. The well-designed, well-staffed, and well-financed New Jersey radon program and the manner in which Clinton was handled by cooperating officials at all levels are unique aspects of the Clinton experience. By way of comparison, nearly two years after Clinton, the authors observed how New York State handled a high radon home. A highly visible and intrusive state radon swat team arrived quickly to conduct a comprehensive diagnosis, but there were serious delays in testing, confirmatory testing, and subsequent action that left the family in limbo for months. Although the home was eventually mitigated and the family's sense of safety restored, the state-financed effort was a far cry from the efficiency and supportive climate found in Clinton.

7. The CIAQ called for a national assessment of radon exposure in structures, development of radon mitigation techniques, improvements in radon measurement technologies, and improved information about radon health effects and risk (GAO, 1986).

8. It was true that there was a lack of any mandate in existing legislation authorizing the federal government to do more than conduct research or to provide technical assistance for a natural environmental hazard manifested in the private home (GAO, 1986).

9. In arguing that the characteristics of the radon hazard, rather than Reaganomics per se, had determined the most appropriate form of federal response, Erdman was in basic agreement with EPA officials (Daggett, 1988; Egan, 1988) and the assistant surgeon general (Houk, 1989).

Chapter 3

Federal Response to Geologic Radon

> Environmental issues generally require some advocate to force the issue to
> be selected. The advocates are usually public interest groups, legislators,
> victims groups or attorneys. What is unique about radon is that EPA advo-
> cated an issue that did not have a great constituency outside the agency.
> —Richard Guimond

With its uncanny levels of radiation, the Watras discovery catapulted geologic
radon from an issue lacking sufficient impetus to the status of a full-fledged national environmental and health priority. The issue was quickly broadened from
a localized crisis in Colebrookdale Township, Pennsylvania, to a national problem, affecting millions of citizens in all states. But the response to this problem
still had to overcome governmental barriers to costly new environmental programs, barriers that had helped to hold back earlier response to natural radon.
Despite these barriers, by 1988, radon appeared to have emerged as a consensual
contaminant, with a president loath to support environmental initiatives signing
major radon legislation.

Richard Guimond and the EPA Approach to Radon

If the Watras discovery was to provide the magic needed to demand federal radon action, then Richard Guimond, a career officer in the public health service
assigned by EPA to respond to Colebrookdale Township was to prove to be the
magician capable of conjuring up acceptable policy initiatives. Guimond had cut
his teeth in the EPA with his first assignment in the early 1970s in addressing
mill tailings in Grand Junction, Colorado. Subsequently, he went to Florida to
develop a program for dealing with the excessive radon levels found in homes
built out of phosphate materials. In the early 1980s, he became involved in addressing the discovery of serious radon contamination in Montclair, New Jersey
(Coyle and Drachler, 1986; Guimond, 1988c).

Given his experience with radon, Guimond was quick to realize the implications of the Watras incident. From the onset, he became the driving force behind
the very construction of the indoor radon issue. There is reason to believe that
geologic radon might never have surfaced as a major issue had it not been for
Guimond's tutelage. The selling of the radon issue to an initially hostile administration reflected moxie in using the media, tailoring programs, and currying
support of the right allies at crucial junctures. Recognizing the overwhelming re-

53

sistance to creating another Superfund-type program in the early Reagan period, Guimond pragmatically crafted a politically acceptable response to radon. The program was deliberately made modest so as to not run afoul of the OMB. Radon's pragmatic quality—that it can be defined as a blameless natural occurrence having a very great risk—was played up. Furthermore, radon could be seen as a private problem beyond the scope of regulation. Any response to this problem would have to be decentralized, falling on the backs of the states and, more directly, upon individuals. In these ways, Guimond nurtured the radon issue, converting it from a response to the Watras incident into a proactive program through a careful strategy of policy orchestration (Coyle and Drachler, 1986; Guimond, 1988b).[1]

The success of this issue advocacy was demonstrated by the ability of EPA's radon program to survive and grow under the Reagan/Bush administrations, even as other environmental programs were under attack. In fact, the EPA program even appeared to justify Reaganomics, as one EPA insider suggested (Page, 1988). "How do you get environmental work done in the Reagan Era? Not from on high, but from below. The question is what you can do given few resources. Guimond set a network quickly. The network is working well. The irony is that we justify the Reagan agenda. If we made radon look like a Federal package, the OMB and the White House would not let us initiate it. . . . [But because] it's not regulatory, we can be the 'white knights.'"

The EPA Radon Action Program

In the wake of Watras, representatives from some fifteen states helped Guimond mold EPA's role in developing a scientific and technical understanding of radon, bridging local, state, and private sector radon activities and providing information to homeowners (Guimond, 1988b). By September 1985, a skeleton program had been launched to identify the scope of the radon problem and develop means to reduce or prevent residential radon exposure (EPA/CRCPD, 1987). Initial activities were justified under the broad discretionary authority vested in the EPA under the Clean Air Act, Section 103, to establish a national research and development program aimed at the control and prevention of air pollution (GAO, 1988; GAO, 1986). However, EPA's response suffered from the limits of this authority, as well as from a challenge to its jurisdiction by the Department of Energy (DOE) (GAO, 1986) and from the lack of targeted funding (Coyle and Drachler, 1986; Guimond, 1988c). However, as a former deputy EPA administrator explained, "A lot more money early on would not have made a difference. We needed to sort out the task and get underway with a good game plan. Radon continued to get more funding at a time when the environmental budget was flat" (Barnes, 1988).

However, it is notable that during this period EPA expended significantly less on radon than either the states of Pennsylvania or New Jersey. Moreover, state officials were caught in a bind, trapped between a call for prompt action by the Centers for Disease Control (CDC) and yet stymied by the slowly developing federal policy (Coyle and Drachler, 1986), as Colebrookdale's State Senator Michael O'Pake explained in spring 1986 (O'Pake, 1988). "Unfortunately, while the CDC was sending major health warning signals and our Department of Environmental Resources was discovering many homes with high levels of radon gas contamination, the national government was slow to act. The EPA had not set a national radon standard. There existed no reliable low-cost remediation technique, and Congress had not provided direct federal assistance to homeowners" (p. 364).

O'Pake's concerns were echoed at the federal level by Senator George Mitchell of Maine, where a radon-in-water problem had been recognized since the 1970s. Long a lone voice on radon, now Mitchell was joined by a new block of proradon congressmen spawned instantly by the headline writer for the *New York Times* who bannered Philip Shabecoff's May 1985 article about the Reading Prong with the words "radioactive gas in soil raises concern in three-state area" (Mazur, 1987). An especially active new advocate for radon action was New Jersey's Junior Senator Frank Lautenberg, whose Montclair home was only a few blocks from the houses affected by radon from radium-contaminated soil. In January 1986, Lautenberg led a three-day tour of Sweden. His accompanying task force included EPA's Guimond, New Jersey State Senator John Dorsey, and a number of representatives of the building and real estate fields. During the visit, the group met with Swedish officials and scientists involved with radon response, a realtor, and residents of a home contaminated with high radon levels. The task force report, issued on February 11, 1986, set forth the basic outlines of a radon action program that EPA and Congress could agree upon (Lautenberg, 1986). In 1986 this congressional radon coalition was able to outmaneuver a still reluctant president in order to significantly fund the developing federal radon program and to grant EPA a clear mandate to address the issue. In order to assure congressional support, the Radon Gas and Indoor Air Quality Research Act of 1986 was included as Title IV of the popular Superfund Amendments and Reauthorization Act of 1986 (commonly known as SARA) that became law only after a showdown between a supportive Congress and the reluctant President.[2]

Key Components of the Radon Action Program

Through most of geologic radon's first decade, EPA's Radon Action Program was based in the Radon Division, within the Office of Radiation, itself within the Office of Air and Radiation.[3] The Radon Division contained three subdivisions: Problem Assessment, Measurement Proficiency and Quality Assurance, and Policy and Public Information. EPA's Office of Research and Development also played a key support role within the agency. Significantly, the program embodied the key myths framed by the Colebrookdale and Clinton experiences, evident in the focus on identifying hot houses (i.e., the myth of the hot house, see chapter 5) and areas where radon risk is extreme (i.e., the myth of the Reading Prong, see chapter 5), through the use of screening measurements employing short-term tests (i.e., the myth of the quick test, see chapter 6), and the promise of a quick fix (i.e., the myth of the quick fix, see chapter 7). Simultaneously, the program fit the tenets of Reaganomics by limiting the federal role primarily to research and dissemination of information to the states, stimulation of the private market, and promotion of the homeowner as risk consumer. These goals were approached through the following four specific task areas:

1. Assessment of the Problem

Both the "myth of the Reading Prong" and "the myth of the hot houses" were central to the Radon Action Program's efforts to locate high-radon-potential regions. Two approaches were employed. First, state radon surveys were used to identify the extent and magnitude of the problem. Although only seventeen states and several Indian Nations had completed radon surveys by 1988, by 1992, all but two of the fifty states had conducted such surveys. A composite map based on these surveys was then employed to suggest U.S. counties having high, medium, and low levels of radon. A second approach used geological mapping to create a radon-potential map distinguishing high-radon areas. Further efforts included a national survey of radon levels in workplaces, schools and homes. By 1992, with a specific mandate from the Indoor Radon Abatement Act, 20 percent of U.S. Schools had been tested with a target of 75 percent to be tested by the year 2000 (Maconaughey, 1988; EPA 1992b).

2. Establishing Quality Control for Radon Testing

The Radon Measurement Proficiency Program (RMP) was developed to assess the capabilities of private and public testing firms. Participating companies submitted to the EPA a specified number of radon detectors, which were then exposed to a known amount of radon at a federal laboratory. The detectors were then returned to the company for analysis. Subsequently, EPA compared the company's findings with the known levels of exposure. By 1988, in RMP's fifth round, 1,011 firms had participated (EPA, 1988d). By 1993, 1,650 firms and 550 individuals were listed as proficient in radon testing. The RMP was voluntary and not intended to accredit, certify, recommend, or endorse participating companies. Rather the program sought to make available a list of companies with demonstrated radon-measurement competence (Gearo, 1988).[4]

3. Mitigation Research and Training

An effort to develop effective and inexpensive mitigation and prevention techniques occurred through the Radon Mitigation Research Program. The EPA Office of Research and Development undertook to find cost-effective methods for radon reduction. More than 600 houses were remediated through 1987, including the two major early "hotspots"—the Pennsylvania Reading Prong and Clinton, New Jersey (GAO, 1986). The HEP (House Evaluation Program) was developed to provide training in hands-on radon diagnosis and mitigation for state and business employees, in part through a week-long field course involving the diagnosis and mitigation of actual houses. In addition, through HEP, 130 houses in six states were remediated through 1988 by contractors hired by homeowners but using remediation plans developed by EPA. Another 110 homes in eleven states were addressed in 1989. Both HEP programs were useful for evaluating the effectiveness and cost associated with different mitigation techniques. Meanwhile, through NEWHEP (New House Evaluation Program), EPA also began working with eight building contractors from four states to evaluate the effectiveness of the interim guide for radon resistant new construction. More than 140 homes were evaluated, with another 100 homes assessed in New Jersey. EPA also undertook a survey of mitigation firms to identify the effectiveness, cost, and extent of mitigation efforts (Mardis, 1988).

The Radon Contractor Proficiency (RCP) program was begun under the Indoor Radon Abatement Act to evaluate the proficiency of mitigation companies. Like the RMP, EPA considered the RCP to be a voluntary program, while many states considered successful participation in the program to be a requisite for demonstration of basic competency in the field. By 1993, 902 mitigators had been found proficient under the program. Finally, to support the development of contractor (and testing) proficiency, EPA also funded the creation of regional training centers located at Rutgers University, Auburn University, Colorado State University, and the University of Minnesota.

4. Providing Radon Information to the Public

EPA undertook an extensive public information campaign in support of the Radon Action Program. Beyond producing information for homeowners, a comprehensive media campaign was mounted and outreach efforts occurred through an expanding list of organizational partners, including at the onset the American Medical Association, the American Lung Association, and the National Conference of State Legislatures (see chapter 11). A program of research on risk communication was also undertaken (Page, 1988; Fisher, 1988; see chapter 8).

The EPA research strategy was put to use in the effort to build a national consensus for radon. New data were used to prove that the radon issue is widespread in nature and that hot spots would be found across the nation. With the growing recognition that radon affects all states, legislative support for the issue grew proportionately. While some radon initiatives stalled in congressional committees, such as Senator Lautenberg's effort to get tax breaks for remediating radon problems—hampered by its fiscal impacts at a time of belt tightening—the Senate developed a consensus for action on the issue. The absence of a "bad guy" was a central factor in winning congressional support for radon legislation (Erdman, 1988). There appeared to be few political costs in supporting radon action; given spreading concern about the issue, there were clear political gains. However, a broad consensus on radon faced other roadblocks.

Conflict and Consensus over Major Policy Issues

Despite the backing of Congress and the administration for EPA's radon program, serious challenges to a radon consensus remained. Turf battles were fought between agencies over ownership of the radon issue and, within the EPA, geologic radon had to attract support, even where it competed for resources with institutionally entrenched environmental concerns.

The EPA/DOE Radon Turf War

Even after SARA formally mandated EPA's lead in addressing radon and other indoor air contaminants, a turf war raged between EPA and the rival Department of Energy (DOE) over control of radon funding and programs. The DOE had a major interest in radon given its long-standing role in remediating anthropogenic sources of radiation exposure, its program of basic radon research, and its concern with the relationship between energy efficiency and indoor air pollution.[5]

Although EPA had won the support of Congress, DOE was backed by the administration's OMB, as evidenced by budget appropriations, particularly in fiscal year 1988. DOE's popularity with the Office of Management and Budget probably reflected the fact that the energy department's basic research approach was comparatively nonthreatening to the Reaganomic agenda as contrasted to EPA's applied Radon Action Program. Furthermore, DOE personnel favored a much higher action level for radon (of around 20 pCi/l) that promised to have much less fiscal impact than did the EPA's 4 pCi/l guidance. And DOE's health research confirmed OMB's doubts about the severity of radon risk. One participant in the OMB's so-called confidential information meetings anonymously described that agency's favoritism for DOE: "DOE got the money because the OMB was concerned about a strong EPA program that would stimulate action and have a greater impact on the federal budget. They recalled the early days when there was talk of a Superfund for radon. Their concern continues. DOE spends $100 million per year for research but no one knows about it. The EPA spends $2 million and its all over the press."

Given that Congress had just granted EPA the lead radon role under SARA, Maine's Senator Mitchell challenged OMB, creating a half year of turmoil that exacerbated EPA tension with the DOE. One result was that Congress used SARA in 1988 to add $2 million to the EPA budget that the agency had not even requested, allowing for the addition of fifteen radon positions (Guimond, 1988c; Page, 1988; Erdman, 1988).

To address the interagency competition, assistant administrators of both EPA and DOE jointly developed a "memo of understanding," signed in September 1987. The memo granted areas of primary responsibility to each agency—to the EPA for applied research and operational indoor radon programs and to the DOE for basic research into methods for reducing overall exposure to radiation, for investigation of health and environmental effects of radon exposure, and for issues relating to the further development of energy efficient conservation (Martin, 1987). By 1989 a pattern had emerged whereby EPA dominated radon action and DOE dominated basic research on radon (Committee on Indoor Air Quality Radon Work Group, 1989).

Despite these areas of mandated cooperation, considerable tension continued to simmer between the agencies. DOE radon experts, principally Tony Nero, published blistering attacks on EPA policy. An EPA official told the authors in an off-the-record conversation that the DOE was fanning the flames by "working the press heavily" in an effort to undermine the EPA policy. Given that the DOE's narrow mandate was to conduct basic research, the official questioned the appropriateness of the DOE's role as EPA critic. This anger surfaced at EPA's 1991 radon conference in Philadelphia when DOE's radon guru Susan Rose was unceremoniously raked over the coals by Guimond's successor and head of the EPA radon program, Margo Oge. Rose's revenge was to invite Guimond to address a DOE journalist conference on the topic "EPA's overregulation of radon."

Turf Wars within EPA

Within EPA, support for geologic radon programs had to overcome challenges as well. Administrative backing awaited Reagan's third appointment to the administrator's office, Lee Thomas. Thomas and his deputy Jim Barnes provided internal funding for Guimond to build his program. Additionally, radon had to win its place beside EPA's mandated programs, which serve as its bread and butter. EPA employees often feel such strong allegiance to these programs that one observer irreverently referred to them as fiefdoms. Radon was an interloper issue. It required legitimacy to be accepted, both in its own right and as a possible threat to other programs. Guimond (1988c) observed that it took time to make radon believers out of agency professionals. "We were not without skeptics. New issues need an infrastructure—middle managers need to believe that it is an important issue. We're beginning to see this at EPA. It needs a few more years to grow. We made positive gains, but not as quickly as I would have liked."

During his time at EPA, Thomas emphasized risk assessment, the quantitative estimation of the likelihood of adverse consequences. Quantitative risk assessment can be traced back to the early days of EPA, when the agency sought to develop a uniform method for ranking pesticides. Within the Reagan administration, risk assessment became the EPA's analog of cost/benefit analysis, a process central to the work of the OMB and the administration's overall effort to reduce regulation.

Thomas undertook an evaluation of agency priorities through a comparative study of risks associated with thirty-one environmental problems, given existing levels of control. The study was carried out by a special task force of seventy-five EPA career managers and technical experts (EPA, 1987a; Shabecoff, 1988a). The impetus for the report is clearly laid out in the introduction by Thomas: "In a world of limited resources, it may be wise to give priority attention to those pollutants and problems that pose the greatest risks to our society. That is the measure this study begins to apply. It represents, in my view, the first few sketchy lines of what might become the future picture of environmental protection in America" (EPA, 1987a, p. ii).

As the result of this comparative risk assessment, radon was consensually ranked as the number one carcinogen (tied with cumulative worker exposures to chemicals). Radon was also given a medium rank in terms of noncancer risks (given some potential for birth defects) and was ranked as the fourth most significant environmental problem overall. The report recognized, importantly, that the high risk associated with radon did not fit with its low priority in agency programming, legitimating an increased agency emphasis on radon. These findings were repeated in subsequent EPA rankings of risk (see chapters 9 and 10). The comparative approach did not, however, resolve controversy and conflict over radon's risk.

It is instructive that the workplace, where workers lacked control over their environment, was regulated for radon. But the home was presumed to be under the residents' control. This difference was not particularly important with the human-caused radon exposures that the federal government was mandated to remediate anyway. It was particularly salient, however, with natural radon, where protective measures required that the resident act. But, at what level of radon exposure was action to be taken?

Five Views of Radon Risk

At the root of radon controversy were fundamental questions of how much risk from radon was acceptable. Before the Colebrookdale discovery, various national and international groups and agencies had addressed this question, but with conclusions that diverged from tolerance of exposures from as low as 1 all the way to 50 pCi/l.[6] Given this divergence of numbers, it is not surprising that the setting of a geologic radon action level by EPA would prove to be controversial. Figure 3.1 displays five distinctive views of radon risk placed on a continuum of risk tolerance. At the extreme left of this continuum have been advocates for pushing radon exposure to its lowest limits—EPA regulators implementing the Safe Drinking Water Act standards for radon in water and congresspeople advocating the ambient level for airborne radon. On the far right of the continuum are critics who challenge the view that radon is a serious hazard requiring government response, the radon rejectionists. In the center of this continuum have been the two involved federal agencies, the DOE on the right and EPA on the left. Let's explore the center of the continuum first (see also Cole, 1993).

EPA safe drinking water proposed standard	Congress's ambient goal	EPA/CDC guidance	DOE preferred guidance	Radon rejectionism
0.12 pCi/l air equivalent	0.2–0.5 pCi/l	4 pCi/l	20 pCi/l	no action

Fig. 3.1   Five views of acceptable radon risk.

The EPA and CDC: The 4 pCi/l Guidance Level

Facing demands for federal guidance on naturally occurring radon in the wake of the Colebrookdale discovery, EPA and CDC adopted a 4 pCi/l action level. The origin of the 4 pCi/l level stemmed from Canadian efforts to address contamination from radioactive materials processing in the 1970s. The level was statistically derived from background radon progeny levels found in an uncontaminated town chosen for comparison to another town where an early radium refinery had been located. The goal of remediation was to bring the contaminated town down to the level of radon exposure found in the comparison community. The figure later was justified based upon health risk (Eaton, 1988).

The first adoption of the 4 pCi/l level in the United States came in Florida, one of the earliest states to grapple with indoor radon because of its reclaimed phosphate lands. The level was selected by EPA based upon the mill tailings experience in response to a formal request for guidance from Florida's governor (Page, 1988). Subsequently, the 4 pCi/l level was adopted for use in Essex County, New Jersey, where radium-contaminated soil from the old watch dial factory had been used as fill for housing sites (BPA, 1984; also GAO, 1986).

However, the 4 pCi/l guidance was not immediately communicated to the public because of internal EPA debate over the terminology to be used to describe when to take action in response to naturally occurring residential radon. Reflecting the impasse created by this delay, Pennsylvania's Senator O'Pake surmised in the spring of 1986 that the EPA had failed to promulgate an action level "because they are not prepared to follow through and make the kind of commitment that is needed in light of the seriousness of the problem" (Makofske and Edelstein, 1988, p. 376). EPA argued that delays were caused by states that feared a mitigatory gap, where public radon concern would outstrip the ability to address the problem. An EPA staff member paraphrased this fear, as follows: "that EPA would announce the guidance and there would be no follow through. Who pays? How do we measure? Who does it? What do we do after we measure? There was concern for what the *Citizens Guide* would precipitate" (Page, 1988).

In fact the guidance was not formally stated until the 1986 publication of the EPA/CDC's *Citizens Guide to Radon*. The guidance was not intended to be a standard that determined safe and legal levels from dangerous and illegal levels regulated by government, but rather a statement of governmental advice to citizens who must take action themselves. As EPA's Guimond (1988c) explained,

> People have a lot of individual freedom in deciding what to do about risks in their lives. They choose whether to smoke or not and whether to drive a race car or not. Nonetheless, from extensive discussions with people throughout the country who participated in EPA focus groups, it is clear to us that people need to have guidelines and recommendations that are as clear as possible. These provide benchmarks about when there is a hazard, what kind of action they should take, and how rapidly they should take that action.

In the guide, EPA presented various exposure levels and the actions EPA suggested that citizens undertake for each. For test results over 200 pCi/l, EPA advised action within several weeks to reduce levels and, in some cases, interim relocation. It was advised that exposures between 20 and 200 pCi/l be reduced within several months, and results between 4 and 20 pCi/l within a few years. The document states clearly that exposures at or below 4 pCi/l "do present some risk of lung cancer, [however] reductions of levels this low may be difficult, and sometimes impossible, to achieve" (EPA, 1986, p. 11).

Thus, EPA did not maintain that radon levels below its guidance of 4 pCi/l (0.02 WL) were acceptable. It was acutely aware that differences between 3.9 and 4 pCi/l are meaningless. Furthermore, in congressional testimony in 1986, EPA asserted that there are no safe levels of radon exposure and that the 4 pCi/l level was set for economic as well as health reasons. In fact, the EPA estimated that ten to fifty people out of one thousand would die due to lifetime exposure at this level (GAO, 1986). While a level based upon safety might push well below 4 pCi/l, Guimond stressed that EPA feared that a lower guideline would be achievable by such a small percentage of the population that it would discourage people from addressing radon (Guimond, 1988c; Eheman, 1988).

The DOE: Advocates for a 20 pCi/l Policy Focus

EPA was heavily criticized by its rivals at the Department of Energy for its choice of a 4 pCi/l guidance level. The point man for the DOE was scientist Tony Nero (see Nero, 1989, and Nero et al., 1990). In a series of articles and reports, Nero argued for a policy of taking care of the people over 20 pCi/l first. He raised the comparative risk issues and asked where the dead bodies were. He charged that 4 pCi/l served as a de facto regulation. Similarly, Nero's DOE colleague Richard Sextro (1991) argued that 4 pCi/l was the minimum "cut point" for radon, a risk equivalent to accepted probabilities for car or home accidents. What was needed, he suggested, was "a reasonable upper boundary," in the range of 20 pCi/l or even higher, to avoid addressing situations with too little risk. The problem was not so much with the 4 pCi/l guidance per se, Sextro explained in an interview, but with the false impression created by screening tests and with the sloppy use of the guidance.

> Few people say that 4 is wrong. The problem has been that EPA has been unwilling to have more than one number out there for fear they'll confuse the public. So we are stuck with 4. We have to stand on the sideline while people use 4 for any use—basement or upstairs, short or long term, any season. It's like a doctor making more x-rays for fear that you'll sue—for similar reasons everyone now uses 4. That is what is driving the problem. EPA is culpable for not weighing in and straightening this out and interpreting the numbers. At 4 you are significantly above one percent risk and one percent should be the cut off line. The EPA is pathologically regulating at ppb (parts per billion).

The answer, Sextro suggested, was to develop different guidances for different situations, as EPA had done with outdoor air pollutants such as ozone. He dismissed EPA's insistence on a single, simple "bright line."

EPA took angry exception to DOE's criticism, suggesting that arguments that the guidance should be around 20 pCi/l were based solely on cost, that those arguing for 20 pCi/l are the same people who protect people at even lower radiation hazards, as with the Nuclear Regulatory Commission ruling for nuclear plants that created a level of exposure twenty times lower than 4 pCi/l, and that an emphasis upon the hottest homes is inappropriate because only 2 percent of the risk is over 20 pCi/l and the real risk is around 4 pCi/l, with 60 percent of homes capable of being reduced as low as 2 pCi/l. Furthermore, it was noted that the cost of an avoided death for radon, at $400–500,000 per life saved for those exposed to more than 4 pCi/l, is comparable to the costs associated with seat belts and smoke detectors. And, finally, the argument that the risks at 4 pCi/l are mundane because they equate to the risks of normal daily life distort the fact that no such catastrophes are acceptably routine. In arguing all this before a conference audience, EPA's Margo Oge (1991a) brought the issue of risk down to a personal level. "Some want us to find the hottest homes—over 20 pCi/l. Some argue that 20 pCi/l is the real risk and 4 pCi/l is a routine accepted risk like home falls and car accidents. This bothers me. Let me ask the audience if they think that having a home fire or a car accident is routine."

Radon Rejectionism

At the root of radon rejectionism is the myth of the dead bodies (see chapter 4). This myth suggests that, in the absence of dedicated fatalities that can be directly linked to radon exposure, there is no provable radon hazard. The radon-rejectionist view embodying this myth has been exemplified by *Science* magazine editorialist Philip Abelson (1990, 1991, 1992). Abelson discounted the validity of radon measurements taken in the lowest part of the house and in winter because such screening measures can exaggerate radon scores fourfold over year-long radon measurements (1990; see chapter 6). He rejected EPA risk projections based on the 1988 report by the National Research Council for relying on a linear extrapolation model instead of the more conservative threshold theory, which discounts the impact of smaller doses of radon (1991; see chapter 4). Abselson denied the applicability of uranium miner cancer data to radon in homes because of numerous differences in condition between the two environments (see chapter 4). He found that smoking accounts for the effect being attributed to radon, citing Nobel prize winner Rosalee Yallow's argument that lung cancer rates were low prior to the advent of widespread smoking, even though radon levels were comparable. Finally, he referred to studies by other radon rejectionists in concluding "EPA is on shaky ground when it tries to frighten the public about radon using as a basis a large extrapolation of data obtained from mines laden with mineral dusts. EPA has no solid evidence that exposures to 4 pCi/l of radon causes lung cancer in either smokers or nonsmokers. Indeed, there is abundant evidence to the contrary in the fact that in states with high levels of radon, inhabitants have less lung cancer than those in states with low levels" (1991, p. 777).[7]

Another example of radon rejectionism is found in a conservative policy review in the journal *Public Interest* (Bolch and Lyons, 1990), which charged that, by inducing a "radon panic" that benefited both private entrepreneurs and itself, the EPA had used radon as an excuse to begin regulating "one of our last bastions of privacy, the home" (p. 61). Natural radiation should not be feared, it is argued, because "mankind has lived with natural radiation for millions of years. . . . (Radioactive isotopes) . . . like many other naturally occurring products (such as salt) . . . can be fatal in sufficiently large dosages" (p. 62, 67). Furthermore, radon's risks are comparable to risks from accepted everyday hazards, such as falls or fires in the home. For these reasons, it is argued that it is premature to actively address geologic radon. In chapter 4, we examine the factual basis for radon rejectionism and the myth of the dead bodies.

The Proposed Waterborne Standard

But if one were to impose a standard of safety for radon, where would the levels be? Even as it avoided this question with airborne radon, EPA was forced to address this issue because of litigation enforcing the agency's obligations to impose standards for radionuclides in public water systems under the Safe Drinking Water Act. As a result, even as the Radon Action Program advocated its 4 pCi/l action level, the EPA water safety staff was in the process of suggesting much more stringent levels of protection applied to radon in water.

Since the 1960s it has been recognized that groundwater in some parts of the United States contains significant amounts of radon. As this water is pulled into buildings, radon outgases, escaping to the air, where it contributes to indoor radon concentrations. In September 1986, an advance notice of rule making was issued by the drinking water group at EPA that proposed maximum contaminant levels (MCLs) for radon in community water systems (MacMullin, 1988). Four regulatory scenarios were offered for comment, ranging from a 200 pCi/l water standard to 2,000 pCi/l. It should be kept in mind that 4 pCi/l of radon in the air is roughly the equivalent of 10,000 in water. Thus, while 2,000 pCi/l in water equals 0.8 pCi/l in air, 200 pCi/l in water is only 0.08 pCi/l airborne radon. In short, the equivalences for the considered waterborne radon standards were in the range of one-fifth to one-fiftieth of the guidance for airborne radon!

The proposed rule was finally published in the *Federal Register* on July 18, 1991 (EPA, 1991). It set forth maximum contaminant level goals and national primary drinking water regulations for radon-222 and six other radionuclides classified as "Group A" carcinogens under Section 1412 of the Safe Drinking Water Act. A MCL (maximum contaminant level) for radon of 300 pCi/l was proposed for all public water systems (excluding private systems serving twenty-five or fewer households). The rule required initial quarterly testing for one year followed by yearly testing for radionuclides. Public water systems violating the MCL would be required to test quarterly until the yearly average fell below the MCL. The rule, originally slated to go into effect in April 1993, was delayed by the 104th Congress's attack on new regulation, later to be reproposed in different form (see chapter 12). Several provocative issues raised by this effort to regulate radon in water were worthy of closer examination.

Comparative Risk Impacts

Radon offers an unfavorable point of comparison to contaminants that are central to the EPA's regulatory role. It is recognized by EPA that more people die from radon than from causes regulated under the Clean Air Act (Oge, 1991b). And, as a waterborne hazard, a review of risk estimates associated with eighty-three regulated water contaminants revealed that not only was radon a greater risk than other unregulated waterborne contaminants, but the risk associated with waterborne radon exceeded that for all water pollutants for which standards have already been set. By way of comparison, it is estimated that radon in water adds an estimated eighty to eight hundred additional lung cancer deaths per year; vinyl chloride, the most hazardous chemical carcinogen currently regulated in drinking water, is estimated to cause twenty-seven fatalities per year and all volatile organics together adds another thirty-two deaths (EPA, 1991a). For the EPA, these numbers sliced two ways. While these comparatively extreme numbers for radon in water favored setting of new radon standards because the resulting savings of life is substantial compared to other drinking water regulations and other EPA regulatory programs, the recognition of the risk magnitude of radon in water also threatened the legitimacy of the entire program of costly regulation for human-caused chemical contaminants.

Waterborne Radon Escapes to Air

As a further complication, waterborne radon's primary known risk stems from its contribution to levels of airborne radon. The move to regulate radon in water thus rendered as absurd the agency's determination not to regulate radon in air. Furthermore, next to unregulated airborne radon, regulated radon in water is comparatively unrisky. Nevertheless, a radon water standard of 300 pCi/l means that residential radon originating in water would be treated as if it were more dangerous than radon emanating from soil gas, even though it represents only 3–7 percent of the total air risk. Former EPA Deputy Administrator Barnes admitted to one of the authors in 1988 that the proposed regulation would not significantly reduce the overall radon risk. "Drinking water regulations create small pockets of clean. You go into the shower and find lower levels of radon than are found outside or in the home. This won't reduce the overall threat."

The disparity of risk between airborne and waterborne radon was additionally a potential source of confusion. Given that 4 pCi/l in the air is the equivalent of 40,000 pCi/l in the water, levels in water appear to be much higher in many cases, but in fact are considerably less risky than much lower air levels. Accordingly, EPA's Richard Guimond (1988c) worried that a strict radon water standard would give a false impression that water is the source of the major risk.

There is a major ongoing public concern over water. One third of the public does something about their water. There is a Roper poll that showed that groundwater issues are the foremost. Radon and air were at the bottom. My concern is that people will now think that the real risk is from radon in water because that is what the government has regulated. We've already seen this confusion. For example, we heard about a lady who had 50 pCi/l in her air and 1000 pCi/l in her water. She spent $1000 to take her water down. It dropped her air level to 49.9.

The proposed rule acknowledged the air radon group's concerns, noting that water treatment should not be a first step in mitigating indoor radon. The rule also addressed the disparity between the risks of radon in air and water, acknowledging that, at 300 pCi/l, the fifty-seven to one hundred annual cancer cases to be avoided by regulating radon in water were only minuscule compared to eight thousand to forty thousand cancer cases caused by radon exposure, overall.

Tension between EPA Programs

In these ways, the promulgation of radon standards under the Safe Drinking Water Act posed major contradictions for the 4 pCi/l guidance for airborne radon. Although the air radon group at EPA could rationalize the drinking water standard, given the greater technical feasibility for reduction of radon in water as compared to air (Mardis, 1988), they viewed it as a direct threat to the assumptions underlying their programs. The issue pitted the radon group against the water division within EPA.

However, these concerns did not have the opportunity for full internal debate within the EPA at that time. Nervous that impending elections meant the likely departure of the sympathetic administrator of EPA, Lee Thomas, the water group bypassed two tiers of internal EPA review by skipping from the staff-level Work Group, where a stalemate had developed, directly to Thomas. In so doing, they cut the air-radon group out of the debate about the proposed rule (Page, 1988). Although the water staff claimed that it had no hidden agendas in going directly to Thomas (MacMullen, 1988), the procedural flap fanned the anger between the divisions. Guimond was forced to lobby heavily with Thomas for a standard that would not undermine the 4 pCi/l airborne radon guidance (Page 1988). In any case, slow review of the regulatory impacts of the regulation by the OMB pushed the decision into the new administration anyway.

The Costs of Regulation

Also influential in delaying implementation of the regulation has been the projected cost. There are forty-eight thousand community and twenty-thousand noncommunity public water systems in the United States served by groundwater sources. EPA had surveyed different-sized public water systems in the mid-1980s. For radon, EPA had found that 72 percent of systems exceeded 100 pCi/l, 30 percent exceeded 300 pCi/l, 11 percent exceeded 1000 pCi/l, and 1 percent exceeded 10,000 pCi/l. Smaller systems were most likely to be in excess (EPA, 1991a). The EPA determined that the cost of a 300 pCi/l standard would be $4 per household per year for larger systems and $170 per household per year for smaller systems. Annual nationwide costs were estimated at $180 million (EPA, 1991a).

However, other estimates pushed the potential costs much higher. For example, as many as 98 percent of all of the water systems in the State of Georgia and more than 75 percent of the 3,300 public water supply wells in New Jersey were said to be out of compliance with the proposed rule (*IAR*, June 1992b; Silverman, 1992b). Given the magnitude of the impact and the fact that many of the affected water systems service areas are as small as fifteen connections and twenty-five people, cost, not technology, became a key driving factor for the water division as to where to set the standard (MacMullen, 1988). Even allies in the war on radon questioned these expenditures. The New Jersey DEP noted that the costs of remediating these systems (some $125 million) is totally out of proportion to what was being spent to correct the principal source of danger, namely airborne radon. EPA was faulted for not doing a comparative study of all routes of radon exposure (*IAR*, June 1992b and December 1992a).

Environmental Concerns over a Mitigatory Gap

The proposed rule concluded that the best available technology for addressing radon in water was aeration (see chapter 7). However, concern was raised that this preferred mitigation would cause adverse secondary impacts. Aeration systems could generate ambient air pCi/l levels of a billion or more. Furthermore, some state health officials expressed concern that home aeration would remove chlorine, resulting in bacteriological exposures to the affected homes (*IAR*, December 1992). Meanwhile, the alternative of using charcoal filter systems may create radiation hazards by concentrating the daughter products of radon to the extent that the filters became sources of significant radioactivity.

The Ambient Goal

The water standard thus became a many-headed hydra, challenging regulation of chemicals in water, the nonregulation of airborne radon, and the priority for radon action. However, the proposal for water standards was not the only forum for questioning whether 4 pCi/l is sufficiently protective. The question of an acceptable level for radon was central to debate leading to the Radon Pollution Control Act, the first major legislative mandate to explicitly address radon, signed by President Reagan on October 28, 1988. Public Law 100-551 added a Title III to the Toxic Substances Control Act addressing "Indoor Radon Abatement." A fifth view of risk was to emerge during the passage of this legislation that underscored the lack of consensus on radon risk.

Thus, in contrast to the DOE scientists who advocated a more relaxed guidance, other critics such as activist Gloria Reins of the Florida organization Manasota 88 considered the risk at 4 pCi/l to be unacceptably high (Page, 1988). Even more vociferous in favor of a more protective standard was Congressman Henry Waxman, chair of the Subcommittee on Health and Environment. Waxman found his opportunity to raise the radon ante during congressional debate over the Radon Pollution Control Act in 1987 and 1988. The core of that bill reinforced the emerging consensus around radon.

The bill had begun in the Senate under the bipartisan leadership of Senators George Mitchell and John Chafee. At the heart of the proposed legislation was an expensive plan to provide seed money to build state radon programs. Despite the costs, the bill captured the very logic of Reaganomics. EPA had completed its state surveys, waking up states to the fact that the problem of radon was not merely isolated in the Reading Prong states. Now it sought to enable the full decentralization of the program. EPA Deputy Administrator James Barnes (1988) explained in an interview how this approach convinced the OMB: "We used the surveys to motivate the states. Now we wanted to give them money to develop their programs. When we went to OMB, we told them 'We've been playing this out just the way you said we should.'" The OMB did insist that the federal share of support would decline over a three-year period. With this proviso, the Reagan administration supported the Senate bill, terming it "a prudent and balanced approach to addressing a difficult public health problem" (Chafee, 1987). With a mix of other program elements to satisfy a broad coalition of congresspersons, the bill appeared ready to sail through to passage in the summer of 1987. However, the pending bill left intact the 4 pCi/l guidance.

Enter Congressman Waxman

In mid-1987, Henry Waxman claimed jurisdiction over the formative Radon Pollution Control Act in the House, even though the Senate version of the bill had already unanimously passed the rival House Subcommittee on Transportation, Tourism, and Hazardous Materials. Waxman then spent the next year attempting to introduce a radon standard. He failed. However, by the time the radon bill was finally reported out of the Health and Environment Subcommittee, in August 1988, two fundamental policy changes regarding the question of acceptable levels of radon had been introduced. First, the House bill now included language setting a national radon goal of ambient (background) levels—specifically that radon levels inside buildings should be no higher than levels in the outdoor air, typically between 0.2 and 1.0 pCi/l (Gesell, 1983; Hopper, 1991; Sextro, 1988a). Furthermore, Waxman's language would direct the EPA to revise the *Citizen's Guide* to clearly inform the public of risks below 4 pCi/l.

Waxman was assisted by several factors in convincing Congress to adopt an ambient goal. First, there was his ability to hold out for a compromise, delaying the legislation entirely. Further influencing willingness to support the ambient goal were general doubts about the 4 pCi/l guidance. In his congressional testimony, EPA Deputy Administrator James Barnes stated that the 4 pCi/l action level was not intended as a health-based standard, but rather as an amalgamation of information regarding health risk, population exposure, and the feasibility and cost of mitigation—all merged into one action level to avoid confusion. Congress had found, however, that the action level had caused rather than avoided confusion because 4 pCi/l was interpreted by the public as a safe level. Specifically, it was concluded "that many people have misinterpreted EPA's designated action level and the statements in the current *Citizen's Guide* as meaning that there is little or no risk from radon levels below 4 picocuries per liter" (Dingell, 1988, p.12).[8]

Furthermore, congressional support for these revisions was heightened when EPA's Barnes testified before the Subcommittee on Health and the Environment that "we really want to try in this country to drive those indoor radon levels down as low as we can, so that we are protecting the public health."[9] In an election year, it was difficult for a congressperson to argue for a less protective approach (Guimond, 1988c). Finally, the ambient goal fell short of a more restrictive standard for radon. In his analysis of the final bill, Congressman John Dingell, chair of the Committee on Energy and Commerce, stressed that ambient levels are a "long-term aspirational goal for the public" not a practical and achievable goal in the short run.[10]

EPA's View of the Ambient Goal

EPA had staked its reputation on the 4 pCi/l guidance. Despite the claims of some critics, EPA did not appear to be directly behind Waxman's efforts to push radon exposure below 4 pCi/l and was certainly ambivalent about being given a mandate to create a standard.[11] At the same time, the agency realized that Waxman's efforts were more to its benefit than would be a counter push aimed at increasing the action level. In the push and pull over risk that underlay much of the funding and support for radon programming, too much protectiveness was a very healthy sign, indeed.

Furthermore, the EPA radon staff saw the ambient goal as legitimating their efforts. Scientists at the DOE and elsewhere who thought that radon risk was being overstated had painted Guimond as a radical for selecting the 4 pCi/l guidance. With the ambient goal, 4 pCi/l had to be rethought. It was no longer so radical. As one of Guimond's colleague's noted, "Rich has been vindicated. . . . the risk estimate of 4 pCi/l turns out to be middle of the road" (Page, 1988).

EPA Forces Action on the Law

Of more immediate concern to the agency was the fact that EPA's radon program was placed in limbo for a year while congressional debate dragged on. EPA had a strong interest in helping to break the log jam in the House. The agency was also concerned with just how easily radon had dropped from the public's attention, reducing efforts to test and mitigate. Lagging public concern, in turn, further reduced pressure on Congress to resolve the impasse. As a result, EPA hatched a grand strategy to force congressional agreement on the bill, to ensure administration support, to attract public attention to radon, and to cement EPA's firm lead on the radon issue. The strategy involved using the Public Health Service, whose leader—Surgeon General C. Everett Koop—had established a public presence in defining such major health threats as cigarette smoking and AIDS. The plan was to attract Koop to champion radon as his latest public health priority.

The Public Health Service is formally a branch of the military. Recruits are posted to various agencies, where they work on matters related to the public health. EPA was well linked to the Public Health Service because a number of key agency officials, including Rich Guimond, were actually PHS officers on loan to EPA.[12] This fact is particularly noticeable on Wednesdays, when PHS officers must wear their uniforms. Thus, the radon group had the connections to enlist Dr. Koop. On its end, the Public Health Service placed certain conditions on its involvement. The Public Health Service recalled the public confusion caused by government warnings about asbestos earlier in the decade at a time when there were no available means to remediate the problem. As a result, it refused to support EPA on radon until after the seven-state study was completed, quality control for testing was in place, and mitigation techniques were ready to be implemented. The EPA had met these stipulations by the summer of 1988, and the joint EPA/PHS announcement was planned for August. However, there were snags as the plot unfolded. First, implementation was delayed through the summer of 1988 into the fall. Then, in the end, Guimond lost Surgeon General Koop's direct involvement.

Guimond wore his PHS uniform on a Monday when the time finally arrived. On September 12, 1988, a well-publicized joint PHS-EPA press conference was held. The PHS was represented by Assistant Surgeon General Vernon Houk, head of the Centers for Disease Control in Atlanta. Houk joined EPA administrator Lee Thomas in announcing a national health advisory urging the testing of homes for radon (EPA, 1988b). The advisory read, in part, "Indoor radon gas is a national health problem. Radon causes thousands of deaths each year. Millions of homes have elevated radon levels. Most homes should be tested for radon. When elevated levels are confirmed, the problem should be corrected."

The effort successfully made radon a headline that grabbed the public's attention (see chapter 9).[13] With the help of the heightened concern resulting from the public health service strategy, radon received the political push needed to move the pending legislation out of committee and quickly through the House. With strong administration backing, the bill received bipartisan support, speeding through the joint house conference committee to become Public Law 100-551, the Indoor Radon Abatement Act, on October 4, 1988. The revised legislation survived review by the Office of Management and Budget and was then signed by President Reagan.

Public Law 100-551

The Indoor Radon Abatement Act provides the most comprehensive policy statement about radon to date, drawing upon the concerns of both senators and representatives. Against the alternative views of radon risk—tied to the 4 pCi/l guidance, the DOE advocacy for 20 pCi/l, and the waterborne radon standard—Congress set forth a bold vision with a national goal of ambient exposure (Sec. 301 of the Toxic Substances Control Act [15 U.S.C. 2661]): "The national long-term goal of the United States with respect to radon levels in buildings is that the air within buildings in the United States should be as free of radon as the ambient air outside of buildings." Among many other provisions, a revised *Citizen's Guide to Radon* was mandated for mid-1989 that would identify ambient radon levels, clarify the relationships between short-term and long-term testing, discuss costs and feasibilities of reducing radon in new and existing buildings, indicate how behaviors such as cigarette smoking increase the radon risk, and identify potentially sensitive populations.

Conclusion: Divergent Views of Risk United— Consensus or Confusion?

United States radon policy now incorporated elements of at least four different views of risk. The *Citizen's Guide* was based upon 4 pCi/l, with exhortations to push even lower. At the same time, EPA's testing strategies remained grounded in screening tests that sought the hottest houses. In effect, the DOE's argument was embodied in this practice, even if Waxman's push for more protection was embodied in rhetoric. Meanwhile, promulgation of dramatically stricter water standards proceeded. However, the cohabitation of these four views of risk hardly constituted a consensus. For example, to the DOE's Susan Rose, Guimond had engineering a policy rout that bypassed "a legitimate scientific conflict over risk at the lower levels." As a result, even at 4 pCi/l, EPA had created a "de facto regulation" for radon, a "pathology" that was Guimond's "effort to outguess OMB" (Rose, 1988). And, if critics from the DOE had been unhappy with the 4 pCi/l guidance, they were livid with the ambient goal. Thus, DOE's Rose gestured accusingly toward a conference hall where EPA radon staffers gathered as she seethed with frustration, "It's all worthless with the ambient.

There is a legitimate conflict over the risk at the lower levels. The bureaucrats in the other room won't hear it" (Rose, 1991). On a lighter note, Pennsylvania's radon program head, Tom Gerusky, dubbed this legislation the "Full Employment for Health Physicists Act of 1988" (1991).

While controversy continued to boil around the basic risk assumptions underlying radon policy (see chapters 4 and 10), these conflicting views of risk were still tangled when, in 1992, the EPA brought out the revised *Citizen's Guide to Radon*, as well as a new consumers guide and guides to remediation, new construction, and real estate (see chapter 10). Similarly, the dissensus on risk was deeply embedded in a 1992 Radon Program Review, its recommendations for reform, the agency's reply, and a subsequent congressional investigation (EPA, 1992a, 1993c; GAO 1992; see chapter 12). Thus, although seemingly the radon issue had progressed by September 1988 along the environmental policy cycle to the point that effective consensus had been achieved on key issues, in fact dissensus was inherent in the EPA radon program, as well as in Congress, which subsequently failed to reauthorize the Indoor Radon Abatement Act or pass any of several additional pieces of radon legislation (see chapter 12).[14]

Conclusions—The Federal Role

We have seen that EPA succeeded in mounting a quick and surprisingly successful radon program after the Colebrookdale Township discovery by embracing the general principles of Reaganomics—nonregulatory, market-based, consumer-driven, and decentralized in responsibility. Even critics of the federal radon program were forced to admit that EPA accomplished much with comparatively few resources (Lautenberg, 1988; Erdman, 1988). Former Assistant Surgeon General Houk commented in an interview (1989), "There are not many issues that find me and the EPA on the same side. But the way they've handled radon has been exemplary. The taxpayer has got his money worth."

EPA itself viewed the radon program as a radically different approach for solving a new breed of environmental problems that emerged in the late 1980s. Thus, while he admitted that "all the returns aren't in on this one yet," former Deputy Administrator Barnes (1988) commented in an interview that he viewed radon as a prototype for "a lot of problems that the agency is looking at that cannot be solved by going after a few big sources. These problems include indoor air, municipal waste, and farm-and-lawn runoff. We need models that work based on providing information and technology and motivating people to take action. There are a lot of risks and there aren't enough EPA inspectors to deal with the individual level of society."

Of particular importance to Barnes was the movement away from the federal government as an isolated actor. Instead, he found one of the strongest points of the program to be its built-in need for coordination among different levels of government and with the private sector. As a result, the radon program is "un-like established environmental programs which have an overlap and duplication and an inefficient use of resources" (Barnes, 1988). The innovations found in the federal radon program thus represent a test of the assumptions of Reaganom-ics. Given the building crescendo of the Reaganomic movement into the "Neo-Reaganomic" Contract with America period in the mid-1990s, this test has important implications, explored throughout this volume.

Beyond Reaganomics, the federal radon program was inherently shaped by the Colebrookdale Township experience. In its concern with hot spots and hot buildings, the use of screening tests, and its belief in a quick and easy technolog-ical fix, radon programming drew heavily upon the myths formed during the Colebrookdale and Clinton experiences. As we continue, we will also explore how effective these myths have been as a guide to radon policy.

Finally, we have shown that the question of risk is central to the federal ra-don program, contributing to conflict and policy confusion. In order to further dissect the varied views of risk discussed above, we must turn to the basic as-sumption underlying governmental response to radon, namely that radon is a significant threat to health. Here policy based on "assumptive risk" meets critics who ask "Where are the dead bodies?" This question is the focus of the next chapter.

Notes

1. In presenting the radon issue as a construction of EPA, we do not wish to over-look the importance of public pressure in spurring the agency's early action. Advocates included PAR, EDF, and the Reading Prong congressmen, as well as a Florida group, Manassota 88. The effect of these groups is sharply seen when U.S. radon policy is con-trasted to the Canadian experience. Lacking the advocacy of "policy entrepreneurs," the Canadian government abandoned the 4 pCi/l guidance as too protective and sought to downplay the risk (Harrison and Hoberg, 1991). At the same time, it is important to note that radon benefited by comparatively minimal public advocacy in the U.S. as compared to that found with other environmental and public issues. Generally, the radon issue was an EPA construction supported by a well-timed dose of public advocacy.

2. Recognizing that federal research on radon is "fragmented and underfunded," Ti-tle IV required EPA to undertake research and disseminate findings for all facets of radon and indoor air contamination, including research on geology and building types useful for predicting radon levels. The act particularly highlighted two applied research projects. Section 118(k) of the act mandated that EPA prepare a report to Congress by 1987 based on a national radon assessment. The study was to identify U.S. locations where radon is found in homes, workplaces, and schools; to assess the amount of radon found, and to identify the level of radon that threatens health; and, finally, to carry out a demonstration

program testing means for reducing or eliminating radon in buildings. Second, the Radon Mitigation Demonstration Program was to be developed, centered in the Reading Prong. Authorization of the act included $5 million per year from 1987 to 1989 for the purposes of research. Overall, EPA was appropriated $7.6 million in fiscal year 1987 to address the mandates in section 118(k) and Title IV of the law (GAO, 1988).

3. In 1995, the Division of Indoor Air Pollution merged with the Radon Division into the newly formed Office of Radiation and Indoor Air (see chapter 12).

4. However, as we discuss in chapter 8, the RMP quickly took on a quasi-regulatory role, with states requiring testing companies to successfully complete the RMP as a requirement for their own certification programs.

5. The DOE's broad authority to do radon research derived from the Atomic Energy Act, the Energy Reorganization Act, and the Federal Non-Nuclear Energy Research and Development Act. It had three research objectives: to improve understanding about radon's health risks, to understand and predict radon entry to buildings, and to develop and evaluate radon reduction techniques (GAO, 1986).

6. The lack of a pre-Watras consensus on radon risk is evidenced by these divergent guidances. The U.S. National Council on Radiation Protection and Measurements (NCRP) recommended a total indoor nonoccupational exposure of no more than 2 WLM/yr (about 10 pCi/l at 75 percent occupancy) in 1984. In contrast, the American Society of Heating, Refrigeration, and Air Conditioning Engineers (ASHRAE) recommended an action level of 2 pCi/l. Meanwhile, the federal Bonneville Power Administration revised its 3 pCi/l action level for radon mitigation in conjunction with its weatherization program to 5 pCi/l (BPA, 1987). The International Commission on Radiation Protection (ICRP) suggested a 10 pCi/l guidance for remedial action in existing homes where remediation can easily be accomplished, but higher levels would be tolerated in houses difficult to mitigate. New houses would not exceed 5 pCi/l. The United Kingdom proposed a 20 pCi/l remedial action level and a 4 pCi/l design limit for new housing. Canada had adopted a guidance of 3 pCi/l for further investigation, 7 pCi/l for primary action, and 50 pCi/l for prompt action; 20 pCi/l is the remedial action guideline for existing houses. In Belgium, at 40 pCi/l a house is considered to be uninhabitable, at 8 pCi/l remedial action is called for, and new houses are to fall below 4 pCi/l. And in Sweden, regulations set levels at about 4 pCi/l (0.02 WL) for new dwellings (with a design objective of 1 pCi/l), about 10 pCi/l (0.054 WL) for rebuilt homes, and about 20 pCi/l (0.108 WL) for existing dwellings (Guimond, 1988b; BPA, 1984).

EPA's Kirk Macaunaughey, in an interview on April 4, 1991, reported success in the agency's effort to exert leadership within the international radon community to move toward a consensus and support of EPA's guidance, in part, by inviting foreign scholars and officials to its 1991 radon conference. "The international community is coming lower. The CEC and U.K. were at 20, now they are at 6. There is more and more agreement, which we want to encourage. The ICRP, WHO and IARP have produced documents that reassess their positions, existing and new standards are continuing to be worked on. We all understand one another. There is a more unified position."

7. Abelson was rebutted by EPA's director of the Office of Radiation, Margo Oge (Oge and Farland, 1992). Oge cited scientific agreement regarding the validity of the uranium miner cancer risk from radon, the validity of the linear theory, and the invalidity of studies attempting to correlate radon in a geographic area with individual exposure.

8. There are many examples of the confusion of the guidance for a standard (see Makofske and Edelstein, 1988, for a discussion of this issue). For example, two Associated Press releases describing the EPA announcement in April 1989 of the results from the initial sixteen-state school survey repeatedly referred to 4 pCi/l as a standard and a "safety standard" (Associated Press, 1989a and 1989b).

9. Hearing of the House Subcommittee on Health and Environment, November 5, 1987, p. 57.

10. See Report 100–1047, p. 11. The House committee also raised concern regarding the accuracy and reliability of short-term radon tests, citing fluctuations in radon levels over time. The committee charged the EPA with determining whether to recommend only the use of long-term tests. These concerns, as well, were reflected in the formative legislation.

11. Assistant Surgeon General Houk credited Robert Yuenke of the Environmental Defense Fund for the language relating to the national goal of ambient levels of radon in the bill.

12. By June of 1989, Guimond had been promoted by surgeon general Koop to the dual ranks of rear admiral and assistant surgeon general.

13. In April 1989, EPA once again released a carefully orchestrated radon bombshell—the results of a sixteen-state survey of schools showed many exceeded the 4 pCi/l guidance (Associated Press, 1989a and 1989b).

14. Despite the failure to pass new radon legislation, a total of $25 million was spent on the federal radon program in fiscal year 1992, more than had been appropriated by the Indoor Radon Abatement Act, whose $15.5 million per year for three years included $10 million for state grants. The 1992 funding included $8.1 million to continue the state radon program grants for an additional year (GAO, 1992). These grants have since continued rather than being phased out. However, radon appropriations within EPA saw a 10 percent reduction during across-the-board cutbacks early in the Clinton administration in the mid-1990s.

Part II

The Scientific Myths of Radon

Chapter 4

The Myth of the Dead Bodies

The American people do not want to become health physicists. They want information they can use to sort out radon.
—Richard Guimond

Basic to the radon issue from the onset was the claim that radon (or more specifically, radon-daughter decay) is one of the major causes of lung cancer, an illness responsible in 1996 alone for some 158,700 deaths and 177,000 new cases in the United States (ACS, 1996a). Slowly developing, often asymptomatic until it is too late to treat, allowing few survivors—nine out of ten victims die within five years (ACS, 1996b)—lung cancer has become one of the most dreaded of diseases. While the bulk of lung cancers have been attributed to smoking, post-Watras it has generally been claimed that radon is the second leading cause of the illness. Estimates of lung cancer deaths caused by radon vary from a few hundred to as high as thirty thousand, with the EPA suggesting five thousand to thirty thousand deaths per year as a reasonable range (EPA, 1986, 1992f).

These figures may sound very factual, but behind them lies a great deal of ambiguity. As an invisible contaminant, radon is shrouded in uncertainty. One often does not know whether or when the exposure is actually occurring, to what degree, and for how long. Furthermore, this uncertainty extends to the consequences of the exposure. One cannot sense the effects of these unspecified possible exposures. Nor could physicians measure such effects and predict outcomes. And because of illness latencies, there may be periods of as much as twenty years before any symptoms become manifest, a time of "medical invisibility" during which victims do not know that they are developing the disease. Diagnosis of the disease may be uncertain, the cause of the disease is unlikely to be known with any certitude, and the course, prognosis, and treatment of the disease or condition may be subject to speculation (see Vyner, 1988). Also, little is understood about the interaction and synergy of different dispositional and environmental factors. However, the likelihood of interactions—or rather the unlikelihood that single factors cause simple consequences in isolation—adds a level of complexity to the real world that is baffling to scientists trained to want the level of control found in the laboratory. The result of these multiple uncertainties and others that will become evident throughout this chapter is that the exact health consequences of radon are inherently complex and difficult to measure and, therefore, subject to divergent interpretation, disagreement, and controversy.

Given the lack of consensus, one must resolve the ambiguity by determining the level of proof required for invisible effects of invisible contaminants. At root,

79

the criteria demanded for proof is a matter of values rather than facts. And, a fundamental division of values is evident in the area of environmental risk. On the one hand, the norms of traditional science suggest a cautionary approach that avoids drawing conclusions that cannot be proven to a high level of certitude. In contrast, environmental and health advocates have increasingly demanded a precautionary approach, where one accepts a lower level of scientific proof before taking protective action. Inherent to a precautionary approach is the realization that one may not succeed in proving many environmental hazards to a high level of certitude and that to demand traditional levels of proof is tantamount to denying the hazard.[1]

Following the efforts of Congressman James J. Delaney and the 1958 food and drug clause he championed, American laws have embodied the precautionary approach, at least regarding carcinogens. EPA adopted this precautionary strategy in its approach to radon, making assumptions necessary for projecting potential invisible risks. In contrast, a considerable number of health and other scientists hold that risks must be concretely proven. Regarding radon, their arguments tend to embody what we call the myth of the dead bodies—the notion that absent actual lung cancer fatalities directly linked to residential radon exposure, it is implausible that radon is as dangerous to the general public as EPA claims. Heated disagreement has surrounded the basic premises behind EPA's approach to radon.

In this chapter, we examine two areas of broad agreement about the risks from radon that have generally stayed beyond the controversy, and we then examine four areas of dispute.

Areas of Broad Agreement about Radon and Lung Cancer

There are two central issues upon which there is broad agreement surrounding radon and lung cancer. First, we have compelling epidemiological evidence that radon causes lung cancer in humans. Lung cancer incidence in uranium and hard rock miners has been well documented (see chapter 2). Second, toxicological evidence plausibly accounts for a mechanism whereby radon exposure can cause lung cancer.

Radon Causes Lung Cancer

For the past 50 years, there have been numerous scientific epidemiological studies of uranium and other hard-rock miners that show significantly higher rates of lung cancer mortality compared to nonexposed populations. In addition, the data show enhanced lung cancer incidence that strongly correlates with increased cumulative exposure to radon daughters as measured through WLM values (Cross, 1987). And this excess lung cancer is not accounted for by smoking

(Jackson et al., 1987). It is generally agreed among the scientific establishment that these studies of miner populations have demonstrated to a high order of certitude that radon exposure actually causes lung cancer (Lubin et al., 1994a; NRC, 1994). Importantly, the strength of these findings supercedes much disagreement within the health physics profession over how to use the uranium miner data to estimate radon risk for the general population. Such estimates of radon deaths are derived by using a risk projection model to extrapolate the risk of lung cancer to the general public based on the distribution of radon exposures to that population. The validity of these complex calculations rests on the soundness of underlying assumptions relating to such factors as the latency period for cancer and average exposure to radon. Health researchers have argued extensively about some of these assumptions, particularly whether risk is relative or absolute and how much risk drops off over time. In table 4.1 we have listed the key assumptions and the resulting lung cancer deaths predicted by year for three of the major radon risk projection studies (EPA, 1987e; NCRP, 1984b; and BEIR IV, 1988). The table illustrates that varying assumptions about the nature of radon risk do not alter the common finding from all three studies that radon is a major cause of lung cancer deaths. Indeed, most researchers come up with a similar range of radon deaths (Lubin and Boice, 1989; Nero et al., 1990; Lubin et al., 1994a). While health scientists may view these differences as having great significance, the severity of radon as a serious public health issue is affected very little according to whether the estimate of radon deaths is five thousand, twenty thousand, or forty thousand deaths per year.

We Know How Radon Causes Lung Cancer

We also have compelling toxicological evidence that provides a plausible physiological explanation for how radon might cause cancer. The current theory of carcinogenesis, based upon studies of populations exposed to radiation, accounts for the impact of the alpha radiation associated with radon decay. Essentially, incoming radiation breaks apart molecules, damaging the proper functioning or reproduction of cells. The absorbed dose from this ionizing radiation, measured in units of "rads" or "millirads," represents the amount of energy absorbed by cells or tissues, linking the radiation and the resulting radiation-caused cancer (see Crawford-Brown, 1987). Compared with beta and gamma radiation, alpha radiation has the highest rate of energy transfer and, therefore, the highest ionization for a given distance traveled in matter. When an alpha particle slams into cell tissue, DNA molecules may be harmed directly by collision or through attack by "free radicals," highly reactive chemical compounds formed by ionization. Subdividing DNA from incorrectly repaired cells may then pass on the damage to the daughter cells through mutation, potentially resulting in cancer. The biological damage to the organism from radiation, measured in "rem," is a product of both the dose of energy absorbed and the relative biological effectiveness of the radiation resulting from the way that energy is spread out or distributed among the affected cells.

The convergence of findings from both tissue-based studies of cancer and from actual populations of miners exposed to high radon levels provides a basis for general agreement on the fundamental fact that exposure to radon may result in the incidence of lung cancer.

Table 4.1   Comparison of Assumptions Made by EPA, NCRP, and BEIR IV

Assumption	EPA	NCRP	BEIR IV
Dose-response linearity	Yes	Yes	Yes
Risk model assumed	Relative 1–4% increase per WLM; life table analysis	Absolute 10x10⁻⁶	Relative
Latency period	10 years	5 years; no cancers before age 40	*
Smoking and radon	Synergistic	*	Synergistic
Dose/WLM in home and mine	*	40% higher	Same
Drop off of risk with time	None	Exponential $T_{1/2}$ = 20 yrs.	Decreasing with time since exposure
Average indoor radon concentration	0.8 pCi/l	1 pCi/l	1 pCi/l
Equilibrium ratio	0.5	0.5	*
Lung cancer deaths from radon per year	5,000–20,000	10,000	13,000

Sources: EPA, 1987; NCRP, 1984b; and BEIR IV, 1988.
*The particular assumption was not clearly specified in the reference.

Areas of Disagreement about Radon and Lung Cancer

As discussed in chapter 3, radon rejectionists take exception to the threat of radon to the general public. In general, those who argue for higher risk levels or who reject radon outright as a significant health issue tend to be raising at least one of four generic questions challenging the EPA/CDC formulation about geologic radon. First, EPA's concrete, if broad, projections for radon's death toll are viewed as unfounded exaggerations in the eyes of critics who ask, "where are all these dead bodies?" Second, critics question "can data from uranium mines serve as a valid basis for projecting radon risks in homes?" Third, critics ask "given the dominant role of cigarette smoking in causing lung cancer, of what significance is radon?" Finally, critics question "where is the proof of harm due to such small doses of radiation as 4 pCi/l?" Let's explore these challenges more closely.

Where Are All These Dead Bodies Due to Radon?

As noted, EPA has generally estimated that between five thousand and thirty thousand U.S. lung cancer deaths per year are due to radon, although the range has been pushed as high as forty thousand deaths. While the wide range reflects real uncertainties, estimates of so many radon deaths caused controversy. Some professionals in the health fields, unable to find upwards of twenty or thirty thousand lung cancer deaths unaccounted for in a given year, questioned the absence of the dead bodies suggested by these figures. Meanwhile, the potential for other illnesses caused by radon also emerged.

Disputed Body Counts

The dead body controversy was rooted in skepticism by local health officials, who challenged radon's risk because the estimated total number of deaths from smoking, radon, and other known causes exceeds total lung cancer mortality. And Nobel Laureate Rosalee Yallow expressed the views of many health scientists when she cited smoking as the predominant cause of lung cancer and, thus, the primary target for prevention (1988). Indeed, the fact that radon shares its signature illness with a dominating causal agent complicates the accounting for dead bodies.

However, the illusive dead-body issue is not as substantive a problem as it appears to be on the surface. The exact relationship between smoking and lung cancer is itself surrounded by considerable uncertainty (Doll and Petro, 1981). The American Cancer Society estimates that between 70 percent and 83 percent of lung cancer deaths are caused by smoking (ACS, 1996). Given this range, between twenty-seven thousand and forty-seven thousand lung cancer deaths are left to be accounted for by radon and all other causes. Thus, there is enough lung cancer death to go around to make both smoking and radon serious hazards. Furthermore, given a likely synergistic effect between radon and smoking, discussed below, it may be a false exercise to think of radon and smoking as separate causes of lung cancer (EPA, 1987e). In short, enough dead bodies exist to make the threat of radon credible.

However, the myth of the dead bodies has been reinforced by findings from correlational research, principally Cohen's examination of county lung cancer rates for women in the period 1950–1969 (1989a,b). Not only did Cohen fail to find a positive correlation between higher lung cancer death rates and areas known to have higher radon levels, but, in some cases, a negative correlation appeared. Cohen, thus, asked, "Do such findings suggest that higher radon levels actually make lung cancer less likely?" While this work has had enormous influence in questioning EPA's claims about radon risk, in fact, Cohen's research suffers from severe methodological problems that robs his findings of both validity and utility.[2]

Radon and Other Causes of Mortality beside Lung Cancer

It should be noted that most examinations of mortality due to radon focus exclusively upon lung cancer from inhaled radon daughters. Nonetheless, there has been some concern about the risk associated with ingested radon in water supplies and, more recently, about ecological studies that link radon with other forms of cancer. Raised is the possibility that there might be "dead bodies" associated with radon that have been missed due to the focus on lung cancer.

When water is ingested, the stomach is the primary recipient of the radioactive dose (Suomela and Kahlos, 1972). Most of the radon moves quickly out of the stomach to the gastrointestinal tract, into the bloodstream, and ultimately to the lungs where it is exhaled. The biological half-life of radon in ingested water is thought to be 30–70 minutes compared to the physical half-life of 3.9 days. Based on normal consumption of water with a radon concentration of 1,000 pCi/l, an adult would get a yearly dose to the stomach of 100 mrem and a whole body dose of 2 mrem.[3] While the risk from ingesting radon in water is hardly negligible, it appears to be much less than the risk associated with the inhalation of radon (and, ultimately, the daughters), which outgasses from the same water (Crawford-Brown, 1987; Eichholz, 1987).

Residential ecological studies using data from fifteen countries have found strong correlations between the incidence of myeloid leukemia, kidney cancer, prostate cancer, melanoma, and certain childhood cancers with increasing home radon exposure (Henshaw et al., 1990; Eatough and Henshaw, 1990).[4] A study of uranium miners failed to find a statistically significant increase in liver cancer or leukemia with radon exposure, although increased risk of cancer of the gallbladder and extrahepatic bile ducts, and multiple myeloma, were associated with radon (Tomasek et al., 1993). Finally, EPA (1987a) has cited the potential for birth defects associated with radon. Although important, these additional radon risks appear to be at least an order of magnitude less than the risk of lung cancer from radon exposure. There is a continual process of reassessment of the health effects of radon exposure, and a new BEIR VI study is underway to investigate all the existing evidence on the health effects of radon-induced cancer (NRC, 1994).

In sum, we consider the challenges to the severity of radon based upon identification of dead bodies to be merely a myth. Given the uncertainties surrounding smoking and lung cancer, and the possible synergisms between radon and smoking, to reject the possibility of radon risk for this reason is eroneous and ignores substantial evidence to the contrary.

Can We Generalize from Uranium Mines to Residences?

While it is generally accepted that the miners' data demonstrate a causal relationship between radon and lung cancer, critics have argued that these findings cannot be legitimately generalized from mines to homes. Absent epidemiological data proving that residential radon also causes lung cancer, the presence of a hazard to the general population would, therefore, be unsubstantiated.

Differences Between Mines and Homes

Indeed, there are significant differences between the mine and home environments, including differences in radon concentrations, aerosol characteristics, breathing rates, and populations exposed. We will explore the significance of each difference.

Different Radon Concentrations. One complication of using the miner studies is that the mines generally have higher cumulative radon exposures that must be extrapolated to the lower environmental radon exposures found in most houses. However, exposure time is likely to be greater in the home. These differences may be accounted for by calculating the cumulative dose to the lungs as measured by the working level month (WLM—defined on page 5 in chapter 1). When exposed to an average indoor radon level of 1 pCi/l, a person would receive approximately 0.2–0.3 WLM/yr. under normal household conditions or a cumulative lifetime exposure of around 15–20 WLM, far below miner exposures. In contrast, a lifetime of exposure at the EPA guidance level of 4 pCi/l gives exposures that are at the lower end of miner exposure data. And people living in homes with exposures to higher radon levels of between 10 and 20 pCi/l do not require any extrapolation to be comparable to WLM exposures received by some miners showing excess cancers.

While this type of comparison provides a basis for extrapolation, there is still the question of whether a dose concentrated into a smaller time interval gives the same risks as the identical dose distributed over longer time periods (BEIR IV, 1988). Data from a joint analysis of eleven miner studies support a higher lung cancer risk at lower exposure rates. This suggests that low exposure rate, long durations of exposure, or both, may be particularly risky, at least based on the miner data (Lubin et al., 1994a). Unfortunately, the data could not provide sufficient evidence for this inverse dose rate effect at the lower levels found in homes.

Different Aerosol Characteristics. An important difference between mines and homes involves the amount and types of suspended dust and dirt particles found in the air. Such aerosol characteristics are important because they affect the ability of radon daughters to deliver a dose to lung tissue. Two aerosol characteristics of particular importance in determining dose are the particle size and the percentage of "unattached daughters."[5] Corrections may be made for these interdependent aerosol characteristics by modeling the dose of radioactivity received by the lungs.

It might seem that dirty and dusty mines would be much more dangerous than comparatively cleaner homes. However, when particle size is considered, it turns out that the smaller particles found in homes (averaging 0.12 micrometers) will penetrate more deeply in the lungs and provide a greater dose to sensitive lung tissue than will the generally larger particles found in the mine environment (averaging 0.17 micrometers). Therefore, the dose in homes could be as much as 1.4 times greater than in mines (NRC, 1991).

Similarly, the fraction of unattached radon daughters—radon daughters floating around not attached to some particle of dust or dirt—also points to greater risks in homes than in mines. As aerosol concentrations decrease (i.e., there is less dust), the fraction of unattached daughters increases.[6] Because these daughters have not attached or "plated out" on dust, they are more likely to reach the sensitive target areas in the tracheal and basal areas of the lungs. Therefore, a less-dusty, cleaner environment may be more hazardous than a dirty one. Some data on the unattached fraction in homes and mines indicate that homes may have twice the unattached daughters as mines do, leading to an increased dose in homes by a factor of about 1.2 (BEIR IV, 1988).

Different Breathing Patterns. Patterns of respiration are also likely to differ between adult male miners and home dwellers. One key difference in breathing pattern involves tidal volume (the amount of air moved through the lungs). Increased tidal volume is associated with aerobic exercise, when radon daughters are pulled deep into the lungs and deposited. Working miners would be expected to have greater tidal volume than a person relaxing at home. Differences are also found with the percentage of mouth/nose breathing and the overall frequency of breathing. Breathing through the nose tends to plate out unattached particles (i.e., the particles become attached to the nasal mucosa), reducing the bronchial dose. Again, working miners are at greater risk because they are more likely to breathe through their mouths than less-active persons at home. Finally, as one breathes more frequently, air is held in the lungs for less time. Therefore, fewer particles are deposited on lung tissue. This difference is particularly significant for children. Because their rate of respiration is much higher than adults, they have lower average exposure. When these three characteristics of respiration are combined, miners are exposed to nearly twice the dose of radon found in the home (BEIR IV, 1988; NRC, 1991).

Different Populations Exposed to Radon. There is one further problem in extrapolating the miner lung cancer data to the general population, the so-called healthy worker effect. Miners tend to be a fairly homogeneous population, healthy males in the prime of life. In contrast, any random group selected from the general population as a control for miners is likely to evidence comparatively more cases of illness and cancer. As a result, epidemiological studies may overestimate cancer cases in residential settings, therefore, underestimating the cancer rate among miners. This effect is difficult to make corrections for (Steinhausler, 1988, p.350).

Conclusions on Extrapolating from Mines to Homes. Correction factors can be computed to account for most of these differences while making extrapolations between settings (BEIR IV, 1988, pp. 149–59; NRC 1991; Samet 1991). When the discussed differences in radon concentrations, aerosols, and breathing patterns between mines and homes were combined in one study, all of the differences balanced out (i.e., the correction factor was computed as $1.4 \times 1.2 \times 0.56 = 1$), suggesting that the mine and the home hold comparable dangers (BEIR IV, 1988). However, a later analysis by a National Academy of Sciences panel recalculated this correction factor as 0.7 for adults and 0.8 for children. Use of these results would reduce the estimated radon deaths in homes discussed previously by perhaps 20–30 percent, an insignificant difference at the policy level (NAS, 1991; Samet, 1991). A recent joint analysis using eleven miner studies and following the BEIR IV extrapolation methodology resulted in an estimate of fifteen thousand lung cancer deaths in the United States in 1993 from radon exposure in homes (Lubin et al., 1994a).

Epidemiological Studies in the Home

Of course, the most direct way to deal with the limitations of generalizing the miner data to homes would be to collect epidemiological data directly on home environments. Epidemiological studies look at the actual incidence of disease among the population exposed to radon concentrations in the environment. There are two approaches for residential studies of radon. The case study approach begins with a population of lung cancer victims and seeks to identify their radon exposures. In contrast, the cohort approach takes a population exposed to high levels of radon and watches to see if predicted health effects occur. As with the miners' studies, the ideal residential cohort study should have a large radon exposure group for statistical reliability, an appropriately selected control group, accurate radon measurements for both populations, and sufficient follow-up to identify cancer cases over the lifetime of the group's members. Two of the biggest difficulties of all such studies are determining the lifetime radon exposure of a given individual and adjusting for differences in smoking habits. No environmental study has been able to incorporate all these elements to give a decisive result (see Jackson et al., 1987; Lubin, 1994).

With some nine case-control studies reported in the literature through 1996, results have been inconsistent. Some epidemiological studies such as the New Jersey Department of Health (1989) study and the Swedish studies (Pershagan et al., 1992; Pershagen et al., 1994) show some positive correlation between radon exposure and lung cancer, while studies from Missouri (Alavanja et al., 1994), Finland (Auvinen et al., 1996; Ruosteenoja et al., 1996), and Canada (Letourneau et al., 1994) show no trend at all. There are a considerable number of additional or expanded case studies in progress (Lubin et al., 1990; Samet et al., 1991; Neuberger, 1992). Unfortunately, all of the results reported so far have low statistical power, as well as other weaknesses, and therefore have little ability by themselves to unambiguously define the health effects of residential radon exposure (Lubin, 1994). While in principle studies can be pooled to improve the statistical power, differences in methodology often make it difficult to combine studies. One analysis combining three such studies has found a sufficient range in the resulting radon risk so as to be consistent with both the miner studies and also with no effect (Lubin, 1994). It appears that considerably more time is needed before epidemiological studies will provide definitive information on the radon risk in homes. Until then, the miner data continue to represent the best available information for assessing the health risks from radon.

In the absence of causal epidemiological research, correlational or ecologic studies of the home environment have received considerable attention. These studies attempt to show the relationship between lung cancer and radon levels based on average radon data for a geographic area. Results have been mixed. Research in Sweden using background gamma radiation and in Maine using radon in water (Hess, 1983) indicate positive correlations between radon exposure and lung cancer (i.e., higher radon rates were associated with higher cancer rates). However, other studies have failed to give positive correlations, including work in China and Finland comparing lung cancer rates in high-radon and low-radon areas, as well as Cohen's previously discussed comparisons of county lung cancer rates for women and county radon levels (1989a,b). Such studies suffer methodological problems and are not considered definitive by many in the radiation community (Jackson et al., 1987; Neuberger, 1991; Lubin, 1994).[7]

How Important Is Radon vs. Smoking As Causes of Lung Cancer?

Radon and smoking are inexorably bound together. They share causality of the same disease—lung cancer. The uranium miner data show significant excess cancer deaths above those that would be expected after correcting for smoking. However, in practice, any attempt to determine risk estimates due to radon must take into account the indisputable fact that cigarette smoke is such a strong carcinogen that it readily masks the effects of low levels of radon.

Epidemiological Difficulties in Separating Smoking and Radon

Given the complexity of their individual relationships to cancer induction, it has been difficult to sort out the combined effect of smoking and radon exposure. The simple risk models that have been used typically consider only cumulative exposure in WLM and either duration or intensity of smoking patterns. However, many factors such as age, time since exposure, age at first exposure, dose rate, gender, diet, and even genetic predisposition may be important in determining risk from radiation. Besides duration and intensity of smoking, the type of tobacco, inhalation habits, and time since quitting may be important factors in determining the biological impact of smoking. The sequencing and overlap of radiation and smoking may also have considerable impact. It is known that exposure to both smoking and radon shortens the latency period, resulting in the earlier onset of cancer. This synergy between smoking and radon threatens to bias epidemiological studies of radon (Cross, 1987; Jackson, 1987).

Toxicological Difficulties in Separating Smoking and Radon

An inability to distinguish between the types of cancers caused by smoking and/or radon adds to the dilemma. Neither produces a distinctive or recognizable pattern of lung cancer cell types (Jackson, 1987). Furthermore, the simple model of cancer induction suggests that the smoking/radon interaction may be described as a multistage process (Cross, 1987). In the first or "initiation" stage, damage to a cell occurs from radon. A second "promotion" stage is then required where an additional insult, smoking, causes the cell to reach the "cancer expression" stage. However, the reality of the smoking/radon interaction may be more complex, when, for instance, a single occurrence affects both initiation and promotion. For example, under certain circumstances, exposure to smoking and dust enhances mucus production, which prevents radon daughters from reaching the lungs and provides for their removal. Meanwhile, the same mucus traps longer lived cancer-causing substances from cigarette smoke, enhancing cancer promotion (Cross, 1987). While the contribution of smoking or radon to an eventual incidence of cancer may vary, the net cumulative effect is an increase in risk. It is merely a question of how much the risk is enhanced.

Interactions between Smoking and Radon

The inability to epidemiologically or toxicologically distinguish between cancers caused by exposure to smoking and to radon raises the question of how the risk from smoking and radon combines. There are many possibilities. If smoking and radon combine additively, then the risk from both is found by adding the separate risks from each, and there is no interaction between them. If smoking and radon combine multiplicatively, then the risk to smokers from a given radon exposure is significantly enhanced over the additive model. Whenever the effect is greater than additive, the interaction is referred to as "synergistic," where the results of exposure to two pollutants is greater than the exposure to either separately. However, there can be a continuum of possibilities, from the subadditive (less than the sum of both), to the submultiplicative (less than the product of both), to even the supramultiplicative (greater than the product of both). Indeed, studies demonstrate everything from radon acting alone all the way up to a fully multiplicative mode between smoking and radon.[8] Figure 4.1 illustrates a multiplicative relative risk model, showing deaths caused by smoking, radon, radon and smoking, and other possible causes of lung cancer. While smoking is still the leading cause of lung cancer, the model identifies most of the lung cancer fatalities from radon as being in the joint radon and smoking category, occurring for smokers and former smokers. This strong synergistic effect suggests that deaths from the combination of smoking and radon cannot be attributed to either separately but must be considered to be caused by both.

Illustrated Breakdown of U.S. Lung Cancer Deaths*

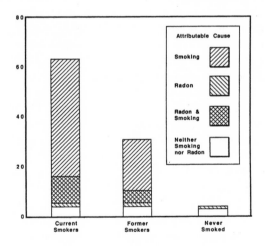

Fig. 4.1   Breakdown of lung cancer mortality by cause.
Source: EPA 1987e.

*Presumes a 20 percent attributable fraction for radon in each category. Attributable fraction for smoking in current smokers is 92 percent, in former smokers is 83 percent, and in all categories combined is 85 percent. Effects of passive smoking are not considered.

If these strong synergistic effects are a reality, then beyond the potential for both smoking and radon to independently cause lung cancer, it is quite likely that many, if not most, lung cancers result from both. Thus, smokers would suffer an enhanced risk due to radon exposure. Precisely just such a geometrically increased risk is emphasized in the 1992 *Citizen's Guide to Radon* (EPA, 1992f), which explicitly separates out the risk to smokers and the risk to those who have never smoked (see fig. 4.2). The chart shows that the risk to smokers is about fifteen times the risk to never-smokers. Of course, the concept of a never-smoker also requires examination. The prevalence of secondhand smoke or ETS (environmental tobacco smoke) makes smoking an ambient hazard in the same manner as radon.

Radon Risk If You Smoke (If you are a former smoker, your risk may be lower)

Radon Level	If 1,000 people who smoked were exposed to this level over a lifetime...	The risk of cancer from radon exposure compares to...	WHAT TO DO: Stop smoking and...
20 pCi/l	about 135 people could get lung cancer.	100 times the risk of drowning.	fix your home.
10 pCi/l	about 71 people could get lung cancer.	100 times the risk of dying in a home fire.	fix your home.
8 pCi/l	about 57 people could get lung cancer.		fix your home.
4 pCi/l	about 29 people could get lung cancer.	100 times the risk of dying in a plane crash.	fix your home.
2 pCi/l	about 15 people could get lung cancer.	2 times the risk of dying in a car crash.	consider fixing between 2 and 4 pCi/l.
1.3 pCi/l	about 9 people could get lung cancer.	(Average indoor radon level)	Reducing radon levels below 2 pCi/l is difficult.
0.4 pCi/l	about 3 people could get lung cancer.	(Average outdoor radon level)	

Radon Risk If You've Never Smoked (If you are a former smoker, your risk may be higher)

Radon Level	If 1,000 people who never smoked were exposed to this level over a lifetime...	The risk of cancer from radon exposures compares to...	WHAT TO DO:
20 pCi/l	about 8 people could get lung cancer.	the risk of being killed in a violent crime.	fix your home.
10 pCi/l	about 4 people could get lung cancer.		fix your home.
8 pCi/l	about 3 people could get lung cancer.	10 times the risk of dying in an airplane crash	fix your home.
4 pCi/l	about 2 people could get lung cancer.	the risk of drowning.	fix your home.
2 pCi/l	about 1 person could get lung cancer.	the risk of dying in a home fire.	consider fixing between 2 and 4 pCi/l.
1.3 pCi/l	less than 1 person could get lung cancer.	(Average indoor radon level)	reducing radon levels below 2 pCi/l is difficult.
0.4 pCi/l	less than 1 person could get lung cancer.	(Average outdoor radon level)	

Fig. 4.2   Comparative risk for smokers and for those who have never smoked
(Source: *Citizen's Guide*, EPA CDC 1992f)

The exact nature of the interaction between radon and smoking has not yet been determined. In a joint analysis of eleven underground miner studies (Lubin et al., 1994a), the relationship between smoking and radon was consistent with an interaction intermediate between additive and multiplicative. Although the data was inadequate to clearly define the relationship, it appears that the smoking/radon synergism may not be as strong as suggested by the EPA multiplicative models shown in figures 4.1 and 4.2. When the new data is applied to residential radon exposures, radon may account for 10 to 12 percent of the total lung cancer deaths among smokers (i.e., ten thousand deaths) and 28 to 31 percent of the lung cancer deaths among nonsmokers (i.e., five thousand deaths). If this data proves correct, radon by itself must be considered a major public health threat.

The Policy Implications of Synergy

What are the implications of a strong multiplicative effect for radon abatement policy? With so few radon-only lung cancers predicted, critics can argue that the emphasis of a program to protect the public should focus more on the elimination of smoking than on radon. That strategy would have the added advantage of reducing many of the other health effects of cigarette smoking besides lung cancer, which account for so much of the mortality and morbidity in the United States.

Regardless of the strength of the synergy, many health officials, scientists, and policymakers cite as marginal the benefits of mitigating homes close to the 4 pCi/l action level. Instead, it is suggested that cost-effective action on radon should focus on higher radon levels where individual risk is excessive; otherwise, funds would be better spent to reduce smoking (Nero et al., 1990; Nazaroff and Teichman, 1990; Mossman and Sollitto, 1991; Yallow, 1988).

On the other hand, there are also compelling reasons to disregard the "smoking only" argument. Increased public health efforts to decrease smoking have shown some important successes, with a 40 percent decline in cigarette smoking among U.S. adults between 1965 and 1990. However, more than a quarter of U.S. adults—forty six million people—continue to smoke. In a counter trend, moreover, a significant increase in smoking has occurred among high school seniors in recent years (CDC, 1994). Furthermore, the growing assault against public smoking has not extended to the private domain. The widespread exposure to passive smoking in the home, the workplace, and in public is estimated to cause five thousand lung cancer deaths per year in the nonsmoking population (Repace and Lowrey, 1985). Combined with the rather extensive distribution of radon in homes and buildings, passive smoking guarantees that exposure to both radon and smoke is ubiquitous. In addition, there are rather large uncertainties in the multiplicative interaction itself. If the synergism were less strong, which is certainly possible given the existing data, many more people would be dying from radon exposure alone. Given the difficulties of reducing exposure to smoke, the magnitude of the potential public health problem, and the other considerations discussed above, the suggestion to concentrate only on smoking and ignore radon is dubious at best.

Is There a Threshold for Radon Exposure?

All the current models for estimating the risk from radon share an important assumption—linearity. In simple language, a linear model predicts that any exposure to radon in the general population will cause additional deaths. In other words, no amount of radon is safe; exposure carries with it a risk that increases proportionally with the exposure. Current radon policy is based upon the linear assumption. There is general agreement that the linear assumption works for higher dose exposures. However, there is continuing controversy over whether the linear model applies to lower dose exposures. Some argue for a threshold model at lower doses, under which small amounts of radon that fall beneath some as-yet-to-be-determined threshold value are viewed as safe.

Uncertainty at Lower Doses

The effects of radiation on a population are typically plotted in the form of a dose-response curve. Confidence in the shape of this curve varies dramatically from high to low dose. At higher levels, evidence from atomic bomb victims, nuclear accident victims, and uranium miners clearly demonstrates linear outcomes in both deaths caused and cancers produced. In this higher dose region, the number of cancers is directly proportional to the dose received, and a sudden whole-body dose in the 400–500 rem range is known to bring death to half a human population within a few weeks. There is general agreement about such outcomes. Likewise, exposure to an intermediate amount, say 50–100 rem at one time, will not generally cause acute short-term symptoms, although it is believed to increase the lifetime risk of cancer (Kaku and Trainer, 1982).

The controversial portion of the dose-response curve is at the lower end. It is generally assumed that the linear relationship found at much higher doses continues down to zero added dose. However, there is no evidence comparable to that for high doses for what happens as the curve approaches zero. Thus, there is much conjecture over the effects of, say, a 0.1 or 0.2 rem per year dose over seventy years. In such a case, the number of predicted cancers would depend on which of several models is used to describe how the curve approaches zero

(Kaku and Trainer, 1982; Gofman, 1990). Figure 4.3 illustrates the low-dose portion of a dose-response curve showing how the dose approaches zero. In addition to the linear or straight-line hypothesis, the sublinear or quadratic hypothesis, the supralinear hypothesis, and the threshold hypothesis are shown.

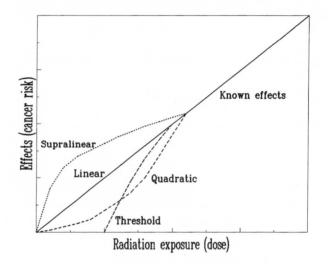

Fig. 4.3   Dose-effect comparison of four hypotheses:
supralinear, linear, quadratic, and threshold (*Source:* Kaku and Trainer, 1982)

The Threshold Model

The most tenaciously advocated alternative to the linear theory is the threshold model. The threshold model has retained a small but consistent following, particularly among advocates of the safety of nuclear power. In the threshold model, there is a level below which radiation does no apparent harm; it is only when some magic point—the threshold—is passed that danger appears. The model is justified on the basis that cells have the ability to repair themselves from the many thousands of particles per second that hit our bodies from background radiation. It is only when the dose exceeds the repair level, threshold advocates argue, that the risk of cancer is introduced. Cohen's work (1989a,b) mentioned above, showing an absence of positive correlation between lung cancer deaths and radon exposure, has been cited as supporting a threshold model over a linear hypothesis. There are some scientists who even go further, suggesting that small doses of radiation stimulate a protective effect, as purportedly shown in Cohen's findings, a phenomenon known as radiation hormosis (Hickey et al., 1983; Luckey, 1991). However, the threshold theory is subject to substantial criticism. First, the relation between repair processes and cancer induction is a complex one, and the fact that body repair normally occurs does not in itself demonstrate a threshold level. Second, there is no experimental evidence for a threshold. Cohen's research is generally dismissed as a serious challenge to linearity for reasons previously noted. As a result of these limitations, the major radiation standard-setting organizations have rejected the threshold hypothesis.

Known Limitations of Linearity

Rejection of a threshold model does not imply the lack of serious questions about linearity. First, inaccuracies in the handling of low doses by the linear model are evident in the research on uranium miners and on the shortening of life due to neutron radiation. As a result, it can be concluded that the linear model may overestimate the risk for beta and gamma radiation and underestimate the risk for alpha and neutron radiation. In short, the linear hypothesis may underestimate radon risk (Jackson, 1987). Second, the linear model has difficulty accounting for differences in susceptibility to DNA damage and accompanying cancer risk between different human genotypes. In the case of radon, individuals whose basal cells are unusually deep in the epithelium tissue have some protection from alpha radiation. Conversely, others have high vulnerability. Greater basal cell susceptibility would cause more cancers at very low doses and less cancers at very high doses than would be predicted by a linear model.

Third, at very high doses, there is a departure from linearity known as the saturation effect. For example, miner data show that cancer incidence per unit dose drops off at high doses. This counterintuitive outcome reflects the fact that cells are killed outright at high doses and, therefore, do not have a chance to reproduce incorrectly (Jackson, 1987). An implication of this finding is that extrapolation from high doses may overestimate the effect at low doses. It is, therefore, necessary to extrapolate from the lowest dose data available. Fourth, evidence for linearity at low levels is sparse. The only direct experimental evidence for radon at very low cumulative doses comes from experiments on rats exposed as low as 20 WLM that suggests a linear relationship down to this level (Cross, 1994; Steinhausler, 1987). Additional insight comes when miner data are generalized to the home environment. The lower end of the miner data indicates excess cancer risk for about 80 to 100 WLM, corresponding to a seventy-year lifetime home exposure (75 percent occupancy, with an equilibrium ratio of 0.5) of about 5.7 to 7.1 pCi/l. Initial reports of newer miner data reflecting the imposition of lower exposure standards may demonstrate linearity to below 50 WLM (EPA, 1987). Such findings, if replicated, would push documented linearity below the 4 pCi/l guidance level, since a person exposed in the home at 4 pCi/l for a lifetime accumulates about 60 WLM. However important, these findings still fail to provide direct evidence for linearity at the average level of residential radon exposure, about 1 pCi/l.

Additional evidence at the level of micro dosimetry and cell biology suggests that even a single alpha particle can transform a cell and cause a cancer. However, the extrapolation down to background levels below 1 pCi/l is still in some sense a leap of faith given the lack of direct evidence on humans, either through mining data or through environmental exposures, that cancers are caused at extremely low radon levels. Animal studies, while showing an effect down to 20 WLM (1.3 pCi/l in the home), are at different dose rates and may not be directly applicable to residential exposures (Cross, 1994). In spite of these ambiguities, most scientists and the health physicists accept linearity as the proper curve, assuming that any additional exposure to radiation of any type will have negative effects. The linearity hypothesis is considered to be a conservative approach in the absence of further specific information (Jackson, 1987).

Policy Implications of Linearity

The linear model presents policy challenges that the threshold model avoids—namely the need to recognize and respond to risk at quite low levels of exposure. Given that there is such a large population exposed to low levels of radon, in a linear model, much of the predicted exposure and risk—perhaps as many as two-thirds of the deaths—is seen as occurring among the population exposed at levels at or below the federal guideline of 4 pCi/l (EPA, 1992c; see also chapters 5 and 10). In this view, while the relatively few people exposed to higher radon values have substantially elevated risk, even an average radon level of around 1 pCi/l poses a public health problem.

Another way of viewing this question is to extrapolate from the miner data one order of magnitude past the 4 pCi/l guideline—to 0.4 pCi/l, a value approximating outdoor background levels for radon. If the average risk for lifetime exposure to 4 pCi/l (using EPA risk estimates) is about three per hundred, the risk (under a linear model) at 0.4 pCi/l would be three per thousand. The three per thousand risk is large when compared to many other potential carcinogens we are exposed to in the environment and would itself trigger a standard setting regulatory response for human-caused contaminants. These risk levels underlie the ambient goal for radon levels in homes and the relatively stringent proposed radon standard for the water supply.

Conclusions

In this chapter, we have described the uncommonly solid health evidence behind radon risk, so often obscured by side controversies such as the myth of the dead bodies. These controversies have, at times, detracted from the implementation of radon policy and raised a fundamental issue of how much information is needed or required to take effective public policy action. More importantly, these controversies have publicized relatively obscure disagreements over the severity of the issue. Disagreements among experts serve to discourage the public's action on the radon issue, action that is easily sidetracked. This chapter also points to major gaps in our knowledge about the health effects of radon that would resolve current uncertainties. Indeed, were it not for the uranium miner studies, the present health data would not be sufficiently compelling. In the end, the epidemiological opportunity afforded by the miner exposures has been the saving grace of the natural radon issue.

Notes

1. This conflict over radon is often discussed in terms of the scientific dichotomy between "Type I and Type II error" as represented, respectively, by the DOE and EPA (see Paigen, 1982; Levine, 1982; Edelstein, 1982, 1988; Shrader-Frechette, 1991). The "myth of the dead bodies" reflects Type I thinking, whereby caution is defined so as to minimize the chance of mistakenly concluding that an effect (e.g., lung cancer) is due to an environmental cause (e.g., radon). Proof of an effect (i.e., "dead bodies") is demanded before public action is taken to protect or help potential victims. A policy based upon hot houses is thus demanded. In contrast, a policy more concerned with Type II errors would guard against the chance of concluding no effect when there actually is one. Given uncertainty, this paradigm defines precaution in terms of the need to be protective of health in the face of a potential threat. While the first approach is willing to accept false negatives in order to avoid false positives, the second is more tolerant of false positives. With radon, the tolerance for Type I versus Type II error correlates, to some degree, with whether a scientist ascribes to the linear or threshold theory of effect. If radon is believed to cause a proportionately diminishing effect according to dose, then the most significant risk is to the large number of people exposed to lower amounts of radon. While the individual risk is comparatively low here, the population risk is extremely high. Conversely, scientists who believe that there is a threshold dose below which no adverse effect from radon will be found will see the significant risk as falling upon the relatively few individuals exposed to higher levels of radon.

2. Probably the most significant criticism of Cohen's work is his reliance on relatively old mortality records. As a database, these records are widely recognized as being inaccurate and incomplete. The mobility of Americans further means that there may be a very weak correlation between those dying in a given county and their exposure to radon in that county. Likewise, the data used to distinguish high from low radon areas may have been inadequate, both in terms of the number of samples and the fact that mostly screening measures were used. Finally, one may question whether mortality data are even going to be a good indication of the incidence of a long latency disease. During a

twenty to thirty year latency period, many other causes of mortality may occur, with the lung cancer either never being discovered or not being the actual listed cause of death (see Oge, 1990 and Cohen, 1990 for further discussion of the county lung cancer study).

3. There is some evidence that, under certain circumstances, the biological lifetime of radon ingested in water may be as long as twelve hours, and therefore contributes to an even greater whole body dose (Gosink et al., 1990).

4. In order to explain myeloid leukemia, a dosimetry model has been proposed based on the enhanced solubility of radon in fat cells compared to surrounding marrow. At an exposure level of about 6 pCi/l, yearly doses to bone marrow are comparable to that received from natural background gamma and cosmic ray radiation. Furthermore, at the world average radon exposure of 1.3 pCi/l, 13–25 percent of all myeloid leukemia might be radon induced.

5. Another aerosol characteristic of interest is the equilibrium ratio, reflecting the relative balance between radon and its daughter products. However, while the equilibrium ratio reflects the extent to which the more dangerous radon daughters are present in the air and does depend on ventilation rate, it appears to have little affect on the actual dose (James, 1988, p. 295).

6. For this reason, the EPA has not generally recommended the use of air cleaning devices for removing the particles containing radon daughters; the unattached fraction of radon daughters increases in the cleaner environment, thereby potentially increasing the risk (see Cook and Egan, 1987, p. 269; Jonassen and McLaughlin, 1988, p. 496).

7. Methodological problems with correlational studies include the problem of smoking as a confounding variable, the lack of detail on accumulated exposures, the problem of population mobility, changes in residence, modifications to houses over time that may affect radon levels, and statistical accuracy (see also note 2).

8. Several studies have demonstrated some form of interaction between smoking and radon. The Colorado uranium miner data, containing the most extensive individual smoking information, supports a more than additive effect. A Swedish residential study with smoking data supports a synergistic effect, as do some animal studies. Both the BEIR IV report and the EPA study indicate something between a submultiplicative to multiplicative model. On the other hand, other data from a Swedish miner study, the atomic bomb survivor study, and other animal studies, are consistent with either an additive or even subadditive effect. New Mexico uranium miner data where smoking incidence is low even suggest that radon exposure alone might cause lung cancer (Jackson, 1987).

Chapter 5

The Myth of the Reading Prong

We have identified an area (in Minnesota and North Dakota) similar in severity to the Reading Prong.

— Second EPA State Survey, September 1988

In this chapter, we confront two key myths about radon that emerged from the early Watras experience. The myth of the hot house involves the fixation of radon policy on finding and remediating "hot houses," hypercontaminated buildings, such as those found in Colebrookdale Township, Pennsylvania. Radon policy after the Watras case never got past the inconceivable risk faced by the occupants of such hot houses, resolving to attempt their identification by fast and dirty screening tests. The myth of the Reading Prong, also dating from that time, refers to the early association of the high radon levels in Colebrookdale Township with the granite/gneiss rock formation stretching east along the Appalachian chain from Reading, Pennsylvania, up the spine of western New Jersey, along southeastern New York, and into Connecticut (see fig. 5.1). The myth of the Reading Prong triggered a search for other radon hot spots having definable boundaries, for a geological understanding of why these hot spots occurred, and for the means to use geologic and geographic features as a predictive tool for locating hot areas. Along with the myth of the hot house, the myth of the Reading Prong represents a fundamental confusion about how radon is manifested that, in turn, has confounded radon policy.

Fig. 5.1   Reading Prong region [Source: (Middletown, New York) *Times-Herald Record*, file graphic by Lance Theraux]

99

Chapter Five

The Myth of the Hot House

Ever since the Watras house was discovered, there has been an obsession with
"hot" houses. While there is no formal definition for a hot house, clearly, houses
with radon values in the hundreds or thousands of pCi/l qualify. Here we opera-
tionally define a hot house as one having an annual average radon concentration
of 20 pCi/l or higher, a level at which home occupants would receive an annual
dose equivalent to the maximum level allowed to mine workers. While we save
for the next chapter the issue of how we test for these hot houses, here we examine the prevalence and threat from hot houses and question whether hot houses
are a sound basis for government policy.

Are There Many Hot Houses Out There?

Shortly after the Watras discovery, a rough idea of the theoretical distribution of radon in U.S. homes was developed. Scientists at Lawrence Berkeley
Laboratory (LBL) examined existing data for 817 homes adjusted to show annual averages (Nero et al., 1986), while University of Pittsburgh physicist Bernie
Cohen (1986) analyzed one-year average radon measurements collected from
the homes of 453 physics professors. The distribution of residential radon from
both studies follows a lognormal curve (see fig. 5.2); that is, while most houses
have fairly low radon values—the studies show an average radon value in homes
of 1.5 pCi/l—there is a long tail on the distribution showing that a significant
number of houses have radon values much higher than average.[1]

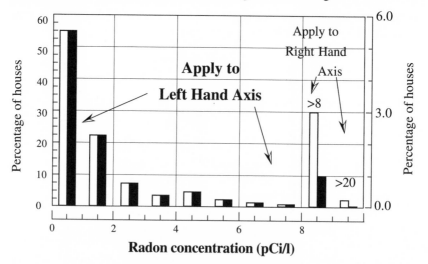

Fig. 5.2   Probability distribution of radon concentrations in 552 U.S. homes.
See endnote 1 for discussion of figure
(Source: Data from Nero, 1986, and Cohen, 1986)

Because of the small sample sizes and sample bias, these results were viewed as tentative. The basic problem in determining a valid distribution for radon exposure in homes is getting a representative sample that is large enough. A good representative sample would also reflect all regions of the country, represent different housing types, and consider the full range of geological diversity. Ideally, testing procedures would be standardized so that measurements were made using the same kind of detector, in appropriate locations in the home, and at the same time of the year. If the annual average radon concentration was not measured directly, corrections would be made.

Initial efforts to verify the LBL/Cohen lognormal distribution using existing large data samples were not particularly fruitful. By 1992, more than a million radon measurements had been taken from all over the country and larger testing firms such as Terradex, the Radon Project at the University of Pittsburgh, and Key Technology had collected many tens of thousands of measurements each. Despite the large sample size, however, the data came with severe limitations. Illustrative of such bias was a Terradex survey of ninety-one thousand measurements that found ten times the LBL and a hundred times the Cohen estimate of homes projected to be over 20 pCi/l (Alter and Oswald, 1988).[2] It is likely that the Terradex data exaggerated the number of hot houses. The data set included many confirmatory tests following up on initially high radon levels and a disproportionate number of tests from radon elevated regions of the country. Additionally, many of these tests did not measure annual average radon exposure to occupants and, thus, were unrepresentative. Similar problems affected government research, as well. The joint State/EPA Residential Radon Survey (SRRS) incorporated more than fifty-nine thousand randomly selected measurements from forty-two states in order to avoid geographic, geologic, and housing diversity biases (Philips et al., 1991; Philips and Marcinowski, n.d.). However, the findings, depicted in the summary map shown as figure 5.3, are based on data representing short-term screening measurements made under closed house conditions in the lowest livable area of the house. As explained in the next chapter, these results fail to reflect the homeowners' average annual radon exposure level.[3] As a result, there is no precise definition of the magnitude of the radon health threat. In addition, such test results have sometimes been reported in a misleading way by comparing them to the annual average EPA guideline of 4 pCi/l (see EPA 1987c). This misinterpretation falsely suggests that over 20 percent of homes in many states have annual averages exceeding the guideline. EPA has been rightly criticized for inflating the data to advance the radon issue.

To address the limitations of previous studies, EPA undertook another project, the National Residential Radon Survey (NRRS), to measure annual average concentrations using year-long alpha track detectors on each lived-in floor of the house (EPA 1992c). The survey covered single-family, attached homes, multiunit structures, and mobile homes, ultimately collecting data from a randomly selected sample of 5,694 homes throughout the United States. Results released in October 1992 are shown in figure 5.4. The annual average radon con

Chapter Five

STATE/EPA RESIDENTIAL RADON
SURVEY SCREENING MEASUREMENTS

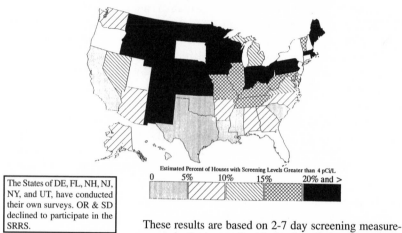

The States of DE, FL, NH, NJ, NY, and UT, have conducted their own surveys. OR & SD declined to participate in the SRRS.

These results are based on 2-7 day screening measure-ments in the lowest livable levels and should not be used to estimate annual averages or health risks.

Fig. 5.3   Estimated percentage of houses with screening levels greater than 4 pCi/l from State/EPA Residential Radon Survey screening measurements (*Source*: EPA, Philips and Marcinowski - undated)

centration in the U.S. housing stock was found to be 1.25 pCi/l (+/- 9 percent), with about 6 percent of homes having annual average radon values greater than 4 pCi/l, 0.7 percent greater than 10 pCi/l, and 0.1 percent greater than 20 pCi/l. These data indicate that about 5.8 million homes (+/- 22 percent) have annual average radon levels greater than 4 pCi/l, while perhaps 72,000 houses (0.1%) have annual averages greater than 20 pCi/l. The black bars in figure 5.4 show how radon risk is distributed across the U.S. housing stock and indicates that the bulk of the risk is in homes below 4 pCi/l. The results confirm the earlier LBL analysis. Based on the NRRS data, EPA estimates that radon is responsible for seven thousand to thirty thousand lung cancer deaths per year in the United States (EPA 1992c).

A Case of the Tail Wagging the Curve: Limits of Hot-House-Based Policy

Using the NRRS data, we can draw a crucial observation about population exposure. Most radon exposure (about 65 percent)—and the bulk of radon health risk—is at levels of radon below the 4 pCi/l guidance. Hot houses (i.e., over 20 pCi/l) account for only 1 percent of the aggregate risk. Even if all hous-

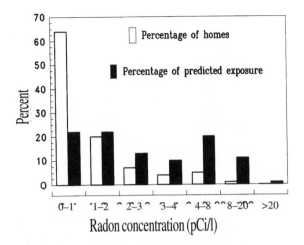

Radon concentration (pCi/l)

Fig. 5.4   Distribution of homes and total exposure at selected radon levels
for all homes (*Source*: EPA, 1992c)

es above 4 pCi/l were identified and remediated to 4 pCi/l, only a third or less of
the risk would be addressed.[4] This basic realization has been obscured by the
state/EPA radon surveys, designed to screen for hot houses, hot clusters, hot regions, and hot states, discussed further in chapter 6. This concern over hot houses reflects their high individual risk, but ignores the important policy
implication (i.e., that the overall aggregate risk from hot houses is small). Furthermore, very hot houses (over 100 pCi/l annual average) are even rarer. Nero
and colleagues (1990) estimate that perhaps one in twenty thousand homes in
the United States, or a total of four thousand homes, may exceed 100 pCi/l. Beyond representing a small portion of the overall risk, there is difficulty in finding these extreme buildings, discussed later in this chapter.

The Myth of the Reading Prong

Since the Watras experience, federal and state radon policy has rested on the
myth of the Reading Prong, the assumption that radon incidence is geographically and geologically bounded. Indeed, certain regions, such as the Reading
Prong, are high in radon. However, given the broader geographic distribution of
radon, it makes little sense to speak of high-radon versus low-radon regions. Radon is not so readily bounded. This conclusion can be drawn both because high
levels of radon are found in significant amounts outside of such hot regions and
because low-radon houses and areas exist within these regions. In fact, evidence
for rebutting the myth of the Reading Prong was present in the very circumstances that gave birth to this myth.

The Puzzling Geology of Colebrookdale Township, Pennsylvania

The area around the Watras house in Colebrookdale Township, Pennsylvania, became an early "laboratory" for geologist Linda Gunderson and her colleagues from the United States Geological Survey as they sought to discover what geological conditions might account for such extremely elevated indoor radon levels. Colebrookdale was puzzling because it combined a cluster of extremely hot houses with houses with low radon levels. Gunderson discovered that the area around Boyertown consists of the three different types of underlying rock and soil shown in table 5.1. By matching soil and indoor radon data to these bedrock microregions, the Colebrookdale mystery was explained.

Table 5.1   Rock and Soil Types and Characteristics in the Boyertown (Colebrookdale Township) Area

Rock and Soil type	Maximum Uranium Concentration	Soil Permeability
hornblende gneiss	less than 5 ppm	low
quartz feldspar and biotite gneiss (QFB)	10–25 ppm	moderate
mylonite	50 ppm	high

Source: Gunderson et al., 1991b.

When we plot indoor radon levels over the local geology of Colebrookdale Township, as shown in figure 5.5, we discover that the hot cluster was located at the boundary of two different types of gneiss bedrock, quartz-feldspar/biotite and hornblende, separated by a sheared fault zone. The "foliated mylonite" rock within this fault zone was created by pressure, temperature, and ductile shear conditions that altered the microstructure, porosity, permeability, and chemical composition of the surrounding parent rock and redistributed and concentrated its component uranium. As a result, radon concentration, emanation, and permeability were all enhanced. Not only are high amounts of radon generated in the rock, creating a high radon source strength, but the conditions for easy movement are present, allowing extremely high volumes of radon to pass easily to the surface and enter homes built atop the shear zone (Gunderson et al., 1987; Gunderson and Wanty, 1991; Agard and Gunderson, 1991).

Comparable local conditions have been documented around the United States (see Gunderson and Wanty, 1991). While the geological details may differ, the outcome is much the same. Smaller areas of very high radon potential can be imbedded even in regions of relatively average potential. And, importantly, knowledge of the higher than average radon potential of the Reading Prong was in itself not predictive of the high radon levels found in the Colebrookdale cluster. Thus, identification of generally elevated regions contributes little to the discovery of extremely hot areas. And, it should also be noted that we are far from having available the kind of in-depth understanding of the entire United States that the USGS study made available for Colebrookdale Township. Thus, microscale geologic research cannot currently serve as a predictive tool for finding hot areas; rather, its use is retrospective in explaining extreme radon levels after they have been identified through some other means.

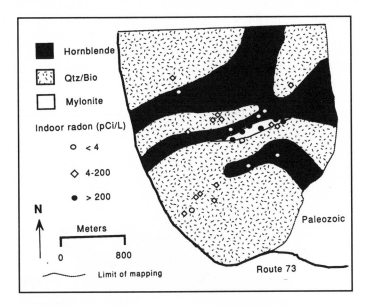

Fig. 5.5   Indoor radon concentrations in pCi/l for the Boyertown (Colebrookdale Township), Pennsylvania area shown with underlying geology (*Source*: Gunderson, et al., 1991b)

Regional Geographic Surveys

Despite the clear lesson of Colebrookdale that microscale rather than macroscale geology is indicative of hot areas, EPA, as well as such states as New Jersey, Pennsylvania, and New York, persisted in using regional geology in an effort to statistically predict the distribution of indoor radon levels in the regional housing stock. Their rationale was that even a crude delineation of radon potential would allow public and private efforts to be targeted in areas likely to yield the highest percentages of hot houses. This approach is exemplified by the EPA/USGS Indoor Radon Potential Study.

Chapter Five

The EPA/USGS Indoor Radon Potential Study

In the most extensive effort to map radon to date, EPA and USGS combined data on geological radon potential and indoor radon measurements to create a map of indoor radon potential for the entire United States (Gunderson et al., 1991). Radon potential is predicted from five factors: indoor radon levels, aerial radioactivity measurements, geology, soil permeability, and architecture type. Each factor is given a point value and the total defines one of three categories of indoor radon potential—high, moderate, and low (Gunderson et al., 1991, EPA, 1993d). Based on the results, the United States was divided into three provinces as depicted in figure 5.6: highest risk (those with predicted average screening measurements over 4 pCi/l), moderate risk (between 2 and 4 pCi/l), and low risk (under 2 pCi/l). It would appear that two-thirds to three-quarters of the country has moderate to high indoor radon potential. The conclusion is clear. Radon risk is too diffuse to be meaningfully bounded. There is little to be gained by following the myth of the Reading Prong.

National Geologic Radon Province Map

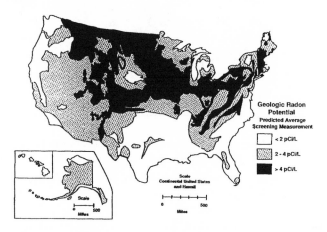

Fig. 5.6   National geologic radon province (indoor radon potential) map of the United States (draft). (*Source*: EPA 1993d).

Undaunted by this demonstration of the futility of its approach, EPA continued work on the geologic radon potential data, breaking it down to the county-by-county level by mid-1993. The resulting EPA Map of Radon Zones was intended to help state and local organizations target their limited resources on the worst areas and to provide impetus for accepting radon-resistant building codes (EPA, 1993d). Yet these goals are hardly advanced given the limitations of the study. For example, in order to designate a county partitioned by several different zones, the largest zone was chosen, thus, masking variations within counties. Accordingly, a county containing a known hot spot might nevertheless be depicted as having only moderate to even low radon potential. EPA admits that the mapping cannot define the boundaries of hot spots and even that homes in all zones should still be tested since elevated radon is found in substantial numbers of houses in all three zones (EPA 1993d). Given the disclaimers, of what purpose is the mapping? For policy purposes, drawing boundaries around radon is misleading.

Conclusion

While the limits of viewing radon as a bounded hazard have been clear since early in the geologic radon issue, the myth of the Reading Prong persists.[5] Despite somewhat elevated uranium levels for the entire region, not every area of the prong is hot, as Colebrookdale demonstrated. Nor were areas off the prong cold, as Clinton, New Jersey, quickly proved. Why then the persistence of this myth? Perhaps the myth of the Reading Prong reveals something about the underlying psychology of hazard. It is reassuring to believe that an invisible hazard is somehow kept within boundaries where it can be confronted, outside of which one can feel safe. And the resulting false sense of control is so convincing that it can mindlessly underlie government policy. We return to the perception of radon risk in chapter 9.

Predicting Indoor Radon from Local Outdoor Conditions

The cause of radon levels in a given building can ultimately be traced to the mother material (uranium and radium) in the rock and soil surrounding a house. Radon potential depends on the strength of the radon source in that location. But can indoor radon levels in a particular house be correlated with local geology? Can a knowledge of local site characteristics serve as a predictive tool for anticipating radon levels in a planned house or development? Here we show that the attempt to bound radon at a more local level is merely an extension of the myth of the Reading Prong.

Use of Local Soil and Rock to Predict Indoor Radon

Much data has been collected on the types and distribution of rock most likely to be associated with higher indoor radon levels in homes. Rock types containing higher natural uranium concentrations (typically greater than 2 to 3 ppm) are widely distributed throughout the United States.[6] However, rock types with lower uranium concentrations may have localized uranium deposits that lead to radon problems.[7] Structural features such as faults and shear zones have also been found to lead to localized high indoor concentrations, as found in Colebrookdale Township (Gunderson and Wanty, 1991).

Soils may also supply radon to homes. In many cases, soils are representative of local rock types and, therefore, have similar properties. However, in some cases, soils may be deposited from other areas and may differ from underlying bedrock. And even if soil is from underlying rock, weathering can cause redistribution of minerals and accumulation of uranium/radium in certain soil layers (Gunderson and Wanty, 1991).

Given that the primary radon source to buildings is soil gas, tests of radium or radon in surrounding soil might potentially be predictive of interior radon levels. However, research has failed to correlate radon or radium concentrations in the soil and indoor radon levels (Osborne, 1988). The reason is quite simple. Radium and the resulting soil radon are only one factor out of several that determine how much radon will enter the house. These other factors include the permeability of the soil, shrink-swell potential, depth to seasonal high water table, the existence of faults and fissures in surrounding soil and rock, soil to foundation openings, and the driving forces due to house operation and natural weather influences that move soil gas into the house (Gunderson and Wanty, 1991).

Radon Availability or Potential

Given the complexity of the local geologic environment around houses, geologists have developed a number of methods to estimate the ability of local sources and soil transport to contribute radon to a home (Tanner, 1987; Kunz et al., 1988; and Sextro, 1988b). Such approaches combine source strength (i.e., concentration of radium or radon in soil) with a measure of gas movement in soil (typically permeability, but sometimes diffusion as well) to provide a number that is then compared with indoor radon concentrations. Significant correlations have been found where the local geologic environment is simple and uniform (Kunz et al., 1988).

However, it is not uncommon for the local environment to be complex. For example, soil permeability may locally vary by four or five orders of magnitude while soil radon concentrations may differ by a few orders of magnitude. Soil radon around a given building shows wide spatial and temporal variability. For example, tests of varied depth and distance around fourteen buildings in Florida and New Jersey found soil radon values to vary by as much as a multiplicative factor of 3.1 to 12.9. In New Jersey, longitudinal soil tests using three-month alpha track measurements differed by an order of magnitude between fall and winter/spring, and did not correlate with cross-sectional grab sample measurements.

Another New Jersey study found large spatial and temporal variations in soil permeability (Clarkin and Brennan, 1991). Furthermore, predictions based on soil radon potential do not work over fractured bedrock, clay, or construction areas (Scott, 1992). And the New Jersey Statewide Scientific Study of Radon found that if the radon source potential was low, having high transport potential (e.g., permeable soil, etc.) had little affect on indoor radon levels. However, medium source potential coupled with high permeability gave high overall indoor radon potential (Cattafe, 1988).

Given this variability, precise prediction of radon potential is impossible (Clarkin and Brennan, 1991; Scott, 1992). Estimating an indoor radon concentration between 1 and 10 pCi/l for a future house is not all that useful to a builder or homeowner deciding whether radon-resistant construction techniques are needed. And when we recall house-to-house variations in Colebrookdale Township, where the Watrases' house was over 2,000 pCi/l and the adjacent home below 4 pCi/l, local variability appears to defy geologic predictability.

As a result, even a complex approach to using outside conditions to predict interior radon may not work. For example, Sweden employs soil radon potential in determining building restrictions. The Swedish method for soil risk classification incorporates factors such as ground humidity and soil thickness in addition to taking soil radon concentrations and soil permeability into account. However, when Florida tested the Swedish soil radon concentration recommendations, it found that 40 percent of the houses fitting the high risk category (and thus requiring radon-safe construction) actually fell under 4 pCi/l without any special construction techniques. At the same time, 13.5 percent of the houses falling in the lowest risk classification based on soil radon levels had indoor radon levels greater than 4 pCi/l (Clarkin and Brennan, 1991). Clearly, an accurate assessment of other factors having wide local spatial and temporal variations is necessary if substantial error in classification is to be avoided. With the current state of the art, these approaches can provide at best perhaps 50 percent predictiveness of basement radon levels based on outside soil permeability and radon source measurements (Gunderson, 1990).

Conclusion

At the present time it is impossible to reliably characterize or predict the indoor radon level of a building lot, or an existing house for that matter, based on a few simple soil measurements. In the case of a new building site, it is even more complicated because until the site is graded and the foundation dug, access to the soil next to the foundation is limited. This is not to say that sites cannot be characterized as to their radon potential if enough measurements are taken or if the local geology is simple and uniform. However, the cost-effectiveness of such an approach is questionable (Scott, 1992). Even successful predictions based on radon potential would only correlate to the basement radon level, having in most buildings little relevance to the radon health risk in living areas. It is cheaper and easier to just build in radon resistance, particularly if the concern is whether or not the indoor level will be above or below 4 pCi/l, or even 2 pCi/l, the value suggested by EPA as a goal for new homes (Clarkin and Brennan, 1991).

Searching for Hot Spots

While indisputable points of extreme risk, hot houses are not a proper focus for radon policy precisely because finding them is rather like finding needles in a haystack. The effort to find a shortcut method may in the end be more exhaustive and less fruitful than just systematically searching through it. Nevertheless, two approaches that have been employed with some success to find hot spots deserve mention. The first is analogous to using a metal detector to find the needles; the second asks where the needles are most likely to fall.

Aerial Measurement

In chapter 2, mention was made of airborne radiometric surveys called the National Uranium Resource Evaluation (NURE) study. Conducted in the 1950s and 1960s, when the United States was eager to locate its uranium resources for use in the cold war, NURE overflights involved detecting gamma decay from bismuth-214 in the top foot of soil. While NURE successfully identified human-caused hot spots in Essex County, New Jersey, can it also be used to find much smaller natural hot spots or clusters? The hot area in Clinton, New Jersey, was clearly visible in the NURE data taken in 1963, before the Clinton Knolls subdivision was built, although no one followed up on the data. Later on, as part of the New Jersey Statewide Scientific Study of Radon, NURE data were used to try to locate hot spots and some areas were reflown to search for high-radon clusters of homes. Table 5.2 displays anomalies in radiometric readings together with the distribution of indoor radon measurements,[8] The numbers are striking. Clusters of high houses can be identified, particularly with one-fourth-mile flight spacing, where anomalies are detected on multiple flight lines (Muessig, 1988). Aeroradiometric readings were also useful in California, which is generally low in radon levels, in the discovery of an organic Rincon shale unit outside of Los Angeles where 76 percent of the screening measurements were over 4 pCi/l, 26 percent were over 20 pCi/l, and over four thousand homes were potential candidates for high radon levels (Carlisle and Azzouz, 1991).

Table 5.2 Anomalous NURE Values for Indoor Radon Cluster Areas and Percentage of Homes above 4, 20, and 200 pCi/l Based on Screening Measurements

Location	NUR eU in ppm*	Percentage greater than 4 pCi/l	Percentage greater than 20 pCi/l	Percentage greater than 200 pCi/l
Clinton	10	96	80	35
Montgomery	9	67	27	7
Ewing	8	78	40	5
Princeton	9	75	28	2
Bethlehem	7	75	35	11
Hampton	11	100	64	14
Bernardsville	9	87	45	9
Mansfield	10	88	65	7
Washington	10	87	57	13

Source: Meussig, 1988.
*Peak values for the anomaly in the NURE area.

Unfortunately, NURE data have serious limitations. The technique is very costly. And most existing NURE data employed wider spacing of flights than is optimal for locating radon hot spots. NURE data are also limited to the first foot of soil. However, radioactive bedrock or a radium source may lie at deeper levels (Muessig, 1988).

Geological Investigations for Hot Areas

Another approach for finding hot areas involves the search for geologic formations and soil features known to harbor high radon levels, such as fissures, faults, and the boundaries between geological formations. Local geological features can be reconnoitered using geochemical analysis and radon soil sampling to identify areas worth further investigation (Reimer et al., 1991). A comprehensive method for county-scale radon mapping using such techniques combined with indoor radon testing has been developed by Gunderson and her colleagues at the U.S. Geological Survey (Gunderson et al., 1988). In a study of Montgomery County, Maryland, the researchers combined hundreds of measurements of radon in soil gas and equivalent uranium in soils from across the county with permeability data and voluntarily reported private indoor radon test results. The different rock units in the county were then outlined on a map and rated for either low, medium, or high radon potential.[9]

As with previously discussed efforts at mapping radon potential, there are serious limitations of this approach for making real estate purchase decisions, radon-resistant building standard requirements, or even individual testing decisions. These limitations are evident in the researchers' own disclaimers that "the map should not be used as a sole source for predicting indoor radon levels," that a low rating "does not mean that radon will not be found in these areas, but that the radon potential is low relative to the rest of Montgomery County," and that "no area of the county is free from the potential for indoor radon levels greater than the U.S. EPA remediation level of 4 pCi/l." While calling attention to the overall radon threat, as a predictive tool, little certainty is added by this method. Meanwhile, some residents will test and others will not, some property values will be deflated and others enhanced, and the safety of some areas will be demeaned while others are enhanced, perhaps falsely.

In sum, neither NURE nor a local geologic study is likely to find the needle.

Radon in Water

Much as with airborne radon, radon in water also reflects the myth of the Reading Prong. Here the historic association is with New England, where the issue was first discovered, and where the highest values of radon in well water, levels of over a million pCi/l, have been discovered (Hall et al., 1988). Here, we find another sin of omission: the emerging data show that higher levels of radon in water are widely distributed throughout the country (Hess et al., 1985; Horton, 1985).The granitic rock of the Appalachians is rich in uranium and radium, as evidenced in eastern groundwater. In Florida, the high radium content in the phosphate rock causes high water levels of radon. Other higher values may be found scattered throughout the West and upper Midwest (Brookins, 1990). Reminiscent of the ill conceived effort to map radon in air, figure 5.7 shows three ranges of radon for U.S. groundwater (Brookins, 1990).

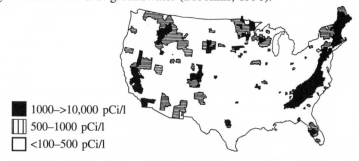

■ 1000–>10,000 pCi/l
▥ 500–1000 pCi/l
☐ <100–500 pCi/l

Fig. 5.7   Distribution of radon in groundwater in the United States
(*Source*: Brookins, 1990, 98)

Table 5.3 demonstrates that homes with individual wells have the highest potential for radon from the water supply. More specifically, perhaps 11 percent of the households with private wells may have radon contributions exceeding the estimated mean air radon concentration (1.5 pCi/l). While the contribution to the overall public health risk from radon in water is small (see chapter 3), for those homes with higher radon concentrations in well water, the water contribution may provide a significant health risk. An analysis of data from public groundwater supplies for the United States further reveals a similar lognormal distribution to that discussed earlier for airborne radon.[10] It is implied that a significant number of groundwater supplies will have radon concentrations much greater than the mean (Nazaroff et al., 1988a).

Table 5.3   Water, Population, and Geometric Mean Values for Radon Concentrations for the United States

Type of water supply	Population Served (%)	Population-weighted geometric mean radon concentration
public surface	49.5	8 pCi/l (300 Bq/m^3)
public groundwater	32.2	140 pCi/l (5,200 Bq/m^3)
private well	18.3	970 pCi/l (36,000 Bq/m^3)

Source: Nazaroff et al., 1988a
Note: 1 pCi/l = 37 Bq/m^3.

Similar to the radon distribution in soil gas, the localized geology determines the potential for high waterborne radon levels. Likewise, there may be significant variations in well water radon concentrations from nearby houses; for example, differing well depths may draw water from different rock layers with much different radon concentrations (Clarkin and Brennan, 1991). In every way, despite evidence of its pervasiveness, radon in water has been subjected to myths suggesting that it is bounded and futile efforts to identify hot areas have been undertaken.

Conclusions

We finally understand just how anomalous the Watras discovery was. The average annual radon exposure in the United States is 1.25 pCi/l, and the number of homes with annual average exposures above 4 pCi/l is about 6 percent of the housing stock, or 5.8 million homes. The number of homes with annual average exposure levels greater than 20 pCi/l might be around seventy to eighty thousand, and only a relative few have been found so far. An important question is whether a concerted effort along the lines we have discussed in this section (more NURE-type mapping, detailed county mapping, follow-up on local high radon test results, and so forth) could identify the majority of those hot houses remaining and at what cost? On the other hand, is a massive effort to find these houses warranted if it only eliminates about 0.1–1.0 percent of the overall radon risk when 100 percent implemented? This distribution of radon risk poses a dilemma for radon policy. Clearly shown is that a radon policy focused on hot houses and reducing the highest risk hardly dents the overall public health risk.

In our desperation to find hot houses, hot clusters, and hot regions, we have grasped at many tools, ranging from macroscale to microscale geological investigation, site soil testing, and use of aerial reconnaissance. It is sobering that identified hot spots have been found through serendipity, the accidental anomaly of Stanley Watras being crapped up on his way into work or of the individual homeowner from the Clinton Knolls subdivision who decided to conduct a home radon test. Regional macroscale efforts have been shown to demonstrate little and distort a lot. And while studies of the correlation of indoor radon levels and localized geology provide important information for advancing our understanding of radon dynamics, they provide misleading information, both for radon policy as well as for people considering whether to test, buy, or build a home. Even the most sensitive studies of site-specific radon potential cannot predict house construction, design, and operation variables; geological data are not sufficiently predictive to be protective. Clearly, there is no better alternative for finding the hot needle in the haystack than to test radon levels in all buildings, as discussed in the next chapter. Indeed, EPA has recommended that every house be tested (EPA, 1988b, 1992f) and, in setting a new construction goal of 2 pCi/l, it has made including radon resistance in new homes preferable (see chapter 7). While these orientations conflict with the actual policies in place that depend on hot houses and regional radon boundaries, the very fact that they exist among the mixed messages of radon policy underscores the absurdity of continued efforts at geological and geographic prediction.

Perhaps the most important policy implication from the study of geology and radon is simply this: the radon problem is caused by localized geology; therefore the radon problem cannot be bounded. The myth of the Reading Prong, the idea that certain regions are safe while others are not, is totally false. Even within regions of relatively low indoor radon values, localized concentrations of uranium/radium, soil conditions, weather, house construction and operation factors could provide much higher radon levels in certain homes. And, conversely, even in regions of extremely high radon availability, many houses will be low. Unfortunately, the very attempt to delineate regions into categories (high, moderate, and low risk) sends a double message. To those living in the high-risk region, the message is to test. But the other regions also receive a message: that radon testing is not as urgent. Thus, the exhortation to test based on the assumption of boundedness, no matter how well qualified and explained, may actually backfire against the goal of protecting public health. As we discuss in chapter 9, the myth of the Reading Prong is a significant misleading influence on public perception of the radon problem. Furthermore, it appears that the EPA believes that the accumulation of ever more detailed grids of indoor radon potential will convince states and the public to take radon more seriously. Carried to its logical conclusion, such a belief might have each acre in the United States classified as to its radon potential. Such a strategy might be a good way to employ geologists, but it is unlikely to provide effective radon policy.

Notes

1. The two studies diverged at higher radon levels. Projections for single family homes with annual average radon concentrations greater than 4 pCi/l were 7 percent (four million homes) for LBL and 6 percent for Cohen; for homes exceeding 8 pCi/l, 1–3 percent for LBL and only 1 percent for Cohen; and for homes with radon values above 20 pCi/l, 0.1–0.2 percent for the LBL study and only 0.02 percent for the Cohen study.

2. For the Terradex data, the arithmetic mean is between 3 and 4 pCi/l, and the data imply that around 2 percent, or 1.6 million homes, may exceed 20 pCi/l.

3. Screening measurements before the new *Citizen's Guide* was issued in 1991 were defined in the lowest livable level of the house, in winter, under closed house conditions, thus including many basements that were not occupied. In 1991, EPA recommended that they be taken in the lowest lived-in level.

4. If one factors in American's high mobility, the chance of any one person receiving a maximum dose from a lifetime of living in a hot house is greatly reduced. For example, if the distribution of radon exposures is corrected to assume that every person moves every seven years to a randomly selected house instead of spending their lifetime in the same building, the projected percentage of the population expected to have annual average lifetime exposures over 4 pCi/l drops to one-tenth the prior estimate (from 6.0–7.0 percent to 0.6 percent) (Nero et al., 1986, 1990). Of course, since some people may not move as often, the actual percentage of people exceeding a lifetime average of 4 pCi/l will lie somewhere between these estimates. Significantly, the overall public health risk is not diminished by mobility, but is just redistributed. As the individual high risk associated with high radon houses is further reduced, a policy based on finding hot houses is even harder to justify.

5. The myth of the Reading Prong was reinforced by the media, as well as by government. For example, a 1986 public presentation on radon by the New Jersey Department of Environmental Protection included color slides of the Reading Prong, even though it was already well known that there was a substantial radon problem outside of the prong. Even the EPA, who also should have known better, kept using the Reading Prong image long after it had been discounted by accumulating data. For example, based on state/EPA screening surveys, the EPA referred to parts of Minnesota and North Dako-

ta as "similar in severity to the Reading Prong" (EPA 1987c). Indeed, there were very few "hot houses" in the region, but there were many houses that were slightly elevated above 4 pCi/l. Testing since 1985 has found elevated radon levels in practically every state. Radon is ubiquitous on the planet.

6. These rock types include carbonaceous black shale, glauconite-bearing sandstones, some fluvial sandstones, phosphorites and phosphatic sediments, chalk, some carbonates, some glacial deposits, bauxite, lignite and some coals, uranium-bearing granites and pegmatites, metamorphic rocks of granitic composition, felsic and alkalic volcanoclastic and pyroclastic volcanic rocks, syenites and carbonatites, and many sheared and faulted rocks (Gunderson et al., 1991).

7. These include marine quartz sands, some shales, siltstones and clays, and some mafic rock (Gunderson et al., 1991).

8. Bismuth-214 counts were converted to equivalent uranium (eU). Anomalies were defined as exceedances of 6 eU compared to the mean statewide value of 2.4 eU.

9. Low potential areas have less than a 40 percent chance that levels of radon greater than 4 pCi/l will be found in a home in the area (based on screening tests in the basement or lowest livable area of the house). A moderate rating has a 50 percent chance of a home being elevated, with 10 percent of the homes exceeding 20 pCi/l. A high rating has a greater than 60 percent chance of a home having elevated radon with as many as 30 percent of the houses greater than 20 pCi/l.

10. The data collected on public groundwater supplies are limited to public supplies serving one thousand or more people (accounting for 86 percent of the public groundwater supplies). Smaller supplies serving fewer people appear to have somewhat higher concentrations (see Nazaroff et al., 1988a).

Chapter 6

The Myth of the Quick Test

The use of short-term measures for mitigation decisions creates all kind of problems.
—Richard Sextro

The context of radon testing is explained directly by the myths of the hot house and Reading Prong. The U.S. geologic radon policy has been driven by the image of the Watras experience and by the tail of the lognormal curve, the specter of extreme hot houses exposing their residents to extraordinary risk. Abetted by the scientific consensus over risks in hot houses, EPA has crafted a policy that espouses much broader goals (the 4 pCi/l guidance and even ambient levels), but in effect focuses on finding hot houses and hot regions. Given this policy focus, the primary objective of radon testing has been to "screen" buildings to find the hot ones, to the exclusion of other objectives that should be central to a comprehensive policy for radon risk reduction.

Moreover, this emphasis upon screening for hot houses demanded a quick, inexpensive, and easy measurement approach that came to dominate U.S. radon testing. By the myth of the quick test, we refer to the inherent delusion underlying radon policy that such screening measurements, made over time intervals of only a few days, accurately reflect the risk from radon exposure in a given building. Despite serious validity questions, such tests have been widely employed for all uses. As a result, the majority of those testing have used inappropriate tests for their objectives and possibly drawn inaccurate conclusions regarding the safety of buildings, the need to remediate, and whether to proceed to purchase a house. The myth of the quick test has led policymakers, experts, and even consumer groups to create misleading programs and to provide wrong advice. We see this impact clearly when we examine error in radon testing.

Errors in Radon Testing

In our view, the challenge in radon testing has less to do with the technical problems of how to detect radon than with the central question of whether information gleaned from tests provides a valid indication of the average radon level and, particularly, the exposure of building occupants to radon. Validity requires the elimination of testing errors that might lead us to obtain false results, to make false conclusions, and to make inappropriate responses. Also requisite for validity is repeatability, since we can have no confidence in results that cannot

117

be replicated. Validity is threatened by six potentially interacting types of error, all found in the U.S. radon testing program.

- *Error of Policy.* Are we asking the right questions? Are we clear enough about what our goals are to select the appropriate testing methodology and technique?
- *Methodological Error.* Have we adequately sampled for radon so that our findings represent radon levels in the test setting?
- *Device Error.* Might error result from the inherent shortcomings of the radon detector that we are using, whether a charcoal canister, an alpha track detector, or an electret?
- *Measurement Error.* Is the testing device properly used and are there situational factors that might contribute to error?
- *Analysis Error.* What are the potential laboratory errors in the analysis of the radon collected in test devices?
- *Interpretation Error.* Are correct conclusions drawn from the measurement?

We will now examine how each of these errors affects radon testing policy and practice.

Errors in Policy

The primary cause of "policy error" has been a failure to clearly delineate the different goals that exist for testing and to consider whether given testing techniques achieve desired objectives. Tests valid in all other ways may fail simply because the information they provide is neither what we need to know nor, having been misled, what we think it is.

At least seven different testing goals and objectives are reflected in common practice (see table 6.1), yet these goals and the techniques most appropriate for achieving them have never been adequately differentiated in radon policy. When a careful comparison of the goals and objectives is made, some striking conclusions about radon testing and measurement can be drawn that reflect policy error. After reviewing the key questions posed by the seven different policy goals and objectives, we will examine the case of screening and the myth of the quick test more closely. Note that EPA testing protocols cited here were originally published in the 1986 *Citizens' Guide to Radon*; reference to updated protocols relies upon the revised 1992 *Citizens' Guide* (EPA 1986; 1992f). Unless noted, these two protocols were in agreement.

Table 6.1   Goals, Objectives, Location, Time, Cost, and Problems of Various Types of Measurements

Goal	Objective	Location	Time	Cost	Problems
Screening	Is the house hot? Is it above 4 pCi/l?	Lowest potential livable (lived-in) space	Short—days to a few months	Low	High false negatives and positves
Follow-up	Is remediation needed and how soon?	2(1) lived-in levels	1 yr. if greater than 4 or less than 20; short if greater than 20	Low	Inaccurate if closed house or short test
Household character- ization	What is the health risk?	2 lived-in levels	1 year	Low	Long testing Interval
Diagnostis	What is the best mitigation choice?	Suspected entryways	Short—grab or sniffing	High	Requires high tester skill level
Mitigation evaluation	Did mitigation work?	2 lived-in levels	Same as premitiga- tion	Low–high	Unreliable
Realty transfer	Can safety be warranted?	Generally in lowest livable (lived-in) space	Short	Low–high	Unreliable
Institutional exposure	Are public buildings safe?	Generally in lowest occupied space	Short	Low–high	Unreliable

Source: Summarized from NYSEO, 1989; EPA, 1986; EPA, 1989a; and EPA, 1992f.
Note: Items in parentheses reflect May 1992 EPA recommendations.

Screening: Is the House Hot?

"Screening measurements" are quick initial tests for identifying houses having high concentrations of radon—the so-called hot houses. Screening seeks to measure the highest radon concentration in a building. To achieve this end, "closed-house" conditions are employed and tests were originally taken in the lowest potentially livable level of the building, later changed to the actual lowest lived-in level. Because screening measurements theoretically capture the highest radon levels found in the home, it is well recognized that they have an inherent tendency to exaggerate results. Therefore, the intended use of the screening measure is to sort buildings into those requiring further confirmatory measurements and those deemed to be safe (i.e., not a hot house). Accordingly, screening measurements are by definition quick and dirty—and relatively cheap. But, while helpful, perhaps, for a rough sorting of houses, the screening test is not helpful in determining the actual risks associated with a building or in determining whether remedial action is required. Moreover, because of sampling and other errors discussed below, short-term testing is an unreliable method for estimating lower radon levels, particularly around 4 pCi/l.

Follow-up: Is Remediation Necessary?

"Confirmatory testing" involves follow-up measurements made in upper levels or lived-in portions of the house for the purpose of estimating potential health risks and the need for remedial action. EPA recommended confirmatory testing after an initial screening test indicated a result in excess of 4 pCi/l. The urgency of the follow-up test and the resulting actions are determined by the radon level found. Screening results between 4 and 20 pCi/l (later revised to between 4 and 10 pCi/l) were to be followed by a year-long radon characterization study (now revised to a long-term test over ninety days unless results are needed quickly).[1] Should levels be confirmed, remediation is to occur within a few years. Radon screening results between 20 (now 10) and 200 pCi/l are to be followed by confirmatory tests under closed house conditions and, if confirmed, remediation is to occur within several months.[2] And screening values over 200 pCi/l do not require confirmation, rather remediation is recommended within a few weeks.

Household Characterization: What Is the Health Risk? Is My House Safe?

"Household characterization" seeks to estimate the long-term yearly average radon exposure in living areas in order to provide more reliable information on health risk for the occupants. House characterization should not be confused with confirmatory testing because the latter, as practiced, rarely gives a long-term average. House characterization may be made by using an alpha track detector or electret for a year or averaging four short-term charcoal canister detectors, one over each season. The only context wherein an EPA guidance ever explicitly called for house characterization was in the confirmatory testing recommendation originally made for screening results between 4 and 20 pCi/l. Health risk was to be computed by averaging tests conducted on each occupied level of the building (EPA, 1986). Even this minimal use of house characterization disappeared with the 1992 revised guidance.[3] In any case, we never heard of any testing or mitigation firm that followed the first guidance. For such firms, year-long testing is impractical; if confirmatory tests are done at all, they are most likely to be short-term tests, most often charcoal canisters prone to serious sampling error. Overall, relatively little house characterization has occurred, even though this approach is the only one that addresses the ostensible concern of occupants, namely, determining their actual exposure to radon and the safety of their building.

Diagnosis: What Is the Best Mitigation Choice?

"Diagnostic testing" is sometimes carried out for buildings greater than 4 pCi/l in order to determine the sources and entryways for radon, and, therefore, the likely options for remediation (NYSEO, 1989, III-24). Such testing is generally done by experts, employing short radon gas measurement techniques such as grab sampling (where air is scooped up in a container for testing) or continuous monitoring (capable of "sniffing" or giving a quick, crude indication of relative radon levels). While diagnostic testing is a tool for understanding the radon dynamics in a building, and useful for tailoring a custom solution to the building, mitigators increasingly employ cookbook remediations requiring little if any diagnosis (see chapter 7).

Evaluation: Did the Mitigation Work?

"Postmitigation evaluation" is conducted to see how well a completed mitigation works. In order to reduce the variability of readings, these measures are ideally compared to premitigation radon tests similar in such sampling and measurement characteristics as ventilation and pressure conditions, weather, time of year, and detector placement. The comparison of premitigation and postmitigation measures determines whether the mitigation succeeded in lowering radon levels and whether the reduction is sufficient (NYSEO, 1989, III-23). Preliminary data from such mitigation evaluations indicate that many mitigations fail (see chapter 7). Furthermore, because buildings change over time, it is quite possible that radon levels will also change. For these reasons, whether the house has been mitigated or not, repeated tests over time are prudent. There is no evidence that many such measurements are taken, however.

Realty Transfer: Can a Building Be Warranted As Safe? Is Radon a Threat to a Building's Value?

"Realty" and "new construction" testing involve the effort to warrant that a building is free of radon problems that would be passed on to a new owner. The demands of real estate transfer often require quick answers, leading to a reliance upon short-term testing despite the inability of such measurements to do more than screen the house. As a result, many houses have been mitigated because they fell at 4 pCi/l or just above on a crude measurement, while other buildings deserving of mitigation may have been missed. While this sampling error must be addressed, realty transfer of used or new buildings represents a logical point for finding and lowering radon levels. Indeed, in the absence of government mandate, considerable market pressure has developed to force accountability on radon, particularly in areas where radon problems are known. Yet, EPA has lagged seriously in addressing the realty context. The 1992 *Citizen's Guide* blithely suggested that homeowners test their homes (and fix them) well before they intend to sell, while ignoring the well-known threats to testing validity— fraud and the quick test. It was not until 1993 that a formal guidance on real estate was issued by EPA, the *Home Buyer's and Seller's Guide to Radon*. Overall, real estate transfer has been a blatant instance where science, the radon industry, and government have bowed to economic pressure rather than to sound practice. We return to realty testing in chapter 8.

Institutional Testing: Are Public Buildings Safe?

"Institutional testing," involving measurements in public schools, day care centers, and government office buildings, became a major EPA focus by the late 1980s due to congressional mandate. Preliminary data from around the country indicated that there was some cause for concern. While the health guideline for public buildings is the same as for residences (4 pCi/l), development of testing guidelines is hampered by complex sampling questions, such as whether buildings should be tested while they are occupied or unoccupied; on weekdays or on weekends or evenings; and with heating, ventilation, and cooling on or off. Tight economics and the feared complications and costs of mitigation hampered many school districts from attending to the radon issue quickly.

Policy Error—The Case of Screening

EPA radon policy has focused upon screening measurements, with the goal of identifying hot houses and hot regions. Implementation of screening relied on finding a quick and inexpensive technique of sorting for hot houses. The tool of choice for screening was the charcoal canister, a government developed, inexpensive and easily handled testing device.[4] Screening as a policy was wedded to the charcoal canister and thus to the myth of the quick test, the assumption that radon levels could be assessed in a few days so as to provide valid information about longer term average radon levels in the building. One might even conjecture that screening became the policy goal of choice because the charcoal canister was so readily available and its best application was for screening.

The policy error in emphasizing screening should have been evident from the onset. It was well recognized in 1985 that the greatest public health risk was not to the few families living in hot houses, but to the multitudes living with much lower levels of radon. However, the myth of the hot house was so persuasive with its demand to screen for hot houses that EPA even ignored its own radon guidance, whereby the clear need for testing was to accurately discriminate between values below and above 4 pCi/l. The charcoal canister is particularly ill suited to this task, giving large numbers of false negative and false positive results (see for example, Scott, 1988b; Mose et al., 1988; Steck 1988, 1990, 1992; GAO, 1989). Thus, the primary emphasis on screening at best has been confusing, and, at worst, has provided wrong information to those testing their homes. Significantly, most homeowners who test their homes have a different goal than that embodied in screening; they seek to identify whether their homes are safe.

The issue of safety is best answered by household characterization, which attempts to define the annual average radon level to which occupants of the building are exposed, and not by screening. A strategy based upon household characterization would find the hot houses, but would also give building occupants valid information about their annual average exposure. That information could then be utilized to project risks associated with the building. Informed decisions about needed remediation based on risk could be made. An additional advantage is that testing protocols could be simplified. Furthermore, a characterization-based policy is consistent with the national goal of lowering buildings to ambient radon levels, thought to average somewhere in the 0.3–1.0 pCi/l range. Most homes have a radon problem needing to be addressed according to the ambient goal. While reliable and economical measurement at such low levels is inherently problematic, short-term screening is certainly too inaccurate to reliably measure low radon levels required by this policy.

In summary, the dominant reliance upon screening represents a serious policy error for the EPA. Screening asked the wrong question; by focusing on maximum values in the basement, its findings are hardly applicable to the issue of safety and risk in most houses tested. Neither did screening address the public health risks posed by the vast majority of houses at lower radon values. And screening relied on short-term tests that were highly susceptible to sampling error. By taking on the impractical objective of screening for hot houses, EPA missed the opportunity to implement a policy based upon household characterization that would have both addressed risk and identified hot houses.

While a combination of the Watras discovery and limited available information might excuse EPA's initial adoption of screening, what is surprising is that the policy has persisted in the face of firm evidence of its inadequacy. In the wake of the Indoor Radon Abatement Act of 1988, with its ambient goal, together with the increasingly recognized inadequacy of short-term sampling (see GAO, 1989), a shift away from screening would have been expected. However, in 1991, EPA proposed new guidelines for doing exactly the opposite: a one-step testing process enthroning the screening measurement with all its problems as the predominant radon test. Finally, in May 1992, the new *Citizen's Guide* moved even further from household characterization with its emphasis on shorter term tests, although it did recommend measuring in lived-in (rather than potentially livable) levels.

Methodological or Sampling Error

The key methodological error affecting the validity of radon testing involves sampling error caused by the heavy reliance on short-term testing and resulting insufficient sampling time.[5] Put simply, radon concentrations are often sampled over a time span that is too limited to fully assess the phenomenon being measured: one cannot validly predict a long-term average exposure from a short-term measurement. Blinded by the myth of the quick test, experts in government and the private radon sector continue to ignore ample evidence that radon is just too variable in many cases to reliably measure it over time periods of only a few days or less. Such variability is evident in radon's predictable fluctuations, those for which known variables have been identified related to weather and other natural conditions and to human behavior and house design. Radon also undergoes erratic or unpredictable fluctuations for which there is currently no acceptable explanation.

Radon's Predictable Variability

Radon and daughter concentrations indoors have been related to a variety of natural and human-caused conditions (see NYSEO 1989, II-23 to II-29).

Naturally Induced Radon Variations. Natural environmental factors that affect radon emanation from the soil include specific soil and weather conditions, daily or diurnal (day/night) weather cycles, and longer term cycles. The dynamics of some variations are well understood; in other cases, known variables cause less predictable outcomes.

There are many weather conditions that affect radon levels. For example, high winds can induce pressure-driven flows of soil gas from the ground into the house. Large barometric pressure changes accompanying storms can also affect radon levels. Rain, snow, and freezing ground can enhance the entry of radon into houses by preventing the escape of soil gas directly to the outside air surrounding a building (Nazaroff and Nero, 1984; Nazaroff et al., 1988b, pp. 92–97). Seasonal and even yearly variations in radon levels have been found by many researchers (Cohen and Gromicko, 1988b; George and Hinchcliffe, 1986; Sextro, 1990; Martz et al., 1991b).

There are also short-term fluctuations in radon levels observed on diurnal cycles. As shown in figure 6.1, such differences between night and day are probably caused by temperature and wind changes that accompany day/night changes (Scott, 1988b; Sextro, 1990). Such diurnal differences suggest a pattern of change that can be eliminated as a testing variable if tests begin and end at the same time of day (Scott, 1988b).

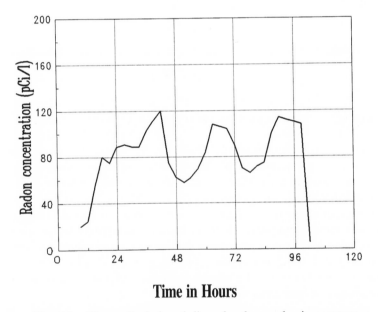

Time in Hours

Fig. 6.1 Thermally induced diurnal radon cycles in summer
(*Source*: Scott, 1988)

However, natural radon cycles of longer term also occur that would not be addressed by diurnal sampling. These longer-term cycles relate to high and low pressure systems, the weather patterns that continually cross over the continent bringing changes in temperature, wind, moisture, and atmospheric pressure. These patterns change approximately every three or four days, as shown on figure 6.2. A sampling interval capable of averaging the variations surrounding several pressure system shifts would require about fifteen days of integrated testing (Scott, 1988b).

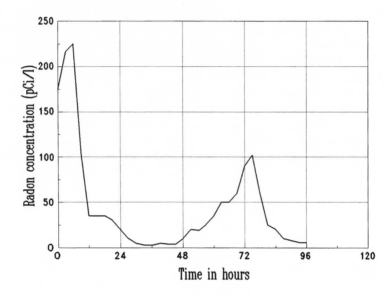

Fig. 6.2   Extreme long-term radon variation (*Source*: Scott, 1988)

Building and Occupant-Induced Variability. It is well documented that radon levels in houses are affected by such house conditions as whether the house
is closed up (doors and windows are shut), whether ventilation fans are on or
off, and whether the furnace is operating (EPA, 1989a; Scott, 1988b). Generally,
open houses during warm weather have lower radon levels because air exchange
dilutes the internal atmosphere. However, there are exceptions to this rule. If air
exchange increases negative pressure in the building, more radon may be drawn
in from the soil. In fact, such actions as blowing air out of a basement window
or using a whole house fan, by serving to increase the negative pressure in a
basement, may enhance radon entry.

Similarly, conventional rules regarding radon concentrations within different spaces in a building can also be proven wrong. Two such rules, that basements have higher radon values than do upper levels of the house, and that
upstairs rooms have less radon than downstairs rooms, may be contradicted if
air handling systems circulate radon from the basement or the ground to upper
levels of a house, causing higher levels there, or if thermal bypasses enhance air
flow and radon to upper-level rooms, again inverting the normal behavior. Radon outgassed from water could give larger values upstairs in rooms where water use is greatest.

Radon has been found to vary spatially for other reasons (Steck, 1992). For
example, rooms over different types of foundations (slab, crawl space, or full
basement) may have varying amounts of radon. Bathrooms and kitchens may be

affected by ventilation devices. Locations near HVAC vents, doors, windows, and exterior walls may be affected by drafts. Locations near the floor or ceiling are often not representative of other locations in the room. These factors are recognized in EPA measurement protocols and are the basis for the recommendations for controlling testing conditions.

Occupant-driven changes in house conditions such as ventilation, water use, or appliance use may also affect radon levels in extreme and sometimes unpredictable ways. The use of cook stove fans, bathroom fans, and clothes dryers may enhance negative pressure, and thus radon entry. If high amounts of radon are found in water, the radon concentrations in the internal air may well vary with water use. An example of this variation is offered in figure 6.3 (Scott, 1988b). The variations shown in figures 6.1–6.3 were all obtained under closed-house conditions and following all EPA protocols for assuring reproducibility. In all of these cases, however, short-term tests are seen to be particularly vulnerable to distortion from fluctuating radon levels.

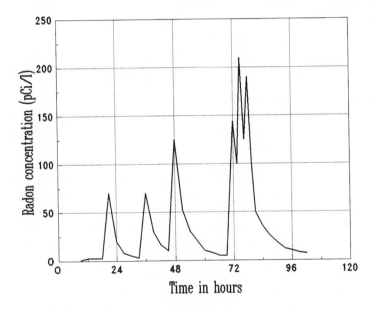

Fig. 6.3   Variations produced by radon in water (*Source:* Scott, 1988)

Radon's Erratic Variability

Aside from the somewhat predictable cycles associated with weather, time of day, and human use of the building, there is also evident an element of the erratic in the behavior of radon that upsets conventional wisdom about where and when to find maximum radon values in a building. Researchers have observed significant changes in radon levels over just a few weeks within a house—sometimes of more than a factor of twenty—that cannot be readily explained by any of the factors discussed above. Such "unusual variations" in radon emanation may be caused by seasonal changes in radon levels in soil air combined with wind direction changes. In other instances, soil and bedrock conditions combined with topographical factors may be involved; examples include conditions of exceptionally high permeability found with limestone cavities, shattered shale, or sand combined with sloping surface land forms (NYSEO, 1989, II-27 and II-29). Such extreme exceptions to the rules are not infrequent; several buildings out of every hundred or so studied seem to defy conventional assumptions about radon behavior (Camroden Associates, 1989).

Implications of Variability for Screening

While a radon measurement of any time interval is likely to introduce some error in estimating average radon levels for a longer time interval, in general this sampling error will increase as the time of measurement decreases. Indeed, studies show that short-term measurement devices such as the charcoal canister have a considerable sampling error (see Scott, 1988b; Mose et al., 1988; Steck, 1988, 1990, 1992; Dudney and Hawthorne, 1989; Granlund and Kaufman, 1987; GAO, 1989; Sextro 1990). Sampling error poses a major problem when using a short-term measurement to screen or characterize radon levels in a building where radon levels are highly variable. Since variability is inherently unknown, the degree of actual sampling error in a given test is also unknown. It cannot be assumed that the shorter term test is representative for the long-term average radon exposure.

There are ample proofs of the limits for generalizing screening tests. When short-term charcoal canister measurements were compared with seasonal and annual average alpha track tests made in Maryland and Virginia, the screening measurements had a 90 percent uncertainty in approximating year-long house characterization radon levels. In other words, the short-term measure is a relatively poor indicator of long-term average results (Mose et al., 1988).[6] Similar problems were found in a Minnesota and Wisconsin study of charcoal measurements. In 20 percent of the houses tested, screening results were less than 4 pCi/l, while long-term house characterization results exceeded 4 pCi/l. In contrast to these false negative results, in another 30 percent of the houses, false positive results were found. That is, screening measurements were greater than 4 pCi/l, but subsequent long-term follow-up measurements were found to be less than 4 pCi/l. In all, 50 percent (20 percent false negative and 30 percent false positive) of the screening measurements gave a wrong message (Steck, 1988, 1990).[7]

Finally, a summary of data from several researchers on the seasonal and spatial variations in indoor radon concentrations found that daily variations in radon cause large inherent measurement uncertainties ranging from 20 to more than 100 percent. Even monthly average radon concentrations were found to vary by large factors, so that measurements taken for periods of less than three months may only be reliable to within a factor of two or greater. In addition, the aggregate data for houses tend to give a ratio between basement screening and annual living space average that varies regionally around the country. There is also a large variability in these ratios within regions indicating that little can be assumed about the individual house based on the basement screening measurements that original EPA guidances recommended (Sextro, 1990; Steck, 1992).[8]

It should be noted that the sampling errors mentioned here are not indigenous to the charcoal canister; it just so happens that the charcoal canister is most often used. Any detector used for short-term measurements may produce similar sampling biases. That it is common practice to engender this error—albeit often unknowingly—suggests that officials, professional testers, and the public have just not recognized sampling error as the problem that it clearly is. The fact that rampant error is found in the EPA's preferred approach to radon testing suggests the need to look more closely at the adequacy of the EPA protocols and quality assurance program.

Inadequacy of EPA Protocols to Address Sampling Error

EPA protocols attempt to address sampling error by recommending minimum sampling times for different kinds of radon test devices, and by recommending a standardized set of conditions (environmental, house, and occupant behavior) for testing. However, because these recommendations were based on early and inadequate information and assumptions, they do not adequately address the issue of what sampling interval is necessary to validly measure radon levels. Clearly the minimum recommended times for screening measurements are often too short to account for radon variability. As a result, conventional wisdom about radon fundamental to the screening approach has been often contradicted. For example, closed-house wintertime conditions have often been found to yield lower radon levels than have characterization tests measuring average annual radon concentrations so that you cannot assume maximum radon levels will be found by screening. Similarly, basements do not always yield highest levels (see Scott, 1988b; Steck, 1988, 1990; Mose et al., 1988; GAO, 1989; Sextro, 1990). Perhaps of even greater concern, the protocols and recommendations are often so complicated that they are hardly followed. As we mentioned earlier, most professional testers did not perform house characterization tests to follow up screening measurements between 4 and 20 pCi/l, even when it was recommended by EPA prior to 1992. The new *Citizen's Guide* recommendations (EPA 1992f), by excluding a specific recommendation for house characterization, makes it unlikely that many homeowners would seriously consider it as well.

There is, of course, an even greater problem. An EPA study showed that over 85 percent of homeowners in the Washington, D.C. area who screened their homes for radon and received greater than 4 pCi/l did not perform a follow-up measurement of any type (GAO, 1989, p. 5). The absence of confirmatory testing places an even stronger onus on screening measurements that the screening approach is totally incapable of meeting.

Cumulative Effects of Sampling Error

The significance of sampling errors was shown by a study examining how cumulative errors affect false negative readings (Bierma et al., 1989). Monte Carlo sampling methods were used to simulate various errors at different radon levels and specified monitoring scenarios. At the guideline of 4 pCi/l, three-day charcoal canisters tests gave 36.6 percent false negatives and three-month alpha track detectors yielded 30.2 percent false readings. At 8 pCi/l, the three-day charcoal gave 11 percent false negatives while the three-month alpha track gave only 2.2 percent. These projections are probably underestimates given conservative assumptions about spatial and seasonal variation (Sextro, 1990). Perhaps more surprising is that the sequential testing approach recommended by the EPA (screening then follow-up) would give 67–70 percent false negatives at 4 pCi/l. This high figure is understandable if one considers that about one-third of the houses didn't follow up because of the false negative reading on the original screening measurement, while about half the remainder could be expected to fall below 4 pCi/l on the follow-up test based on statistical error. These results illustrate the problems of setting an artificial guideline at 4 pCi/l and the inherent futility of the screening approach.

Conclusions Regarding Methodological Error

The evidence on radon variability explains why quick tests are conducive to methodological or sampling error. While some of the factors that affect radon variability are under the control of the tester, many are not. The whole logic of screening with short-term measures relies on the notion of searching for maximum radon levels within a building. In a significant number of cases, however, it is not known where or under what conditions these maximum levels will be found. Maximum levels may not be encountered with basement tests under closed-house conditions. Furthermore, short-term testing cannot, by definition, account for significant radon fluctuations that are not sampled for. For these reasons, any measurements using short-term testing with any type of detector are particularly prone to methodological or sampling error that limits their utility. These problems are further compounded when we examine device error.

Device Error

Each testing device brings significant advantages and disadvantages to the testing task that make it more suitable for application to certain objectives than to others. Here we focus specifically on "device error," the intrinsic or inherent limitations of testing instruments that limit the validity of their findings. Table 6.2 summarizes major characteristics of the three most common passive radon detectors. The shortcomings of the charcoal canister are of particular note given its central role in screening policy. Also notable is the extent to which the myth of the quick test blinded EPA and others to these limitations, as well as to the advantages of the alternatives.

Table 6.2   Comparison of Passive Integrating Radon Detectors

Characteristics	Charcoal canister	Alpha track detector	Electret detector
Integration time	2–7 days	2 weeks to a year	Few days to a year
Cost	Low	Low	Low
Integration ability	Fair	Good	Good
Environmental limitations	Sensitive to temperature and humidity	Few limitations	Sensitive to temperature, background gamma, and temperature during analysis
Precision	Good	Low at low concentrations or short sampling times	Good
Analysis location	Laboratory	Laboratory	Field or laboratory
Major shortcomings	Limited sampling time; desorption with varying radon concentration	Low precision at short sampling times	Care must be taken to not inadvertently discharge electret

Source: NYSEO, 1989; EPA, 1989a; and Kotrappa et al., 1990.

Charcoal Canister

Charcoal canisters use activated carbon to absorb radon by molecular diffusion over an integrating period of between two and seven days. The tight-fitting cover is removed from the canister at the onset of testing and is resealed upon completion, preventing the escape of the charged heavy metal particles belonging to the radon daughters polonium, bismuth, and lead present due to the decay of radon gas that entered the canister during the test period. After return to the laboratory, the canister is placed on a detector that counts gamma rays emitted in a particular energy range from the radon daughters lead 214 and bismuth 214.

The charcoal canister provides relatively precise results over fairly short periods of measurement. Its strength lies in the ability to reduce statistical error through detection from the absorbed radon of a large number of gamma counts given off during daughter decay. This advantage is offset, however, by the characteristics of the physical test device and the fact that charcoal canisters can be used only for tests of brief duration, typically a few days, and are thus highly susceptible to sampling error. This short test time is necessitated by radon's half life of only 3.8 days. Short-lived daughters from radon collected early in sampling preferentially decay away before analysis can take place, weighting the latter part of the measurement. As a result, the canister may easily misrepresent average radon levels if radon variability is sufficiently significant to make the test period unrepresentative of the longer-term average. Furthermore, the ability of charcoal canisters to integrate radon levels over time is limited because radon will desorb from the canister depending on temperature and relative radon concentrations in the canister and the room. Thus, two-day charcoal canister tests will preferentially weight the last twelve or so hours. These variations may add an additional 50 percent uncertainty to the measurement (Sextro, 1990). By using a charcoal canister equipped with a diffusion barrier, the time-integration error can be reduced from 30 percent to 8 percent with additional improvements in averaging over diurnal variations. However, the modified canister requires an exposure of seven days (Martz et al., 1991a; Field and Kross, 1990). The charcoal medium is also sensitive to temperature and humidity effects, a problem that can add to the error associated with these detectors (Bierma et al., 1989).

Alpha Track Detectors

An alpha track detector consists of a plastic film placed inside a small plastic pillbox container. Since only radon diffuses through the filter, any microscopic tracks etched into the plastic from alpha emission will indicate the presence of radon and its daughters. Thus, the more tracks over a given time period, the greater the radon concentration. After its return to the laboratory, the film is "developed" in a sodium hydroxide solution that etches the tracks, which are then counted.

The alpha track detector is one of only two devices (with the electret) that cheaply and easily performs an integrated radon measurement over time periods significantly longer than a week. Alpha track detectors do not exhibit errors due to time integration, temperature, or humidity. Measurements using alpha track detectors are typically made for at least two to three months or for a year where an annual average exposure is desired. The alpha track detector is sometimes used for shorter measurement periods if the expected concentrations of radon are sufficiently high or if, by counting a larger area, a more sensitive reading of the detector is made. A major disadvantage of the device is that precision is limited at relatively low levels of radon and/or for shorter test periods simply because there are few tracks on the film to count (EPA, 1989a). The device has from time to time been plagued by bias and precision errors (Field and Kross, 1990; Martz et al., 1991a; Scott and Robertson, 1991; Yeager et al., 1991; Pearson et al., 1992).

Electret Ionization Chamber

The electret ion chamber emerged as an testing device around 1988, challenging the other passive detectors with its similar range of applications and several distinct advantages. Radon gas enters the chamber by diffusing through filtered openings. A permanently charged electret (an electrostatically charged disk of Teflon) is used to collect ions (charged particles) formed by alpha, beta, and gamma radiation emitted during the subsequent decay of radon and radon daughters. Because negative ions attracted by the electret during decay serve to reduce the electret's surface voltage, the loss of voltage becomes the measure of radon concentration. The average radon level in pCi/l is found directly by dividing the voltage difference by a calibration factor and the time of exposure. A correction may be made for external background gamma radiation. Two versions of the device are made, one for use in short-term tests of between two and fourteen days and one for longer term measurements of between two weeks and a year (NYSEO 1989, III-10; EPA, 1989a; Kotrappa et al., 1988).

The electret shares the advantages of both the charcoal canister and the alpha track detector. Plus, it adds two major advantages of its own. First, while the charcoal canister cannot be used for sampling for longer than several days and the alpha track detector is inadequate for short-term tests, the electret device functions over any time span from a few days to a year. It further avoids the tendency of two-day charcoal canisters to overemphasize the last twelve hours of testing, integrating the entire time period equally. Second, analysis of the electret can be done immediately in the field by testing professionals using a surface voltage meter (EPA, 1989a; Kotrappa et. al., 1988). On the negative side, care must be taken to correct for sensitivity to temperature at the time of analysis and in handling the device when it is removed from its protected plastic case in order to avoid uncontrolled effects on the charge of the unit. The electret ion detector also is subject to correction errors from background gamma radiation. Finally, this test device requires testing by an expert, increasing costs and creating a potential conflict of interest for having analysis done by testing firms having a direct interest in whether mitigation is required.

Conclusions Regarding Device Error

Device error is rarely a major threat to validity in and of itself. Limitations of various instruments are well known and are often subject to correction in analysis. Manufacturers and the EPA provide recommendations for the avoidance of device error. Accordingly, our concern mostly involves device error's compound effect when interacting with already troublesome levels of policy and methodological/sampling error. The charcoal measurement's overall error raises the possibility of unacceptably large numbers of false positives and negatives in detecting whether buildings require remediation.

Measurement Error

Over the time interval during which radon is measured by any given device, there is a risk of measurement error. Such error occurs when conditions before or during the test depart from the standardized conditions for the test and cause the device to give an inaccurate or irreproducible result.

Measurement Error and EPA Protocols

EPA protocols for radon testing devices make recommendations for the standardization of testing in order to enhance the reproducibility of results. These protocols include specifications for house conditions, detector placement, occupant behavior, and operation guidelines for various types of detectors and for different measurement goals (EPA, 1989a). General EPA protocols call for location of detectors away from sources of air turbulence and drafts, away from obstructions that would block radon from reaching the device, away from pets and children who might damage the device, and away from heat sources. Devices are to be located within the average breathing zone, typically three to five feet from the floor. EPA also generally recommends that testing be done under closed-house conditions and in the absence of air exchange systems that would mix inside and outside air. For test samples of three days or less, closed-house conditions are also recommended for at least twelve hours prior to testing. EPA and manufacturers have further developed some targeted protocols for specific testing devices.

Deliberate Measurement Error

We have seen that there are substantial opportunities for error in the way that measurements are done. These may occur accidentally or due to carelessness. However, there is a third possibility—deliberate measurement error. The potential, indeed, the likelihood, of such error exists when test conditions are controlled by those who have a direct vested interest in the test outcome. Such deliberate error has been widely noted in real estate testing, where the person selling the building benefits directly if no appreciable concentrations of radon are found (see chapter 8). Radon testers have also been known to fudge results as well, although most often they hurt validity by being sloppy or incompetent in providing accurate test analysis and adequate quality control (GAO, 1989, p. 5). Overall, measurement error due to any cause is a threat to test validity.

Analysis Error

After the measurement has been taken, an instrument either has recorded a certain number of counts or tracks representing radioactive decays of radon and/ or its daughters or has absorbed radon in charcoal. Analysis error refers to the error introduced when the raw data are read and converted into radon concentrations (pCi/l) or daughter concentrations (WL). Several types of analysis error can be delineated. These are statistical error, calibration error, background error, and human error.

Statistical Error—Getting Enough Counts

Typically, error margins of plus or minus 10–30 percent are assigned to most radon devices, reflecting the statistical error and/or the ability to reproduce the measurement under a fixed set of conditions (NYSEO, 1989, III-30).[9] Generally, less error is expected when greater numbers of decays are counted. Thus, for a given concentration of radon, statistical error is more likely when the device is less sensitive, the air volume tested is small, or when counting times are short. Clearly, decisions made about sampling times and the type of instrument will affect analysis error. Protocols address statistical error by suggesting minimum times for sampling for different test instruments. Additionally, analysis procedures can be modified to reduce this error factor. For alpha track detectors, for example, increasing the area of the film that is analyzed will produce more counts and reduce error. For charcoal canisters, increasing the length of time during which gamma rays from the daughter products are counted gives more counts and reduces statistical error.

Statistical analysis error can affect the overall accuracy of a measurement program. Substantial analysis errors are thought to have occurred after the 1988 assistant surgeon general's pronouncement on the health effects of radon. Tens of thousands of concerned citizens screened their homes in the wake of the warning, and swamped charcoal canister laboratories with detectors way beyond their capacity. As these canisters waited for analysis, radon and radon daughters decayed away, leaving fewer counts for analysis. Some laboratories also reduced counting times to deal with the overload. While a statistical error of between 10 percent and 30 percent is typical for such analysis, in this instance, analysis error was thought to be considerably increased.

Calibration Error—Are Instruments Calibrated to a Standard?

All analysis methods depend on a calibration factor used to convert counts measured over some time interval into a radon concentration in pCi/l or a radon daughter concentration in WL. However, if the calibration number obtained is either too high or too low, a bias or systematic error is introduced into the analysis. By analogy, the biased calibration factor is the rough equivalent of measuring distances with a ruler that is stretched or contracted; all measurements would be off in one direction or the other. EPA's Radon Measurement Proficiency (RMP) program provides for a check of bias error by comparing the average of a large number of detector measurements of the same type with a standardized value. Most detectors reviewed under the RMP program have been found to produce a bias error of less than 10 percent (Wing and Mardis, 1987), although it appears that actual bias under more realistic conditions might be greater (Yeager et al., 1991).

Background Error—Is the Analysis Contaminated from Another Source?

Background radiation may also limit the accuracy of measurement. This source of error is particularly a problem for low counting rates associated with low radon concentration samples because, in these samples, background makes up a comparatively large proportion of the measured counts. The EPA provides device-specific recommendations for reducing the background error (EPA, 1989a).

Human Error

There are numerous mistakes that can be made during analysis, all exacting a toll on accuracy. Canisters can get mixed up, numbers can be misread, incorrect calibration factors can be used, and delays in analysis can occur. The number of possibilities are almost endless, indicating a vast human ingenuity for fulfilling Murphy's Law—if it can go wrong, it will. Performance evaluation tests of detector firms indicate that human errors are not uncommon (Yeager et al., 1991).

The Radon Measurement Proficiency (RMP) Program

The EPA, through its RMP program, has tried to limit some of the analysis error, including statistical, bias, background, and human errors, that are inherent when a testing company produces a radon or radon daughter measurement with a testing device. The RMP program was initiated in 1986 by the EPA "to allow organizations offering measurement services to consumers a means to demonstrate their proficiency in measuring radon" (Jalbert et al., 1991). This voluntary quality assurance program has a twofold purpose. First, it promotes standard measurement procedures. Second, it encourages quality assurance procedures by all companies in the radon measurement business. In effect, the RMP program focuses on analysis and device error.

In the RMP program, detectors belonging to participating companies are exposed to undisclosed calibrated levels of radon and radon daughters at an EPA radon chamber.[10] The detectors are then analyzed by the testing firm, and results are submitted to EPA for comparison with the radon chamber values. Proficient performance is defined as a screening measurement that lies within plus or minus 25 percent of the chamber value. Companies passing the RMP proficiency tests are listed in a public document that is distributed by EPA to state agencies and to the public. While the RMP program is voluntary, states led by New Jersey quickly began to require passing the RMP proficiency test as a precondition for testing in the state. Firms are required to renew their proficiency on a regular basis. Since its inception, the RMP program has mushroomed with the increasing numbers of test firms and testing devices (see chapters 3, 8, and 10).

The major advantage of such a program is that it provides some degree of control over the proliferation of inept or fraudulent companies and inaccurate testing devices in the radon testing field. It does provide a minimum standard of performance for companies who desire to be on the proficiency list. However, there are some key limitations to the RMP program that relate specifically to measurement and analysis error (GAO, 1989). The program does not test detectors under realistic conditions where radon variability may be large. Testing is often done at much higher radon levels than is typically found in homes. The program hardly measures how well firms do on a day-to-day basis; firms have treated their EPA detectors with special reverence. Even so, the quality of results from different testing firms for the same type of testing device can be quite variable (Martz et al., 1991a; Pearson et al., 1992). Numerous rumors hint of industry cheating on the RMP proficiency tests. And, unless states require participation in the RMP program, it is purely voluntary. Thus, many firms can avoid this minimal quality control altogether. Recognition of these problems has led to the application of remedies such as the use of double-blind testing, where firms would not know which tests coming to their lab were from the RMP program. When EPA applied double-blind tests in 1989, 20 percent of the firms that had shown proficiency in 1988 failed (GAO, 1990). The EPA is also considering radon chamber testing under variable conditions. A GAO (1990) study recommended that EPA require that firms participating in the RMP program demonstrate a minimum quality assurance capability, and that EPA issue guidance on what an effective state program should do to assure accurate radon measurements. In the meantime, the growing number of states requiring RMP participation will close an important loophole. However, the RMP program hardly addresses policy, interpretation, and sampling error (see chapter 10).

Interpretation Error

After a radon test result is received, the findings must be interpreted. Interpretation error occurs when inaccurate conclusions are drawn about the meaning of a test result. Interpretation errors are often secondary effects of other validity threats, such as policy error. In particular, radon policy is plagued by a prevalent interpretation error originating from confusion over the meaning of screening, follow-up, and house-characterization measurements.

Screening and Follow-up Confusion—the Problem of False Negatives

EPA's 1986 and 1992 guidelines for screening and confirmatory testing created rampant false interpretations among testers and the public. The most significant interpretation errors are due to the myth of the quick test, the assumption that short-term tests can provide valid indicators of a building's radon level, and, therefore, give an accurate health risk estimate.[11] The error of interpretation is a secondary impact of methodological and policy errors whereby screening and confirmatory testing are confused with household characterization. When people conclude that their homes are safe based upon screening results less than 4 pCi/l, a confusion invited by EPA guidelines, they are making this serious error. We have seen above that short-term screening tests coupled with radon variability and erraticness can lead to a significant number of false positives and false negatives. Since EPA guidelines invite people receiving scores of 4 pCi/l or more to do additional testing, false positives have a chance of being addressed. However, false negatives are never checked. Those incorrectly told that their levels are less than 4 pCi/l are not likely to do further testing. Such errors were compounded when few homeowners and relatively few testing professionals followed EPA's original recommendations to use household characterization as a means of confirming screening results between 4 and 20 pCi/l. Instead, follow-up testing would use charcoal canisters under closed house conditions. The methodological problems with the charcoal test bias these results. When they are interpreted as though they provided information about the safety of the building and health risk, interpretation error occurs. Revised EPA guidelines assure this error.

Assumption of Safety below 4 pCi/l

Beyond compounded methodological error, there is a serious interpretation error in the very perception that radon levels below 4 pCi/l are safe. Despite EPA's disclaimers that their 4 pCi/l guidance is not a standard separating safe from unsafe levels, the public has clearly treated 4 pCi/l as a magic divide or threshold. The seriousness of this interpretation error was key to Congress's dictate of an ambient goal for radon exposure and its charge to EPA to clarify the meaning of 4 pCi/l in the revised *Citizen's Guide*, which was finally issued in May 1992 (see chapter 9).

Ambiguity in Making Health-Risk Estimates

Another source of interpretation error stems from the inherent uncertainty of estimating unknown health risks. At 4 pCi/l, the EPA estimates that between one and five lung cancers will develop in one hundred people exposed over a lifetime of seventy years. Such ranges of risk, while reflecting our state of scientific knowledge, are confusing. Additionally, these risk estimates are not easily interpreted or understood when applied to shorter exposure times. What is the risk to people who were exposed for only five years, who spend only a small amount of time at home or who are younger than seventy? These points of ambiguity suggest that some members of the public will discount a risk of concern to others.

Ambiguity in Converting from pCi/l to WL

Given that radon daughters, not radon per se, is the source of hazard, conversion between radon and its daughters is necessary in order to project health effects. EPA generally assumes that 200 pCi/l of radon is equivalent to 1 WL of daughter activity based on a condition of equilibrium where half the daughters have plated out and, therefore, do not contribute to health effects. In actual buildings, this assumption may be misleading. For example, buildings with significant airflow, particularly larger buildings with air-handling systems, have conversions on the order of 400 pCi/l for 1 WL. Similarly, there may be less risk in houses with hot-air-circulation systems or whole-house air conditioning. If incorrect assumptions are made about equilibrium conditions, incorrect interpretations about safety are likely.

Conclusion Regarding Interpretation Error

We see that significant interpretation errors are invited by current radon policy. Our tendency has been to discuss these in light of the effort of home occupants to determine their risk. However, interpretation error also has major implications for realty transfer. Perhaps the major "market" for radon testing, we see here that realty decisions based upon short-term measurements are likely to suffer from the same extreme level of error as do the measurements themselves.

Radon Testing in Water and Soil

Many of the validity threats seen with testing for radon in air also occur when we examine radon in water and soil. We previously noted the tendency to over-weight the significance of radon in water, which is in fact unlikely to be a problem in the absence of an airborne radon problem.[12] Still, radon in groundwater has been recognized as a serious issue (see chapters 3, 4, and 10) given values as high as one million pCi/l. Air tests are frequently used to screen for waterborne radon; a low value suggests that little radon is being released from the water supply. Approaches that directly measure radon in water include laboratory analysis of water samples using a liquid scintillation method or by counting gamma emissions, measuring the outgased radon from a sample of water with an electret ion chamber (Kotrappa and Jester, 1993), and placing a special integrating alpha track detector in the toilet tank for several months (NYSEO, 1989). These tests all suffer from various validity errors. However, of greatest interest with radon tests in water are interpretation errors. At a general conversion of 6,000–10,000 pCi/l in water to 1 pCi/l in air, 24,000–40,000 pCi/l in water would be required before the guidance level of 4 pCi/l in air would be triggered. The state of Maine has utilized 20,000 pCi/l in water as a level suggesting the need for mitigation. Nevertheless, the sheer size of these radon amounts can easily frighten an ill-informed homeowner into carrying out water system mitigations not called for by airborne radon levels (NYSEO, 1989).

Soil testing also confronts serious limitations. While it is simple to test soil for radon using grab samples or with integrating devices placed in the soil for a period of time, these tests have little predictive validity. Most critical are measurement or sampling problems due to the variability of radon levels in soil over very short distances and over time. As a result, the number of tests required to accurately represent a complex soil geology is quite large. Furthermore, even if the site is adequately sampled prior to construction, disturbance of the ground may alter the emanation of radon at a given location and make the transport of radon much easier. Of course, soil radon values are only one factor in determining what a house radon value will be. Soil permeability, weather conditions, and house construction and operation are also important (see chapter 5).

Conclusions about the Myth of the Quick Test

We have seen that, of the six types of error discussed, the validity of radon testing is most affected by fundamental policy and methodological errors leading to interpretation error. Simply stated, the combination of screening policy with the use of short-term testing provides too many false negatives and false positives at and around the guideline of 4 pCi/l. Perhaps some 50 percent of those testing for radon under the EPA protocols for screening have received wrong information. Short-term screening, as it is currently done, works for the much fewer hotter houses at the expense of the vast numbers of marginal houses at and around 4 pCi/l where the bulk of the health risk is located (Harley, 1990). Furthermore, screening measurements fail to provide a significant margin of safety. Ultimately, both screening and short-term testing fail due to the nature of radon variability in houses. Given that EPA protocols and the RMP program legitimize these problems, they also fail.

Prospects for House Characterization

Testing error can best be addressed through a change of testing policy to house characterization, based upon the use of an integrated annual radon level. This approach eliminates significant policy error by refocusing radon policy on the actual distribution of risk. Interpretation error is limited because the results of characterization may be directly applied to the radon risk charts. Methodological errors are minimal because house characterization is not affected by radon variability and, therefore, sampling error is not an issue. Also, there is no potentially incorrect assumption of a maximal value in the basement, as in screening. While even a year-long measurement offers a significant statistical chance that a house with a radon value at or slightly above 4 pCi/l will measure below 4, it offers the most valid and reliable information available about risk at a reasonable cost and is the most logical approach to radon measurement (Nero et al., 1990).

A shift to house characterization faces serious obstacles, however. The revised 1992 EPA *Citizen's Guide* avoids any discussion of the accuracy or validity of measurements and removes the minimal recommendation for house characterization found in the 1986 guide. While the agency purports to believe in the myth of the quick test, using elaborate excuses to justify its policy (see chapter 12), another reason for the agency's intransigence may simply be the difficulty of admitting that they were wrong. Reissuing new protocols on lengthening the sampling time for measurements might make EPA look foolish and raise complex questions of liability. All short-term tests below 4 pCi/l would have to be repeated in order to identify the 20 percent of false negatives. The radon industry's heavy reliance upon the short-term test, encouraged by EPA, would cause serious disruptions.The repudiation of short-term tests (including expensive continuous monitor tests) would invalidate the bulk of real estate transaction measurements.

Of course, continuing with the present testing policy has its own set of problems. First, EPA's current screening policy has created a major credibility problem. In many states, EPA and others have found, it is difficult enough to get people to screen for radon, let alone to retest later (GAO, 1989; Evdokimoff and Ozonoff, 1992). As homeowners begin to realize how little they learn from a short-term screening test, there is little motivation to retest or to expend a significant sum of money for mitigation based on relatively unreliable information. Neither can it continue to be argued that the present screening approach is cheaper when it so miserably fails to sort houses by risk and may have resulted in remediation of a substantial number of buildings at sale based upon false positive readings. There is precedent for EPA to revise protocols based on new information, as was done previously to eliminate grab sampling as a screening and follow-up measurement method because of unacceptably high error in sampling. In the instance of the quick test, one would be hard put to argue that the situation is much better.[13]

The real goal of policy should be to motivate accurate house characterization, thereby giving people more reliable information on health effects. EPA's radon policy relies on a screening approach, originally designed to motivate testing, that backfired by asking the wrong questions and failing to provide valid and reliable means of measurement. For a responsive radon policy to exist, the myth of the quick test must be finally laid to rest. In the next chapter, we see that there are also problems with the quick fix.

Notes

1. These tests do not require closed-house conditions and can be made either with a year-long alpha track or electret detector or by repeating a charcoal canister test over each of the four seasons and averaging the results (EPA, 1986).

2. The new version of the *Citizen's Guide* (EPA, 1992f) suggests a second immediate short-term test if the screening result is above 10 pCi/l, or if results are needed quickly. Also, the new guidelines suggest averaging screening and follow-up results rather than taking follow-up results on two lived-in levels of the house.

3. Following screening results between 4 and 10 pCi/l, the 1992 EPA guidelines recommend only a long-term test of greater than ninety days, although there is no explicit recommendation for a full year test. The guide additionally suggests averaging screening and follow-up tests even if they are both short term and ignores taking follow-up tests on two lived-in levels. When screening radon levels are higher than 20 pCi/l (10 pCi/l under the 1992 recommendations), shorter-term testing under closed-house conditions is recommended.

4. There were not really any other options available. Grab samples were fast, but they were known to be inaccurate. Like continuous monitoring, they were extremely expensive because skilled labor was required. The alpha track detector was a patented invention, not available for free use by government. The electret had not as yet been invented.

5. Sampling time refers to the length of time of the test. Three common approaches to sampling radon have been used (George, 1988). Grab sampling collects a sample of air over a short time interval, typically minutes, essentially providing an instantaneous snapshot of the radon or daughters in the building at the time the sample was collected. Because radon levels may vary considerably in a given building over time, grab sampling is unlikely to provide a valid picture of the long-term average radon value. Continuous sampling uses sophisticated monitors to repeatedly sample air, typically averaging over one-half to one-hour intervals, and provides detailed information on the variation of radon over time. This method is limited by complexity and cost. Finally, integrated sampling uses detectors to average radon or daughter concentrations over a few days to a year or more, giving a single number, the average, as the result. The commonly used devices, the alpha track detector, the charcoal canister, and the electret, are based on integrated sampling. We focus on integrated measurements in the text.

6. Interestingly, when three-month alpha track results were also compared to yearly averages, a 50 percent uncertainty was found. Thus, the three-month sample is considerably better, but hardly good, at approximating annual averages.

7. One remedy for addressing the particularly alarming number of false negatives—alarming because they falsely reassure the building occupants—would be to drop the radon action level to 2 pCi/l from 4 pCi/l. Under these circumstances, false negatives might drop to 5 percent, but false positive occurrences would become correspondingly more frequent. Steck suggests that a more reasonable corrective would be to eliminate screening measurements altogether.

8. EPA guidances from 1986 to 1992 called for measuring the radon level in the lowest potentially livable area and, after 1992, measuring in the lowest lived-in area.

9. Typically, two-thirds of the measurements made with the same type of detector under the same conditions and time interval would be expected to give a result within plus or minus 10–30 percent of the result obtained. This statistical error in percent is estimated by dividing the square root of the number of counts by the number of counts and multiplying the entire quantity by one hundred.

10. A radon chamber is simply an air tight box in which a known radon source produces a measured radon concentration. The chamber allows calibration factors to be determined for detectors, or it may be used to check the ability of a company to measure the radon level in the chamber, presumably unknown to them.

11. It is interesting that when EPA decided to get a more accurate distribution of actual radon exposure to the population, they took year-long measurements (see chapter 5). Yet when it comes to individual homeowners making expensive decisions about mitigation, the agency considers the short-term test to be adequate.

12. Radon is unlikely to be concentrated in water when the building draws its water supply from a large municipal source, since reservoirs will lose their radon to the outdoor air and large systems based on groundwater take so long to deliver water that most radon is decayed.

13. Given evidence of radon variability and an unacceptable rate of false negatives, it would be prudent to increase sampling times for other measurement methods. Indeed,

in December of 1990, the EPA revised its screening and follow-up protocols for testing to a minimum of two days. Although it is a step in the right direction, this clearly doesn't go far enough. Scott (1988b) and Sextro (1990) suggest something on the order of fifteen to thirty days in order to average over recurrent weather cycles. While still having some of the limitations of a quick test, the two-week to one-month measure may be the shortest duration having any possible claims to validity.

Chapter 7

The Myth of the Quick Fix

I am frankly troubled that EPA appears to be telling the public that all is easily fixable, when the truth is that some houses are easily fixed, while others can be no end of trouble.
—Senator Patrick Moynihan
If we wanted to design an effective radon collector to remove radon from the soil, we could do no better than the way we currently design and build houses.
—Terry Brennan

In this chapter, we discuss radon entry, mitigation, and prevention in light of a triad of diverse myths relating to radon in buildings. In examining radon entry and its implications for mitigation and new home design, we first confront the myth of blameless radon, the belief that because the geologic radon threat is naturally occurring, people bear no blame for its presence in buildings and, therefore, a regulatory response is inappropriate. A second myth points to a contradictory belief, the myth of the tight house, according to which energy efficient or tight houses are blamed for high radon levels. The effect of this myth was the reigning in of the energy conservation movement, in line with the anti-environmental tendencies of Reaganomics. Finally, we confront the veracity of the myth of the quick fix, a keystone belief for EPA's public promotion of radon as a solvable problem— that houses can be easily fixed and excessive radon entry can be prevented.

The Myth of Blameless Radon

Were radon not transferred into buildings, its presence in soil gas in the natural environment would have little consequence for humans. Thus, natural or geologic radon, in and of itself, is only the source of the radon hazard. To realize that hazard, the right building conditions must be in effect. While we discuss the implications of the myth of blameless radon in chapter 10, the foundation for this myth is the systematic focus on the source of radon, rather than on the point of exposure in the human-controlled built environment. As we see here, that is a very selective focus indeed.

Building Factors Affecting Radon Transfer

We previously noted the importance of the strength of the radon source and the ability of radon to move through the soil surrounding a building (see chapter 5). But these preconditions for radon entry do not explain how the soil gas is drawn into the building. There are two principal characteristics of a building having a propensity to concentrate radon. First, there are openings where the building connects to the surrounding soil and rock. Second, there are design and use characteristics of the building that, in combination with natural conditions, create driving forces in its pressure dynamics. A crude analogy for these factors is a glass of soda and a straw; the straw is the connecting link while the pressure placed on the straw drives the fluid upward or downward. Without the linkage and the driving forces, the soda remains in the glass.

Building Connections to the Surrounding Soil and Rock

House construction can enhance movement of soil air from surrounding soil and bedrock in numerous ways. Common entry of soil gas is through water-drainage systems around the house, as well as through high-permeability sand and gravel used to backfill the foundation and trenches along water and sewer lines. The house may even sit on normally impermeable clay soil, but pipes, drains, or the foundation may punch through to connect the house to more permeable soil layers beneath the clay. These connections may allow easy transport of radon over long distances. Likewise, radon entry depends partly on the type of foundation that exists. While slabs, crawlspaces, and basements provide a barrier to the soil, they are likely to also offer many possible soil gas entryways (see fig. 7.1), including cracks in slabs and basement walls, joint openings between the slab and wall (e.g., French drains), and penetrations for sewer or septic connections, support posts, water lines, drains, and sump pumps. A tiny crack around the entire perimeter of the basement provides a large cumulative entry area. While a crack on the order of a sixteenth of an inch (the diameter of a pencil point) or less can be sufficient as a radon path, most basements have huge and obvious openings. (NYSEO, II-20, IV-12, 1989).

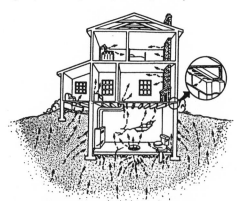

Fig. 7.1   Radon entry routes (*Source*: NYSEO, 1989 [EPA])

Negative Pressure and Driving Forces in Radon Entry

Much as winds are drawn by atmospheric pressure differences, moving from high to low pressure, there must be a similar driving force for radon-laden soil air to enter a building. In a home, driving forces created by lower pressure in the basement than in the surrounding soil suck in soil gases like a powerful vacuum cleaner, accumulating as much as between 5 percent and 20 percent of all the air entering the building (Michaels et al., 1987; Turk, et al., 1987). These pressure differences stem from a combination of built and natural conditions.

Modern houses generally create major negative pressure dynamics through the use of various ventilation devices (e.g., bathroom, kitchen, or whole-house attic fans), as well as the operation of combustion devices (e.g., a furnace, gas dryer, or wood stove) that force combustion gases and make-up air out a chimney or vent while drawing in replacement air from vent openings, around windows and doors, or from soil air surrounding the outside of the basement. Further enhancing negative pressure is the "stack effect," a natural temperature-driven pressure difference caused (particularly in the winter) when less-dense warm air rises and escapes through small openings and cracks at higher levels, particularly in the attic. Some of the escaping air is replaced by soil gas containing radon entering through cracks and openings in the basement. The stack effect is enhanced by such design features as multiple story buildings and the use of thermal bypasses, connections between different zones of the house that allow warm air to easily move to higher levels, including air gaps around chimneys, plumbing chases, recessed lighting, and balloon wall construction (NYSEO, II-9, 1989).

Wind is another significant natural factor influencing pressure characteristics and, thus, radon entry, when high pressure is exerted on the windward side of the house, and a low pressure on the leeward side. This dynamic drives in radon from the soil on one side, while sucking it in on the other (see fig. 7.2) (NYSEO, II-15, 1989). Other weather-related factors influencing radon and soil emergence are barometric pressure changes (radon emerges during low pressure systems and storms) and special conditions, such as frozen soil, snow cover, and rain (radon soil concentrations increase when the gas cannot escape to the atmosphere). All of these factors interact and contribute, given their inherent variability, to fluctuations in radon levels over time (Nazaroff et al., 1988b, NYSEO, II-27, 1989).

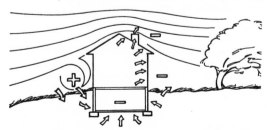

Fig. 7.2   Windblown effect. Arrows show pressure-driven flow while + and − show relative pressure differences (*Source*: NYSEO, 1989 [from EPA])

Conclusions Regarding the Myth of Blameless Radon

The four major factors required for radon entry to buildings from soil air reflect both natural and human-caused factors. First, a source such as radium must be present in the soil relatively close by a building. Second, there must be a transport path, either high-permeability soil, cracks and fissures in rock and soil, or human-made high-permeability paths, which allows the radon to move from the source to the house. Third, there must be entryways into the building itself. Therefore, the type of construction, particularly of the basement, and its connection to the rest of the house, is important. Finally, driving forces must be present in order to power the movement. These driving forces often reflect the way that a building is designed and operated, including negative pressure-producing activities and appliances. These four conditions coalesce often enough to produce annual average radon concentrations in excess of 4 pCi/l in about 6 percent of the housing stock. Thus, it can be seen that geologic radon is natural in its source, but its entry into buildings involves interaction with the construction, condition, and operation of the building. To view radon as a purely natural phenomenon, therefore, is to overlook the synergy that results in the presence of radon in buildings. Radon in buildings is not a purely natural and blameless occurrence. The myth of blameless radon is a form of denial with profound policy implications for radon (see chapters 2 and 10).

The Myth of the Tight House

Even before the discovery of high radon in homes, there had been some concern over whether the energy conservation programs of the late 1970s and early 1980s had increased the risk from indoor air contaminants, including radon. The somewhat publicized early problem with the Nobel house (see chapter 2), an underground building, also helped to call attention to energy innovative designs. These factors helped to set the stage for one of radon's persistent myths, the myth of the tight house, which states that energy efficient houses cause elevated radon levels. A related and converse belief, that well-ventilated "leaky" houses are radon safe, also took hold.

This tight house myth is particularly fascinating given the simultaneous denial that our way of making and using buildings collects indoor radon. It suggests that the cultural risk of blaming the conventional home was too great, but that buildings on the fringe of normal could be safely made the culprit. That alternative and conservation-designed buildings would take the hit for radon at that particular point in time is also instructive. The Reagan administration had succeeded in bringing to a visible end the energy crises of the Carter era. Dramatic cuts in research and implementation of alternative energy and conservation techniques were seen. A return to oil-fueled growth was encouraged. The vilification of the conservation movement because of radon was a natural extension of this trend. Energy conservation became the scapegoat as society struggled with the cultural threat of geologic radon as an attack on the safety of home.

The question of radon levels in energy-efficient houses has sparked considerable discussion and media interest. Unfortunately, the result has been an incorrect belief that energy efficiency causes higher radon levels (i.e., the myth of the tight house). As is generally the case with myths, here we see some basis in fact. For example, the publicized Nobel house was an underground building. Such structures, given the large area of direct contact between the earth and the house, are particularly susceptible to potentially higher radon levels. Extensive wall and floor areas are exposed to the soil, and occupants are always living in the areas of the house that tend to have the higher radon concentrations. Such problems can be mitigated and, in any case, underground houses are rare. However, their publicized vulnerability to high radon levels contributed to the myth of the tight houses. Similarly, some solar houses have unique potential radon entryways, such as attached sunspaces and greenhouses with dirt or rock floors and heat storage areas directly coupled to the surrounding soil. These houses may gain elevated radon levels from the entering soil gas as well as from the radium content of rocks used for storage (George et al., 1983; Fleisher et al., 1983).

However, the principal basis of the myth of the tight house revolves around the perception that "energy efficient" structures concentrate radon. Of the two key factors that make for an energy-efficient building, a high insulation level has virtually no impact on radon levels and merely reduces the heat loss across surfaces. In contrast, the second factor—low air-exchange rates—is more complex. Generally, air exchange brings in ambient level radon air while transferring the higher concentration radon in the house to the outside. Essentially, more air exchange dilutes the radon concentration. Does the inverse follow that a "tight house," having a comparatively smaller volume of outside air moving through it and, therefore, less dilution of radon, would have higher radon levels compared to a comparatively "leaky" building? According to the myth of the tight house, the answer is "yes."

Various studies comparing houses with different air-exchange rates show this myth to be wrong. They demonstrate a random relationship between air exchange rate and radon concentration (see fig. 7.3) whereby energy efficient tight houses as a whole are not prone to high levels of radon (Harris, 1987). This finding can be simply explained. House tightness can only make a difference in those structures having a significant source of radon nearby, mobility for the radon to move through the soil, and access of the radon to the building (see Nero et al., 1983c; Nero, 1988; NYSEO, 1989). However, under these conditions of high radon availability, even drafty houses are likely to be contaminated. The point is that the source strength, not ventilation rate, is the dominant factor in indoor radon rates.

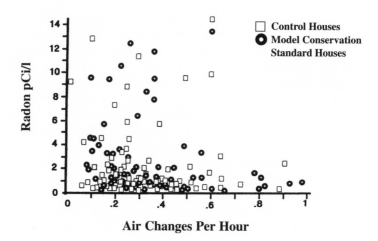

Air Changes Per Hour

Fig. 7.3   Radon concentration versus air changes per hour for energy efficient
and control houses (Source: NYSEO, 1989 [from EPA])

As further confirmation of this finding, no correlation between infiltration
and radon concentration is found in an experimental building where the source
strength is held constant and air-exchange rates are varied (see fig. 7.4). This
finding reflects the fact that source strength and air exchange are not independent of each other. For example, in reducing the air exchange rate, a tightened
house may simultaneously reduce negative pressure from the stack effect, weakening the suction that draws radon into the basement from the soil in the first

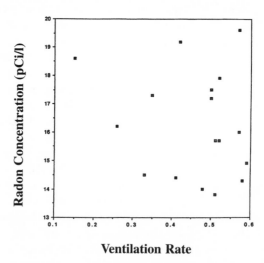

Ventilation Rate

Fig. 7.4   Radon concentration versus natural ventilation rate (in air changes
per hour) for an individual house (*Source*: NYSEO, 1989 [from LBL])

place. In other instances, tightening the house may increase radon (Nazaroff et al., 1988b). Similarly, efforts to dilute radon concentrations by increasing air exchange sometimes fail because the ventilation enhances negative pressure, sucking in more radon. The fact is that tight houses do not necessarily have a high radon level nor do leaky and drafty houses necessarily have low radon levels; it all depends on the source strength and on how much tightening reduces negative pressure. The complexity of the relationship results in the random relationship between tightness and radon concentration (NYSEO, 1989).

There remains the issue of increased risk due to tightened houses where strong source strengths are present. Studies show that existing houses made more energy efficient during the energy crisis of the 1970s reduced the air exchange rate by an average of 10 percent to 30 percent (Nero, 1983a,b). Even using a strict inverse relationship between air-exchange rates and radon levels, tightening houses by 20 percent may have increased radon levels on average by about 25 percent. Thus, a radon value of 1 pCi/l— increased by 25 percent—became, at worst, a level of 1.25 pCi/l. If we take into account that most houses are ventilated over the warmer weather, the 25 percent increase might be halved when estimating the annual average radon increase. Others have estimated a 10 percent effect due to energy conservation (Cohen, 1989a,b). Clearly, energy conservation is not to blame for the radon problem (Nero, 1983a; Nero et al., 1983). One cautionary note is in order. Tightening houses might increase concentrations in those relatively few houses having major internal sources of radon, such as through water supply or material emanation. Furthermore, other sources of indoor air pollution in the home besides radon will generally increase as houses are tightened. Maintenance of adequate ventilation rates when houses are tightened is essential. A better understanding of the interaction of energy efficiency, radon levels, and other indoor pollutants is clearly needed.

The myth of the tight house reflects a culturally biased wrong conclusion drawn from the instance of enhanced radon in some energy-conserving buildings. The problem was not conservation per se, but rather our underlying ignorance of ecological building dynamics that allowed us to tighten these buildings absent an understanding of the relationships between such factors as radon source strength, negative pressure, and ventilation rates. This very same ignorance influences the current conventional mode of building design and operation, making modern buildings generally vulnerable to radon problems, as well as other forms of indoor air pollution. Because energy efficiency and radon reduction are completely compatible if done properly (Mullen and Nevissi, 1990), the myth of the tight house further reflects an instance of lost opportunity, which in combination with the overall failure of the United States to adopt renewable energy and energy efficient approaches to building design, has had serious social and ecological ramifications. The tightening of existing buildings can both reduce radon levels and achieve the benefits of energy conservation. Both objectives are even more easily reached in new construction, as discussed later in this chapter.

The Myth of the Quick Fix

Critical to EPA's efforts to promote the mitigation of homes over 4 pCi/l is the belief that houses can be easily, cheaply, and permanently fixed, a belief based upon the myth of the quick fix.

Changing Perceptions of Mitigation

Given the extraordinary radon levels in Colebrookdale Township, it initially appeared that high radon houses were not easy to fix and that a "mitigatory-gap" was unavoidable, where methods for identification of the problem were out in front of practical solutions and professionals with the necessary expertise were rare. Furthermore, the high cost of early mitigation efforts raised fears that radon remediation would be too costly to be practicable. Perhaps as a response, a contrary view was actively promoted in Pennsylvania just after the Watras discovery (and later by EPA) that homeowners, caulking guns in hand, could conquer radon in their homes by following government self-help guidelines. By extension, the implied simplicity of the endeavor invited a range of people having virtually no applicable prior experience—from Joe the plumber to Harry the house painter—to claim to be professional radon mitigators, enjoying an easy business opportunity in an unregulated free market.

Fortunately, as we show here, the development of radon mitigation expertise over the past decade has reached beyond myth to innovation in theory and practice. While much of the early mitigation experience with radon-contaminated soil and radium residues was not applicable to radon entry from soil gas, new methods based on preventing entry or diluting radon were quickly developed by research mitigators hired by the EPA (and in the case of the Watras house, a private utility) to handle the Colebrookdale and Clinton radon clusters and other early problem houses.[1] These methods included sealing entryways, reducing negative pressure, isolating and ventilating crawlspaces, and reversing and/or diverting the flow of soil air into a house. Subslab depressurization, which emerged as the primary method, involves sealing the basement or slab openings to the soil and then venting or depressurizing under the slab by installing a pipe with a small fan to the roof. Done properly, the technique reverses the pressure difference between soil and basement preventing radon entry.[2] These methods were disseminated at symposia and training courses and quickly adopted by a newly emerging radon mitigation industry (Scott, 1988a; see chapter 8).

Evaluations of the EPA's experimental mitigation research program show good success. Table 7.1 lists the results from four major EPA mitigation research demonstrations, including the average premitigation and postmitigation radon values for all the homes for each project and the percentage reduction in radon. Considering the high initial values of the homes, the results were remarkably good.

Table 7.1   Results from EPA Mitigation Demonstrations

Demonstration program	Number of houses	Avg. radon value premitigation	Avg. radon value postmitigation	Reduction (%)
New York[a]	15	52.8	3.6	93.0
Pennsylvania[b]	34	158.5	3.6	97.7
New Jersey[c]	10	1,075.0	7.0	99.3
Tennessee[d]	13	20.3	4.1	79.8

[a] Average of immediate postmitigation measurements (Nitschke, 1989).
[b] Average of long-term postmitigation measurements, living areas in 1989 (Scott & Robertson, 1990).
[c] Average of long-term postmitigation measurements, April–July 1987 (Carvitti, 1988).
[d] Average of first floor measurements, all crawl space houses (Pyle & Williamson, 1991).

As mitigation techniques matured, affordability of mitigation also was addressed. With more than thirty thousand dollars spent to mitigate the Watras house, it was expected that radon remediation would cost tens of thousands of dollars and might render some houses unsalable. The myth of the quick fix required a cost-effective approach to mitigation that could be used by a large number of quickly trained professionals. As figure 7.5 shows, various approaches to mitigation undertaken in New York State had become cost effective by the late 1980s (NYSEO, 1989). Costs for mitigation in New Jersey were similar, with the reported radon industry average cost of $1,300 per house in 1987 dropping to $1,100 by 1989 (DePierro and Cahill, 1988; DePierro et al., 1990).[3]

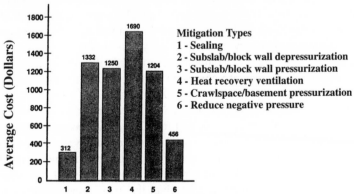

Fig. 7.5   Average cost of mitigation, NYSEO survey
(*Source*: NYSEO, 1989)

A significant factor in reducing costs in New Jersey and Pennsylvania, where the radon industry quickly outgrew the demand, was cost cutting forced by competition. A key casualty here was the virtual abandonment of radon diagnostics in favor of use of cookbook solutions, usually subslab depressurization (see chapter 8). The lack of diagnostics can make mitigations vulnerable to degradation of performance over time, since remediation was not designed on a good understanding of entry dynamics under changing conditions. Thus, the quick fix was not necessarily a sound fix.

Hardly an "Unmitigated" Success

The primary data on mitigation effectiveness come from two surveys by the New Jersey Department of Environmental Protection (DEP). Reporting on post-remediation testing in 716 homes, the first DEP survey (from January 1986 to March 1988) assessed the type and effectiveness of mitigation performed either by homeowners (sometimes with the assistance of noncertified mitigation firms) or by DEP-certified mitigation firms. Three types of mitigation were reported: soil depressurization (in 59 percent of homes), sealing alone (in 28 percent), and use of air-to-air heat exchangers (in 8 percent). In a third of the cases, homeowners performed their own mitigations, generally involving sealing. In contrast, DEP-certified firms preferred soil depressurization (accounting for 85 percent of their reported work).

Were these mitigations successful? An 80 percent reduction of radon was achieved by certified firms using soil depressurization. In contrast, only a 27 percent reduction occurred for homeowners using only sealing. Surprisingly, based on a short-term screening measurement taken on the lowest livable floor, 64 percent of all homes still exceeded 4 pCi/l after remediation, while 36 percent still exceeded 8 pCi/l. Perhaps of even more concern was the fact that 52 percent of homes still having levels over 4 pCi/l were mitigated by DEP-certified firms! As expected, sealing alone and air-to-air heat exchangers were least effective (dropping homes below 4 pCi/l only 15–23 percent of the time) even though these homes had lower radon levels to start with. These results are even more disturbing when they are compared with voluntary reports by DEP-certified firms for 942 homes mitigated in 1987 claiming that 89 percent of the remediated homes were reduced below 4 pCi/l (DePierro and Cahill, 1988).

A follow-up DEP survey conducted for 473 mitigations covering the period between April 1988 and November 1989 revealed improvement in the overall success rate of mitigations: 56 percent of all mitigated buildings were found to be below 4 pCi/l as opposed to 36 percent in the previous study. However, success was not found across the board. Much of the improvement was due to DEP-certified firms, where the success rate increased from 48 percent to 78 percent for all methods of remediation. In contrast, homeowners and noncertified firms did not enhance their success rate of 36 percent. For each of the four methods studied (sealing only, soil depressurization, air-to-air heat exchangers, and "other"), DEP-certified firms typically had a 30 to 40 percent higher success rate compared to noncertified firms and homeowners. Furthermore, in the new survey, noncertified firms and homeowners performed an even larger percentage of all mitigations (52 percent versus 47 percent), and sealing only became even more popular (35 percent versus 28 percent). Over-reporting of success by certified firms was still common in the second survey. Certified firms reported a success rate of 96 percent, significantly in excess of the 78 percent success actually shown in postmitigation testing (DePierro et al., 1990).

The DEP surveys may be interpreted various ways. Optimistically, by 1989 certified firms in New Jersey appear to have made large improvements in their success rate while achieving a 15 percent drop in cost. Increased experience, knowledge, and the DEP technology transfer program may account for this improvement. The effects of competition in a tightening radon market may also be a factor. On the other hand, 44 percent of all attempts at mitigation failed in the fourth year of the nation's most advanced state radon program. Even a 78 percent success rate by certified firms is short of what one would hope for in a maturing industry. Also, because the DEP survey lumped homeowners and noncertified firms together, it is not possible to distinguish the effect of certification on success rate. Thus, it is impossible to evaluate the success of the DEP's certification program and the advantages of mandatory certification from these studies. Furthermore, the large difference between reported and actual success by certified firms is not readily explainable and raises questions about industry ethics. Finally, postremediation testing took place relatively soon after mitigation and, therefore, does not measure the long-term success of mitigation, which is likely to be even less than measured in this research.

The warnings inherent in the DEP survey are echoed by other research findings. A radon reduction demonstration study in New York found that several different mitigation strategies were often needed to reduce radon levels and that subslab depressurization did not always succeed (Nitschke et al., 1988). The latter finding was amplified by a northwest follow-up study of radon mitigation that found failure of subslab depressurization systems over time due to many physical reasons: fans broke, pipes leaked, and cracks from foundation settling or openings from failed caulking occurred. Significantly, reasons for the failure reached beyond improper installation techniques and material failures to include simple homeowner interventions. Thus, people changed the way they operated their houses, closed crawl space vents, or shut the fans off because of noise or vibration, to save electricity, or because they didn't understand the mitigation system. Regardless of the cause, as the depressurization field was reduced in these buildings, radon entry increased (Prill et al., 1988). Similarly, an EPA follow-up study on thirty-four subslab depressurization systems found the systems to perform reliably, except when fans failed (in five instances) or when homeowner intervention occurred (EPA, 1990d; Findlay et al., 1991). What is significant about these studies is that, even when mitigation worked initially, radon levels often did not stay at postmitigation levels. Rather, performance degraded over time due to a mixture of physical and behavioral conditions!

Such questions about mitigation did not escape attention. Senator Patrick Moynihan charged EPA with misleading the public through its simplistic publications, such as the mitigation booklet entitled *Radon Reduction Methods—A Homeowner's Guide* (EPA, 1986). He cited the contrasting disclaimer contained in EPA technical papers, that no two houses are alike due to radon source and building construction, to support his argument that mitigation can be both expensive and difficult (Moynihan, 1987). At his insistence, Congress moved to require EPA to report on the effectiveness of mitigation techniques annually. Instructively, the revision of the EPA pamphlet was entitled a *Consumer's Guide to Radon Reduction: How to Reduce Levels in Your Home* (EPA, 1992f).

While the myth of the quick fix was being challenged, perhaps the most central realization about mitigation has not been addressed. Despite important advances in the techniques that may successfully reduce radon levels at mitigation, there will always be uncertainty about how long these radon reductions will last. A process of long-term testing and reremediation work will be needed if radon levels are to be kept low over time. Mitigation is not a one-step event.

Impacts on Mitigation from Testing Uncertainty

The difficulties surrounding testing (described in chapter 6) affect mitigation, both in terms of whether homeowners have sufficient faith in the results to feel compelled to undertake remediation and also in the ability of professionals to determine whether and what degree of mitigation may be required. EPA guidelines (1992f) offer many reasons to delay action with radon results under 10 pCi/l. Inaction can be rationalized when tests have been taken under closed-house conditions, yet windows are open for almost half the year; when the family spends much time upstairs or away; or if one is aware of measurement uncertainty of 50 to 100 percent or more for quick tests. Such validity questions, augmented by the potential for fraud, also pose difficulties for realty transfer. Even verifying that mitigation has been successful depends on reliable radon test results, a challenge at lower radon levels below 8 pCi/l. The same problem exists for new construction, with desired radon levels of less than 1.5–2.0 pCi/l. In both instances, confidence in professional mitigators is an additional issue. In chapter 8 we address the evolution of the mitigation profession and, in chapter 10, the growing quasi-regulation of the field, including EPA's Radon Contractor Proficiency program.

Can Mitigation Reach Lower pCi/l Levels?

For mitigation to achieve its goal of reducing health risks, it has to be applied to the large number of homes at or around 4 pCi/l besides the smaller number of homes greater than this value. EPA has concluded that the costs of active soil depressurization systems discourage mitigation around the radon guidance value, concluding that other innovative low-cost mitigation technology "will be required if lung cancer deaths due to radon are to be reduced by more than about 14 to 22%" (EPA, 1991b, p. 2). While accounting for the bulk of the health risk, there is no experience with trying to achieve ambient levels, and rough estimates indicate that it might cost ten thousand to sixteen thousand dollars per household to do so (Nero et al., 1990). Therefore, it must be concluded that the ambient level is not achievable economically, and probably not technically, as of this publication. Accordingly, the mitigation technology of the 1980s and 1990s must be considered only as transitional. New, more powerful and cheaper means are needed if we are to achieve ambient radon levels and significantly reduce the radon health problem.

Conclusions Regarding the Myth of the Quick Fix

There are still many questions about radon mitigation. Clearly, the means are at hand to address higher radon levels in houses; yet, the mitigation industry's track record leaves much to be desired. Considerable work is needed to address the lower radon levels that account for the bulk of the risk. Suggested is that a considerable number of mitigations are being conducted with inappropriate technologies. Moreover, given that components of mitigation systems have limited lifetimes and require periodic maintenance, and that houses change over time, any mitigated building will require continued testing, perhaps yearly, and is likely to require ongoing intervention over time to maintain lower radon levels. While these conclusions are clearly established by research to date, expectations of periodic monitoring and update have never been created. Instead, under the myth of the quick fix, mitigation is viewed as a one-shot event.

Radon Resistant New Construction

One other nagging issue remains for our examination in this chapter. Should we continue to build buildings that will attract soil gas, enhancing the need for eventual mitigation of radon, when we alternatively could alter our design and construction of new buildings to be radon resistant from the start? Can we achieve radon-free buildings and, if so, why haven't we done so?

Prospects for Radon-Free Construction Methods

The principles used to achieve radon-resistant new construction come from our basic knowledge of radon entry and mitigation. It is well established that we can prevent radon entry by constructing buildings prepared for subslab ventilation by providing good permeability (four inches of gravel) under the slab, by sealing connections between soil and basement, by building in an active or passive subslab system, and by reducing negative pressure. If these concepts work for retrofitted houses, they should be even easier for new construction.

Benefits of Radon-Proof Design over Postconstruction Mitigation

Research confirms the feasibility of building conventional homes to be radonproof. Thus, a Colorado study of eighty nine homes (Burkhart and Kladder, 1991) suggests that such radon-resistant new construction performs significantly better than mitigation of existing houses. Even with their active systems turned off, houses built with radonproof construction averaged less radon (9.9 pCi/l) than did existing unmitigated homes (12.3 pCi/l). When these existing houses were mitigated, they showed impressive improvements (dropping to 1.7 pCi/l on average). However, when fans were activated in the radon-resistant buildings, even more dramatic results were obtained, dropping to essentially ambient levels (0.93 pCi/l).[4] These results suggest that radon-resistant construction for all new houses is necessary in order to drop radon levels to ambient levels (0.5–1.0 pCi/l), as specified by the Radon Reduction Act of 1988.

Large builders also experimented with the feasibility of radon-proof construction. In Virginia and Maryland, Ryan Homes incorporated a package of radon-resistant features into its new homes. Postconstruction radon measurements in ninety two of the houses indicated that 30 percent still had more than 4 pCi/l in a livable space. An inspection of nineteen of the houses suggested that the quality of installation might have been partly to blame for the poor performance of the systems. In contrast, a more extensive radon-proofing effort by Garnet Homes reported an average of 0.67 pCi/l for the first twenty two houses built with their package, with a range of values spanning 0.0 to 1.4 pCi/l (Osborne 1988).

Costs of Radon-Proof Construction

Beyond technical feasibility, however, the costs of this approach must be low enough to gain acceptance. Several large-scale national homebuilders have incorporated radon-resistant construction guidelines for their homes. The Ryan Homes project noted above added only $200 to the cost of a home. The "Radon Abatement Package" made available by Garnet Homes, in the northern Virginia area, offered sealing ($260), negative pressure control ($664), and an active subslab suction system ($437) at a total cost of $1,361. Other builder packages for radon-resistant construction typically have similar costs (Spears and Novak, 1988). EPA has estimated an average cost of building passive radon-resistant features into new houses of about $300 to $400, while activating the subslab depressurization system with a fan adds another $220 to $300 (EPA, 1990d).[5]

Beyond the initial cost of radonproofing, there are energy and economic drawbacks to current mitigation practices that would also apply to radon-resistant new construction. Given that active systems cost approximately $135 per year for energy and fan replacement, the installation of active systems in one million new homes per year could exceed five billion dollars over thirty years (Saum 1991a). Cumulatively, there is a considerable amount of energy, cost, and pollution associated with the 11 to 12 percent increase in the average residential energy consumption due to the use of active radon-reduction technology. These costs could be minimized if passive (stack-effect driven) instead of active (fan-driven) depressurization was used, a consideration ignored by EPA in its decision to promote active mitigation. In lobbying for a passive approach based upon energy savings, Brennan recalled that he was disturbed by the thought that seventy watt fans running in a half million new homes would demand enough energy for "a small nuke" (Brennan, 1991).

However, it has been argued that passive stack performance is not as reliable as is active mitigation, even in new construction (Henschel, 1988; Nitschke, 1989; Saum and Osborne, 1990). Passive stacks have shown partial success (Nitschke, 1989; Grisham, 1991). An EPA-funded study in 1989–1990 compared passive to active stack performance in new homes (Saum and Osborne, 1990). Passive stacks were able to achieve radon reductions averaging 66 percent. When a forty-five-watt fan was added, the average performance of the sub-slab depressurization systems reached 98 percent, achieving an average radon level of 0.4 pCi/l—essentially ambient outdoor levels (Saum, 1991b). Based upon such findings, EPA analysis (1992a) suggests that more lives are saved with active than passive systems (fifty and thirty lives per year, respectively).

A compromise between active and passive approaches might involve an assisted passive stack, employing only a ten-watt fan, four inches of aggregate under the slab, and well-sealed penetrations. The assisted passive stack would boost passive performance from 65 percent to around 90 percent radon reduction while reducing homeowner costs from $135 to $29 per year (Saum, 1991b). Another possibility would combine passive/active venting by running a fan intermittently depending upon the pressure in the stack. For new construction with an appropriately designed and constructed system, this hybrid approach is likely to reduce fan-related energy costs considerably and to assure low radon levels during times when passive venting alone would not work. In any case, EPA finally began to consider the energy trade-offs of active mitigation, coming to support Brennan's original analysis in favor of passive systems (EPA, 1992a; Harrison, 1991).

Achieving Ecological Design through Innovative Buildings

While the above results suggest that conventional home design can be made radon proof, there is a potential for merging radon-proof construction with other innovations in housing design, such as energy efficiency. An ecological house-systems approach can simultaneously and cost effectively achieve energy efficiency, durability, and healthy indoor air. This approach was demonstrated by the 1991 winner of the EPA Innovative Design Competition. Robert Nuess designed and built his own two-story, 1,780-square-foot house for a cold (over 6,880 degree days) Spokane, Washington, climate. The house is an air-tight superinsulated structure with significant passive solar gain (the space heats up directly from entering sunlight). As figure 7.6 shows, the air in the living space was sealed but not insulated from the crawl space. In heating mode, air is pushed by a small fan from the living space to the crawl space (pressuring the crawl space and preventing radon entry), through an air-to-air heat recovery ventilator (to recover heat), and finally out to a roof vent. In the summer, the system removes heat from the air supply and uses it for water heating (with excess hot air vented to the outside). A small commercially available heating, ventilating, and air conditioning device was used to provide continuous proper ventilation, partial space heating, space cooling, water heating, moisture control, and radon control. Radon levels in the living area upstairs were dropped from 12 pCi/l with the system off to less than 1 pCi/l with the ventilation system on. The crawl space dropped from 120.0 pCi/l to 2.5 pCi/l when the system was activated. And the costs of the entire system were covered by an energy payback of between ten and twenty years, based upon a total heating cost of $216 per year as compared to $596 for the average well-insulated electrically heated home served by the Bonneville Power Authority (Nuess and Prill, 1991).

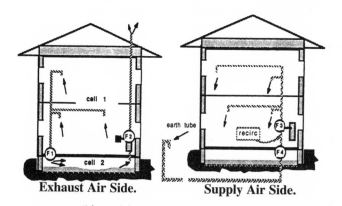

Exhaust Air Side.   Supply Air Side.

Fig. 7.6   Schematic of the Nuess house design. F1, F2, F3, and F4 are fan locations (*Source*: Nuess and Prill, 1991)

Such innovative designs also suggest techniques that can be applied to more conventional buildings. Some researchers have speculated that providing a curtain of air between the soil and the foundation vented to outside air would prevent the entry of soil air (Brennan and Osborne, 1988). While this idea has never been tested, there are commercial drainage materials that could provide the necessary curtain of air. A more detailed double-barrier approach which seals both between the foundation and soil and between the foundation and house has also been suggested (see fig. 7.7). A small porous volume is created between the two barriers that may be passively vented or actively pressurized or depressurized if needed (Kunz, 1991).

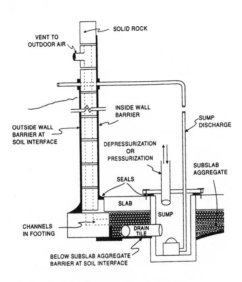

Fig. 7.7   Schematic of double barrier design for basement slab house
(*Source*: Kunz, 1991)

While active systems do reduce radon levels quite successfully, the ideal radon solution would still be a long-lived passive barrier of some type, thereby eliminating energy and ongoing maintenance costs. Yet the perfect passive radon barrier has not yet been built, and we do not know if it can be done and at what cost. And even if it were possible, could commercial firms succeed in building it? Clearly, there is the potential for better radon technology and innovation in passive and hybrid approaches if research support from the EPA or DOE is directed toward that end.

Conclusions on Methods for Radon-Proof Construction

In short, it is possible to design conventional new homes that will attract less radon and allow control of the rest, but the real challenge is to design integrated ecological buildings that solve multiple problems and pay for themselves through energy savings.

Achieving Acceptance in the Building Industry

All of the best techniques on paper will do little to change housing. Low-radon building techniques need to be disseminated to builders, accepted, and then put into practice. They need to reach three groups of builders—the small-scale local builder, the specialized builder concerned with factors such as energy efficiency, and the large-scale national builders. Despite the obvious importance of addressing new construction, these changes have been surprisingly slow in coming.

There are many "small" builders, each erecting twenty or less homes per year, who cumulatively account for about 40 percent of the homes constructed in the United States. For several reasons, these builders have resisted addressing radon. Beyond the newness of the issue and the need for education, there is a natural aversion to viewing something that one has built as being dangerous. Furthermore, an abstract environmental health risk that may occur twenty years down the line is hard to rank above the builders' primary concerns, namely to assure the structural integrity of the building and, in doing so, to aesthetically please the client as well. Radon-proof construction entails additional costs that have to be passed on to the buyer, not an asset in a competitive sales market, particularly if there is not appreciable buyer concern over radon. It has not been clear whether builder liability would be greater having attempted and failed with radon proofing than having ignored it. Finally, small builders are hard to reach with new information because they tend to be independent and to learn by apprenticeship, rather than a central educational source that can disseminate radon information. Local building associations represent one avenue of disseminating radon information about how to respond once radon is discovered locally (Brennan, 1988; Osborne, 1988).

In contrast, specialized builders focused on energy efficiency have proven to be a group naturally interested in experimentation with radon prevention. Beyond innovating in their own homes, as the Nuess house described above illustrates, they have made major contributions to the young mitigation industry, using the new field as a way to compensate for slowdowns in general building and the de-emphasis upon energy-efficient housing. Instructively, a number of progressive associations, including the New England Substainable Energy Association Quality Building Council and the Midwest Energy Efficient Builders Association, were concerned about radon and other indoor air pollutants even prior to the discovery of high radon in homes (Brennan, 1988).

The bulk of U.S. homes is built by a few large builders utilizing factory panelized houses shipped to the site. These large builders tend to be concerned with the problems of development, such as receiving approvals to build, rather than with the details of building construction, which they tend to standardize. Furthermore, at their scale of construction, even a modest additional cost per unit for radon proofing adds up to an impressive sum. As a result, they have a natural resistance to voluntary action on radon. However, in contrast to small contractors, large builders have a more developed central capacity for sharing information. The experience of one builder in finding significant radon levels in finished buildings within a half-built development taught the entire industry that costs for radon-free construction were preferable to those from the delay and uncertainty associated with radon testing and after-the-fact mitigation. As noted previously, large builders, such as Ryan, Garnet, and Ryland, have led the building industry in developing voluntary, radon-free construction measures (Brennan, 1988; Spears and Nowak, 1988).[6]

As a result of the concerns of large builders, the National Association of Home Builders (NAHB) became actively concerned with radon (Brennan, 1988). Through its National Research Center, the NAHB cooperated with EPA on the development of construction guidelines, set up a radon clearinghouse and hotline for the building industry, developed radon seminars, instituted a tracking system for identifying radon-reducing construction techniques, and began to draft model building codes for addressing radon (Spears, 1988). The NAHB has also moved to join other construction industry organizations to create the industry-wide Radon Information Council (VanLaningham, 1988). Independently, the American Society of Testing and Materials (ASTM) began preparing specifications for radon-proof construction along the lines of interim guidelines prepared by EPA (*RIR*, August 1989e).

The involvement of the NAHB and the large builders with radon served to preemptively shape and limit the impacts of radon requirements on building construction. Criticizing the efficacy of soil tests, they sought to escape responsibility for predicting hot spots. They further argued that builders not be saddled with either preoccupancy or postoccupancy testing requirements, citing the limitations of screening measurements, as well as the hardship for builders and the risk of driving up construction loans from both long-term testing or placing radon contingency funds into escrow accounts. Given that radon problems are found in a small minority of houses, furthermore, the NAHB argued that the overall costs of radon testing in new housing are unjustified in light of the limitations of testing. The NAHB also sought to limit the builder's responsibility for radon avoidance. Although recommending the use of construction techniques that limit radon levels, the NAHB has argued that it is impossible to truly warrant a house as safe from radon because this would require nonexistent "foolproof" construction techniques. Noting that radon problems do not necessarily affect the price of a home and that mitigation is a minimal expense in light of the purchase price for most buildings, the builders' organization argued that testing should become the buyer's responsibility, to be done over time after a building's purchase. The new owner would then assume the costs of any mitigation themselves (Ethier, 1988; *RIR*, August 1989f; Spears, 1988; Harrison, 1991).

Perhaps the major obstacle to widespread adoption of radon-resistant construction is the need for it to be incorporated into the wide number of building codes and other regulatory standards affecting the building industry. As discussed in chapter 10, the desirability of several proposed radon codes became a matter of debate rather than action. Proponents of incorporating radon-resistant construction in building codes argue that they are needed to assure health, safety, and economic value; that the approach is cheaper than fixing houses after they are built; that they are needed to assure radon levels much below 4 pCi/l; and that such systems will reduce long-term operating costs by reducing heat losses from the house (from better sealing) and reduced fan energy usage (by allowing passive venting, smaller fans, or perhaps intermittent fan operation) compared to homes that are built without radon resistance. Also, radon control adds to durability, safety, moisture control, comfort, and energy efficiency, all of which have economic value. Since there is no way to predict what the radon levels will be in a newly constructed house, even in a designated "low-risk area," building in radon resistance to every house makes sense in light of the ambient level national goal. It is also argued that present technology, while not perfect, offers effective, affordable, and readily available measures that would achieve levels well below 4 pCi/l.

Opponents to codes argue that, at a cost of $600–$900 per house, it would be cheaper to build houses and mitigate them afterward, even if 50 percent of the houses were over 4 pCi/l. They also claim that better and cheaper technology may be available in the near future so it is premature to act now. Of course, there are also the usual arguments that the building techniques and testing requirements are too complicated and a burden to builders already saddled with too many regulations. Others argue that the currrently proposed codes will not be effective in reducing radon levels because the prescriptive options do not require testing or mitigation and poor quality construction will not be caught.

Indeed, there is a certain truth to the arguments of both sides. Should codes be adopted now only to be changed in the near future? If the long-term goal of achieving ambient radon levels is taken seriously, the argument for radon-resistant construction now is compelling. If technological breakthroughs are imminent, then postponing action may be wise. The proposed codes allow flexibility so that builders can optimize costs, invent innovative systems, receive detailed guidance, and reduce legal responsibility—depending upon which set of concerns predominate. Nonetheless, the introduction of codes has been painstakingly slow (see chapter 10).

Conclusion Regarding Radon Prevention

In our view, the challenges of radon mitigation point in every way to the desirability of preventing radon exposure in the design and construction of new buildings. However, the myth of the quick fix, widely accepted and promoted in Washington, has the reverse effect. Ironically, the myth invites perception that the problem need not be prevented from the start. After all, this inflated view of mitigation suggests that excessive radon can always be found and corrected later.

Mitigation of Domestic Water Supply

While our concern is primarily with radon in air, it is noteworthy that the myth of the quick fix has affected mitigation of waterborne radon, as well. Average radon levels in groundwater supplies in the United States are around 750 pCi/l (NYSEO, 1989). Serious issues affect both competing techniques for removal of radon from water.

Granular activated carbon has been used since the early 1980s as a technique for removing both radon and radon daughters from water (Lowry and Lowry, 1988). Evaluations of the charcoal filter show that the approach works well, with typically a greater than 99 percent removal of radon and daughters. While the activated carbon approach is not inexpensive, the units are expected to have a lifetime exceeding ten years and operation and maintenance costs are negligible (NYSEO, 1989).[7]

Unfortunately, carbon filter technology suffers from radioactive buildup in the filter. Specifically, gamma radiation levels increase from the accumulation of the short-lived radon daughters. In the relatively few houses having water radon levels in excess of 10,000 pCi/l, gamma radiation given off by the filter system may exceed background gamma radiation, even several feet from the charcoal canister! If the canister is located in or adjacent to a living area, a serious problem of radiation exposure may result. The exposure issue is avoided if the canister is installed in a remote location or if it is encapsulated in a water vessel. Additionally, removal of old canisters must be done carefully. Before disposal, the removed canister must sit in a remote location for four weeks to allow for decay of 99 percent of the short-lived radioactivity (NYSEO, 1989; Henschel, 1988). However, even then, there is a further problem involving disposal of the spent canister. Filters are affected by the long-term buildup of lead 210, with a 21-year half-life, and its two shorter lived daughters, bismuth 210 with a 5-day half-life and polonium 210 with a 138-day half-life (Lowry, 1988). As a result, these filters are likely to be defined as low-level radioactive wastes in many states, requiring special disposal (Henschel, 1988).[8]

A competing technology involves the use of aeration units to agitate the water under atmospheric pressure, with the radon that outgases released to the atmosphere through a roof vent. There are several well-developed aeration technologies for large public water supplies, but small units suitable for household use have only been recently developed.[9] New multistaged, diffused-aeration systems achieve greater than 99.9 percent removal of radon, but their cost is high (around $2,200). Operating costs associated with aeration include the need to repressurize the water and the modest electrical operating costs from the operation of a pump and fan (NYSEO, 1989). Removal of high iron and manganese deposits in the water through pretreatment may be required to prevent deposits from clogging the unit (Henschel, 1988).

Thus, the quick and cheap fix for waterborne radon involves granular activated carbon, yet the gamma ray buildup and canister disposal problems are serious drawbacks. Aeration offers an approach that can reach the high levels of treatment demanded by the proposed radon-in-water standard. However, the costs are not appropriate to small applications. Thus, no quick and cheap method exists for cleansing water of radon.

Conclusions: Implications for Myths Related to Radon Transfer

A holistic understanding of the relationship of buildings, their occupants, and their surroundings is required to appreciate the dynamics of radon entry. Simplistic assumptions about isolated factors affecting entry have contributed to the persistent myths of radon that this chapter questions. Our review of radon transfer shows that buildings do not merely passively accumulate radon that happens to be passing through surrounding soil. Rather, our houses, appliances and activities serve to actively pump soil gas and collect it indoors. The recognition that radon is actually a human-caused and technological hazard challenges the myth of blameless radon.

Conversely, the myth of the tight house blames radon problems on one specialized form of technology, energy conserving building practices. This myth has served to dissuade people from taking steps to improve the energy efficiency of their houses or to build new homes designed for energy conservation. We have established that it is possible to have both energy conservation and radon-resistant construction. In fact, good design and construction practice that handles drainage and water problems, that tightens houses with particular care at the upper levels, that provides solutions to negative pressures generated by combustion appliances and fans, and that provides controlled ventilation, is completely compatible with radon control measures. Builder/mitigator Terry Brennan notes that good construction practices mean low radon levels. Energy conserving homes, if intelligently done, will also be radon-resistant buildings. It is only when the building designs reflect an ignorance of ecological building dynamics that problems are encountered. Such problems are evident in poorly thought out and constructed buildings, regardless of their levels of energy efficiency.

Finally, we have explored the myth of the quick fix. Radon mitigation represents one of the most successful areas of development in the entire radon field. Spurred by concerns of a mitigatory gap, EPA developed a model that allowed the very few real radon mitigation experts to correct hot houses while developing generalizable methods available for the private mitigation industry. The development and dissemination of techniques has been remarkably effective and fast. EPA has moved on to also consider the more complex problem of mitigating schools and public buildings. Thus, in many respects, mitigation is a radon success story. The availability of an affordable radon cure gives credibility to the policy that individuals be encouraged to reduce radon levels in their homes.

But while these early radon experiments were carefully evaluated, the subsequent success of mitigation in the field has been poorly assessed. And the few studies that report on long-term success rates of mitigation are disturbing. As we have seen, the long-term and sometimes the short-term success of mitigation by the radon industry has not always been adequately demonstrated. We do not know the real extent to which practice has lagged behind the development of effective techniques. We find that the promise of mitigation as a one-shot cure also is probably a myth.

Four major challenges to how we think about mitigation emerge from our observations of radon policy in practice.

- First, it is likely that mitigated houses will require ongoing monitoring, periodic testing, and system maintenance and adjustment over time.
- Second, cost represents a barrier to mitigation. Present technology is too expensive to represent a realistic solution for homeowners who must voluntarily decide to mitigate. The present emphasis on active systems with their attendant high-energy and economic costs also needs to be reexamined, and research on low-cost innovative passive and hybrid methods needs to be expanded.
- Third, today's active systems generally do not appear to bring radon levels in homes close to ambient levels. Thus, even if the mitigatory gap has been closed regarding meeting the 4 pCi/l EPA guidance, we are far from achieving Congress's goal of no more radon indoors than is found outside.
- A fourth challenge is that relatively few people, finding radon levels greater than 4 pCi/l, choose to mitigate. To close the mitigatory gap for radon requires not only the provision of enough mitigators, remediation methods, and equipment, but also public confidence in the quality of testing and mitigation as a protective package at an acceptable price. Given that risk is associated with long-term exposure, the notion of waiting for better and cheaper remedial techniques is not irrational.

In sum, many of the key issues with mitigation rest on doubts that the existing technology can provide effective long-term reduction of radon at acceptable cost, doubts about the quality of testing results and mitigation, and perhaps a general public disbelief of the seriousness of the radon issue itself. Secondly, the mythical need to construe radon as a blameless hazard (see chapter 10) has abetted the government's denial of the importance of new construction. Along with

other forms of property transfer, new construction is an area where radon exposure can be regulated. The reluctance to move on this regulatory handle reflects
as much the initial ideology of radon programming as it does the problems encountered in implementing regulation of new construction, including dissemination of radon codes. In both the areas of new construction and remediation,
thorough monitoring of the long-term success of mitigation in the field is necessary to bridge the mitigatory gap for radon. Without confidence in an accessible
remedy, public reluctance to test and remediate is understandable.

In the next section, we turn from the myths of radon science to the tenets of
Reaganomics, examining this second context for the geologic radon issue.

Notes

1. Other methods that remove radon or radon daughters after they enter a house
were developed, although such methods never received EPA approval (Henschel, 1988;
EPA, 1992f).

2. In some cases, particularly when radon levels were only slightly elevated, it was
found that sealing alone and/or reducing driving forces could reduce radon levels.

3. It is notable that the affordability of radon mitigation is generally discussed in
terms of short-term individual costs. Yet, the emphasis on active system depressurization
has significant long-term costs. These include the long-term energy and economic costs
associated with continuously running an eighty-watt fan, as well as heat loss due to air
exhausted from the house and fan replacement costs. At an estimated cost of $135 per
year for operation, the some four million single-family dwellings above 4 pCi/l would
entail a cumulative cost of perhaps $20 billion over thirty years (see Saum, 1991a).

4. Other experiments with radon-resistant new construction include several EPA
jointly funded research projects to evaluate radon-resistant construction options on new
houses. These include a fifteen-house project with the New York State Energy Research
and Development Authority (NYSERDA), and one-hundred-house project with the New
Jersey Department of Community Affairs, the New Jersey Builders Association, New
Jersey Central Power and Light Company, and the National Research Center of the National Association of Home Builders. In addition, EPA instituted a New Construction
House Evaluation Program (NEWHEP), which includes builders from around the country (Osborne, 1988; Murane, 1988).

5. The costs listed are actually in fairly close agreement. EPA ignores controlling
negative pressure, which may not improve performance. Sealed combustion appliances
and reducing negative pressure often may be justified on other grounds such as energy
efficiency and safety.

6. Ryan dealt with the radon problem by adding a roughed-in subslab system to its
new buildings at a cost of $230 per house; Ryland spent $500–600 per house on a passive stack ventilation system.

7. In the early 1990s, one filter was recommended for water supplies with less than 5,000 pCi/l at a cost of between $800 and $1,200 and two filters for water supplies over 5,000 pCi/l at a cost between $1,600–2,000.

8. It has been suggested that charcoal filters might be replaced as soon as they approach the state-defined limits for radioactive waste disposal. Depending upon the radon level in the water supply, this could require much more frequent changes than the projected ten-year lifetime, and make the charcoal filter option much less viable. Two other concerns with the charcoal filter deserve note: (1) the potential for biological growth in the charcoal if the organic content of the water is high and (2) high manganese and iron levels in the water supply that can affect filter operation (Henschel, 1988).

9. There are several different types of aeration devices, including packed-tower aerators, diffused-bubble aerators, and spray aerators. While these types have been used for larger water supplies for some time, the technology is now being downscaled for use in individual homes. The state-of-the-art for small systems is, therefore, in rapid flux.

Part III

Testing the Tenets of Reaganomics

Chapter 8

The Myth of the Market Solution:
The Private Sector Response to Radon

> Many persons who have remained in the industry despite the current severe
> recession are discussing whether to hold on a little while longer in the hope
> that the competition will succumb before they do, or whether to begin a
> strike against the increasing government regulation of the industry.
> —David Saum

In this chapter, we explore the development of the radon industry that has been
so central to EPA's nonregulatory and decentralized response to radon. The EPA
approach elevated radon's significance as an environmental health threat while
avoiding federal responsibility by shifting the burden to the public. This strategy
left to the private sector the primary responsibility for mobilizing to provide radon services. As a result, radon became an instant "growth industry." Starting
nearly from scratch, well more than one thousand primary and a host of secondary radon service companies appeared within five years after the Colebrookdale
Township discovery. This dependence upon the private sector as the agent of
government policy was also evident on the state level. Facing an estimated cost
for radon testing and remediation of nearly a billion dollars, New Jersey turned
to the private sector. Within one year, the number of testing firms in the state increased from two to more than seventy (Deieso, 1987) and by three years to two
hundred radon measurement firms and nearly one hundred mitigation firms. Indeed, this type of explosive growth generally characterized the early radon industry.

Creation and Mobilization of a Radon
Industry through 1989

But where did this instant industry come from? Testing firms were required to
screen homes for high radon values or, alternatively, to characterize the long-
term radon risk for the home. The rudiments of a testing industry already existed at the point of the Colebrookdale Township discovery, spurred by the earlier
human-caused radon problems and by other radiation monitoring needs. The alpha track detector had already been developed and put onto the market by industry and the low-cost charcoal canister had been developed for government use by
the Department of Energy. Other more complex measurement techniques exist-

173

ed; some focused upon radon and some upon radon's daughters. Furthermore, an entire branch of physics—health physics—had evolved around instrumentation for radiation. In sum, both the technology and the expertise were present to anchor the dissemination of radon testing.

The case of remediation was quite different, threatening a "mitigatory gap," where identified remediation needs could not be met because of a lag in technology for reducing radon levels or a lack of trained mitigation professionals. The earlier mill tailings experience served as a poor technological model because of the emphasis upon soil removal. And the building-oriented radon mitigation experience in Colebrookdale was mixed, with many homes needing further remediation and testing after modest success with early experimental approaches. Additionally, costs were prohibitive, varying from $35,000 spent on the Watras home to a range between $4,300 and $15,700 in the EPA eighteen-home study. Subsequently, EPA estimated that, depending upon the mitigation technique, it would cost as little as $300 and as much as $5,500 to have existing buildings privately remediated.[1]

Furthermore, where was the required diagnosis and mitigation expertise to come from? Other than a few experimental researchers at Princeton University and at government facilities such as Lawrence Berkeley Labs, there were only a few pockets of expertise in this area. The energy crisis had spawned concern for indoor air contamination among some builders specializing in energy efficient housing. Remediation of the human-caused radon problem had proved a training ground for a few. As a result, researchers in Canada, New York State, Washington State, and Colorado had developed some experimental field expertise in mitigating radon levels in buildings. But there were literally only a handful of qualified mitigators at the time of the Colebrookdale discovery.

Profile of an Emerging Industry

In order to understand the origins and key characteristics of this nascent industry, a content analysis was conducted of listings submitted by companies for inclusion in the *Radon Industry Directory, 1989* (1988), covering both testing and mitigation firms.

Radon Testing Firms

The directory lists 1,450 firms involved in radon detection. A quarter of these identified themselves as operating nationally, another 5 percent operated in more than ten states, and the remaining firms operated at a regional or local level.[2] When firms operating at less than national scope are listed by state (see table 8.1), we see a direct relationship between the development of the radon testing industry and the development of state programs (as discussed in chapter 11), both being driven by data revealing high radon levels in a given state.

Table 8.1 Number of Radon Testing and Mitigation Firms Listed in the 1989 *Radon Industry Directory* by State

Number	Testing firms	Mitigation firms
200+	Pa., N.J.	
150–199	N.Y.	
100–149	Colo., Conn., Md., Va.	Pa.
50–99	Del., D.C., Fla., Ga., Ill., Ky., Mass., N.C., Ohio, R.I., Vt.	N.J.
25–49	Calif., Ind., Iowa, Kans., Maine, Mich., Mo., S.C., Wash., W. Va., Wyo.	Colo., N.Y., Md., Va.
10–24	Ala., Ariz., Idaho, La., Minn., Mont., Nebr., Nev., N. Mex., N. Dak., Oreg., S. Dak., Tex., Utah, Wis.	Conn., Del., D.C., Fla., Ga., Ill., Ind., Iowa, Ky., Maine, Mass., Mo., N.H., N.C., N. Dak., Ohio, R.I., Tenn.
0–9	Alaska, Ark., Hawaii, Miss., Okla., P.R., V.I.	Ala., Alaska, Ariz., Ark., Calif., Hawaii, Idaho, Kans., La., Mich., Minn., Miss., Mont., Nebr., Nev., N. Mex., Okla., Oreg., P.R., S.C., S.Dak., Tex., Utah, Vt., V.I., Wash., W. Va., Wis., Wyo.

Note: Excludes national firms.

The EPA voluntary radon measurement proficiency program (RMP), begun in 1986, provides a further indication of this meteoric growth of the radon testing industry. In the first year of the program, 35 companies participated, with 42 in the second. By 1988, 1,000 companies participated in the program (Gearo, 1988). By 1989, 1,568 firms participated; the EPA RMP report listed 700 primary testing firms, as well as some 7,000 secondary testing firms (RIR, February 1990a; Jalbert et al., 1991). Some two-thirds of these firms appear to have been new enterprises focused on geologic radon. From the corporate names of the remaining firms, it would appear that they were probably existing professional firms that expanded into radon testing (see table 8.2). Of these crossover firms, more than a third were already involved in environmental testing, another third in the overall area of building inspection services, and the remainder comprised of construction firms, pest control services, energy conservation companies, heating and ventilation firms, and university and government testing efforts.

Table 8.2   Approximation of Professions Crossing over into Radon Testing and Mitigation Work

Type of Crossover firm	Number / (%) of 445 radon testing firms	Number / (%) of 195 radon mitigation firms
General environmental services	174 (39%)	53 (27%)
Building inspection services	167 (38%)	19 (10%)
Construction companies	34 (8%)	43 (22%)
Pest control companies	31 (7%)	1 (<1%)
Energy companies and services	29 (7%)	20 (10%)
Heating and ventilation companies	10 (2%)	4 (2%)
Engineering companies	0	25 (13%)
Waterproofing companies	0	23 (12%)
Meteorology and geology firms	0	7 (4%)

Source: *Radon Industry Directory,* 1989.

The fast proliferation of firms reflects, in part, how easy it originally was to enter the field. Firms purchased bulk testing kits from a laboratory, or they might combine a $6,000 piece of nuclear counting equipment with a personal computer. With the charcoal test costing only about $5 to make and mail, profits on tests for which as much as $50 was charged were impressive. Among the early firms establishing themselves in the charcoal testing field were Air Chek, a direct mail testing firm based in North Carolina began in 1986. At a charge of only $11.95 per test, the firm grossed more than $1 million the first year in business. The attractiveness of radon as an investment is indicated by the ability of Radon Testing Corporation of America to attract $2.6 million in investments when it went public in early 1987 (Berreby, 1987).

Along with the growth of the industry, there was considerable development and diffusion of technology. Perhaps most notable was the introduction of the electret, a reusable measurement device, originally developed by the New York State Energy Research and Development Authority, that allows for immediate analysis and integrates over either short- or long-term intervals. By 1989, the electret's rising popularity was indicated by its use in about half of the primary EPA Radon Measurement Proficiency entries (*RIR*, February 1990a).

At the same time, a key focus was establishing control over existing measuring devices. For the first year after Colebrookdale Township, firms marketing alpha track detectors were met continually by patent defense efforts initiated by two claimants of the technology, Terradex and Landauer. By 1986 the firms were consolidated under a $3 million plus buyout by Tech/OPS. The new firm was called Tech/OPS Landauer, marketing under the names of Terradex and Radtrak (Berreby, 1987). In fall 1989, Tech/OPS Landauer filed a suit against Radon Environmental Monitoring, Inc. (REM) for infringement on its May 21, 1985, alpha track detector patent (*RIR*, November 1989b). A settlement of the dispute out of court required REM to modify its detectors and to pay Tech/OPS Landauer an undisclosed amount (*RIR*, January 1990b). But the monopoly had been broken and by the end of the radon's first decade, there was a proliferation of alpha detector devices.

Mitigation Firms

The analysis of the 1989 directory also provides insight regarding the evolution of the radon mitigation industry. Four hundred and thirty-two mitigation firms were listed, most engaged in radon testing, as well. Of these, nearly one quarter (107) appeared to be operating on a nationwide basis, with the remaining firms distributed unevenly across the states in a pattern that generally reflects the spread of testing firms and state radon programs (see table 8.1). Compared to the testing industry, the mitigation industry was even more dependent upon existing areas of professional work as a base (see table 8.2). Nearly half (45 percent or 195) of the mitigation firms appear to have evolved directly from an existing professional service area, most prominently general environmental services and the construction industry, as well as from engineering firms, waterproofing services, energy service firms, and home inspection companies. In contrast to testing, there appeared to be virtually no direct university or government involvement in remediation.

Professional Organizations

This emerging radon industry struggled with the challenges of addressing a nonregulated hazard. One of the key innovations in the field was the fast development of professional organizations aimed at providing self-regulation and guidance. The American Association of Radon Scientists and Technologists (AARST) was formed in 1986 at the request of New Jersey radon officials concerned that the radon crisis in that state was attracting unqualified radon entrepreneurs. The goal, as articulated by AARST's first president, Donald Schutz, was to bolster public confidence in a rapidly growing field. The organization sponsored conferences and training programs, and published a quarterly newsletter. By 1989, some 1,100 members had joined, reflecting a broad range of radon professionals (Schutz, 1989). Two additional professional organizations, the National Radon Association (NRA) based in Georgia and the Ohio-based American Radon Association (ARA), were also formed. Membership in these organizations was limited, however. Only 12 percent of the testing firms listed in the 1989 directory reported membership in one of these three radon professional organizations, with nearly four out of five of those belonging to AARST. In contrast, membership in one of the three radon professional associations was reported by nearly 19 percent of the mitigation firms, in roughly the same proportion as found for testers—60 belonging to AARST, 11 to NRA, and 10 in ARA. Firms did not tend to belong to more than one professional association.

Concern over the fragmentation of the industry as well as competition between these groups became a force for speedy consolidation. By January 1989, NRA and ARA had combined to form the North American Radon Association (NARA). AARST and NARA subsequently formed the Radon Industry Coordinating Council, which by mid-1989 facilitated the further creation of the Radon Industry Manufacturers Committee, made up of executives of more than thirty radon-manufacturing companies (*RIR*, August 1989a). And by late 1989, the industry had also formed RIPAC, the Radon Industry Political Action Committee, to promote radon legislation across the states, particularly on behalf of mandated testing during real estate transactions (*RIR*, November 1989c). In lobbying members of Congress to expand portions of the draft Clean Air Act that address radon, RIPAC claimed to represent six thousand radon firms, twenty-five thousand related employees and to be capable of mobilizing one-hundred thousand people concerned with radon (*RIR*, October 1989a).

Beyond the association newsletters, several specialized periodicals emerged to service the radon industry. The *Radon Industry Review* was a publication of the Maryland-based Radon Press. Provided free to members of the radon profession between 1988 and 1990, the journal then switched to a modestly priced subscription basis. The press also had planned a quarterly dealing specifically with radon and government. By 1991, the journal had been merged into a new publication called *Indoor Air Review*, combining radon news with information about indoor air quality, lead, and asbestos. Other radon publications included *Radon International*, *Radon News Digest*, *Radon Week*, and the *Indoor Air Quality Update*. A yearly directory was inaugurated in 1989 by Radon Press, listing individuals and companies involved in all aspects of the radon field. A second directory was published in 1990, but thereafter the market for such specialized tools of the trade went noticeably into decline. By the end of geologic radon's first decade, AARST was the only surviving radon professional organization.

Decline of the Radon Industry

Far from the sure shot investment originally promised, radon businesses faced a tumultuous and uncertain period by the end of the decade. The radon industry slump was brought on by the slow pace of testing and mitigation, the intensified competition invited during the prior era of promise, and a downturn in the economy, generally, and the construction industry in particular. The decline did not distinguish the radon industry from many other areas of risky entrepreneurship, but the key difference from the standpoint of the public good is that the radon industry—like few others—was society's agent for addressing a major environmental hazard.

By the time of the EPA radon conference in Philadelphia in 1991, this downturn had created noticeable results, as profiled by EPA's Jed Harrison during an interview (1991):

> As an indication that the industry is not healthy, there were only 18 booths this year. At the last AARST conference, there were some 50. There were 60 in Atlanta and 45 at Denver. As other indicators, in this round of RMP, we sent a survey to all who were on Round Six asking them to update their listing. Only 60% returned them. The canister companies are going left and right. The instrument companies are staying the same—they are diversified. The survivors are doing better. It scares me with quality control when a company is in trouble.

Industry officials at the conference reported that the number of major charcoal canister companies had dropped from thirty to three or four, one losing $2.5 million over three years. They noted that radon companies were diversifying to survive. Then president of AARST, Radon Engineering's Harvey Greenberg, confirmed the severity of the downturn to the authors (1991a): "1989 was a killer year. I lost $70,000. I had to trim back. AARST has been cut by two-thirds to one-half. There were 1,200–1,300 members at one time. Now I wouldn't be surprised if we weren't under 600 renewals. Small shops in the industry find it hard to go to conferences and meetings. How do you get people who earn $30,000 per year to come to a conference twice a year?"

Testing was not the only radon field hurting. In an interview, EPA's Harrison (1991) described the economic effects on radon mitigation firms.

> Mitigation is hurting too. There are very few individuals or firms that are supporting themselves strictly on radon mitigation. They are primarily on relocation jobs. Other mitigators are general contractors too. A lot of guys

jumped into this expecting that there would be a million jobs, but it hasn't happened. The industry is only doing well in parts of the country where there are enough home sales and relocation has supported a few mitigation specialists. Radon mitigators in the future will be full service contractors.

Similarly, Harrison noted that the slump in the radon field had made it difficult for four new EPA-sponsored radon training centers to move toward self-sufficiency. The expected numbers of new radon professionals needing to be trained did not materialize.

The radon industry downturn was rooted in a basic fact of life about the radon issue. While, on the supply side, the promise of profitability and need had brought an overwhelming response from entrepreneurs, on the demand side, radon had not caught on. The only real growth centers of the industry, realty and new construction, were heavily affected by a period of economic stagnancy. EPA's Steve Page (1991) told the authors that he saw the downturn in the radon industry as a natural part of the business cycle, heavily driven by the realty market. "In any new industry, there is a fallout and shake out. People come in thinking that they will make a quick million. After a while, a shake out is natural. The bigger and wiser prevail. The radon industry has been subject to the whims of the realty market. In a hot market, radon contingencies are dismissed. People ignore radon. If it bottoms out and becomes a buyer's market, then radon can really count."

Despite these reports of attrition from the industry, private sector participation in the proficiency programs continued to surge through 1993. At this peak, more than 2,000 firms were found to be proficient in testing and another 1,000 in mitigation. While EPA staff were aware that fewer firms were subsequently operating in the field, their data did not clarify whether provision of radon services had declined or merely that remaining firms had consolidated the business left by others' failure. But the pessimism surrounding the industry continued to suggest a downturn. Thus, one former head of the radon division still on the scene reported in 1996 "We heard in 1991 that it was drying up. We heard in 1993 that it was drying up. And we hear now it is drying up" (Rowson, 1996).

Beyond the basic uncertainties of the marketplace that confronted the fledgling industry, however, there was an additional source of significant uncertainty, namely, government policy. What had begun as a true free market was becoming progressively more regulated (see chapter 10).

Uncertainties Faced by the Radon Market

The success of federal radon policy was completely dependent upon a viable radon industry. Accordingly, EPA was reluctant to take actions threatening to the industry. This dependence may explain EPA's persistence in using short-term screening measures as the basis for mitigation decisions, as suggested in an interview by DOE's Richard Sextro (1991): "In the decision to do this, the EPA aided and abetted in creating something that they knew was wrong. They are now not willing to pull the plug. The industry would go crazy over it." But the reverse was equally true. The emerging radon industry was in no way independent of government radon policy and initiative. As a result, the industry faced numerous challenges.

Dependence on Government Policy

The emerging shape of the Radon Action Program had major implications for the new industry. EPA actions set important constraints for the radon private sector. For example, the agency's testing protocols, demanding closed-house conditions indicative of cold weather in the North, made testing into a seasonal phenomenon. Companies had to carry over inventory and lay off staff in the summer (*RIR*, August 1989b; *RIR*, September 1989a).

EPA policy initiatives could also create entirely new markets for radon services. A prime example was the focus on radon in schools. Because children spend only a fraction of their time at school and in a given classroom, schools were not a logical target for radon programs. The EPA radon group had itself been surprised by the legislative push that mandated school testing and mitigation. Agency staff hoped that the radon issue in schools would at least help to raise parents' concern for their childrens' exposure at home, getting at the real risk.[3] By spring of 1989, the agency published an interim report on radon in schools, and EPA Administrator William Reilly announced that over half of three thousand schools tested in sixteen states had elevated radon levels (EPA, 1989b). Subsequent research found almost 20 percent of schools to have at least one classroom over the federal guidance (EPA, 1993a). By 1996, EPA estimated that between 25 and 50 percent of U.S. schools had been tested for radon. While numbers on mitigation were not available, several states had completed testing and were mitigating all their schools (Rowson, 1996).

While the radon in schools issue promised a windfall for radon testing firms, there were significant barriers to be encountered. Congress balked at requiring school testing (Lautenberg, 1993). The radon problem came on the back of other expensive environmental problems, including lead in water systems and asbestos, that confronted schools strapped for funding. Furthermore, the vagueness of the EPA guidelines for school testing and the expectation that the interim guidelines would be substantially revised led many schools to delay testing. And, rather than using expensive radon professionals, there was a move toward self-testing. The radon industry campaigned against a Florida policy allowing maintenance men to test schools (*RIR*, September 1989e).

Industry Dependence upon Government to Promote the Radon Issue

Private industry was never in a position to create a legitimate public belief in radon risk. Rather, the industry was totally dependent upon government to motivate testing, and thus generate business for the radon industry. EPA increasingly sought to "market" the radon issue through escalating efforts to induce radon fear. In 1988 it enlisted the surgeon general to place radon into the same category of risk as smoking. The carefully engineered joint EPA/surgeon general's announcement on the hazards of radon produced a tidal wave of radon calls that overwhelmed the fledgling industry. Things were looking promising. However, the surge was only temporary. The major windfall expected for the emerging radon industry did not materialize in proportion to expectations, leading to the irony that, as of 1989, supply of radon services far exceeded demand. A sense of urgency pervaded an industry where livelihood depended upon agency initiative.

As their failure to win public action on radon depressed business, the pressure to act to bolster the radon industry became a new force shaping EPA actions. What was good for the industry had become fully synonymous with what was good for EPA. This codependency was evident when, in fall 1989, a press conference was called by EPA to unveil an advertising campaign developed by the Ad Council, as well as to release results from the most recent state survey. But a catastrophic earthquake that devastated San Francisco the prior day dominated the national news, and the opportunity for a surge of business to help the slumping industry was lost (*RIR*, November 1989d).

The agency's failure to market radon at a time when the industry was being increasingly regulated brought resentment and desperation from the business-hungry radon industry. EPA's next solution, the fear-inducing Ad Council marketing program (discussed in chapter 9), was almost canceled when so many radon businessmen called their local stations to urge the showing of the spots so as to threaten the nonprofit nature of the effort (*RIR*, January 1990a; see also February 1990b).

Competition from Government Programs

The basic EPA approach has involved the development and dissemination of information and skills. A primary example is the Housing Evaluation Program (HEP), which was based upon technology transfer. Ten typical homes were chosen by EPA and a participating state. EPA then did the radon diagnosis and remedial design as part of a training program for local radon mitigators (Mardis, 1988). HEP represented government action that built the private sector's capabilities. In contrast to HEP, other federal programs directly competed with private services. At the federal level, the issue of training is a case in point. EPA originally funded a fledgling training program for radon professionals. Between 1986 and 1988, thirty-one courses were offered, hardly approaching the demand. Clearly there was a need to educate the radon professionals who were needed to address the issue. To fill the gap, a private training industry emerged. However, beginning in 1989, EPA issued grants totaling $1.5 million to university consortia based at Colorado State, Rutgers, and Auburn Universities, and the University of Michigan/University of Minnesota for the purpose of creating regional radon training centers (*RIR*, August 1989c). In the first two years, nearly seven thousand people received training at these centers, directly competing with private radon training professionals, now forced to apply to give courses at the centers using government-developed materials (Barron, 1991).

Other competition came through the use of the RMP to offer, effectively, a "certification of calibration." As participation in the RMP became requisite, the private sector was excluded from providing calibration services for testing firms (Saum, 1991a). Meanwhile, state programs also sometimes competed with private radon companies. For example, the New York State program to provide low-cost radon test kits, discussed in chapter 11, directly impeded the private sector.

Pressures of the Market Place

While careful diagnosis of the building was central to early government-sponsored mitigation, as remediation was forced to operate within the marketplace, diagnostics testing proved a luxury that few employed. Diagnostics requires good training and access to expensive equipment. Furthermore, in highly competitive states, such as New Jersey, diagnosis became a liability. Because mitigators could not afford to do extensive extra work without charging for it, those employing diagnostics could not be competitive with firms that skipped it. The industry was dominated by cookbook mitigation measures likely to work in most situations. In this view, it was cheaper to remitigate a few problem houses that did not fit the norm than to carefully examine all houses initially (Norton, 1989). And with so little mitigation evaluation testing occurring, no one might ever know that a mitigation had failed, anyway.

Secondary Regulation Due to the Need for Consumer Protection

The fast growth of a geologic radon testing and mitigation industry revealed problems of competence and unethical practice that led to demands for secondary regulation. The ironic result was that a government unwilling to protect people from this major health hazard through primary regulation was called upon to protect people from the radon industry itself.

A Fraudulent Start—The Mayonnaise Test. The early radon period in the Reading Prong states featured a demand for radon services that preceded training, government regulation, and development of professional organizations. Radon test and mitigation scams were reported with alarming frequency. Stanley Watras recalled that one company that asked him for an endorsement claimed that its device—when placed on the toilet—would remove radon with each flush

(Watras, 1987). In New Hampshire, door-to-door salesmen offered elderly homeowners a purported radon removal device—requiring monthly replacement—that looked suspiciously like a "no-pest strip" (Berreby, 1987). At the suggestion of one of the authors, New Jersey acted to remove from the market the "raydon," described as "a pen like device worn in the pocket or carried in the handbag and designed to deflect and neutralize harmful radiations" (*Whole Life Times*, Mid-April–May 1985, p. 48). In New Jersey, one radon company was said to have collected air samples in plastic foam cups. When two plastic foam balls were dropped into the cup, they would float due to static electricity. Customers were told that the amount of radon was indicated by the rate at which the balls fell. But perhaps the most famous scam—given its persistence as a cliche in the radon field—was the use of mayonnaise jars to collect air samples by alleged "testing firms" in New Jersey (Higham, 1986).

Failure to Regulate the Testing Industry. Responding to the need for quality control in the testing field, EPA wrote a number of protocols to guide testing and mitigation (see chapters 6 and 7). They also created the Radon Measurement Proficiency (RMP) program to compare testing-firm results to a predetermined controlled radon exposure. However, in keeping with the nonregulatory approach, the RMP program was made voluntary. Its purpose was to provide firms with feedback on their testing quality, not to control the industry. Firms were not compelled to participate. Failure on the RMP led to no greater punishment than omission from a list of firms that passed the test. Furthermore, since participants in the RMP program were aware of when they were being evaluated, they could take special precautions not normally in place. There were rampant rumors of cheating on the test. As a result of these limitations, the initial RMP, in and of itself, did little to protect the public from fraud (Public Citizen, 1989). Similar criticisms could be directed at the subsequent Radon Contractor Proficiency program, designed for mitigators. States were no more effectual in assuring quality control. Even New Jersey's pioneering decision in 1986 to develop a state licensing program took four years to implement. Professional radon associations, such as AARST, created to establish industry standards that would head off government regulation, were only able to control member behavior by peer pressure. In short, only the most blatant frauds could be addressed quickly.

Role of Consumer Advocates. Given the failure to enforce quality in radon professional services, it was not surprising to find scrutiny from consumer advocates.[4] In January 1989, the Ralph Nader affiliated group Public Citizen issued a "Buyers Up" guide on home radon testing. After a one year study of the home test kit industry, Buyers Up ranked thirty-four testing laboratories on their quality control procedures, making available to the public a comparative rating sheet (Public Citizen, 1989). Three of seven large radon measurement laboratories subjected to blind testing were listed as failing to meet EPA quality assurance standards (Associated Press, 1989b). Public Citizen was immediately attacked by the failed companies. The president of Air Chek charged, in a letter to the *Radon Industry Review*, that Public Citizen's independence had been tainted by its arrangement to receive a fifty-cent-per-test fee from the radon firms that it recommended as competent (Alvarez, 1989). And Douglas Martin & Associates promptly sued Public Citizen, charging that the group had deliberately falsified information about test exposure times in its investigation (*Johnstown Tribune-Democrat*, 1989).[5]

While the Public Citizen study indeed suffered from serious limitations, it fulfilled a real consumer need for apparent scrutiny of the testing industry.[6] In fact, Air Chek's Alvarez argued that Public Citizen had successfully stolen from the EPA the legitimacy and authority to make scientific judgments about radon (Alvarez, 1989). An unexpected outcome of this negative scrutiny was increased industry support for a stronger EPA quality control program; more stringent yet more protective of a business's reputation.

Uncertainties Relating to Corporate Liability

Another area of uncertainty for the radon industry involves questions of liability. The threat that testers and mitigators might be held liable for misdiagnosis and failed remediation was sufficient to dissuade Sears, Roebuck, Inc., from seriously considering getting into the mitigation field as part of its home improvement business. Despite initial corporate interest, Sears balked when its lawyers recommended that mitigators carry a minimum of $200 million in liability insurance (*RIR*, October 1989b). The potential for former workers to develop lung cancer emerged as a second area of potential liability. Suggestions within the industry for addressing employee exposure include the use of alpha track detectors as personal dosimeters to track cumulative worker exposure (Pollack, 1989) and thorough employee training (Eason, 1989). Insurers also began to develop tailored liability insurance for radon specialists.

De Facto Industry Regulation

As the abuses of the radon free market continued to go unabated, the pressure for mandatory government programs increased. EPA's two quality control programs, the RMP and the RCP, emerged as the anchors of the EPA's efforts to create a nationally consistent quality control program (Hoornbeck and Zakheim, 1991). The proposed but never enacted 1993 revisions to the Indoor Radon Reauthorization Act even included provisions requiring radon professionals to participate (Lautenberg, 1993).

The Radon Measurement Proficiency Program

The initial EPA Radon Measurement Proficiency program was structured as a voluntary, quality-control program without penalties for failure. States had the option to regulate the industry more stringently. Instead, states adopted the RMP to screen which companies to list as radon service providers (Gearo, 1988). By 1989, twenty-five states had adopted the RMP as the basis for approval for these listings. Thus, a nonregulatory federal program became the sole criterion for state regulation and licensing. In short, the RMP became a de facto form of regulation.

This use of the RMP had severe repercussions for the participating companies. Under the original program, if a firm failed to demonstrate proficiency through the RMP, it was forced to wait an entire year to try again. There was no appeal process. A small firm might not survive being delisted that long; a large firm might be forced to lay off employees (Koopersmith, 1989; *RIR*, September 1989b). Even as firms feared the outcomes, pressure mounted for participation in the RMP. As a result, by the 1989 RMP Round 6, EPA was overwhelmed by some twelve thousand applications, including 700 primary and 1,500 secondary testing companies.[7] One quarter of these submissions failed, destabilizing and angering the radon industry (*RIR*, December 1989a). This backlash led to major evaluations of the RMP by the EPA's Science Advisory Board, congressional hearings, the General Accounting Office (GAO), and an EPA task force (Jalbert et al., 1991).

Particularly damaging was the GAO's conclusion that the voluntary RMP failed to provide homeowners with adequate assurance of professional competency or test accuracy, allowing untested devices and inadequate services to be marketed. Specifically, GAO found that almost half of a sample of testing firms was not calibrating equipment, resulting in unchecked error rates as high as 100 percent. Because the RMP did not employ double-blind tests, where the testing firm was unaware of which tests had been submitted by the EPA rather than a regular homeowner, the testing situation was artificial. The GAO found that some 20 percent of firms that passed regular scheduled testing failed double-blind tests. Nine measurement devices that were either untested in the RMP program or which did not meet the RMP requirements were being marketed, in some cases by large firms. Twenty-four small companies that had failed to establish proficiency in the 1988 RMP were still marketing test devices (GAO, 1989; 1990).

The GAO further concluded that, contrary to EPA's expectations, only a few states had developed complementary quality assurance programs beyond participation in the RMP program. Only nine states had some type of certification program, with only five of these mandatory. Furthermore, wide variations existed between these programs. This failure of states to compensate for the limitations of the RMP led GAO to recommend that passing the RMP program be made mandatory for measurement firms, that adequate quality assurance programs be required as a prerequisite for entry into the program, and that the EPA issue a guidance to states on actions needed to assure quality testing (GAO, 1990).

As a result of these reviews and because of industry complaint, EPA instituted significant changes in the fully subscribed 1990 RMP program. A distinction was made between primary and secondary measurement companies—those doing laboratory analysis of devices for radon and those merely placing testing devices in the field and then sending them to primary testers for analysis. While all were required to have a quality assurance plan, only the primary participants were now required to show measurement proficiency in analyzing results from the specific test devices they process. Additionally, the RMP program moved into a continuous mode of operation, allowing for companies to retest if their results were not more than 50 percent off. Blind tests were now combined with announced tests in order to control for bias and cheating. More normal testing conditions were now employed, reflecting testing levels anywhere between 2 and 200 pCi/l. The agency undertook development of revised protocols, guidance on quality assurance, and written tests for operators testing in the field (Jalbert et al., 1991; Page, 1991; Harrison, 1991).

The changes in the RMP program made it even harder for participants to pass. While previously the average of four samples could show no more than a 25 percent error, the new procedures demanded that each of four submitted samples be within 25 percent of the actual level (Jalbert et al., 1991). Consequently, while 78 percent of the applicants passed the original procedure, now only 68 percent passed. In 1992, EPA delisted both the original and the improved Radtrak model alpha track detector, resulting in further instability in the industry and raising the complex question of whether alpha track customers had to be notified of the delisting. Defenders of the alpha track charged that they were victims of a program designed for the charcoal canister (*IAR*, November 1992; Silverman, 1992d).

The RMP program was now a far cry from its origin as a voluntary and easy-to-pass program seeking to give participants feedback on their testing accuracy. EPA's Jed Harrison (1991) noted the shift during an interview.

> The RMP has been completely overhauled. It is definitely headed toward being a regulatory tool—not by our decision. Legislation . . . will mandate . . . that anyone in the U.S. who offers radon measurements to consumers has to participate. A mandatory program will have to emphasize enforcement. We will have to make sure that people meet the requirements. This will have an effect on the number of companies participating. The other significant impact is that companies will have to pay user fees with a mandatory program. They will have to play and have to pay as well. The RMP will lose more companies than predicted. It is not just fees but the cost of participating. There is the cost of travel, schooling, fees. When you add it together, you have to do a lot of tests to make it back.

Nevertheless, the 1993 RMP program showed continued growth: 553 firms were listed as proficient for providing primary radon measurements (analyzing measurements) and another 1,493 firms and 550 individuals for doing secondary measurement (making test measurements). Another 357 firms were cross-listed (EPA, 1993e). As noted above, however, there was a subsequent drop off of participation.

The Radon Contractor Proficiency Program

As the RMP developed as an increasingly regulatory tool for controlling the radon testing industry, a parallel development occurred for the mitigation industry. The Indoor Radon Abatement Act mandated a Radon Contractor Proficiency (RCP) program. Industry strongly supported the program's inauguration in 1989 (RIR, November 1989e), as indicated when more than one thousand contractors signed up for a required exam. However, requirements became increasingly stringent. By mid-1991, a sixteen-hour hands-on training course run by the four radon training centers was required, to be repeated every second year to assure that the contractor remained current. Contractors also faced record keeping requirements and were forced to follow EPA's radon mitigation guidelines (EPA, 1989c). By 1991, 1,123 contractors had met RCP requirements, representing 71 percent of the applicants. User fees were planned in order to support the program (Harrison, 1991; Salmon et al., 1991).[8] As with the RMP, states increasingly relied upon RCP lists to determine proficient contractors, with seven of the fifteen states licensing radon professionals by 1991 using the RCP as a requirement. Procedures for delisting contractors who failed exams were under development. The RCP was later incorporated into the EPA Guidance to States on Radon Certification Programs (Harrison, 1991; Salmon et al., 1991). By 1993, 902 contractors were listed as proficient under the RCP (EPA, 1993e).

Other Federal Actions

By 1991, EPA had moved to try to control the industry through a guidance to the states on radon certification programs. The guidance dealt with options by which states could set up certification programs while providing for mutual reciprocity. The guidance placed in federal hands the monitoring of standards for manufacturers of radon test devices, calibration facilities, and most measurment laboratories. In contrast, monitoring of standards for radon testers and mitigators was viewed as principally under the purview of the states. The federal RMP and RCP were the primary tools for supporting this guidance (Hoornbeek and Zakheim, 1991).

In 1992, EPA brought out *The Consumer's Guide to Radon Reduction* to augment the new *Citizen's Guide,* emphasizing that radon mitigation be done by professionals rather than by homeowners themselves and that only state-certified contractors or those listed under EPA's RCP be hired (Silverman, 1992c). While the RCP was not required per se under the emerging practice, it also clearly served as a de facto regulation.

Emergent but Divergent State Certification Programs

The decentralized federal policy provided the RMP and RCP programs at the federal level and left all other decisions to the individual states. As a result, the emerging radon industry faced the prospect of fifty different radon certification programs and fifty different sets of regulations. The GAO review of the RMP identified significant differences just among the nine states that had initially moved to set up certification programs (GAO, 1990). A later review of pending state legislation by the Environmental Law Institute (see chapter 11) projected an even more heterogeneous future regulatory environment (1993a). For the radon industry, the disparity between state policies had became a formula for confusion, expense, and frustration (Koopersmith, 1989, p. 6). EPA's Harrison (1991) described the agency's belated effort to organize the confusion.

> The problem is that we have left things to themselves, and all of a sudden you have so many different requirements for companies operating in all states. Even now the states are not reciprocating. We are developing a model state certification guidance—a recipe book. We start at the bottom line— participation in the RMP. The radon program will start giving technical aid to states to assure consistency between states. There are the same issues for the RCP. We want to encourage states to make it mandatory, to add enforcement, labs, blind testing, etc. We will make sure that they will not have to meet 50 different sets of requirements.

Despite Harrison's optimism, a high ranking staff person reflected five years later that "We have not seen a wholesale adoption of the EPA RMP. We had higher expectations" (Feldman, 1996). Furthermore, federal action to create coherent state policy after states' policies already had diverged was both too little and too late.

The transition from an unregulated radon industry to mandatory certification and licensing was to be no simple matter, as seen with New Jersey's pioneer radon certification, authorized in August 1986. By late in 1988, 175 testing and 60 mitigation firms had applied for approval in the voluntary program, with 87 testing and 35 mitigation firms accepted (Tuccillo et al., 1988). But as New Jersey subsequently moved from voluntary to mandatory certification, testing and mitigation activities in the state could only be carried out by certified personnel (Nicholls and Stern, 1988). Stringent and costly requirements for certification were imposed.[9] By 1990, the radon industry was funding a half-million dollars in training and administration costs needed for the certification program. Angry contractors predicted that the program would force small contractors to subcontract to larger companies that could employ the required specialists and meet the need for computerized record keeping to track the some twenty-nine different items to be reported for each job. The industry also feared harassment by state inspectors who could charge $400 per inspection and visit an unlimited number of times (Greenberg, 1991a,b).

These concerns were echoed by the owner of a small New Jersey-based mitigation firm, interviewed in 1991. Because of concern over retaliation in inspections, he asked not to be identified. He charged that the DEP was adopting a "bullying" approach to radon businesses, citing state quarterly reporting deadlines that, if missed by even one day, could result in delisting a firm. Furthermore, the certification standards were not conducive to helping firms stay in business. Small companies would now require personal and corporate certification, a costly step in terms of the fees. Furthermore, newly evolving OSHA (Occupational Safety and Health Administration) rules on worker exposure to radon threatened to burden the mitigator with so much record keeping that the cost of mitigation would be forced to double or even triple. Finally, the regulation failed to address the needs of real estate transfer, the contractor's major source of business, because the requirement for postmitigation testing contradicted the need of realtors for action within two weeks. Overall, the New Jersey program was seen as "bureaucratic overkill" that would threaten the survival of small radon businesses, promising a consolidation of firms toward the scale able to viably meet regulatory demands.

AARST opposed the new regulations, as its then-president Harvey Greenberg described in an interview (1991a). "N.J. AARST got a lawyer to fight the certificate. The N.J. regulation is the most overkill regulation in the industry. It is all a bit ridiculous. They don't regulate furnace repairs and other industries that break the soil! They are regulating us when we are just learning about levels of radon. They are regulating the industry that is most knowledgeable. We spent $6,000 to hire a lawyer. Fifty people gave testimony on the draft certification." Despite AARST's opposition, the regulations creating the program were put in place.

However, once the regulation passed, Greenberg saw its silver lining. Some contractors would be knocked out by the certification program, culling a competitive market. Others would now need to subcontract with firms like his Radon Engineering, which already had the required technical personnel on staff. In a 1991 letter to New Jersey home inspectors, Greenberg invited them to avoid the certification costs by becoming subcontractors to his firm. Under this plan, Radon Engineering would register as a Radon Measurement Business, paying thousands in fees, while the inspector would only need to become certified as a measurement technician at a cost of only hundreds (Greenberg, 1991b). Similar issues later arose with certification programs in Pennsylvania (Granland, 1988; Pennsylvania Environmental Quality Board, 1988), Florida, Indiana, and proposed programs in eight other states (*RIR*, October 1989c,d,e).

Overall Industry Response to Federal Regulation

As states increasingly required participation in EPA's "voluntary" programs, industry representatives accused the agency of enacting de facto regulation. In the view of Infiltec's David Saum (1991a), the use of such "pseudo-certification" as an industry quality standard was unfair to firms whose reputation was based upon comparatively greater competence. Ironically, unlike actual regulations, Saum charged that such de facto regulations bypassed public input: "All the EPA guidelines, recommendations, and proficiency demonstrations quickly become de facto rules because the states are quick to incorporate them into law or local regulations. But the EPA is not required to subject these de facto rules to the same level of public scrutiny as their other formal rule making activity" (p. 5). As a result, companies were required to participate and pay for programs that they might see as impeding industry quality.

Nevertheless, a GAO survey (1990) of industry representatives found a strong majority supporting federal regulation of quality assurance requirements. "The primary reason they gave for preferring federal regulation was the need for uniformity in the requirements. Among the problems associated with state regulation mentioned by individual representatives were overlapping jurisdictions, inconsistencies and conflicts between state requirements, and general confusion for the industry" (p. 23).

Ironically, while responsible members of the industry supported regulation, the impetus for quality control remained grounded in the public fear of fraud. For example, the 1987 Pennsylvania certification statute was intended to protect "property owners from unqualified and unscrupulous consultants and firms" (Granland, 1989, p. 2). Reacting to what was seen as unjust punishment for consumer fraud perpetrated by others, one radon industry spokesperson charged, "We read more headlines concerning nefarious radon firms using mayonnaise jar kits than we do about the ability of radon to kill" (Koopersmith, 1989, p. 6). Furthermore, regulation took time and resources from the "essential goal" of educating the public to test (*RIR*, October 1989f). Fair or not, the need to regulate the industry had forced a fast reevaluation of the free market response to radon. The industry was no longer the solution; it had become part of the problem.

Realty and the Hope for a Resurgent Market

The downward spiral faced by the radon industry brought on a desperate search for hopeful signs. Some market analysts predicted a coming resurgence due to the general concern for indoor air quality.[10] However, radon abatement comprised only one-twentieth of the nearly $5 billion spent on indoor air quality in 1991. In fact, the inability to motivate widespread voluntary testing for radon might have killed the newly emergent radon industry were it not for one special lucrative context—real estate transfer.

The real estate transaction has provided the context in which the public is most willing to deal with radon (Doyle et al., 1990; Locke, 1990; Pratt, 1991). In fact, 90 percent of all radon tests have occurred in a realty context. As many as 15 to 25 percent of homes sold were being tested for radon into the 1990s.

Furthermore, as many as 25 to 50 percent of homes for sale above 4 pCi/l were being mitigated, in contrast to fewer than 10 percent being mitigated outside of realty transfer. The trend less reflects voluntary concern than market demand, fear of liability, and, increasingly, the rules of government regulation. For similar reasons, the National Association of Realtors has supported testing of all homes, as well as providing radon information during sale (EPA, 1992d).

Problems of Realty Testing

As an unregulated area, addressing radon in the realty context has been fraught with inconsistency, abuse, and inaction. Some of the pressure comes with the demand for quick radon results by realtors anxious to close the deal. As a result, real estate testing buys into the myth of the quick test, suffering the inherent potential for false negative and positive results.

Beyond the problems of honest invalidity in testing, fraud has proven to be a particular problem with real estate transfer. Fraudulent testing has usually been practiced by the seller of the property, whose personal interest is served by preventing or minimizing discovery of radon problems. It has been estimated that between 40 percent and 60 percent of real estate radon tests involve seller tampering to reduce radon levels.[11] Such efforts usually involve ventilating the building during the period of testing, although direct tampering with test devices may also occur (e.g., covering them up or moving them outside). In a sense, the professional radon tester joins the buyer as a victim of such deception. It has been difficult for testing firms to discover tampering. There may be no detectable signs that interference has occurred. Posting someone to guard the testing equipment is excessively expensive. And there are obvious problems created for the contractor/client relationship if the tester tries to surprise the homeowner cheating. Visible methods for tampering detection have been employed by some testing firms in an effort to deter seller fraud (Harbuck, 1989; Sachs, 1988).[12] Additionally, the issue of radon disclosure has been addressed by states and the courts (see chapter 10).

Proposals to address both the limitations of quick testing and the potential for fraud usually attempt to shift the burden of testing to the buyer, who is presumed desirous of the most accurate results. One approach is the use of escrow accounts. The buyer of the property conducts long-term testing during the first year of occupancy. A sum paid by the seller into an escrow account is tapped only if a radon level requiring mitigation is discovered. Conversely, if no radon problem is discovered, the amount is returned to the seller (Sachs, 1988). The use of escrow accounts in amounts of $5,000 for radon testing and remediation has been supported by influential environmental attorneys (Kass and Gerard, 1987), even if it has not caught on with realtors. Another novel concept for allowing the buyer to test the home is the concept of radon insurance, to be provided at sale. If mitigation proved necessary after long-term testing by the property buyer, the insurance would pay (Jordan, 1988). Such insurance might also back a warranty by builders or mitigators that their work provides acceptable reductions in radon levels (*RIR*, December 1989c). So far, insurers have been unwilling to offer these services (EPA 1992a). In chapter 11, we examine the potential for realty fraud to be controlled by disclosure laws and by the threat of litigation over failure to disclose known high radon levels.

Conclusion

In this chapter, we have charted consequences from defining radon as a private matter requiring private action. The fast growth of a radon industry capable of assisting the homeowner with testing and mitigation affected radon policy in three ways. First, a need for government regulation of the industry was created. As a result, de facto regulation of the industry became increasingly evident, despite the strictures of Reaganomics against regulation (see chapters 10 and 11). Second, the new industry lobbied against government competition and on behalf of government efforts to stimulate demand in the radon marketplace. There was an increasing pressure on government to threaten rather than educate the consumer about radon. Finally, when the resulting Reaganomic policies to "market" radon as a voluntary issue failed, the industry became dependent upon the less-voluntary aspects of the radon issue. The threat of radon liability in real estate rather than the threat of illness due to radon exposure became the driving force for testing and mitigation. Our review of the radon private sector, thus, tests the assumption that the market and government are independent sectors, and that the public will voluntarily consume private radon services at government's behest without the active involvement of government in the process. In chapter 9, we examine the public's role under Reaganomics as consumers in the radon marketplace.

Notes

1. The General Accounting Office deemed EPA's figures too low. GAO's estimates were higher than EPA's because GAO assumed the need to do additional work on some buildings and the involvement of radon experts to guide contractors (GAO, 1986). By 1993, EPA research showed the actual costs of mitigation to be in the $500 to $2,500 range (EPA, 1993b).

2. A regional or local radon firm was defined as a firm that operates in ten or less states. Note that several firms were franchised to operate as separate companies in different states, most notably the thirty-two branches of Radon Detection Services and the thirteen branches of Radon Testing Services.

3. Given their initially limited knowledge of schools, the agency had to "swim up-stream" to create a guidance. They quickly found that radon problems in schools were associated with poor ventilation systems, which caused other indoor air problems as well, demanding a comprehensive approach to remediation (Maconaughey, 1991; Page, 1991; Harrison, 1991).

4. Beyond several articles covering the topic, *Consumer Reports* published a book on radon entitled *Radon: A Homeowner's Guide to Detection and Control* in 1987, by Bernard Cohen and the editors of Consumer Reports Books. Coming early in the radon issue, the book bought into the logic of the EPA radon program. Short-term charcoal canister screening measurements were recommended, in keeping with the concern for hot houses. Cohen, while known as a critic of EPA radon policy, was, however, deeply involved with a radon-testing business using charcoal canisters. Thus, the volume is hardly a critical review of the consumer issues relating to radon.

5. Central to the charges were the recollections of Andreas George, a leading developer of charcoal canister technology for the DOE, who served as a consultant to Public Citizen. George apparently told both the Martin firm and a reporter that false information had been given to the testing firm by Public Citizen. George then rechecked his records, and, this time he concluded that Public Citizen had not misled the testing firm, after all (*The Johnstown Tribune-Democrat,* 1989).

6. Public Citizen's materials do not supply sufficient information about the conduct of their study. The information released by the group is unclear as to which companies failed its quality control tests; rankings are provided of various companies without a clear indication of the quality of their test outcomes. Even more significant was Public Citizen's failure to address the consumer choice between long- and short-term testing. While the group correctly calls attention to the problem of false negative results received from poor laboratories, it succumbs to the myth of the quick test. Thus, consumers are not warned that their use of the short-term charcoal canister test might result in a false negative conclusion despite competent analysis. Furthermore, alpha track companies were not rated for quality. As a result, a consumer influenced by the Buyers Up guide would be likely to utilize a charcoal test. Buyers Up even offered an incentive for using two large canister laboratories whose quality control and price policy they found to be particularly strong.

7. Firms were often involved in numerous applications when they used multiple radon measuring devices.

8. It is interesting to note that the states with the largest number of radon contractors showing proficiency in the RCP program were the Reading Prong states of New York (with 185), New Jersey (with 163), and Pennsylvania (with 148). Thus, we see a continuation of the trend begun from the start of the radon issue (see chapter 11).

9. Every testing firm would have to employ a "certified radon measurement specialist," having a bachelor's degree in science or engineering, a year of experience, and sixty-four hours of additional education in radiation. The specialist would have to take an examination and face other course requirements. "Radon measurement technicians" would need one year of applicable experience, sixteen hours of approved training, and

would have to pass an examination. Every mitigation firm would be required to employ a "Radon Mitigation Specialist" holding a degree in architecture, engineering, or the study of heating and ventilation systems, six months of relevant work experience, twenty-four hours of training in radon and mitigation, and a passing grade on an examination and course. While the specialist would design mitigation systems, they would be implemented by "radon mitigation technicians" having two years of construction experience, one year of experience with radon mitigation, sixteen hours of approved training, and a passing grade on an examination (*New Jersey Register*, 1990).

10. According to a report by Richard Miller and Associates entitled *Environmental Markets 1992–95*, the radon abatement market was $240 million, with 20 percent anticipated growth through 1995. Another $5 million was spent on radon instrumentation in 1990, with a projected doubling of the market by 1995. Of course, the usual caveat was offered, namely that growth in the radon field depends upon growth in public concern, rendering the projections unrealistic.

11. In contrast, it is interesting that 84 percent of the realtors surveyed by the GAO in Pennsylvania and New Jersey claimed that they had not encountered radon fraud (GAO 1992).

12. Some radon-testing firms have attempted to detect fraud by developing methodological practices designed to detect suspect variations in test levels. For example, the use of a grab sample at the time that a test device is placed provides a comparison point for examining the actual test result. Or a continuous monitor can be used in combination with another device. Alternatively, a device for checking ventilation can be included with the radon test. If the ventilation rate in the house is excessive enough to dilute the radon level significantly, it would be detected at a level beyond what would normally be expected for a building of that size. In all of these cases, if interference is suggested statistically in comparing the results, the buyer can be made aware that tampering was likely.

Chapter 9

The Market As Regulator: Risk Perception and the Radon Consumer

Two children are shown cuddled on their living room couch playfully. Near-by, a toddler stands by the family dog. Another youngster throws himself onto his father's shoulder while mother plays with two other children. **A voice over announces: "A radioactive gas has been found in homes in your area. It's called radon. And it's so deadly. It's the second leading cause of lung cancer."** *Zap: X-ray images of the mother and children replace their figures.* The picture returns to normal again. As the camera pans past a boy sitting on the couch to a toddler looking at the newspaper, the voice begins again: **"High radon levels will expose your home to as much radiation as having literally hundreds of chest X rays in one year."** *Zap: The toddler's X-ray image replaces the last frame.* Then, as mother speaks on the phone and her daughter draws lounging on the couch, *Zap: The girl becomes an X-ray image.* Father is then shown sitting with the paper while two children play behind him. *Zap: They become X-ray images. . . .*
—Ad Council/EPA television spot

This chapter addresses the root assumption in Reaganomics that radon gas expo-sure can be addressed by the public as a private consumer problem. In effect, the radon issue was thereby decentralized right down to the individual household, with each building occupant given the role of self-regulator. In this approach, the public was given the option to privately remedy radon through the marketplace.

There is an important confusion here between the terms "public" and "pri-vate" that demands comment. The role of publics devolved under Reaganomics so that the term "public" is often utilized when the correct word might best be "the private." The entire thrust of both Reaganomic and neo-Reaganomic per-spectives is to deny public or community values (such as environmental health and protection or the commons of clean air and water) in favor of private inter-ests. In crucial areas, the public was disenfranchised from meaningful participa-tion. Thus, the term public was expropriated to mean an aggregate of "privates" acting, in the sense of Adam Smith, in their own private interests. It was the pri-vate citizen, not the public, that was the target of radon policy during this era.

Given the formidable risk profile and, at least in the view of EPA, the ease with which radon can be identified and addressed (based upon the myths of the quick test and the quick fix), the demand generated by consumers seeking radon

197

protection was expected to maintain the supply side of the marketplace. Consumers, not government, would foot the bill. However, it has been a paradox of radon that the hazard has been widely recognized but generally ignored. Thus, even after fear-rousing advertising was used to motivate action, the number of American homes tested for radon had only reached 5.4 million, or about 6 percent of occupied buildings, by July 1991 (EPA, 1992d), 9 percent (8.1 million homes) by spring of 1993 (EPA, 1993g), and 10 percent (some 10.5 million homes) by early 1995 (Feldman, 1996). By July of 1991, some 140,000 to 170,000 U.S. homes had been mitigated by contractors (EPA, 1992d); the number of mitigations reported through early 1995 was 300,000 (EPA, 1993g; Feldman, 1996; Rowson, 1996).

Perhaps the public—or the collection of private citizens—did not view radon in the same light as the experts who as a group have tended to rate radon as among the most risky environmental hazards (e.g., EPA, 1990a). The views of these experts were rendered moot when radon policy placed the essential response to the hazard into the hands of the average person. And public perception of radon risk could not diverge more diametrically from that of the experts. This divergence is crystal clear when one contrasts the ranking of radon by EPA's Scientific Advisory Board as third in risk for all environmental hazards with a public ranking of radon as twenty-eighth in a March 1990 Roper Poll (Roberts, 1990, p. 616). Precisely this same contrast is shown in figure 9.1, drawn from a 1991 analysis entitled "Risks to Vermont and Vermonters" (Vermont Agency of Natural Resources, 1991). The left portion of the figure displays results from a spring 1990 survey of four hundred members of the general pub-

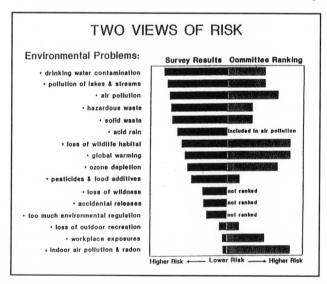

Fig. 9.1   Disparity between public and expert views of risk for various environmental hazards (*Source*: Vermont Agency of Natural Resources, 1991)

lic; the right portion the rankings of risk by an advisory committee of experts influenced by technical information and reports. While indoor air pollution and radon were ranked as a risk of the highest priority by the experts, they appear at the absolute bottom of the public's list of concerns. Such a dramatic discrepancy explains why motivating the public to become private radon consumers has become the driving concern behind the evolution of federal and state radon policy. It did not begin that way.

The Early Fear of Radon Panic

The initial concern of public health and environmental officials after the events in Colebrookdale Township was over panic, not apathy. Experience with rising public fears over even minute quantities of pesticides and other toxins (e.g., Edelstein, 1988a) had taught health and environmental officials that contamination was not a topic to be taken lightly. Indeed, the geologic radon issue had begun with an explosive start.

Unseen dangers must be publicized to cause fear. University of Syracuse sociologist Alan Mazur's (1987, 1990) analysis of media coverage of the radon issue from 1984 to 1986 demonstrates that there was no shortage of potentially fear-inducing publicity. Coverage of natural radon began with the early radon problem in the Nobel house in Pennsylvania (see chapter 2). Despite regional and national media coverage, the Nobel problem did not create a "critical mass" of coverage needed to create a public radon issue. However, Mazur believes that criticism of the Department of Environmental Resources (DER) during the appearance of the Nobels and their radon consultant Harvy Sachs on CBS television just the week before the Watras discovery may have motivated the subsequent strenuous search for radon throughout the Watrases' neighborhood, allowing the radon issue to quickly balloon from local to regional and then to national coverage. On January 7, 1985, a DER spokeswoman blamed the high levels of radon found in the Watras house on the "Reading Prong." This assertion was reported in the first newspaper coverage of the discovery, in the weekly *Boyertown Area Times*. By January 12, Watras's identity had been uncovered by a reporter for the *Pottstown Mercury*. The radon story became a focus of regional media and briefly went nationwide. Watras, Jones, and Varady became key press contacts on the issue (Mazur, 1987).

Mazur notes that for a story to become national, it must first be picked up by one of the national media, such as the *New York Times*. Philip Shabecoff of the *Times* learned of the radon story on a tip from Robert Yuenke, the Environmental Defense Fund attorney who had helped Kay Jones. When Shabecoff's first major story appeared on May 19, 1985, the *Times* set the elements for virtually all of the massive subsequent national attention to the radon issue: the Watras story, the Reading Prong as the source, the EPA estimates of five to twenty thousand yearly cancer deaths, and the role of Jones and Varady as concerned activists (Mazur, 1987). As a further spin-off of Shabecoff's first story, headlined "Radioactive Gas in Soil Raises Concern in Three-State Areas," the state of New Jersey was forced into action on natural radon by public concern (Nichols and Cahill, 1988).

Fear of public panic over radon drove early government response. The resulting strategy to minimize the problem appeared to succeed. For example, after the DER's effort to reassure the residents of Colebrookdale described in chapter 1, public attention to the issue dropped off, with local press coverage diminishing by February 1985 (Mazur, 1987). The subsequent initial EPA informational approach reflected a strategy was demanded in order to address EPA's new challenge, indifference toward radon. Let's examine the program's transformation toward a focus on public apathy.

Policy for an "Apathetic" Public

When the federal government chose not to regulate radon, but rather to exhort the public to voluntarily test, they based their strategy of risk communication on the assumption, consistent with market economic theory, that homeowners are rational decision makers (see Mazur and Hall, 1990). The homeowner's own judgment would determine what level of risk would be accepted. This approach to defining "acceptable risk" was consistent with the contemporary literature on nuclear and toxic hazards that highlighted the importance of public, rather than expert-based, perceptions of risk (see, for example, Slovic et al., 1988). This view of the public's role was evident in the comments of Dr. William Schull, who headed the EPA advisory committee that recommended the use of the 4 pCi/l guidance for radon (Eckholm, 1986). "The individual homeowner will have to be aware of the alternatives and then decide where to put his money— what level of costs and risks are acceptable. And people must realize that the scientific information isn't cast in concrete" (pp. c1, c7). In short, the citizen, and not the experts at EPA, would call the shots. A key result of this perspective was that agency success depended upon its ability to inspire public action without inducing panic. The challenge, then, was to educate the public to make informed decisions without dictating the exact outcomes. This challenge was confronted by EPA in the crafting of its principal public guidance document on geologic radon, the 1986 pamphlet *A Citizen's Guide to Radon: What It Is and What to Do about It*, coissued by the Centers for Disease Control.

The Citizen's Guide—A Rational and Educational Tool

The *Citizen's Guide*'s function of preparing homeowners to interpret their radon test results was aided by two graphs. The first (see fig. 9.2) depicts the expected number of lung cancer deaths per group of one hundred people exposed to a building with either 4, 20, or 200 pCi/l for 75 percent of the time over a seventy-year period. A second illustration (fig. 9.3) contrasts the corresponding estimated lung cancer deaths from radon to those from cigarette smoking and X rays. The urgency of action to reduce radon exposure is related to the level found, ranging from immediate action at 200 pCi/l to action within a few years for levels between 4 and 20 pCi/l (see chapters 3, 6, and 7).

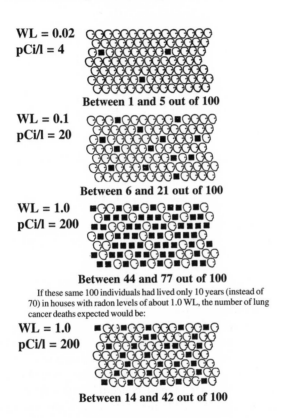

WL = 0.02
pCi/l = 4

Between 1 and 5 out of 100

WL = 0.1
pCi/l = 20

Between 6 and 21 out of 100

WL = 1.0
pCi/l = 200

Between 44 and 77 out of 100

If these same 100 individuals had lived only 10 years (instead of 70) in houses with radon levels of about 1.0 WL, the number of lung cancer deaths expected would be:

WL = 1.0
pCi/l = 200

Between 14 and 42 out of 100

Fig. 9.2   Lung cancer deaths per one hundred people exposed to 4, 20, or 200 pCi/l of radon at 75 percent occupancy for a lifetime (seventy years) (*Source*: EPA, 1986)

Critical reaction to this nonprescriptive guidance focused upon the extensive responsibility that it placed on the citizen, as *New York Times* reporter Eric Eckholm (1986) noted: "Private citizens will be required to make unfamiliar, uncomfortable judgments of cost and benefit on the basis of uncertain data. How much money will one spend to avoid a possible increase in odds of lung cancer of one in 100?" (p. C1). Eckholm, thus, verbalized EPA's anxiety over whether people could handle this decisional freedom. Indeed, the public balked when it came to making any decisions about radon.

PCi/l	WL	Estimated number of lung cancer deaths due to radon exposure (out of 1000)	Comparable exposure levels	Continuum of Risk	Comparable risk
				HIGHEST RISK	
200	1	440-770			
			1000 times average outdoor level	> <	More than 60 times non-smoker risk
100	0.5	270-630		>	4 pack-a-day smoker
			100 times average indoor level	<	
40	0.2	120-380		>	20,000 chest x-rays per year
20	0.1	60-210	100 times average outdoor level	> <	2 pack-a-day smoker
10	0.05	30-120		>	1 pack-a-day smoker
			10 times average indoor level	<	
4	0.02	13-50		>	5 times non-smoker risk
				>	200 chest x-rays per year
2	0.01	7-30	10 times average outdoor level	<	
				>	Non-smoker risk of dying from lung cancer
1	0.005	3-13	Average indoor level	<	
0.2	0.001	1-3		>	20 chest x-rays per year
			Average outdoor level	<	
				LOWEST RISK	

Fig. 9.3   Risk from radon compared to cigarette smoking and X rays
(After: EPA, 1986). Arrows show roughly where the risk falls
on the continuum of risk values.

Motivating the "Apathetic" Public

Problems with the educational approach were quickly evident. By our first conversation with Richard Guimond, in 1986, he already recognized that the primary challenge for EPA was less to understand radon than to understand how to motivate the public. Two years later, EPA's Steve Page (1988) reiterated that "the risk communication stuff is our biggest concern." EPA's efforts to overcome "public apathy" included what Page termed "low cost, high impact approaches." Several magazine interviews were given per week. EPA sought support from groups seen to hold special influence in their home communities, such as the American Medical Association, the National Association of Homebuilders, the National Conference of State Legislators, the American Lung Association, PTAs, and various consumer groups (Page, 1988; see also chapter 11). Beginning in late 1990, an annual Radon Awareness Week was held under the sponsorship of the American Lung Association. The promotion featured community programs nationwide, including poster contests in which five hundred schools participated after a feature in the *Weekly Reader* magazine informed some three million students about radon. The American Medical Association sent communications to some four-hundred thousand doctors. In all, the promotion brought an eight-fold surge of ten thousand calls to the EPA radon hotline, leading to the distribution of sixty-five thousand radon brochures (Miller, 1991). However, while such efforts might yield long-term results, they accomplished little in the short run. The agency was desperate to understand how to motivate radon action.

Risk Communication Research

Compared to the more entrenched, regulatory programs at EPA, the Radon Action Program was uncommonly open to guidance on risk communication provided by the agency's Office of Policy, Planning, and Evaluation (Fisher, 1988). In the office's first effort to study radon risk communication, participants in a study of lung cancer epidemiology conducted by the Maine Medical Center were given an information pamphlet along with their radon results. As a consequence, significantly more participants perceived that their radon exposure was serious and half undertook some form of remedial activity addressing radon, usually involving altered use of their homes. However, there was no relationship between radon level and whether the person mitigated; as many low-risk subjects as high-risk subjects took remedial action and many people mitigated unnecessarily (EPA, 1988e; Fisher, 1988). In short, receiving information about radon's risks was more influential than was the actual radon level.

EPA next experimented with the form of risk communication, employing the New York State Energy Research and Development Authority's (NYSERDA's) radon study of 2,300 randomly distributed New York households. The best understanding of radon risk came from quantitative and directive information that told how much risk there was and what to do about it. In contrast, a minimal fact sheet caused the most concern over radon, even among those with low radon levels, suggesting once again that respondents with the least information were most likely to overreact in evaluating their own risk (EPA, 1988e).

In a third study, a team of researchers from Rutgers University (Weinstein et al., 1989a) asked two thousand homeowners who had never tested for either radon or asbestos to evaluate the risk associated with hypothetical test results for their home for both hazards. They found that while respondents understood information about risk probabilities and could use it to more accurately predict health risks, knowing the risks had less influence over how people felt about the threat or their plans to mitigate than did knowledge of where they stood against the guidance level. Thus, the use of action levels appeared to serve as a "bright line," much as EPA had said it would, allowing for consistent interpretation of findings, with those scoring over the action level being more likely to plan to remediate than those scoring below. The use of action levels did not appear to create a significant false dichotomy between safe and unsafe (Weinstein et al., 1989a).[1]

An Evolving Focus on Television

These studies suggested the importance of how risk information is presented. But, the agency also realized the importance of the medium as well as the message. Early in the radon issue, a model media campaign was developed by Channel 7 (WJLA) in the Washington, D.C. area. Special programming and public service announcements were combined with discounted testing kits available at a major grocery store chain and a follow-up program conducted by the American Cancer and Lung Societies. The Channel 7 program created such a demand for test kits that people had to wait in long lines to get them and their supply in the supermarkets was exhausted. Some one hundred thousand tests were completed (Fisher and Sjoberg, 1987). Richard Guimond (1988c) drew a clear conclusion from the WJLA experiment: "The message is that to motivate the homeowner one has to use TV + TV + TV."

EPA officials envied the success of the contemporary Alar scare, spurred by actress Meryl Streep's televised advocacy of the need to protect children from apples sprayed with that chemical. Richard Guimond (1988c) admitted that he was looking for a celebrity to play Streep's role with radon. Thereafter, the EPA became increasingly preoccupied with ways to get television coverage. Their first attempt was the 1988 release of the first EPA state survey, with EPA head Lee Thomas announcing that every American home needed to be tested for radon (Page, 1991). The EPA then turned to Surgeon General Koop, widely known and respected for his outspoken stands on AIDS and smoking. In September 1988, with Koop represented by the significantly less charismatic Assistant Surgeon General Vernon Houk, EPA and CDC officials issued the National Radon Health Advisory calling for radon testing in all homes below the third floor. The advisory read, in part, "Indoor radon gas is a national health problem. Radon causes thousands of deaths each year. Millions of homes have elevated radon levels. Most homes should be tested for radon. When elevated levels are confirmed, the problem should be corrected."

Then head of communications for the radon division, Steve Page (1991), recalled in an interview how this strategy moved radon testing beyond a meager less than 1 percent of 80 million homes: "We left the informational approach when the surgeon general came in. That was when we came out of the closet. It caused a tremendous surge after that. We had a million measures after that. We'd only had 500,000 before that."

Indeed, in the wake of the radon advisory, calls and requests for radon testing inundated government agencies and private firms. The New York State Health Department registered nearly nine thousand calls in each of September and October 1988, as compared with one-tenth that number in the same months of the prior year (see fig. 9.4; NYDOH, 1989). Nationwide, some 1.2 million tests were taken immediately thereafter. Alpha track manufacturer Tech/Ops Landauer evidenced a 34 percent increase in its stock on the American Stock Exchange, making it the largest percentage gainer on the market (Wagner and Dickson, 1991; *New York Times*, September 14, 1988).

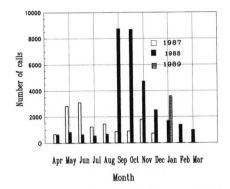

Fig. 9.4 Response of public to 1988 National Radon Health Advisory as measured by phone calls to the New York State Health Department (*Source*: NYDOH, 1989). The graph covers the period from April 1987 to January 1989.

But the agency attack on apathy stalled when a press conference by the next head of EPA, William Reilly, expected to generate another million tests, instead was crowded from the media by a catastrophic earthquake in San Francisco. Subsequently, it was difficult to get radon back into the news. Thus, Mazur's analysis of radon coverage by the media in the late 1980s and 1990 shows an opposite trend to that seen earlier. Figure 9.5 depicts Mazur's findings for radon coverage in the *New York Times*, magazines, and television news through 1990. As can be seen, radon coverage took a nosedive after 1986, with virtually no coverage by 1990, a condition that continued through the mid-1990s. Much-publicized radon had fallen from public attention. It had undergone several media half-lives. It was now as invisible in the media as it was in the home. At the same time, EPA was under increased pressure from Congress, anxious to reduce radon levels down to ambient outdoor levels. Informative publicity about radon proved hard to obtain and control and, even worse, it failed to motivate individuals to act. The fall from public attention was to prove the major step in the sequential abandonment of EPA's rational approach.

The Ad Council Campaign: Madison and Pennsylvania Avenues Team Up

Given the view that radon testing was a private decision made by the individual consumer, it was not a major leap for the radon problem to be reclassified as a marketing problem. Radon would now be promoted in much the same manner as a new brand of cleanser or toothpaste or snack. Consumer preference would be induced by deliberately molded selective information. The basis for this marketing campaign would be television, identified as the most powerful tool for addressing the issue. With backing from the surgeon general, the Ameri-

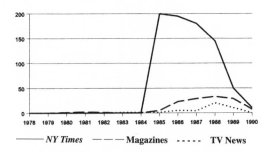

Fig. 9.5   Media coverage of the radon issue, 1978–1990
(*Source*: Adapted from Mazur, 1990a)

can Medical Association, and the American Lung Association, EPA successfully applied to the Ad Council, a consortium of marketers who yearly select a few public benefit causes for advertising campaigns based upon their potential benefit to society (Page, 1988; Wagner and Dickson, 1991).

Based upon survey results, the major New York advertising firm TWBA concluded that radon was not perceived by the public as a serious risk, that testing was being done only by those who were educated and self-starters, and that the public readily denied its vulnerability to radon risk. As a result, TWBA identified the need for "a no-holds-barred approach . . . to move the viewer out of complacency" (*RIR*, February, 1990c). A radon hotline would be used as a quick and easy first step to launch people on the path to dealing with radon. Comparisons of radon to cigarette smoking would be dropped because both smokers and nonsmokers could deny radon risk, the first because they were subjecting themselves to an even greater risk and the latter because they had already avoided the greatest cause of lung cancer. Instead of smoking, X rays were chosen as a tangible comparative risk within the average person's experience. Radon testing would be compared to concrete protective steps already undertaken by people in their homes. And radon was to be portrayed as a problem in the viewer's own home and community, rather than a distant and abstract problem, with a focus on family protection (Wagner and Dickson, 1991).

In fall 1989, the Ad Council unveiled its radon awareness campaign. As showcased at the beginning of this chapter, flashing skeletal X-ray views made visible the attack of decaying radon-daughters on an innocent family secure in its home. Despite controversy over the sensationalism (*RIR*, November, 1989a, d), the campaign was distributed to more than six hundred television stations, three thousand radio stations, and four thousand newspapers and magazines in thirty-three states with known radon problems. Additionally, six thousand billboards and ten thousand transit cards were distributed and brochures were sent to hotline callers and customers of testing firms (Wagner and Dickson, 1991). By January of 1990, the campaign was generating four hundred phone calls a day to the "Radon S.O.S. Hotline" (*RIR*, February, 1990c).[2]

Evaluations of the ad campaign showed that it held people's attention and was simultaneously informative. Watchers were more likely to act on radon. In the campaign's first year, some one hundred thousand people called the radon hotline. Calls particularly surged when radon was featured on the *Today Show* and during the annual radon awareness week (Wagner and Dickson, 1991). But, when the scary Ad Council campaign had run its course, still only a small fraction of American homes had been tested for radon. Apparently, the dreadful images in the campaign invited denial and dismissal. The lesson appeared to be simple—if radon was so serious, people didn't want to hear about it.

In response, a second Ad Council campaign was constructed to treat the topic with humor and low-key persuasion. In one ad, a turbaned woman—"the bird lady"—tells her caged crow Hector to "smile for mommy" while she snaps flash pictures. When she begins singing "four and twenty blackbirds baked in a pie," the crow caws raucously. This bit of foolishness is used to hold the viewers' attention while a voice over asks "What are you doing this weekend that you can't take a little time to test for radon? After all, it's the second leading cause of lung cancer. And a radon test kit is inexpensive. You can pick up one on your way to get more film." A second ad features a similar voice message over the image of a henpecked (as opposed to crow-pecked) husband frantically moving gnome statues around his backyard under the dictatorial direction of his disapproving wife. The viewer is told to pick up a radon kit "on the way to get a few things for the yard." Neither ad makes it clear that the moral of the story is "test for radon." Instead, one might imagine the announcement "crow felled by lung cancer, yard gnomes recognized by EPA as new radon detectors for upcoming RMP test round."

Thus, two approaches, "Radon-Heavy" and "Radon-Lite," were served to consumers through major national advertising campaigns. Neither approach produced a major radon testing breakthrough. If anything, by the early 1990s, radon had ceased to be a fad—to the extent it ever was. Because it was no longer newsworthy, little reinforcement for testing was provided by the media. The free advertising campaigns were finished. EPA had moved from educating the public about radon to motivating them through fear and then humor with only modest success. But, why was the public unresponsive? Was this truly a case of "apathy?" In our view, apathy is one of those words that explains everything while explaining nothing. What were some plausible reasons why the market approach to radon was failing to generate demand?

Alternative Explanations for Public Inaction

While apathy may play a role in the public's inaction on radon, other contributors to the evident hesitancy of the public to respond to the EPA's Radon Action Program deserve recognition. Distrust of testing and mitigation may have accounted for some resistance (see chapters 6, 7, and 8). Here we examine several additional factors—the mixed risk profile found for radon, the failure of radon policy to distinguish between divergent publics, the lack of social discourse about radon, confusions contained in EPA policy and the *Citizen's Guide*, scientific conflict regarding radon as publicized by the media, and the influence of radon's myths.

Radon's Risk Profile

How does the public select risks? Given the plethora of potential hazards that people face, risk factors are screened to determine which risks should be taken seriously. Three factors stand out as crucial to radon's risk evaluation. The cause of the hazard is the first evaluative factor. As discussed below, radon is an invisible, unbounded, radioactive natural hazard. Second, the consequences of the hazard serve as a basis for the person's initial risk appraisal, assessing the expected severity of the outcomes and the estimated likelihood of occurrence. These outcomes are most threatening when the risk is seen as personal rather than abstract and/or the observer is viewed as particularly susceptible or vulnerable. Even a catastrophic and likely hazard won't rouse someone who is convinced that the consequences "won't happen to me." Finally, the controllability of the hazard influences further examination of the threat. We are understandably less threatened by hazards that can be prevented and controlled, and whose consequences can be mitigated.

Radon exhibits a number of key traits related to the hazard's cause, consequences, and control (see table 9.1). The totality of these traits comprises a distinctive risk personality, evident since early in the radon issue (e.g., Sandman, 1988). What is instructive about each of these traits of radon is its dual influence—the way that it simultaneously *contributes to* and *discourages* action on radon.

Table 9.1   Radon's Risk Personality

Causal traits	Consequences	Controllability
Invisible	Carcinogenic	Identifiable
Natural	Impacts the home	Preventable exposure
Radioactive	Stigma	Remediable
Unbounded	Delayed effect	
and ambient		

Radon Is Invisible

For any risk, an absence of perception is tantamount to a "tree falling in the forest" nonexistence. In radon's case, the gas and all but its longest term effects are invisible. For the general public, its invisibility (absent scientific instrumentation) renders radon as unbelievable and thus deniable. For believers in the threat, the fact that radon cannot be directly sensed contributes to the fear it arouses (see chapter 1). As with other invisible contaminants, this fear is enhanced by the difficulty of taking protective action against a force that one neither knows with certainty to be present nor absent; even if a test provides a crude snapshot of exposure for one point in time, one may not know one's exposure before or since the test was done (see Pearson, 1980; Vyner, 1988; Edelstein, 1988a). Believers in the hazard must ask, as did the Ad Council campaign, whether the unseen gas is seeping into their secure home and making witless victims of their family. Furthermore, radon not only has environmental invisibility, but also has medical invisibility. Absent medical tests or clear symptoms, lung cancer remains an undetectable affliction. The consequences of radon exposure are further clouded by the uncertainty caused by its long latency (Vyner, 1988).

Radon Is Natural and, Therefore, Blameless

In contrast to radon issues before the Colebrookdale Township discovery, the subsequent geologic radon hazard was carefully defined as a natural phenomenon, resulting from the unpreventable upward movement of soil gases. Ironically, the definition of radon as natural acted to sanitize it. Radon did not spoil natural conditions through some undesired change created by human hands. The absence of blame made radon exposure a faultless hazard, producing no sense of outrage at others for causing the risk (Sandman et al., 1987; Edelstein, 1982, 1988a). The absence of a target for blame robs geologic radon of an impetus to address the hazard, rendering radon, in Rich Guimond's words (1988b), a "benevolent hazard." As a result, action on radon rests largely upon risk aversion. In contrast, "malevolent hazards," where others are perceived to have caused harm due to greed, incompetence, or malevolence that government and others failed to prevent, inspire anger and distrust, as well as a desire for setting things right. Radon, much as other "acts of God" became an acceptable and even purified hazard. Furthermore, unlike new hazards associated with synthetic toxins, radon had been around during the entire of human history on the planet. As radon risk rejectionists enjoy noting, radon is an unavoidable risk of living on this earth. From a public perspective, such events are seen as fateful; they are acceptable because there is nothing that can really be done to control them.

Radon's natural status impeded government efforts to motivate public action, as suggested by Dr. Vernon Houk, then head of the Centers for Disease Control and the assistant surgeon general, who acted to commit the Public Health Service to the radon issue (June 1989).

> We're not doing terribly well to reach the public—you can't sue God! If this was something that somebody did, people would be up in arms. But no

one did it to them, so they accept it. In Montclair you see the focus was on radium, it wasn't natural. The point is that there is no one to blame with radon, so no one pays attention. People are not concerned with radon because you can't sue anyone because of radon. If you contrast the radon issue to Alar, Alar isn't going to hurt anybody. Yet you came close to destroying the apple industry. Radon isn't pizazzy enough for Meryl Streep.[3]

Indeed, media coverage of radon reflects exactly this bias. Mazur notes that between July and December 1986 nearly half of the thirty-eight articles on radon in the *New York Times* were about the inability of the DEP to dispose of the radium-contaminated soil in Montclair (Mazur, 1987). Thus, a great deal of the media hype and public concern about "radon" was really about a human-caused radioactive industrial waste requiring disposal and not about natural radon (see Edelstein, 1988a; 1991). Not surprisingly, New Jersey residents who had tested and found 4 pCi/l or more of radon in their homes viewed geologic radon as a blameless issue (Weinstein et al., 1989b).[4]

Radon Invades the Home

Central to our perception of radon is it's locus of effect. Radon is an indoor air pollutant that harms people right in their own homes. The home is the place of greatest perceived personal freedom, the private realm where people can choose their risks and remedies. Indeed, EPA radon policy recognizes the individual's right to choose whether to test for radon. In the face of an environmental threat, people can be expected to act to protect their home and family, as anticipated by the Ad Council campaign. Then, why would they not be responsive to radon? Several reasons come to mind.

First, publicity about Colebrookdale and Montclair offered images of serious disruption to home life, including protracted relocation. For those remaining, an "inversion of home" was evident, with the place where people formerly felt most secure transformed into a place of perceived danger (Edelstein, 1988a). As a response to these images, for members of the untested public, the consequences of testing may have seemed so severe that denial or delay was preferred. Second, the Ad Council campaign suggested that many homes were already contaminated and exposure had already occurred, which may have tapped feelings of resignation (e.g., "It's too late to prevent it.") rather than vigilant defense. Third, because radon is a natural result of the buildings' interface with the surrounding environment, it is less an intruder—as characterized by the Ad Council campaign—than a routine part of the home environment. How can something natural, ubiquitous, and historically everpresent be an intruder? Finally, radon action may face competing demands (the new roof versus radonproofing), limited resources (food versus radon), transience ("we won't be here long enough to be affected or to want the responsibility of fixing the place"), competing threats ("do we do asbestos next or radon?"; "I'm smoking anyway!"), feared responsibility from knowing ("If we sell the house and I don't know about a problem, I don't have to disclose it."), and so forth. Thus, radon testing may command a high priority within "public" reasoning but not in "private" reasoning within the isolation of the home.

Radon is Radioactive

Radioactivity is perhaps the most dreaded of all environmental hazards (Slovic, 1987; Dunlap et al., 1993; Vyner, 1988). One would expect, therefore—as did the Ad Council—that a great deal of anxiety would accompany knowledge of potential radon gas exposure. The absence of fear, we suspect, is the result of radon's natural and blameless character. Radon may be a major source of exposure to ionizing radiation, but it is, after all, only "background" radiation—a fact of life. Unlike artificial sources of preventable radiation risk created through human action, natural radon, while not safe, is easily viewed as acceptable. An additional factor may be that radon's primary hazard is through the action of alpha particles, which are too weak to pierce the skin. It may be that more acutely dangerous radioactive particles, principally gamma and beta particles, may generate more active fear.

Radon Is an Unbounded and Ambient Geologic Hazard

Radon is a geologically caused but geographically diffuse phenomenon. With little exception, radon is everywhere, although in varied amounts, and is the dominant source of ambient radioactivity. It is a truly ubiquitous hazard. The area of radon contamination can not be fenced in the manner of a Love Canal, where boundaries were drawn (albeit somewhat arbitrarily and erroneously) around the chemically polluted area. If people believed that radon was truly unbounded, they might have a reason to fear it. However, the myth of the Reading Prong offered the public a cognitive as well as geographic map of the alleged contours of the radon problem that affected radon testing. This myth fostered the tendency to see radon as confined to identifiable hot areas. Even the Ad Council campaign embodied this myth, being targeted to "high-risk areas." As previously noted, New Jersey DEP officials continued for many years to show slides of the Reading Prong during their public presentations, even long after the Clinton hot spot was discovered off the prong. It was hardly surprising that the public would be confused on this point.

Evidence of this confusion comes from several sources. New Jersey State policy was governed by the mapping of three tiers of geographically graduated risk. "Tier I," the perceived highest risk area, was the Reading Prong. The second highest risk area, "Tier II," comprised parts of the state adjacent to and influenced by the prong. It was not surprising when a review of forty-one articles printed about radon over a three-year period in northern New Jersey's *Bergen Record* found that most of them suggested that radon is *only* a threat in the Reading Prong, depicted in the media as "the Radon Belt," and, conversely, not a threat elsewhere. The myth of the Reading Prong also influenced perceptions among the nontesting public. In a subsequent study, risk information in articles about radon was perceived by a sample of New Jersey residents to be abstract and thus nonthreatening, with the exception of information regarding the Reading Prong, which aroused personal feelings of vulnerability and heightened the estimation of personal risk for those living there (Edelstein and Boyle, 1988).

Various early studies of what motivated people to test for radon suggested that testing was inspired by a belief that the home was likely to have a problem, notably the sense of "geographic susceptibility" found with proximity to the Reading Prong. Residents who tested for radon in Orange County, New York, were significantly more likely to identify themselves as living on or near the Reading Prong than were "nontesters," and perceived proximity to the Reading Prong as a major reason for their testing. Proximity to the prong significantly enhanced expectations of finding "worrisome" results; proximity also heightened concern that family health would be affected by radon (Edelstein et al., 1989).

Similarly, Rutgers University studies found that respondents from higher risk areas knew more about radon, recognized that they had a greater likelihood of a problem because of their location (although most did not see the likelihood as great), and were more likely to know others who had tested or mitigated for radon. They were more likely to have tested their current home (nearly all tests were done in the high risk "Tier I") as well as one they might purchase. The high-risk-area residents appeared to be more adjusted to radon issues. They reported less anger and helplessness. They were more optimistic about mitigation and less likely to say that they would give up a house deal if radon were found. They were less likely to blame others or to expect others to pay for their radon problems (Weinstein, Sandman, and Klotz, 1987a, b; Sandman, 1988; Weinstein, 1988; Weinstein, Sandman, and Roberts, 1989a, b, 1990; see also EPA, 1990c). Of course, many residents of high-risk areas continued to rationalize inaction. For example, as participants in a Maryland EPA study became convinced that there was radon in their area, they were less likely to believe that they had radon in their own homes (EPA, 1988e). Some residents of the Reading Prong in Orange County, New York justified not testing for radon because they felt safe because their houses were so drafty (Edelstein et al., 1989).

Radon Is Carcinogenic

While genetic mutation was a major preoccupation of cold war nuclear anxiety (Weart, 1988), perhaps the dominant health association for radioactive exposure has been cancer. More than any other physical problem, cancer is most feared by the public, in part because it often results in prolonged and painful suffering, disfigurement, and social stigma (see Berman and Wandersman, 1990). Given radon's association with lung cancer, one might add the term "death" to this list. The relative incurability of lung cancer suggests that fears of cancer would be maximized for this type of malignancy. Indeed, as we have seen, radon's uncommonly high risk has been central to government response. EPA consistently refers to radon as the second leading cause of lung cancer. Despite controversy over the number of actual deaths, there is little scientific dispute that the risk is serious. Internal EPA risk reviews have consistently named radon as one of the top environmental risks (see chapters 3 and 11), as have similar state risk evaluations (EPA, 1990a).[5]

Why then doesn't fear of lung cancer motivate widespread radon testing? One key problem is that radon risk is overshadowed by (and perhaps interactive with) smoking risk, a topic shrouded by personal and social denial. With the leading cause of lung cancer long tolerated, the secondary cause is unlikely to cause much of a stir, even if it is less voluntary. Interestingly, the rise of the radon issue corresponds to the fall of public smoking in the United States. However, smoking is still a discretionary activity within the private home. The urgency of addressing smoking risk has made lung cancer's second cause appear as a secondary priority, as long suggested by many health officials and critics of EPA radon policy (e.g., Cole, 1993).

Radon Is Stigmatizing

The longtime head of Pennsylvania's radon program, Thomas Gerusky (1988), recalled to the authors an occasion when his boss at the DER visited with a congressional committee to discuss the Reading Prong. "In congressional testimony, the Secretary of the Department suggested that the name of the Prong be changed to the 'Passaic Prong.' But the New Jersey delegation on the Committee had no sense of humor." Similar reticence characterized two New Jersey communities protesting the state's listing of high radon communities for fear that real estate values would be adversely affected (Melamed, 1992).

These instances recognize "environmental stigma," the discrediting of settings, places, and objects, as well as associated individuals, families, and communities, as the result of a feared environmental condition. Environmental stigma affects property values and sales, social relationships, and self-concept (Edelstein, 1991, 1988a). Radon stigma is influenced by other attributes of the hazard's risk personality—its carcinogeneity, radioactivity, invisibility, and its invasion of the private dwelling. When these feared conditions become visibly associated with a physical setting, the place becomes marked as dangerous and undesirable. By extension, the people associated with the place are also marginalized. Stigmatized communities are characterized by blame directed at victims, at unprotective parents, at those who failed to disclose the hazard, and at activists whose activities publicize the hazard. As a result of such consequences, even when there is little fear from the hazard, there may be considerable fear of the stigma.

Radon's potential for stigma is a disincentive to testing and mitigation. There is some evidence that known radon-contaminated homes are harder to sell and may bring lower value. Radon testing and mitigation is obtrusive and some forms of mitigation may permanently mark the house. While mitigated homes may offset their stigma with the knowledge that they have been "cured," the efficacy and duration of the cure must be trusted. As a result, it may be rational for homeowners to choose ignorance of their radon levels as an alternative to unleashing this chain of consequences. Fear of radon stigma is also explained, in part, by the myth of Reading Prong, which was the expectation that this diffuse and pervasive hazard will be manifest only in bounded hot spots, such as Colebrookdale Township, or geographic regions, such as the Reading Prong. A hazard perceived to be truly pervasive would hardly be stigmatizing (Edelstein, 1991).

Radon's Impacts Are Delayed—Another Day of Exposure Is Unlikely to Matter

Radon lacks immediacy as a hazard. Its best-known consequence, long latency lung cancer, occurs potentially far in the future. And were lung cancer actually to be manifested, it would be difficult to relate the disease to some identifiable radon exposure because such exposures will have been chronic and invisible. Furthermore, the risk from radon, as described by the EPA, involves a cumulative, lifetime exposure. The risk is placed somewhere into the same eventual realm as are the other risks of aging, merging with the certitude that something, sometime, is going to kill us. And, until people pass middle age, seventy years of exposure is outside any temporal boundary for urgency. And, by then, any significant exposure has probably already occurred.

Adding to these other invitations for delay, lifetimes are rarely passed in one building, and people suffer cumulative exposure across places. Even a vigilant individual could control radon in only a portion of these cumulative settings. And, while there may be a high fear of lung cancer per se, the perceived risk of "catching" lung cancer from any given point of exposure is negligible. Even the *Citizen's Guide* suggests that some time delay in mitigating all but extreme exceedances of the guidance is unlikely to be harmful—in some cases even a delay of several years. By creating a temporal—as well as spatial—relativity to radon risk, there is a sense of continuing slide built into radon perception. All things considered, another day or delay is not going to matter. Thus, action is easily put off even if intention to act is aroused.

It follows that radon exposure in the existing home does not trigger urgent decisions. Unless a home is to be sold, bought, or built, one has already made decisions relevant to the building. The risk and the decision making are both in the future. The urgency of acting on radon is, thus, easily lost in the context of other competing threats that demand our attention. As the former head of the American Lung Association, Thomas Godar told a lunchtime audience at the 1991 EPA radon conference, "People are facing a circuit overload of bad news: AIDS, cancer, drugs . . . they are not going to be as concerned about something that is not an immediate threat."

Radon—A Controllable Hazard

The characteristic of radon risk that is thought to present the greatest hope for inspiring action involves its controllability—that an aware public will act to avoid the risk because an avenue of action is available. However, while radon is viewed by the public as extremely dangerous, beyond its natural occurrence, controllability is the key factor explaining why radon generates relatively little stress, making it easier to delay or avoid action. The perception of controllability is created by the myths of the quick test and quick fix. On the other hand, as previously discussed, radon may not be as controllable as the EPA suggests. Doubts over the validity of testing or the efficacy of mitigation (i.e., the mitigatory gap) further serve to invite delayed action. Thus, for radon action, in a sense, the issue is damned if it is controllable and damned if it isn't.

Summary: Mobilizing Versus Qualifying Risk Characteristics

Inaction on radon is a consequence of the hazard's ambivalent risk personality. That radon is radioactive and carcinogenic, and invisibly invades the home represent mobilizing characteristics, factors that invite public response. Indeed, the Ad Council campaign targeted these very themes. Yet, radon action is offset because it is a natural and pervasive long-latency hazard easily perceived as bounded to specific areas. Action on radon may be socially stigmatizing. And whether one believes or doubts the hazard's controllability, action is discouraged. In other words, despite the recognition of its severity as a hazard and the possible recognition of its remediability, radon is not necessarily seen by the public as a likely threat and, therefore, it is not viewed as a personal risk demanding action. The general public is fairly resistant to active vigilance against radon. Perhaps, then, radon policy is targeted on the wrong public.

A Failure to Distinguish Divergent Radon Publics

The perception of radon risk rests as much on the attributes of the perceiver as it does on the attributes of the risk to be perceived. Most geologic radon programs have targeted "the public," the amorphous mass of citizens who must be convinced to voluntarily test their homes. The tendency has been to treat this public as if it were homogenous. However, on closer examination, one can define the following different subpublics, each with distinctive interpretations of radon risk:

- *Apathetic subpublic*. Members do not attend to environmental risk issues in general and view radon as irrelevant to their lives. Because little attention is paid to the hazard, apathy invites the person to be uninformed, assuring radon's continued unimportance unless forced by external events.
- *Fearful subpublic*. Members know enough about radon to dread it. Their fear may cause them to remove the threat by addressing radon, to remove their fear by denying the threat, or, if no other recourse is understood to be available, to panic.
- *Vigilant subpublic*. Members are informed and choose to act upon radon after weighing the evidence and options available. Vigilance does not guarantee a response to radon. Rather, the weight of information may favor delay or inaction on radon. Other issues may urgently compete for attention.
- *Pragmatic subpublic*. Members respond to situational demands to act on radon. They test and remediate for radon in order to sell their homes, regardless of their personal concern for radon. They find it prudent to test a home they intend to purchase while responsibility for addressing problems belongs to the seller. Radon is just part of the transaction, like termite inspections.
- *Victimized subpublic*. For those coping with identified "significant" levels of radon in their homes combined with uncertainty over remediation, radon may become a central organizing issue in the way they live and think about their lives (see chapter 1).

A recognition of the differential response of subpublics to radon risk suggests that no single strategy to motivate radon testing and mitigation will reach the entire public. Efforts based upon education, rational persuasion, and fear will succeed with some subpublics while failing with others. The apathetic require a change of context, making radon relevant, before information has any impact. Those engaging in issue denial are less needing of information about the risk of radon than motivation to shift to action. Panic is mitigated by clear courses of feasible action. The vigilant portion of the public, amenable to rational decision making, must be approached in a manner that addresses radon's myths and the limitations of existing testing and mitigation in order to prove that now is the time to act on this issue. Pragmatists are readily accessible in a regulatory or market context that will require radon testing for real estate transfer, including new construction. For the pragmatic subpublic, radon action is a mundane necessary financial transaction, rather than a voluntary decision influenced by personal and social characteristics affecting the choice to act or not.

EPA policy has shifted over time from a focus on the panicked, to the vigilant, and then to the apathetic public. However, there is ample evidence that the pragmatic public would be the most fruitful target for policy. Indeed, by 1988, field staff were telling EPA's Washington radon office that "The radon issue would disappear if it were not for the real estate people" (Page, 1988). EPA risk communication research similarly found the public more willing to reduce radon risk during a real estate transaction than otherwise (Doyle et al., 1990). The 1992 review of EPA's radon program recommended a shift in focus to real estate and new construction. Nevertheless, a shift of focus to realty transactions was not anticipated in the near term (Melamed and Rasmussen, 1992).

Finally, subpublic differences might be further aggregated along class, cultural, racial, and geographic/regional factors. Federal radon policy has been targeted to the middle-class homeowner, presumed to have the interest, control, and resources to address the issue. Renters lack similar authority to act. Most are dependent upon landlords for testing and mitigation, a responsibility that has not been mandated. Furthermore, the poor may be unable to afford the "luxury" of radon testing and mitigation absent a social commitment for assistance. Accordingly, radon policy has a built-in economic bias, whereby it has alerted the economically disadvantaged of still another environmental hazard without enabling them to act.[6]

The focus of the EPA radon program upon voluntary action by homeowners has invited charges of environmental racism. EPA was very sensitive to this issue. After Carol Browner took office as EPA administrator in 1993, she issued a five-point strategy for implementing environmental justice in EPA programs and activities. Subsequently, such steps became national policy when, on February 11, 1994, President Clinton issued Executive Order 12898, entitled "Federal Actions to Address Environmental Justice in Minority Populations and Low-Income Populations." That order set a goal of achieving equal environmental protection for all communities regardless of race, income, ethnicity, or culture (see Gaylord and Bell, 1995).

About the same time as Browner was setting clear agency policy, the radon group was reviewing data on radon action that clearly showed that lower income and minority people were taking less action than others to address radon (see table 9.2).[7] The radon group, with its characteristic assertiveness, determined to use the environmental justice bandwagon in order to address the inequities. Taking leadership within EPA, a staff team was created to address these differences by intensifying efforts to reach a wider audience with information about the radon threat and by identifying resources that might support low income action. The staff implemented a major outreach program with the assistance of new organizational partners funded by EPA to help reach various minority groups. As table 9.2 illustrates, subsequent survey data showed some closing of the gap in radon awareness and testing (Rowson, 1996; Carpentier, 1996), although results are very uneven. EPA still has a way to go if it is to achieve its goal of equality between groups by the year 2000. One bright spot, reflected in the data, is the comparatively successful effort to address radon on Indian reservations.

Table 9.2   Survey Results Showing Differences in Radon Awareness and Testing by Race for 1993 and 1994

Subgroup	% Aware of Radon		% Testing for Radon	
	1993	1994	1993	1994
White	73	80	10	11
Black	47	50	5	6
Hispanic	29	47	4	6
Asian	47	46	3	6
Native American	64	70	8	14

Source: EPA data provided by Carpentier, 1996.

Lack of Social and Media Support for Radon Action

Radon testing, given the hypothetical nature of the hazard, involves an abstract situation easily influenced by information about radon. Strong social pressure, such as from the media or from family and friends is required to encourage testing (Mazur and Hall, 1990). Inaccurate beliefs about radon are reinforced by the media or by word of mouth, leading to a confused understanding of the hazard, greater denial of the problem, and rationalization of inaction.

Social Support and Perception of Radon

Rutgers University studies reveal that a significant source of influence in people's thinking about radon comes from their social reference groups, such as their family and friends. Frequently people start to pay attention to radon only when they learn that others take it seriously. Significant increases in the social recognition of radon were found among New Jersey residents between 1986 and 1988–89, with an increase of those who knew someone who had tested from 15 percent to nearly half and knowledge of others mitigating for radon increasing from 1 to 15 percent. Ironically, while influenced by others to attend to radon, people reported that they shared their own radon test results with five or fewer people. This limited sharing less reflected people's unwillingness to talk about their radon results than disinterest by others to listen to them (Weinstein, Sandman, and Roberts, 1989a and b; Weinstein et al., 1990). But can social support be mobilized on behalf of radon testing? A 1988 EPA study that compared radon testing rates in three Maryland communities exposed to different risk communication strategies confirms the importance of community outreach and the impact of informal communication. However, even the most successful approach resulted in testing by less than 10 percent of the residents (EPA, 1988e).

These limits of social influence on radon testing may reflect the fractured nature of modern society. Indeed, federal radon policy assumes that the American homeowner has become so divorced from community that the nuclear family is the only access point for radon policy. However, in an effort to enhance social influence for radon action, the EPA has attempted to educate influential groups and respected community leaders, such as physicians. They have also integrated locally based national organizations, such as the American Lung Association, into their program. Recent efforts to reach into minority communities have led EPA to network with several national organizations that have a community presence, including the National Medical Association, the National Coalition of Hispanic Health and Human Services, the Association of Asian and Pacific Community Health Organizations, and the National Council of Negro Women (see chapter 11). However, with some exceptions (see chapter 1, also EPA, 1988e; Makofske and Edelstein, 1989; Edelstein and Hoodes, 1988), radon has failed to become a grassroots issue, and social networks have not generally been mobilized in support of testing.

Media As a Factor in Perception of Radon

We have already seen how myths, such as the myth of the Reading Prong, become established and reinforced in public understanding through the media. We have also seen many instances where media coverage of radon rejectionists has given currency to the myth of dead bodies or other challenges to radon's risk. In an experiment by the first author and one of his students, Valerie Boyle, reported scientific disagreement over radon was found to diminish perceptions of personal threat from radon. Some subjects read a newspaper article, "Radon May Threaten the Health of Millions," which depicted radon as a high risk. Others read a generally reassuring article, "Scientists Discount Radon Risk." Readers of the article about high risk recalled many more details about radon than did those reading the article about low risk. They also evaluated radon as a more serious hazard and indicated a greater intention to test a home they considered for purchase (Edelstein and Boyle, 1988).

The effect of reporting of radon dissensus should not be minimized. From the onset of the radon issue, visible controversy—often exceeding actual substantive disagreement—has eroded EPA's claims about the urgency of addressing radon. Reporting of controversy may diminish the public's perceived risk or may just confound people as to the appropriate response. Take, as a case in point, the Albany paper's article "State Scientists Debate Radon Threat in Voorheesville" (Thurman, 1986, p. C1). When Karim Rimawi, director of New

York State's Bureau of Environmental Radiation Protection, met with residents of Voorheesville, New York, to discuss finding that forty local homes had excessive radon levels, the validity of the findings was repeatedly challenged from the audience by John Matuszek, director of the state's radiological sciences laboratory. The article cites two reasons for Matuszek's vociferous criticism, his belief that radon risk was overstated given the inapplicability of miner's data to the home and his view that EPA guidelines were "19,000-times stricter than those set for nuclear power plants." The article proceeds to provide an indication of the confusion caused by the controversy, including Voorheesville Mayor Edward Clark's observations: "They were dueling with scientific esoterica . . . literally arguing over what is right or wrong, testing devices and how findings should be interpreted. We were there to get clarification but we got confusion. . . .The community is less well off right now in terms of information and guidances than it was yesterday. They literally confused everybody." As an interesting commentary on environmental stigma and radon, the mayor reported that residents now felt that the state was using the village as a "hot spot proving ground."

Readers of this article were vicariously confused, without having to attend the meeting. Other reporting on radon establishes similar ambivalence. For example, would a rational member of the public rush to remediate even a serious radon problem after reading that mitigation is "a technology that is still being developed. The cost of remediation can range from $100 to $40,000" (Swift, 1987)? Similarly, criticism of testing may dissuade people from finding out their radon levels (see Harley, 1990), and publicity about radon scams has been blamed for creating a reticence among people to trust radon firms (Scripps Howard, 1991).

Most questioning of EPA's program has come from a cadre of highly visible scientific critics in the rival Department of Energy, as well as from several independent scientists. Such critics have seemingly had no trouble attracting media attention in the general press, the professional press, and the scholarly journal. For example, Eckholm cites Naomi Harley's charge that EPA's risk estimates for radon are "outlandishly high" (1986, p. c7). An editorialist in the *Washington Times* relied on two other persistent radon critics in attacking EPA radon policy. Ralph Lapp, credited as the scientist who originally developed the 4 pCi/l "standard," is cited criticizing the use of this "standard." A table illustrates Lapp's findings of "far higher" lung cancer deaths in the low-radon coastal area of New Jersey than in the high-radon Reading Prong. And a cartoon depicts Rambo-type warriors dressed in protective clothing firing into the "radon zone." The "seminal" and "exhaustive" work of University of Pittsburgh physicist Bernie Cohen is next cited to assert that higher radon levels are actually therapeutic and that the "single flawed" study of uranium miners upon which EPA's risk estimates are based actually shows that the risk of lung cancer from radon in the residential setting was less than that "from drinking tap water in normal quantities." Summarizing these criticisms, the editorialist attacks the Bush administration's effort to achieve "zero-risk . . . even though there is not the slightest epidemiological evidence that radon poses any significant health hazard in America, unless you happen to be a uranium miner who smokes heavily" (Brookes, 1989, p. f1). To similar effect, a University of Rochester biophysicist minimized the risk of radon through comparison to common everyday risk factors, concluding that "indoor radon is about as much of a hazard as living in your own home" (Associated Press, 1988, p. 6).

The contradiction and ambiguity found in press coverage of radon is illustrated by the headlines of two articles appearing in the same newspaper *(Middletown Times-Herald Record)* only a half year apart with no other radon coverage in between: "Radon Threat Reduced: Study Can't Link Gas, Cancer" *(Chicago Tribune*, 1994) and "Study Calls Radon Big Risk" (Associated Press, June 6, 1995). Contradictory risk statements are often found mixed together within a single article, as found in the text of this 1993 item from Knight-Ridder Newspapers [bold is added to highlight risk-enhancing messages, while italics is used to display risk-qualifying messages].

One of every five schools in the United States has unacceptably high levels of radioactive radon gas, according to federal officials. . . . *The numbers are not quite as bad as they look, because schools tested for the EPA survey were listed if just one measurement taken within the building exceeded the federal safety standard.* . . . **The EPA has labeled radon the nation's second leading cause of lung cancer.** . . . *Should parents worry? Probably not, Rep. Henry Waxman (D.-Calif.), co-chairman of the House Commerce Committee's subcommittee on health and the environment, said in Washington.* . . . *"Radon causes lung cancer only after years of exposure," Waxman said, adding that there is no evidence children are suffering immediate, acute illnesses because of radon exposure at school.* . . . **Radon is considered a serious health problem,** *but no federal regulations require schools to test for it or do anything about high levels if they are found.* . . . *Exceeding the EPA safety standard is not considered a matter of urgency, even by the EPA. The EPA recommends that steps be taken to control a radon problem within a year of its discovery.* . . . **But ignoring it is foolish because there is no way, short of testing, to know where it will show up in dangerous quantities, experts said** (p. 7).

In sum, at the same time that the EPA exerted extensive efforts to carefully mold the radon issue, the media gave the issue a very different shape. The media, with its lust for "news" (a.k.a., controversy), is less configured to support a permanent public service effort than to respond to divergent opinions that criticize government programs. The net effect has been to amplify scientific controversy over relatively narrow issues into what seem, in print, to be wholesale dismissals of the entire radon threat. Much as the EPA has tried to use the media to serve its ends, the agency's critics have proven capable of using the media to embarrass the agency. Confused and ambivalent messages prevail. The observant citizen cannot help but to see this mixed scientific environment as a disincentive to radon action.

The Question of Radon Mitigation

An early experience with mitigation suggested that remediation faces a potential for denial comparable to that faced by testing. Thus, few confirmatory tests and credible mitigations followed the successful community testing effort conducted by WJLA in Washington, D.C., despite many thousands of completed radon tests (Fisher and Sjoberg, 1987; Doyle et al., 1990; EPA, 1992d). However, subsequent experience suggests a somewhat different picture.

Earlier in the chapter it was suggested that 300,000 homes had been mitigated for radon by contractors as of spring 1993 (EPA, 1993g). But what does this number mean? On one extreme, if we assume that 6 percent of the 8.1 million homes tested are over the federal guidance, and that remediations occurred among these 486,000 homes, then as many as 62 percent of homes testing over 4 pCi/l would have been remediated by contractors. Thus, although nearly 40 percent of those presumably requiring remediation have not done so, these numbers certainly suggest a greater level of response than does testing. On the other extreme, perhaps as many as 20 percent of the 8.1 million homes exceeded the federal guidance, in which case only 18 percent of those homes have been remediated.[8]

In any case, it would seem that the decision to mitigate is quite different from the decision to test. Testers having found high radon levels face an imminent and concrete personal hazard—represented by their test scores—that should be likely to motivate remediation. Mitigation, unlike testing, is, therefore, governed by a direct sense of objective risk. The difference between mitigation and testing decisions is illuminated by research. In one New York study, while relatively few tested for radon, those receiving scores indicating the need for mitigation tended to undertake remedial efforts (Mazur and Hall, 1990). And a July 1990 survey of 135 homeowners having tested over 4 pCi/l found one-quarter reporting completed mitigation and the remainder planning it (Wagner and Dickson, 1991). Rutgers researchers found those testing over 4 pCi/l to be more predisposed to action than worry. Nearly 70 percent reported changing their behavior while at home—keeping windows open or avoiding high-radon areas of the home. Such behavioral mitigations were particularly adopted by people having fewer resources. More well-to-do people tended to make structural changes to their homes; more than half of the respondents overall planned future structural changes to reduce their homes below 4 pCi/l. Mitigation was driven specifically by the perception of in-

creased likelihood of getting lung cancer due to exposure, not by the specific radon level or a general fear of cancer per se. The perception of danger was enhanced by knowledge that one's radon level was higher than others. Mitigation was inspired by the belief that it is an effective means for preventing lung cancer (Weinstein et al., 1990). In sum, receiving a radon test over 4 pCi/l increases protective vigilance and predisposes one to action.

Of course, the subpublic most prone to undertake mitigation are the pragmatists, heavily represented in the testing public. For example, research found high mitigation levels among workers subject to frequent job transfer and needing to easily and quickly sell their homes (Fisher and Sjoberg, 1987). In other words, many mitigations are likely to be done by people attempting to sell their property, and thus occur for pragmatic rather than risk reduction reasons. Perceived victimization by radon is another factor demanding action on remediation, as we saw in chapter 1, and the social context can also be influential, as it was in Clinton, New Jersey. There, the fact that local officials recruited state and federal assistance to test and mitigate the excessive radon levels found in 1986 meant that residents were not left in a personal vacuum regarding how to proceed. While most homeowners paid for their own remediation, government organized and managed the remediation process. A social context reinforcing radon remediation prevailed, making it possible for people to address the radon problem effectively with minimal personal stress (see chapter 2).

All of these factors explain why rates of mitigation may be greater tha testing. Yet, we can also identify factors that may impede some people fro undertaking mitigation. Media controversy may cause a distrust of mitigati techniques or firms. If people disbelieve the myth of the quick test, then th have no foundation for proceeding to remediate. Mitigation measures have times been unsightly, detracting from the home. Mitigation measures may viewed as insufficiently developed, reflecting a mitigatory gap. In a poor ec omy the resources for mitigating may be tight, especially when unemployr and poor house sales combine to create uncertainty about the duration that dents may stay at their addresses. The evidence cited here suggests that pe may undertake behavioral mitigations as interim or permanent substitute structural mitigations. Finally, the lag time allowed for response to radon below 20 pCi/l by the *Citizen's Guide* may suggest that delay is accep inviting procrastination; allowable delays are on the order of the average A can mobility time.

Overall, the factors influencing testing and mitigation for radon do n port the prevalent EPA policy assumption governed by the need to make testing simple and convenient in order to fit into the lifestyle of the ap homeowner. Yet, the agency's belief in an apathetic public dominated the *Citizen's Guide to Radon*. We now look to the original and revised gu potential influences on public perception of risk.

Mixed Messages Inherent in the
Citizen's Guide and EPA Policy

While the 1986 *Citizen's Guide* served as the primary public statement of risk communication and EPA radon policy, in numerous ways the document became part of the problem that it was supposed to solve. Figure 9.6 summarizes the key messages conveyed by the guide. As can be seen, the rational reader confronts a highly qualified and restrained message, full of contradiction. Yes, radon causes thousands of cancers, but it is much less serious than is voluntary smoking. Factors such as duration and dose contribute to radon risk, but this risk is portrayed as inherently uncertain. Most houses don't have a radon problem, and if you haven't heard that others have a problem nearby, don't worry about it. The recommended screening test does not reliably measure actual radon exposure, and further tests would be needed before any action was required, anyway. It was not surprising that an EPA/New York State Energy Research and Development Authority study found the mixture of quantitative and qualitative information and directive and nondirective language in the *Citizen's Guide* to be the least successful of six approaches compared for imparting an understanding of radon risk (EPA, 1988e).

---

* Radon is responsible for between 5,000 and 20,000 yearly lung cancers.
* In contrast, smoking accounts for 85 percent of all lung cancers.
* Risk is related both to the amount of radon exposure and to the duration.
* There is uncertainty over the actual risk.
* Most houses are unlikely to have a radon problem.
* In deciding whether to test, concerned citizens should check to see if any high radon levels have been found in their area.
* Residents are recommended to do a screening measurement in the lowest livable area of the home.
* Because of the variability of radon levels, screening tests do not reliably measure average radon exposures.
* Follow-up measures including long-term testing are recommended for tests exceeding 4 pCi/l, with the urgency dictated by the level of radon.

Fig. 9.6   Selected messages from the 1986 *Citizen's Guide to Radon*
(After EPA, 1986)

The Draft Revision

These problems were compounded, rather than fixed, in the 1992 revision of the guide. In their effort to conquer public apathy, EPA officials drew heavily from the risk communication research and the marketing studies that accompanied the Ad Council campaign. Six summary findings from this research, listed in fig. 9.7, were used to direct the revision of the *Citizen's Guide*.

---

1. *Be prescriptive as well as informative.* Clear guidance avoids perceptions of uncertainty, a possible basis for avoiding radon action.

2. *Streamline guidelines on testing and mitigation to minimize barriers to public action.* Because the 1986 *Citizen's Guide* demanded technical decision making involving three steps (test-test-fix) and multiple people and skills, it invited people to drop out of the process. It is difficult enough to get people to test once, let alone twice. People are particularly unwilling to do long-term testing.

3. *Overcome public denial through the use of persuasive appeals such as concern for the family.* There is a tendency to deny that radon levels will "affect me." Information about radon is used to enhance such denial. Denial can be overcome by rousing concerns for family protection.

4. *Provide an appropriate level of radon information, since too much or too little information may result in an undesired effect.* Research suggests that too little data may cause unjustified concern, whereas too much detail feeds denial because some basis for rationalizing away personal risk is likely to be found. Information suggesting uncertainty is particularly likely to excuse inaction.

5. *Personalize the radon threat with tangible, relevant comparisons to familiar risk.* Because the public is reluctant to believe in radon as a risk, such belief can be fostered through comparisons to other health risks that have already been recognized—associations with lung cancer and smoking for example. Quantitative risk information allows people to form rational risk estimates.

6. *Stress that radon problems can be corrected but do not overstate the ease of fixing them.* People readily believe that mitigation is expensive and ineffective and that contractors can't be trusted. They are suspicious of claims to the contrary. Thus, dismissals of such beliefs cannot be overstated.

Fig. 9.7   Key risk communications findings
(After EPA, Radon Division, 1992a, 6–2).

Based upon these principles, a revision for the *Citizen's Guide* was announced in the *Federal Register* in fall 1990. EPA distributed for comment some eight hundred copies of the proposed brochure, *A Citizen's Guide to Radon: Don't Let a Dangerous Intruder Invade Your Home,* which embodied the fear-inducing approach developed for the Ad Council campaign. Note the language: "There is an intruder invading your neighborhood. And unfortunately, locking the doors and windows in your home won't keep the intruder out. Or keep you and your family safe. You can't see this intruder. You can't smell it. You can't taste it. But this intruder is a problem in 1 out of every 5 homes. This intruder isn't human, it's a radioactive gas. The intruder's name is radon. And it can be deadly" (p. X).

The draft review was also considerably more prescriptive than the original guide: readers were bluntly told that they should test their homes for radon, fix their homes if radon levels exceeded 4 pCi/l, and consider reducing their risk through mitigation even if their levels were below 4 pCi/l. Three alternative risk charts were shown, one for the general risk of radon, a second breaking down smokers and never-smokers, and a third demonstrating the risk only for never-smokers. Each chart displayed the lifetime lung cancer risk per one thousand people at different radon levels. The number of chest X rays necessary to give an equivalent risk was also displayed, as was a column of recommendations for action. Each chart stressed that radon risk is greater for smokers, that children may be more at risk than adults, and that radon risk is comparatively greater than that from other pollutants.

It is not surprising that much of the seven hundred pages of comment received on the draft dealt with issues of risk. While risk communication research indicated that the fear-inducing "dangerous intruder" cover and theme were most likely to inspire radon action, the majority of the 147 comments on the draft found the approach to be "patronizing and misleading" (EPA, 1992d). In response, the new *Citizen's Guide* actually issued in 1992 backed away from this approach.

A New *Citizen's Guide*

The final document substituted "family protection" as its theme, depicting on the cover framed portraits of a cluster of three racially diverse families. Graphics throughout the 1992 *Citizen's Guide* similarly avoid any fear-inducing messages. At fifteen pages, the document balanced findings that too much technical information would make it easier for readers to rationalize radon risk and forgo protective action with the concerns of state radon officials that a sparse guide would shift the major burden for providing information to the public onto their shoulders (see EPA, 1992d).[9] The guide kept the prescriptive recommendations of the draft, warning that radon is estimated to cause thousands of yearly cancer deaths in the United States, while stressing the "facts" that radon is a cancer-causing radioactive gas found nationwide, that testing is "inexpensive and easy," and that the problem is "simple" and "inexpensive" to fix. EPA even lists a series of radon "myths," some of which parallel those we have cited.

A shift in risk comparison was made in the new guide. Because research proved it was not frightening, the use of comparisons of radon risk to X rays was abandoned. Instead, an effort was made to personalize the risk by comparing radon to more generally feared causes of death, such as drowning, home fires, and airplane and car crashes (see fig. 9.8). According to the risk comparison charts used in the final guide, radon kills about fourteen thousand people per year, about two-thirds of the number killed by drunk driving, but more than twice the number attributed to drownings. Fires and airline crashes are shown to cause even fewer deaths (EPA, 1992f). Separate charts (see fig. 4.2) are used to show radon health risk for smokers and never-smokers in order for nonsmokers to realize that they have significant risks from radon, even if they don't smoke. Meanwhile, smokers ostensibly learn that their already huge risks are enhanced by radon exposure.

Perhaps the most fascinating issues in the revised guide involve EPA's evident desperation to market radon even at the sacrifice of scientific validity. As a result, findings from risk communication research about how to arouse radon concern were given preference to issues of scientific validity in shaping EPA policy. This bias is evident with the issues of both testing approach and test location.

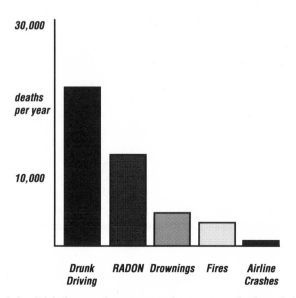

Fig. 9.8   Risk from radon compared to commonly feared risks
(After EPA, 1992f)

The Need for Simplified Testing

The new radon testing guidelines were less stringent than the prior guide, allowing short-term tests to be used for initial screening and, although acknowledging that long-term tests are better, allowing short-term tests to be used for confirmatory testing, as well. This ambiguous guidance resulted from research findings that demonstrated that homeowners are likely to drop out of a two-stage testing process—where initial results are confirmed by a second round of testing—and were certainly unwilling to wait a year for long-term confirmatory results. EPA rationalized this confusing policy shift despite its own findings that exposed the weakness of short-term testing. Instead, the agency relied upon a "decision analysis" comparing the presumed accuracy of varied consumer decisions to retest, to mitigate, or to do nothing (EPA, 1992f). As a result of this analysis,

1. Long-term follow-up testing was rejected, despite the greater accuracy (i.e., less false positives and false negatives), for fear that long-term tests would reduce compliance.
2. The guidance used in 1986 was also rejected because those receiving radon scores below 4 pCi/l were originally given no reason to do confirmatory testing. On this point, EPA thus concurred with the analysis made in chapter 6 that the guidances encouraged false negative decisions.
3. Similarly, a guidance based entirely on short-term tests for initial and follow-up measurement was rejected for fear of false negatives, despite the convenience to consumers.

Because none of these choices was satisfactory, EPA was left in a bind. Grasping straws, they chose to combine initial screening with the tester's choice of long- or short-term follow-up. Given the agency's assumption that 91 percent of testers would use short-term tests for confirmatory testing given the choice, the guidance embodies the same acknowledged error that had already led the agency to reject a policy based solely on short-term testing. The only significant difference is that the new wording shifts responsibility from EPA to the consumer. The choice to do poor testing is left in the hands of the homeowner, who can then be blamed for doing just that. Thus, the guidance addressed the agency's bind by accepting invalid testing as an inevitable consumer choice. With these verbal gymnastics, EPA claimed that it had achieved the best balance between testing accuracy and convenience (EPA, 1992d). The trade-off was justified by the need to remove any barriers to testing and mitigation that might discourage an apathetic public: "Although EPA recognized the technical superiority of long-term versus short-term testing, after extensive evaluation of the issue, it had to accept the compelling practical limitation that the public at large is more likely to use short-term testing. A lot of 'good testing, after all, will provide greater public health protection than a more limited amount of 'perfect' testing" (p. 7-7).

Ironically, the revised policy promised not only the potential for more false negatives but also by inviting testers to skip confirmatory testing altogether, potential false positives. The absurdity of this position was not lost on EPA's critics. For example, the DOE's Richard Sextro (1991) told the authors: "EPA feels that you can look at everything from their side of the Potomac—they have Potomac fever. They make sweeping generalizations and they are not getting anyone to test. Few are mitigating. What is wrong with the picture? Their answer is that if you can't get people to test the first time, you have less of a chance the second time (i.e., in confirmatory testing); and if you work your way down the curve, you will get no one to mitigate. So they chopped out the middle test. You just test and fix. But does 10 [pCi/l] on a screening test mean more than 4? The 95 percent confidence level is so big that it may drop below 4!"

Testing in Lived-in Areas

The new guidance relied upon research findings about where consumers actually tested in recommending that testing should occur in "the lowest lived in level of the home (for example, the basement if it is frequently used, otherwise, the first floor)." This recommendation contradicted the first *Citizen's Guide*'s direction to test the lowest livable area of the house (EPA, 1992f). Much as with the issue of confirmatory testing, the decision of where testing should occur was, thus, transferred from EPA to the consumer.

This shift was justified because people don't seem to care what the level of radon is in an area that no one ever occupies; homeowner's know their own lifestyle and, thus, where testing makes the most sense. However, the changed guidance introduced an important new source of confusion (and, thus, error) into radon testing (see also chapter 6). What if an existing homeowner tested an upper floor (probably less likely to have as high a radon level as lower floors) because they rarely used the lower floor. Yet, an eventual buyer might have a different use pattern, resulting in greater exposure to radon. Buyers of a "radon-free house" might not realize that the tests disclosed before sale were done upstairs. While their "lowest living area" might have significant radon levels, levels were acceptable at the prior owner's lowest area of living. Radon testing professionals were particularly concerned about being trapped in the resulting confusion, as radon professional Bill Broadhead noted: "Can you realize the legal nightmare when a buyer sues because no one asked him if he planned to live in the basement when they tested his first floor? It would be a disaster!" (Silverman, 1992a, p. 29). Requirements for testing with closed-house conditions were also eased.

While these significant changes were implemented, the new guide opted to keep the same 4 pCi/l level of acceptable risk found in the original, while alerting the homeowner that pushing radon levels lower was even better. The agency fully expected to be raked over the coals by Congress for failing to lower the guidance. EPA's Steve Page (1991) told the authors, "When Congress passed the Indoor Radon Abatement Act, they made it clear that the risks were way out of line with the regulatory side. We were told to get them in line. When EPA goes before Congressman Waxman's committee, they will ask if EPA has a hearing problem. The new *Citizen's Guide* talks about 4 pCi/l. He will ask, 'You say that you can fix 80 percent of the homes at 2 pCi/l?'"

The issue of risk level, much like the issues of location for testing and choice of testing protocol, illustrates the extent to which the agency was unable to resolve the nagging policy questions regarding radon. Even as it feared public apathy, the only efforts to overcome it were in the form of the document. And the substance of the guidance was perhaps even more ambiguous than the prior version. Thus, an apathetic public was given even more choice points to be indecisive about. Agency indecisiveness was, thus, decentralized.

Conclusions about Radon and Apathy

In allowing radon to shift from an issue driven by the institutional fear of public panic to that governed by the belief that the public is apathetic, EPA placed the issue of geologic radon firmly into the model of the marketplace. The rational consumer required motivation by education and information in order to become vigilant about radon. He or she would then compute a cost/benefit calculation favoring action on radon. However, when this inherently interested citizen was found to be rare, its opposite—an inherently disinterested person—was substituted. Unobservant and oblivious, the apathetic person had to be awakened through "Madison Avenue" tactics of persuasion and emotional arousal.

But why was the rational or "economic" person so basic to radon policy (and the marketplace ideology of Reaganomics) so scarce? For all the attention paid to risk perception by EPA, the basic finding of the field is ignored. Namely, while the general public understands the severity of radon exposure, there is often lacking a sense of personal vulnerability that suggests that these consequences are likely to affect any given person or family. As a result, the fact that testing and mitigation are relatively easy does little to inspire action. Radon may be a problem, but it is readily viewed as somebody else's problem.

Meanwhile, EPA also continued to ignore the major exception to this disinterest in radon. In real estate transfer and new home purchase, the character of the rational and economic person was in full evidence. In a pragmatic vein, radon could be addressed without direct appeal to issues of safety. All indicators pointed to the promise of realty and new construction.

Even as they denied the most promising entry point for successful radon policy, EPA officials began to actively rationalize their failure to mobilize urgent public action against geologic radon. They began to reconcile themselves to viewing radon as a serious risk that would, nevertheless, take time to percolate through the public's consciousness. In making this retreat, they freely drew solace from the campaigns by the Highway Traffic Safety Campaign to encourage use of seatbelts and by the Public Health Service to discourage smoking. Both campaigns did not show significant success until after a decade or more. Both also led eventually to legislative reforms that gave impetus to the desired change in public behavior (Wagner and Dickson, 1991). The need for legislative action was a code word for a move toward regulation that would salvage the wreckage of the voluntary radon program. In the next chapter, we explore the mounting pressures for such a regulatory radon program.

Notes

1. Other findings suggest that the ability to compare one's score to higher levels of exposure was reassuring even when one's own score exceeded levels viewed as safe. And people found it difficult to compare risks from different hazards, failing to appreciate that radon has a risk about twenty-five times greater than that associated with asbestos (Weinstein et al., 1989a).

2. The X-ray ad was genuinely scary to children. The first author's then ten-year-old son was deeply frightened when he saw a tape of the ad, asking many questions about radon. However, a year later the same child was borrowing the radon tape to take to school in the hopes of scaring his classmates.

3. From an interview with Vernon Houk by the first author on June 22, 1989. Houk was referring to the celebrated public rejection of the chemical Alar—and apples grown by an Alar-dependent apple industry—after a campaign visibly championed by actress Meryl Streep.

4. Nevertheless, many respondents still blamed government, industry, and builders. Blame placed upon state and local government may have reflected a general expectation for government to prevent public health hazards. To some extent it also—much as the blame directed to industry—probably reflects the persistent confusion of the industrial radium contamination problem in New Jersey with radon. Blame toward builders may reflect a recognition that radon is drawn into buildings because of their design and construction (see chapter 7). Overall, natural radon is viewed as blameless (see chapters 7 and 10).

5. In 1989, the New Jersey Department of Environmental Protection termed radon the most serious environmental health hazard in that state, in a bid to promote testing. The DEP commissioner, Christopher Daggot, noted that even in the lowest risk areas of the state, the risk from radon exposure was greater than that from other environmental causes. The agency released a comparative risk study that predicted 320 yearly radon deaths in New Jersey, against 21 cancer cases from hazardous waste sites, 10 from drinking water contamination, and 184 from pesticide residues consumed with food (Associated Press, 1989d).

6. Meanwhile, the economic difficulties faced by the middle class in the late 1980s and early 1990s of course created major obstacles to discretionary spending even in that group.

7. The 1990 National Health Survey had previously shown a significant gap between whites and blacks in perception of radon. Against 69 percent of the 41,000 people surveyed who had heard of radon, 73 percent of whites but only 48 percent of blacks were aware of radon. However, blacks who had heard of radon were significantly more likely than whites to consider radon exposure to be unhealthy (Eheman et al., 1996).

8. Presumably, the number of homes potentially needing mitigation represents the proportion of the 8.1 million homes tested that exceeded the federal guidance of 4 pCi/l. Our first estimation is based on EPA's National Residential Radon Survey, where a random survey showed that only 6 percent of American homes have annual averages greater than 4 pCi/l. The second estimate uses figures derived from large private radon firms that found 20 percent of homes tested to exceed 4 pCi/l. The latter data is biased, as actual testing patterns may be, in favor of conditions that are likely to produce higher than national average radon values. See chapter 5 for a comparison of these data sets.

9. The length was also a major concern to members of the radon-testing industry, afraid that the public would be deterred from reading the guide (Silverman, 1992a).

Chapter 10

Avoidance of Regulation

> Note that the purpose of government intervention is to achieve efficient risk
> taking and risk bearing, not necessarily to reduce risk. We reject the con-
> ventional wisdom that risk is always bad, and that it should be eradicated
> from the face of the earth.
> —Richard Belzer

In this chapter, we review the forces behind the nonregulatory approach to radon.[1] While the retreat from regulatory programs and large government was basic to the ideology of Reaganomics, cost containment may have exceeded
ideology as an inspiration for the nonregulatory direction of the federal radon
program. In the wake of the Watras discovery, the scope of the radon problem
certainly loomed large to federal officials who eagerly sought a way to limit their
responsibility. They seized upon the dimensions of radon's character, on one
hand as a natural and, therefore, blameless hazard, and, on the other, as a hazard of the private home—a sphere said to be placed beyond regulation by our inherent respect for private property. Accordingly, the responsibility—and thus the
costs—for testing and mitigation could be shifted to the homeowner. There were
also counterforces pressuring for regulation of radon. Such regulation was justified by cost-benefit analysis, the predominant method under Reaganomics for le-
gitimizing government action. The issues of radon disclosure in real estate
transfer and of radon-resistant new construction both demanded and made feasible government involvement. And, even if the executive branch failed to act, a
mandate for government action might potentially come from the courts.

The Ideology of Reaganomics

The 1992 budget of the U.S. government clearly places authority for considering
questions of environmental risk under Executive Orders Nos. 12291 and 12498,
which required "that Federal regulation be based on adequate information; that
the benefits of Federal regulations exceed their costs; and that regulatory agencies develop an annual regulatory plan" (Part 2, p. 367). The principles of risk
suggested by Executive Order 12291 were elaborated by an Office of Management and Budget (OMB) economist who helped prepare the budget (Belzer,
1991): "First, regulatory actions should be based on adequate information concerning the nature of the risk to be addressed, and some notion that the proposed
action will actually ameliorate the problem. Second, regulatory policies should

be focused on delivering to the American people regulations that are cost-effective. Third, to the extent permitted by law, regulations should offer more risk-reduction benefits to society than they cost in terms of societal resources consumed" (p. 2).

The enforcer of these executive orders during the Reagan-Bush years was the Office of Management and Budget, where regulatory and risk review was conducted by the OMB's Office of Information and Regulatory Affairs. This office used cost-benefit analysis and performance standards as means of evaluating proposed rules. A key tool in their review was the requirement for "Regulatory Impact Analysis" to be done on all major rules of government. Under President Bush, the office shared this review with the president's Council on Competitiveness, chaired by Vice President Quayle (Belzer, 1991). Federal regulation, while not totally ruled out, became an approach of last resort, as explained by OMB's Belzer (1991).

> Our approach to regulatory policy is unabashedly grounded in the principles of welfare economics. In the absence of a market failure, we believe that individuals are the best arbiters of their own welfare, and they should be free to make their own decisions concerning the risks they take. However, we are not ideologically opposed to government regulation. Where significant market failures exist which inhibit or prevent efficient risk taking and risk avoidance, government may be an effective agent in restoring efficient market performance where markets are imperfect, or stimulating efficient market performance where markets do not exist (pp. 2–3).

Belzer cites other tenets of the Reaganomic approach, namely, the reliance on the marketplace (see chapter 8) and the acceptance of some risk as a necessary cost of progress (see chapter 12). Specifically, under the developing practice of regulatory impact analysis during this period, for a regulatory approach to be justified, several conditions would have been necessary. First, a failure of the market to address the problem; and, second, proof would be needed that alternatives to regulation would not adequately solve the problem (OMB, 1991a). In effect, OMB argued that the dissemination of information about risk is a market-based alternative to regulating human exposures (Center for Risk Analysis, 1991).

The ideology of nonregulation later moved on to become a hallmark of neo-Reaganomics, embodied in the "Contract with America" (Republican National Committee, 1994). The goal was, in part, to control and even countermand the growth of the federal government, containing costs, as well.

Avoidance of Costly Federal Programs

Cost has been central to the definition of the radon issue since its inception, to the point that key policy decisions relating to radon have been driven as much by economic considerations as by the high risk of lung cancer. The nonregulatory approach reflected the desire of the Reagan OMB to avoid setting costly precedents for government radon spending. But what have the costs of the radon issue been and who has borne these costs?

The economic costs of the radon issue have been substantial. Radon quickly became a multimillion dollar industry engaging thousands of businesses. Millions of Americans paid for radon testing and mitigation. The issue was a source of new challenges and costs in the construction, lending, and realty industries. But not all of the costs were privatized. Government programs were developed at the federal, state, and local levels to provide testing and mitigation services and to protect government clients in institutions, the military, municipal water systems, and schools. Taking account of expenditures between EPA, DOE, and other involved agencies, it was estimated that the federal government would spend some seventy million dollars, on radon in the first eight years of its programs (Houk, 1989).

The overall costs associated with EPA radon policy were potentially much greater. One can crudely project these costs using the agency's estimates that some 130 million U.S. buildings (including some 80 million single family homes) require testing for radon (Koopersmith, 1989). Assuming an average of twenty-five dollars per building, testing alone would require three-and-one-quarter billion dollars. If one further assumed that 6 percent of these buildings required mitigation costing an average of fifteen hundred dollars then nearly another twelve billion dollars would be required. And this fifteen-billion-dollar price tag represents only a portion of the radon budget. If this simple estimate appears to be high, then take note of the analysis by Bolch and Lyons (1990), who project the cost for addressing radon in the United States to be in the ten-to one-hundred-billion dollar range, based upon an expenditure of five hundred to five thousand dollars for remediation of one-third of U.S. homes.[2]

That range of estimation is so wide as to be virtually useless. Of course, these cost estimates are subject to many assumptions, not the least of which relates to the five levels of acceptable risk discussed in chapter 3. The 4 pCi/l guidance originally chosen by CDC and EPA was based upon the question of feasibility, naming the lowest level that could be economically achieved rather than a standard of acceptable risk (Eheman, 1988). Assuming this guidance level, Nero and his DOE colleagues estimate a twenty-billion-dollar cost for measurement and remediation.[3] However, the DOE scientists argue that the cost effectiveness of radon policy could be greatly improved if the action guidance were to be increased as much as fourfold. The reduction is due primarily to the combination of use of broad-brush screening measurements to identify hot radon areas and the reduced need for mitigation.[4]

In contrast, Congress pushed policy in the other direction, targeting ambient levels of radon below 1 pCi/l as "acceptable." *Science* editorialist Abelson (1990) estimated that the cost to homeowners of meeting the ambient goal would be in the range of ten thousand dollars each. On their part, the DOE researchers calculate costs for implementing Congress's ambient goal that are even more "staggering." They estimate that, if technically feasible, as much as one trillion dollars would be required to achieve ambient radon levels (Nero et al., 1990; Nazaroff and Teichman, 1990). [5]

Yet, however vast the required expenditures, federal investment was certainly modest for a hazard labeled as one of our most serious environmental hazards. The Reaganomic approach minimized the responsibility of the federal government. Following these Reaganomic proscriptions, federal expenditures were allowed largely for research, demonstration programs, surveys, educational programs, dissemination of information, and a modicum of industry monitoring. State and local governments would spend millions more on radon in line with their own policies. But, the real work was to be left to the private sector, financed by homeowners. This nonregulatory stance could easily be rationalized by citing radon's status as a blameless natural hazard.

Viewing Radon As a Blameless Natural Hazard

A further factor in the classification of radon as a nonregulatory hazard involves the definition of the hazard as natural and thus blameless. In stark contrast to the source of the "human-caused" radon crises that preceded the Colebrookdale Township discovery, geologic radon is a "natural" hazard, entering buildings from the surrounding rock, soil, and water. However, upon reflection, the dichotomy between these two types of disaster is decidedly muddled, as previously discussed in chapter 7.[6]

The False Dichotomy of Natural and Caused Disaster

There is a long cultural tradition of defining floods, hurricanes, earthquakes, and the like as natural disasters. Reflecting the sense that we have no inherent power over such natural forces, we often termed such events as "Acts of God." Two new and contrasting categories of disaster emerged from the realization, in the 1970s and 1980s, that not all environmental hazards are indeed natural. First, technological disasters such as the Three Mile Island accident and, later, Bhopal and Chernobyl demanded recognition for a new type of incident caused by failures of modern technology. These catastrophic or potentially catastrophic acute events were clearly unnatural. They reflected a direct failure of both modern technology and its social support system. As a result, there was a loss of the perceived control over nature that technology had supposedly created. Beyond cataclysmic events, a different form of modern disaster was represented by Love Canal, where slowly spreading, unseen environmental pollutants (including those unleashed by technological disasters) introduced a chronic chain of events, resulting in environmental contamination. The invisibility of such contaminants made the prospect of recognizing and accepting them difficult and the task of avoiding them nearly impossible.

Unseen dangers lurking in the air, water, or soil not only demanded a distrust of a spoiled nature, but a distrust and blaming of the people responsible for the contamination. For, unlike the blameless calamities of nature, what characterized both technological and chronic environmental disasters was that the danger resulted directly from a failure of society. The fact that an unwanted environmental exposure had been *human-caused* was even more significant than the fact that technology had failed. At Love Canal, for example, it wasn't that the chemical factories, per se, were unsafe; it was the lack of social responsibility evidenced in the dumping and later development of the area that was unsafe. Either greed, ignorance, incompetence, carelessness, immorality, or hatefulness was behind the release of toxins that tainted the homes and community. Technological accidents and chronic contamination came to represent the downside of progress, the piper waiting to be paid.

In neither the case of the technological disaster nor environmental contamination could anyone reasonably blame God. The distinction between natural and caused or technological disaster had now become a core distinction in the way that we thought about bad events. The first type of disaster was inherently blameless. In contrast, issues of blame and accountability were central to our psychological, social, economic, and legal responses to contamination. Accordingly, the Superfund laws aimed at cleaning up industrial contamination placed a central focus upon the identification of the "potentially responsible parties" who might be asked to pay the costs.

However, the operative dichotomy between natural and human-caused is in most cases artificial and simplistic. By blaming God or the fates, we denied the ways that human behavior contributed to natural disasters, both in causing catastrophic events and in creating vulnerability to its impact. This can be seen, for example, with floods. Floods are frequently caused by a combination of rainfall and environmental conditions that promote fast drainage. Humans may not produce the rainfall, but their alterations of the landscape create new pathways for the water to collect and move. Furthermore, the human damage due to floods almost entirely results from the fact that people locate themselves in flood plains. The disaster of flooding, therefore, generally results from the interaction of humans with nature; specific actions of humans create the vulnerability. In contrast to the instances of flooding, contamination is more totally a human artifact. Thus, lead contamination less reflects the natural toxicity of lead than the fact that we have used lead in plumbing, paints, and gasoline, assuring that lead pollutes our waters, soils, and ambient air. But the workings of nature, including groundwater flow, air movement, and climatic patterns can hardly be removed from this equation. The true understanding is that all disasters manifest a complex interaction of people and environment. In separating out realms of risk, we have merely demonstrated our ignorance of the interaction of humans, the technological environment, and the natural environment.

Confusions in the Cultural Definition of Radon Hazard

The selective assumption that natural disasters are *natural* sets the mold for defining radon as natural. Geologic radon is an environmental contaminant, in a class with organic chemicals or air pollution. Yet, unlike most environmental contaminants, the source is purely natural; geologic radon would occur whether humans walked the earth or not. In this sense, radon is also blameless—no persons' actions "crapped up" the environment with uranium; and nobody causes the decay of radium to radon, and radon to its daughters.

But from a human-ecological perspective, we must also ask how our actions may contribute to radon exposure. As we discussed in chapters 5 and 7, radon is not generally a severe hazard except in the kind of buildings we build—structures that not only passively allow radon in, but literally suck it from the ground and allow it to collect indoors. Thus, humans may not have *caused* radon, but they surely are *responsible* for their high levels of radon exposure. That exposure reflects a failure of technology—not in the acute and concentrated mode of a Chernobyl—but rather in the decentralized, routine, and subtle dynamics of buildings, their construction, maintenance, and use.

If before Colebrookdale Township, there seemed to be an inability to understand the potential geologic radon problem, it reflected more than a denial of evidence of natural radon. Rather, it reflected an inability to understand the potential relationship between geologic radon and buildings. The fact that we were not prepared to recognize such interactive effects is instructive of why we have constructed buildings that accumulate radon so effectively. Thus, we might further conclude that radon exposure is a manifestation of how poorly we think about and even understand the ecology of our homes and buildings. In a sense, the lack of critical reflection about radon reflects the cultural untouchability of the home—the same denial that causes us to accept life with indoor air pollution, gross energy inefficiency, vulnerabilities to fire, and overconsumption of often unsafe products.

Our limited paradigm of understanding has meant that we do not think about the ecology of radon. Instead, once Watras introduced geologic radon as an issue, it was immediately classified into the false dichotomy according to its origin—as a blameless natural phenomenon. That classification has resulted in our continued denial of the fact that radon itself may be natural but radon exposure is caused. Normal homes and buildings create our vulnerability. The people who design, construct, maintain, and use them must change the way they do things if radon is to be addressed. Radon is not truly a blameless hazard. But blamelessness was a convenient excuse for a nonregulatory program that defined radon as a problem of the private realm of the home.

The Inviolability of the Private Home

Still another element in the mix of factors used to justify a nonregulatory approach to radon was the fundamental belief that government should not intrude into the home—that private property is sacrosanct. Therefore, it followed that homeowners would have to act as their own arbiters of risk, determining for themselves whether or not to act against radon. We have already explored (in chapter 9) the implications of making the individual the lead actor for radon. This decentralization down to the citizen displaced responsibility from the federal government. However, by reducing the citizen to the role of consumer in the marketplace, radon policy become vulnerable to citizen inaction.

While it is understandable that government would seek to avoid bearing high costs for the radon issue, these costs were merely displaced to the homeowner. And such displacement might well backfire. Thus, Bolch and Lyons (1990) predict that major economic losses beyond the costs of testing and attempting remediation will be borne by some homeowners due to the radon issue. Of particular significance, a certain percentage of U.S. houses would be made unsalable should resale of homes require certification of radonproof construction. For the victims, this would constitute the loss of a substantial amount of capital. As a result, these authors predicted that the costs of radon would lead to a homeowner rebellion demanding a Superfund-type government bailout, forcing costs back into government budgets. In the absence of a forcing-mechanism to address radon, serious liability is spared both government and the homeowner.

It is further of interest that radon policy has tended to equate the private sphere with the privately owned home. Yet, there are significant exceptions to this assumption. Rental units, leased property, and other nonoccupant-owned units represent a significant percentage of the national housing stock. Here the responsibility for the safety of the building rests with a landlord or equivalent who is not the occupant being exposed to radon. If the homeowner might be seen as a consumer, landlords could only be considered such if either it were assumed that they would test and prevent radon entry out of a voluntary sense of responsibility for their tenants or due to compelling factors (regulation, legal liability, incentives, etc.). Alternatively, it might be assumed that tenants would address radon, even though they tend to be highly mobile as a group and generally lack any control over the structural nature of their building. Finally, many buildings where radon exposure might occur are not homes at all. While schools and day care centers have received attention in federal and state policy, the notion of radon as a workplace hazard has only been addressed in limited settings, such as some government buildings. In short, there are limits to the image of radon as a hazard in private spheres controlled by the occupants.

Finally, then, the view that radon was a problem of homes and other private buildings placed the issue beyond the reach of government regulation. Only the owners would have the jurisdiction to act on radon. The irony of this view was its inherent contradiction with the myth of blameless radon. In finding no one responsible for radon, the shallow message was that no one was responsible for causing radon. But, the deep meaning is quite opposite, namely, that no one has to accept responsibility for discovering and preventing exposure. Government doesn't want the responsibility. It cannot be placed on the corporate world. There is no social network that will step in. Rather, by default, individuals must act on radon because no one else will protect them. And, they don't seem any more anxious to accept this responsibility than were the institutions granting it to them. In yet a further twist, government has generally accepted responsibility for helping victims of natural hazards. Yet, radon's natural quality has quite the opposite effect, exempting rather than obligating governmental assistance. In sum, no one is truly responsible for radon; it is surrounded by social ambiguities.

Pressures toward Federal Regulation

Even as strong pressures blocked a regulatory program for radon, a series of counterpressures pushed in the other direction. We have already acknowledged in chapter 8 the pressures to regulate the emerging radon industry. Of additional import in moving government toward regulating radon was that, when radon was entered into the calculus of government decision making employed during and after the Reagan presidency, regulatory action was justified based both upon radon's risk assessment and comparative costs as assessed by cost-benefit analysis. Furthermore, there were two ripe issues for regulation, radon disclosure in realty transfer and radonproof new construction.

Cost-Benefit Analysis Supports Radon Action

Cost-benefit analysis was the central calculus of government under Reaganomics and remains so under neo-Reaganomics. It should be noted that critics question the extent to which such risk assessment techniques allow for a meaningful comparison of diverse risks (Goldstein, 1989; Stevens, 1991a and b; Wartenberg and Chess, 1992; Center for Risk Analysis, 1991; Shrader-Frechette, 1991; Freudenberg, 1988) as well as the value assumptions that underlie supposedly objective assessments (Gutin, 1991). There are also questions about what risks are weighted highly (i.e., cancer) and which are overlooked in quantifying risks (see, for example, Colborn et al., 1996). Even Assistant Surgeon General Houk, who led the attack against dioxin risk, complained to one of the authors about risk assessment (1989): "It's got to be something that's come down from the mountains with Moses on tablets. There is an illusion of precision. Risk assessment as now practiced is about as effective as a 5-year weather forecast at best. At worst, it's just voodoo!" Despite much valid criticism, risk assessment and risk comparison have been adopted widely, spreading from the federal government to various states.

While radon did not compete with human-caused risks in rousing public concern, it was clear to experts who compared health risks that radon was a front runner (see, for example, Goldstein, 1989). Cost-benefit analysis easily justified the costs of forceful radon action, as every expert analysis of the subject has shown.

EPA Prioritizes Its Risks

Comparative cost-benefit analysis has played, overall, a central role in EPA's own internal reviews of risk. William Ruckelshaus, retaking EPA's helm in 1983 in order to depoliticize the agency, moved to establish a strong emphasis on quantitative risk assessment as a guide to the agency's priorities (Roberts, 1990; Goldstein, 1989). Ruckelshaus's successor, Lee Thomas, continued the reliance on risk assessment through to the end of the Reagan presidency, declaring that "at the heart of EPA's programs in the future should be a risk-based approach to setting priorities" (1988, p. 3). The keystone of this approach was a self-study entitled *Unfinished Business* conducted by seventy-five EPA senior managers and staff in 1986 and 1987. When the relative risk of thirty-one environmental problems was compared, radon was tied for first place for the category of human cancer risk. Along with climate change, it proved one of the two top-rated risks receiving comparatively minimal attention from the agency (EPA, 1987a; Roberts, 1990; Goldstein, 1989).

The risk-comparison process became even more central during the next administration at EPA, under William Reilly. From the time he took office, Reilly attempted to organize agency priorities around a rating of the risks. He appointed a Scientific Advisory Board (SAB), a panel of nonagency scientists, to review the *Unfinished Business* report. This committee spent a year debating methodology and the prior findings. In the end, as part of what is known as the *Setting Priorities* document, the group charged with examining health risk again recognized radon as one of the primary risks requiring high-priority attention (EPA, 1990a; Roberts, 1990). Later, when EPA calculated the cost of lives saved as part of the regulatory review of its radon policy, the agency concluded that current testing and mitigation averts approximately forty annual deaths at a cost of about $700,000 per life saved (EPA, 1992a).[7]

Radon and Cost-benefit Analysis in the U.S. Budget

As part of this trend, cost-benefit analysis was increasingly used to prioritize environmental hazards during the budget-writing process of the federal government. Thus, the 1992 U.S. budget can be seen as a dress rehearsal for the latter neo-Reaganomic attack on environmental risk. Citing the cost and intrusiveness of regulation, the budget sets forth a goal of "reducing the most risk for the buck" through "risk management budgeting" in order to "reallocate scarce resources to produce both lower risks and lower costs" (Part 2-371). Under the heading "Reforming Regulation and Managing Risk-Reduction Sensibly" (Section IX.C), a cost-benefit analysis is presented for fifty-three health and safety regulations showing both the cost per premature death averted and the number of deaths risked per million people exposed (see table 10.1). There is no direct correlation evident between cost and the number of people protected. The document emphasizes that environmental risks (other than those derived from diet and smoking) are much smaller than other threats to human health (OMB, 1991b; Belzer, 1991; Center for Risk Analysis, 1991).

Table 10.1   Cost-Benefit Analysis Showing the Cost per Premature Death Averted and the Number of Deaths Risked per Million Exposed People (*Source*: OMB (Office of Management and Budget), 1991b)

Baseline Health Regulation	Year Issued	Health or Safety?	Agency	Baseline Mortality Risk million exposed	Cost per Premature Death Averted ($Million 1990)
Unvented Space Heater Ban	1980	S	CPSC	1,890	0.1
Aircraft Cabin Fire Protection Standard	1985	S	FAA	5	0.1
Auto Passive Restraint/Seat Belt Standards	1984	S	NHTSA	6,370	0.1
Steering Column Protection Standard[2]	1967	S	NHTSA	385	0.1
Underground Construction Standards[3]	1989	S	OSHA-S	38,700	0.1
Trihalomethane Drinking Water Standards	1979	H	EPA	420	0.2
Aircraft Seat Cushion Flammability Standard	1984	S	FAA	11	0.4
Alcohol and Drug Control Standards[3]	1985	H	FRA	81	0.4
Auto Fuel-System Integrity Standard	1975	S	NHTSA	343	0.4
Standards for Servicing Auto Wheel Rims[3]	1984	S	OSHA-S	630	0.4
Aircraft Floor Emergency Lighting Standard	1984	S	FAA	2	0.6
Concrete & Masonry Construction Standards[3]	1988	S	OSHA-S	630	0.6
Crane Suspended Personnel Platform Standard[3]	1988	S	OSHA-S	81,000	0.7
Passive Restraints for Trucks and Buses (Proposed)	1989	S	NHTSA	6,370	0.7
Side-Impact Standards for Autos (Dynamic)	1990	S	NHTSA	NA	0.8
Children's Sleepwear Flammability Ban[4]	1973	S	CPSC	29	0.8
Auto Side Door Support Standards	1970	S	NHTSA	2,520	0.8
Low-Altitude Windshear Equipment & Training Standards	1988	S	FAA	NA	1.3
Electrical Equipment Standards (Metal Mines)	1970	S	MSHA	NA	1.4
Trenching and Excavation Standards[3]	1989	S	OSHA-S	14,310	1.5
Traffic Alert and Collision Avoidance (TCAS) Systems	1988	S	FAA	NA	1.5
Hazard Communication Standard[3]	1983	S	OSHA-S	1,800	1.6
Side Impact Stds for Trucks, Buses and MPVs (Proposed)	1989	S	NHTSA	NA	2.2
Grain Dust Explosion Prevention Standards[3]	1987	S	OSHA-S	9,450	2.8

Table 10.1 con't.

Baseline Health Regulation	Year Issued	Health or Safety?	Agency	Baseline Mortality Risk million exposed	Cost per Premature Death Averted ($Million 1990)
Rear Lap/Shoulder Belts for Autos	1989	S	NHTSA	NA	3.2
Standards for Radionuclides in Uranium Mines[3]	1984	H	EPA	6,300	3.4
Benzene NESHAP (Original: Fugitive Emissions)	1984	H	EPA	1,470	3.4
Ethylene Dibromide Drinking Water Standard	1991	H	EPA	NA	5.7
Benzene NESHAP (Revised: Coke By-Products)[3]	1988	H	EPA	NA	6.1
Asbestos Occupational Exposure Limit[3]	1972	H	OSHA-H	3,015	8.3
Benzene Occupational Exposure Limit[3]	1987	H	OSHA-H	39,600	8.9
Electrical Equipment Standards (Coal Mines)[3]	1970	S	MSHA	NA	9.2
Arsenic Emission Standards for Glass Plants	1986	H	EPA	2,660	13.5
Ethylene Oxide Occupational Exposure Limit[3]	1984	H	OSHA-H	1,980	20.5
Arsenic/Copper NESHAP	1986	H	EPA	63,000	23.0
Haz Waste Listing for Petroleum Refining Sludge	1990	H	EPA	210	27.6
Cover/Move Uranium Mill Tailings (Inactive Sites)	1983	H	EPA	30,100	31.7
Benzene NESHAP (Revised: Transfer Operations)	1990	H	EPA	NA	32.9
Cover/Move Uranium Mill Tailings (Active Sites)	1983	H	EPA	30,100	45.0
Acrylonitrile Occupational Exposure Limit[3]	1978	H	OSHA-H	42,300	51.5
Coke Ovens Occupational Exposure Limit[3]	s1976	H	OSHA-H	7,200	63.5
Lockout/Tagout[3]	1989	S	OSHA-S	4	70.9
Asbestos Occupational Exposure Limit[3]	1986	H	OSHA-H	3,015	74.0
Arsenic Occupational Exposure Limit[3]	1978	H	OSHA-H	14,800	106.9
Asbestos Ban	1989	H	EPA	NA	110.7
Diethylstilbestrol (DES) Cattlefeed Ban	1979	H	FDA	22	124.8
Benzene NESHAP (Revised: Waste Operations)	1990	H	EPA	NA	168.2
1,2-Dichloropropane Drinking Water Standard	1991	H	EPA	NA	653.0
Haz Waste Land Disposal Ban (1st 3rd)	1988	H	EPA	2	4,190.4
Municipal Solid Waste Landfill Standards (Proposed)	1988	H	EPA	<1	19,107.0
Formaldehyde Occupational Exposure Limit[3]	1987	H	OSHA-H	31	86,201.8
Atrazine/Alachlor Drinking Water Standard	1991	H	EPA	NA	92,069.7
Haz Waste Listing for Wood Preserving Chemicals	1990	H	EPA	<1	5,700,000.0

[1] 70-year lifetime exposure assumed unless otherwise specified.

[2] 50-year lifetime exposure.

[3] 45-year lifetime exposure.

[4] 12-year exposure period.

NA = Not available.

Agency Abbreviations - CPSC: Consumer Product Safety Commission; MSHA: Mine Safety and Health Administration; EPA: Environmental Protection Agency; NHTSA: National Highway Traffic Safety Administration; FAA: Federal Aviation Administration; FRA: Federal Railroad Administration; FDA: Food and Drug Administration; OSHA-H: Occupational Safety and Health Administration, Health Standards; OSHA-S: Occupational Safety and Health Administration, Safety Standards.

Source: John F. Morrall, III, "A Review of the Record," *Regulation*, Vol. 10, No. 2 (1986), p. 30. Updated by the author, et. al.

The costs range upward from $100,000 per averted death for the ban on un-vented space heaters (affecting nearly two thousand lives per million people ex-posed), fire protection standards for aircraft cabins (affecting only five lives per million exposed), passive restraint/seat belt standards for automobiles (affecting more than six thousand lives per million exposed), steering column protection standards (affecting less than four hundred lives per million exposed), and un-derground construction standards (affecting nearly thirty-nine thousand lives per million exposed). These risks can then be compared to the costs associated with environmental regulation. Other than drinking water standards for trihalom-ethane (affecting just over four hundred lives per million exposed at $200,000 per averted death), the least expensive environmental regulations are in the $3.4 million (for fugitive benzene emissions affecting more than six thousand lives per million exposed) and $5.7 million (for ethylene dibromide in drinking wa-ter) per averted death range. These are contrasted, at the expensive end of the range, with the costs of such environmental regulations as municipal solid waste landfill standards (affecting less than one life per million exposed at $19 billion per averted death), drinking water standards for atrazine/alachlor (at $92 billion per averted death), and the hazardous waste listing for wood preservatives (af-fecting less than one person per million exposed at a cost of $5.7 trillion per averted death).

OMB's Comparison of Risks

OMB calculates the cost effectiveness for each death prevented in govern-ment regulation as part of the Regulatory Impact Analysis required by Executive Orders 12291 and 12498. This work has been extensively used to demonstrate the high costs found with regulations aimed at reducing environmental and oc-cupational cancer risks (see table 10.1). For example, the cost of regulations re-lating to radon in nonresidential environments were calculated by OMB. The 1984 EPA health standards for radionuclides in uranium mines entail a cost of $3.4 million per premature death avoided. And the cost of the 1983 regulations for covering and moving uranium mill tailings at active industrial sites was computed to be $31.7 million per premature death avoided. OMB has not calcu-lated figures for home radon programs because residential radon is not regulat-ed. However, against the costs of environmental regulation generally, even the OMB acknowledged that the nonregulatory radon program addressed one of the highest risk factors known with a minimal federal expense (Belzer, 1991; OMB, 1991b; see also Shabecoff, 1988b).

The DOE Critique of Radon and Environmental Risk

For a cogent analysis of radon's comparative risk, we can turn to EPA's crit-ics at DOE (Nero et al., 1990). Noting that radon's comparative risk depends upon what you are comparing it to, the DOE scientists distinguish between personal, occupational, and environmental risks. Accordingly, they note that radon risk is at the low end of many *personal risks*, often voluntary, that range as high as 10^{-1} or 10^{-2} (i.e., one out of ten or one out of a hundred). These personal risks are exemplified by cigarette smoking, with a mortality risk of at least 25 percent. Given the synergy between radon and smoking, the average cost for radon death averted for smokers is actually much lower ($180,000) than it is for nonsmokers (at $2.7 million). Because smoking so dominates the estimated effect of radon, they argue that a net reduction of 3 percent in the number of cigarette smokers would produce the same benefits in death aversion as would implementation of the EPA/CDC radon recommendations (i.e., the 4 pCi/l guidance).[8] In contrast, the DOE critics find radon risk to be at the high end of *occupational risks*, over which limited personal control occurs, tolerated at levels of 10^{-2} to 10^{-3}. Significantly, they conclude that radon is much greater than other *environmental risks*, over which people exercise no control and that typically are tolerated at risks as low as 10^{-5} or 10^{-6}.

The DOE scientists also contrast costs and benefits for three different regulatory scenarios. Under the EPA/CDC guidelines (of 4 pCi/l) for the current housing stock, Nero and his colleagues estimate that complete implementation of the EPA/CDC policy would reduce the population exposure by 17 percent, avoiding 2,500 lung cancer deaths per year (nearly all among smokers) while leaving 12,000 radon-caused lung cancers. The cost per lung cancer death averted, assuming a thirty-year effectiveness for remediation, would be $270,000. In line with the OMB analysis, the DOE scientists find that this would be an extremely cost-effective program as compared to other environmental programs.[9] As noted earlier, the DOE scientists argue that the cost effectiveness of radon policy could be greatly improved if the action guidance were increased into the 16–20 pCi/l range. These comparatively low-cost risk-reduction programs are then contrasted to efforts to achieve an ambient level of radon. They project that dropping radon levels down to ambient levels would eliminate 75 percent (or about eleven thousand yearly cases) of radon-related lung cancer mortality (still leaving some four thousand deaths from ambient radon). The cost per death averted would be about $3 million assuming thirty-year mitigation effectiveness. The authors suggest that the practicality of achieving ambient levels would be enhanced if one focused only on the million per year new housing units at an annual investment of several billion dollars (Nero et al., 1990; Nazaroff and Teichman, 1990).[10]

What is notable here is that when we place these figures for the ambient goal into a broader framework of comparative analysis such as offered by the 1992 budget, we find that the cost of $3 million per death averted is still in line with regulatory programs addressing chemical contaminants and health. Furthermore, these figures don't rule out regulatory action on airborne radon. Rather, they justify it.[11] In the absence of such regulatory action, various forms of quasi or de facto regulation have developed.

The Move toward Radon Quasi Regulation

Quasi regulation was first evident in the case of secondary regulation of the emerging radon industry, as discussed in chapter 8. It is also evident regarding two clear targets for radon regulation, the cases of realty transfer and new homes. The courts have spurred some movement in this direction.

The Special Case of Real Estate Transfer

The Environmental Law Institute's Paul Locke (1993) argues that disclosure and remedy of radon as part of the real estate transaction is the optimal "trigger point" for radon action, a point at which neither the buyer nor seller is likely to be apathetic about radon, allowing the private sector to serve as the "engine to get stuff done." With 5 percent of homes sold yearly; in fourteen years, half the existing homes in the nation could be addressed in this manner (Locke, 1990).

However, proposed provisions of the Indoor Radon Reauthorization Act that would have mandated radon testing and disclosure during realty transfer were never adopted (Lautenberg, 1993). Opposition was orchestrated by the real estate industry. As one way of heading off regulation, private realty groups developed their own voluntary testing and disclosure initiatives. A 1989 survey by the National Association of Realtors found that realtors in twenty-four states used radon disclosure statements voluntarily in real estate transactions. When the New Jersey Association of Realtors surveyed members near the Reading Prong in 1988 to examine use of its voluntary radon contingency clause, more than 50 percent of the responding realtors reported that half their home sales during the past year had involved radon testing prior to closing and more than 80 percent reported voluntary use of the radon contingency clause. These results were confirmed in a subsequent survey with realtors conducted by the GAO. Similarly, the Pennsylvania Association of Realtors formally adopted a radon disclosure sheet to be appended to standard listing and contract forms. A subsequent survey by the GAO showed widespread use of the disclosure form by realtors, although radon testing occurred in less than half the transactions, even in known high-radon areas (Knox, 1989; GAO, 1992).

The realty industry was also interested in limiting its liability. In 1989, the nationwide Employee Relocation Council advised Fortune 1000 clients to test and mitigate for radon, using professional testers to assure clear and independent test results (*RIR*, August 1989d). Some 40 percent of the council's members reported that they already "automatically" tested homes (Galbraith, 1990). By adopting the EPA screening test as a decision-making tool for building mitigation, the Employee Relocation Council influenced the relocation industry and the broader realty field to rely on short-term tests as a means of minimizing their liability (Pratt, 1991; Page, 1991).

Despite these voluntary industry initiatives, states have increasingly acted to fill the void left by federal inaction on real estate transfer. By 1993, some eighteen states had acted to establish some form of mandatory radon disclosure; three years later the number was twenty-eight (Environmental Law Institute, 1993a; Zanowiak, 1996). Such efforts supporting substantive government intervention into real estate and new construction also faced opposition from the real estate industry.[12] In an interview, Paul Locke, of the Environmental Law Institute, blamed special interests for government inaction on radon disclosure (1993): "The reason that this hasn't moved is that realty is powerfully rooted politically. They have well funded lobby groups. These people don't see realty as the trigger. They don't see it as appropriate to test realty transactions." In part, the industry was reluctant to be drawn into the middle of an immature issue where new evidence might come to light and guidance levels and protocols for testing might well change. Resistance by local realtors also reflected the potential for environmental stigma, whereby the value and desirability of a given house, or even a bounded area, is diminished because of a known environmental hazard. Some early evidence of environmental stigma effects were evident for geologic radon (see Edelstein, 1991).[13]

Considerable evidence exists debunking the concerns raised by real estate interests in opposition to mandated radon testing and notification. In its analysis of radon testing during real estate transactions, the GAO (1992) found that realtors were concerned that testing during real estate transactions might cause a sale to be delayed or canceled and might add to closing costs.[14] The GAO then explicitly tested these assumptions by surveying realtors in Pennsylvania and New Jersey. They found relatively little delay, few cancellations, and costs of around one hundred dollars for radon testing during real estate transactions. Similarly, an earlier survey of real estate agents by the New Jersey Association of Realtors (Knox, 1989) found that radon rarely interfered with a home sale and neither discovery of radon nor the presence of radon mitigation devices caused sellers to reduce their asking price for a home. Houses exceeding the EPA guidance tended to be mitigated at the seller's expense prior to the sale. The New York attorney general cited these results in dismissing realtors' concerns that proposed legislation requiring radon test disclosure would hamper sales (*RIR*, December 1989b). Similar opposition from state and national real estate interests occurred against New Jersey legislation requiring sellers of property to test for radon. Instructively, the argument was made by a spokesperson for the National Association of Realtors (Silverman, 1993a, p. 31) that "radon has never had an impact on sales. The only time it becomes a big deal is when you put a requirement in there to test." In short, the regulation, not the risk, is the real threat.

A third potential force for mandating radon testing and disclosure beyond government and industry is the lending industry. For lenders, the potential for discovery of an environmental hazard such as radon poses major risks affecting commercial loans, real estate investments, and mortgage loans. The collateral value of the property might be diminished. The obligation or ability of the borrower to mitigate might supersede the obligation to repay the loan. And, under some circumstances, the lender might even become liable for the costs of mitigation and for personal and property damages (*RIR*, September 1989d). Furthermore, because of their acquired liability, insurers have increasingly pressured lenders and builders to provide testing and mitigation language in contracts to protect the lender from being enjoined in a suit (*RIR*, November 1989f).

Despite these pressures, mortgage granters did not move quickly to require testing.[15] Their inaction reflected a lack of government requirements or guidance for testing, as well as what the Mortgage Bankers Association termed "unclear and potentially misleading" radon information. Furthermore, the issue of liability is uncertain. Lenders are concerned with some fifty environmental toxins—all threatening potential liability—and there has been no means to address these environmental hazards in an integrated fashion. While radon is particularly easy to test and mitigate for, lenders are caught in a difficult situation generally because if they assess threats in a superficial manner, overall, they may have greater liability than if they don't address environmental hazards at all (*RIR*, August 1989g). Thus, from the lenders' perspective, liability appeared equally great whether they acted on radon or not (*RIR*, November 1989f).

The Environmental Law Institute's Paul Locke, having tracked the radon issue particularly with regard to real estate transfer, advocated a national radon strategy based upon the use of the secondary mortgage market, the federal lenders such as Fannie Mae and Freddy Mack that provide a good deal of the loan capital to primary lenders that is used for mortgages. Locke (1990) argued that these lenders could easily require dissemination of radon information and disclosure of radon test results as part of the portfolio of information assembled for review during the sales transaction. It would then be up to the seller and buyer to negotiate a response to this information. The buyers could insist on mitigation of undesired radon levels or not, as they wished. This process would be free-market driven and self-policing and would provide for national consistency for the real estate industry. In an interview, Locke explained that, despite its non-regulatory nature, his proposal was too aggressive for the Republican ideology of the EPA radon program. "However, Reagan did not want to go too far with even the non-regulatory programs. I proposed requirements for testing to get into the secondary mortgage market. But it will never happen. Steve (Page) and Margo (Oge) told me they couldn't support it. They were all for volunteerism, but they couldn't take it too far" (Locke, 1993).

While stopping far short of Locke's proposal, the Fannie Mae federal loan process for multiple family dwellings does require a specific assessment of radon levels if there has not been a radon test within the last six months that shows less than 4 pCi/l or if nearby structures or local water supplies have elevated radon. A property that fails the environmental screening will not receive a loan (*RIR*, September 1989d).

In sum, while real estate transfer is a logical place to require radon testing, the federal government has failed to use this leverage point, even avoiding compulsory nonregulatory approaches. At the same time, a mix of voluntary and market-driven, as well as state-directed radon mandates suggested development of a quasi-regulatory expectation for realty testing. As a result, between 15 and 25 percent of approximately four million homes sold yearly in the United States were being tested by the 1990s even in the absence of federal regulations requiring radon measurement and disclosure (EPA, 1992a).

Radon Prevention and Disclosure in New Construction

Much as with the realtors' reluctance to address radon, builders have been slow to adopt radon resistant construction practices. As a result, homes continue to be constructed that will subsequently need to be mitigated for radon, even though radon entry could be prevented from the onset through careful building practices. By 1995, some 900,000 homes were listed as having been built with features aimed at defeating radon entry (Feldman, 1996). While yearly improvement has been seen in the percentage of the housing stock with such features, it had only reached an estimated 21 percent by 1996 (Keller, 1996). Absent market demand through radon-aware consumers,[16] a change in building practices requires either voluntary action on the part of builders, changing construction codes, regulation by government, or fear of liability.

Moving Beyond Voluntary Acceptance through Code Modification

Given the absence of any regulatory impetus to force a shift to radon resistant construction, changes in building practices have been voluntary or market-driven. As discussed in chapter 7, voluntary changes to adopt radonproof construction were initially little evident, except among energy efficient small builders. As one EPA staffer working on residential construction noted, "If it is the builders' choice, they will not do it" (Keller, 1996). Moreover, the involvement of building associations in radon programs has appeared to be partially motivated by a desire to head off regulation.

The logical approach for forcing radon-resistant construction would be to amend building codes. However, the federal government lacks the authority to regulate building codes directly. Instead, model building codes are adopted by any of the one national or three regional code organizations and are then available for voluntary adoption by municipalities.[17] It can take three years of political maneuvering to move a proposed model code through to adoption. For example, within one of these model code advisory groups, the ICBO (International Conference of Building Officials), a proposed radon code would first need to be endorsed by the Indoor Air Quality committee as an appendix to the Uni-

form Building Code. The larger membership of the organization would then debate the draft code at the annual convention and decide to accept, amend, or reject it. Successful protocols would then be published and distributed for
comment. In all, some seven or eight steps would lie between proposal and
adoption of the new code (Nuess, 1991). After code adoption, several more years
lapse while localities weigh implemention (Harrison, 1991).

In fall 1989, EPA issued a draft model minimum-standard and techniques
guide for new construction. The draft offered three options to municipalities for
possible inclusion in local codes, depending on whether the site's radon risk is
low, moderate, or high based on EPA's Radon Potential Map (see chapter 5). In
the first option, intended for higher risk areas, full operative mitigation measures were to be included in new houses without any corresponding testing requirements. In the second option, designed for moderate risk areas, roughed-in
mitigation measures would be provided, to be made operative if radon levels exceeding 1.5 to 2.0 pCi/l were found in testing conducted by the builder during
the first year of occupancy. The third option, in low risk areas, would not require
radonproof construction. Rather, testing over the first six years of occupancy
would trigger mitigation, if needed (EPA, 1989e; *RIR*, September 1989c).

Also in 1989, the Bonneville Power Administration published the "Northwest Residential Radon Standard," a code for radon-resistant construction later
adopted by the state of Washington. Although generally similar to the evolving
EPA model code, the Northwest code relied on passive techniques that could be
activated after long-term testing.[18] This difference engendered the opposition of
the building industry. The builders were willing to install active systems in newly constructed buildings, but they did not want to become involved with radon
testing required by the passive approach. They were willing to conduct short-
term tests, if testing were necessary, but nothing longer. In sum, the builders
would accept no code that prolonged and complicated their obligations to the
buyer. It was hardly surprising that the Northwest code ran into trouble before
the Indoor Air Committee when it was submitted to the ICBO. At the annual
convention in 1990, speaker after speaker opposed the code. But, ironically, the
coup de grace came from the EPA.

EPA was approached prior to the conference by the National Association of
Home Builders (NAHB), which offered to collaborate with EPA to develop an
alternative code if EPA opposed the Northwest code. This offer fit EPA's own
agenda of creating one unified national code, as it was obligated to do by the Indoor Radon Abatement Act. Jed Harrison explained to the authors that the agency knew that it could not implement such a code without the NAHB (1991). "We
think that the EPA code is more likely to be implemented. We have been dealing
with the NAHB since the beginning. When we finally drafted our document, we
tried to elicit their support. They have a strong lobby. If we went before the code
organizations without their support, it might kill the code."

Fearing that action on the Northwest code would impede their own ability to act, EPA capitulated. The Northwest code was dropped from consideration in favor of a future joint submittal from EPA and NAHB (Nuess, 1991; Harrison, 1991). EPA's draft code, developed with NAHB input, was issued in 1991. A point of remaining contention was the question of who should test, the builder or the homeowner. As EPA's Harrison explained during an interview (1991): "The NAHB wants the liability to end with the construction. Their preferred approach will ultimately be if they put in the technology, then let the homeowner assume the responsibility to test and do further work. The EPA is not satisfied with that option because people are not even using their test kits; they are turning off active systems."

The draft code contained a fourteen-step guideline for builders to follow. Under the code, passive radon-avoidance measures will be installed in buildings located in high-radon areas. Follow-up testing will be recommended (Silverman, 1993). A the same time, the American Society of Testing and Materials issued an Emergency Standard Guide for radon-resistant new construction in November 1990, followed by a final standard in April 1992. EPA intended to promote both their own and ASTM's models for adoption by the industry (EPA, 1992b). The agency had made some progress in this direction by 1996. Their nationwide code had been accepted by CABO, the Council of American Building Officials, and made part of the one-and two-family dwelling code. However, the success was hardly conclusive. Under the code provision, local code officials were instructed to consult the national radon map to see whether a building site lay within an area designated as requiring radon protective measures. They might also consider local data (wind velocity, seismicity, etc.). They would then use their own discretion in determining whether radon-resistant techniques would be required for buildings constructed on the site. Thus, despite evidence to the contrary, the official was under no compulsion to order radon prevention. The agency's success with other code organizations was even less encouraging (Keller, 1996).[19] In sum, code adoption has proved to be a slow, torturous, and compromising path to radon prevention.

State Mandates for Radon Resistant Construction

While EPA worked with building groups and developed its own model code, it also had the shortcutting option of going directly to local jurisdictions to establish standards for radon-resistant construction. What might well be a six-year-long path could thus be cut in half (Harrison, 1991). In the early 1990s, the state radon grants were being used to provide incentives for adoption of such regulations by individual states (Page, 1991). However, state action on building practices was slow to develop. Into the 1990s, only four states had passed legislation relating to new construction codes, most notably Washington State's adoption of the Northwest code. However, no additional bills addressing new construction were introduced in the 1992 or 1993 legislative sessions (Environmental Law Institute, 1993a). By 1996, no states were legally requiring use of radon-resistant techniques (Keller, 1996). Thus, decentralized state action has not provided for radon-resistant construction.

A Lost Opportunity

In sum, the construction of new generations of buildings that promote radon exposure and are not easily remediated has been assured by the failure of either government or private interests to take definitive action to force a change of building practice. In the absence of market demand for such houses, the primary force toward innovation has been the prospect of builder liability for radon.

Radon in the Courts

Government inaction in regulating radon invited the courts to set de facto radon policy.

Potential Legal Liability

Perhaps, the most fertile area for radon litigation is the real estate transaction, where the potential liability has forced the real estate, construction, and banking industries to attend to radon. The doctrine of *caveat emptor* (let the buyer beware) has traditionally limited the ability of buyers to bring claims against sellers of houses (Kass and Gerard, 1987). However, a variety of implied or explicit warranties of habitability in various jurisdictions may leave architects and contractors liable for building homes in known radon areas, for employing sloppy construction practices, or for otherwise failing to provide a building suitable for habitation due to the radon level (Toomey and Sykes, 1988).

The question of full disclosure is key to radon liability. Where neither party to a real estate transaction knew about a radon problem before the sale, the sale could be rescinded or the terms amended. However, where the seller knew of a radon problem and failed to disclose it, fraud might be alleged (Toomey and Sykes, 1988). Realtors who knew of a problem but failed to reveal it to the buyer would also become liable. Liability would be enhanced where the seller had caused the radon problem through alterations to the building. Contractors whose alterations to a building led to enhanced radon might also be liable (Kass and Gerard, 1987). For a developer, failure to test soils for radon before construction might lead to liability. Lenders who fail to insist on radon testing might become liable for mitigation, and possibly for medical and pain and suffering claims. Likewise, realtors may become responsible for the failure of clients to disclose radon in houses being sold. Beyond the potential for loss in such suits, even defending them would be expensive (*RIR*, November 1989f). Full disclosure has been recommended to real estate attorneys as the best way to protect the seller from liability (Kass and Gerard, 1987).

Radon Case Law

Radon case law predates the Colebrookdale Township discovery. In the 1970s, *Reader's Digest* magazine successfully defended itself against defamation charges stemming from its having described as "quacks" the owners of a "health" spa located in a former uranium mine who claimed that exposure to the inside air could cure arthritis and other diseases. The period of concern over human-caused radon exposure also yielded several precedent-setting decisions. A seller's responsibility for high radon levels was raised in *Wayne v. Tennessee Valley Authority*, where the Wayne family discovered that their house was contaminated by radon emanating from phosphate slag incorporated in the building's concrete block foundation. While in 1969, the court ruled, there was no basis for the seller to know about the dangers of radon, after Stanley Watras's discovery, the same defense would be unlikely to succeed, given the widespread information about radon. In a second case, *Brafford v. Susquehanna Corp.*, owners of a house built on uranium mill tailings were granted the right to seek compensation for forced eviction from their home (Danysh, 1987; Kass and Gerard, 1987). And the government's ability to withhold radon test data for which confidentiality was promised was limited in *Robles v. U.S. Environmental Protection Agency*, where the court found that public interest in matters affecting public health outweighs claims of privacy for residents living in an area where uranium mill tailings had been found. The results have implications for the ability of government to promise confidentiality in radon testing (Toomey and Sykes, 1988).

Nobel v. Kanze, Inc. addressed liability for naturally occurring radon in the home. When the Nobels, owners of the earth-sheltered home in Pennsylvania referred to previously, discovered that they had high radon levels—in the range of 55 pCi/l—they sued all parties involved in the purchase and construction of the building. Based upon a $100,000 effort to diagnose and mitigate the radon problem, it was determined that a seam in the ventilation system was the major radon entry point, which established the ventilation contractor as the primary defendant (Danysh, 1987; Higham and Fleishman, 1986; Stevens, 1986). However, claims by the Nobels that they had suffered increased cancer risk as well as emotional distress were dismissed because there was no proof of physical harm from the radon (Prussman, 1991).

Surprisingly, the flood of expected litigation on radon post–Colebrookdale Township has not yet happened. However, several interesting cases have materialized. Three cases addressed the collapse of real estate contracts due to radon findings. In one of these, *Steiner v. Strano*, the discovery of radon in excess of 4 pCi/l on short-term radon tests was not found to be a sufficient basis for canceling a sales agreement (Sullivan, 1990; Environmental Law Institute, 1993).

Two additional cases have addressed the more interesting issues of liability for failure to disclose high radon levels during the sale of homes. *Wilson v. Koval* (1989; *RIR*, November 1989f) addressed a tangled web of responsibility issues. When Frank and Paula Wilson and their four children moved to Spokane, Washington, in 1986, they rented and then purchased a home from the first owner, with the assistance of a local realtor. The Wilsons were not appraised of any radon problems at the premises. Then, one September day in 1987, when Paula was home, an environmental consultant came by to check instruments present for measuring radon gas. He explained that the home was a "hot house" used for research by the Bonneville Power Administration (BPA) under an incentive program joined by the first owners and the homebuilder. When the Wilsons subsequently tested their home, they indeed found excessive radon levels, apparently in the range of 30 pCi/l. The Wilsons eventually filed suit in Washington Superior Court against the prior homeowners, the realtor and her agency, the listing realtors, the builder, and the Washington State Energy Office, which had served as an agent for the Bonneville Power Authority. In their suit, they charged that the family was exposed to dangerous radon levels because of negligence, fraud, and misrepresentation and that the home was not habitable. The prior owners were charged with hiding their knowledge of a radon problem. The realtor was charged with failing to exercise reasonable care given a known local radon problem, as well as deception for dismissing the Wilsons' explicit questions about radon. The realtor that actually listed the home was similarly charged. The builder was charged with failure to repair the radon problem or to warn subsequent owners of the problem and with breaching a warranty of habitability for the home. Because deception was alleged, it was further charged that consumer protection laws had been violated, making defendants liable for punitive damages. While these charges raised important questions of legal precedent, the case was eventually settled out of court for an undisclosed amount of money and no precedents were set (Johnson, 1996).

Subsequently, a similar well-publicized case took shape on the east coast. After more than a year-long search for a house in the North Hills section of Pittsburgh, Pennsylvania, in 1991, Peter and Sue Ann Radakovich had found and purchased a home on Alydar Drive in Franklin Park for $172,500 from Richard and Sherry Filia. The closing had been contingent upon a radon inspection rider. If a test of the house had exceeded 4 pCi/l, then either the seller would have had to mitigate or the sale would have been voided. However, no radon problem was detected; a home inspector hired by the Radakoviches to test for radon found only 1.6 pCi/l. After the Radakovichs moved in fall 1991, they made extensive use of the house's basement as an exercise and television room and for their offices. The issue of radon did not arise until spring 1993, when they received a surprising letter from Sunn, Gromicko and Associates, a radon mitigation firm. As they learned from the letter, prior to the sale of the house, the Filias sought a mitigator to reduce the building's radon level, later identified as 29.3 pCi/l. The firm wrote to inquire if the mitigation was still desired.

When the Radokovitchs subsequently received the results from charcoal cannister tests they conducted themselves, radon levels as high as 44.2 pCi/l were revealed. In the terminology of their subsequent legal complaint, they had uncovered "a dangerously elevated [radon] level which rendered the premises unsafe and hazardous" (*Radakovitch v. Filia et al.*, 1995, p. 6). The complaint named as defendants the Filias, the three realtors involved in the sale, the two realty firms for which these agents worked (the buying agency, Howard Hanna Real Estate Company; and the sales agency, The Prudential Preferred Realty), and the home inspector. All were charged with fraud and with violation of Pennsylvania's Unfair Trade Practices and Consumer Protection Law. It was alleged that the defendants had failed to share information about previously identified high radon levels with the Radakovichs and had further tampered with a new test in order to lower the test results to be disclosed. The home inspector was additionally charged with negligence. Damages were sought for the Radakovitch's costs in mitigating and retesting the home ($11,641 plus continued retesting and energy costs associated with fans and leaving windows open for ventilation), the alleged loss of property value and inability to recover for improvements to the property, and severe emotional distress and physical symptoms suffered by Mr. Radakovitch due to the radon issue (the last charge was later dropped). Additionally, despite the remediation, the Radakovitch's were deprived of use of their basement due to continued excessive radon levels. In all, $172,620 in damages were sought by the Radakovitch's, in addition to punitive damages and lawyer's fees.

Unlike the Wilson suit, the Radakovitch case actually went to trial. It was described as a "David versus Goliath" situation because the Radakovitchs took on "big players in the residential real estate industry." As many as eight attorneys opposed their counsel at some junctures (Abel, 1996, p. 19). A jury heard the case in Alleghany County court beginning April 29, 1996. Witnesses for the defendants included former head of EPA's Air Division, Richard Girman; the president of AARST, health physicist Raymond Johnson; and well-known radon professional Bill Broadhead. Mitigator Nick Gromicko testified for the plaintiffs that the house was difficult to remediate. Along with the head of a testing lab, Gromicko also testified that tampering with radon results would have been possible. Broadhead went one step further, suggesting that the low results could only be accounted for by tampering. A real estate appraiser also established a value of $120,000 for the house, representing up to a 60 percent loss of value for a building in which the Radakovichs claimed to have invested $280,000. After a ten-day trial, the jury took six hours to reach a verdict awarding the plaintiffs $30,000, representing a $10,000 fine for each realtor for violation of fair trade practices. Otherwise, the defendants were found free of any wrongdoing; jurors

made public reference to their sympathy for the Filias, their belief in the doctrine of caveat emptor, and disbelief in the severity of radon exposure. The
Radakovitchs took the verdict as a defeat; given the power of the judge to triple
the damages and to award costs, their attorney announced the intent to pursue
further penalties.[20]

There are many implications that must be sorted out in the wake of *Radakovitch v. Filia et al.* First, the avowed intention of the suit was to send a message
to the real estate community about its obligations for full disclosure. Indeed, the
realtors bore the brunt of the verdict, not the seller of the home. Yet, the verdict
rested on consumer protection statutes, rather than upon the charges of fraud
and willful deception. The size of the punishment was hardly damaging, particularly to large corporate real estate firms. And it is not clear whether the verdict
will affect the realtors' licenses. In short, although they lost, the realtors suffered
little more than a slap on the wrist. Second, issues relating to the actual claimed
damages did not appear to be compelling for the jury, which was not even convinced to take radon very seriously. Certainly, the jury did not subscribe to a
journalist's words that, for the Radakovichs, the discovery of high radon levels
had "turned their $172,500 dream home into a toxic horror chamber" (Schmitz,
1996, p. A-7).[21] Finally, Pennsylvania had previously defeated a mandatory radon disclosure law; a new bill was under consideration. Had such a law been in
place, the consequences for the defendants might have been greater and the path
for the jury more clearly indicated.

Barriers to Legal Remedies for Radon Exposure

The paucity of litigation about radon may well reflect uncertainties about the
hazard, as well as the lack of standards and regulations. A likely barrier is radon's inherent blamelessness. Perhaps, naturally occurring radon has been slow
to generate tort law because the legal system is so heavily focused on situations
where responsibility for causing some hazard can be assessed (*RIR*, November
1989f). There are additional barriers to a full legal review of the radon issue under conventional "fault based" legal theories. The law demands a showing of direct harm from radon exposure rather than a vague argument of increased risk.
The argument that residents are denied enjoyment of their premises due to radon
confronts so high a level of demanded disturbance that evacuation from the home
or extremely high radon levels would be required of a successful complaint. Violation of a warranty of habitability implies that the owner had notice that a radon
problem existed. Arguments that landlords or sellers who failed to test for radon
were negligent confront prevailing norms under which buildings are not tested
before occupancy. The long latency found for lung cancer and the uncertainty of
the cause of any given cancer make it difficult to prove "present physical harm."
Given these roadblocks, Prussman (1991) argues that explicit legislation setting

forth a duty to test and remediate is a necessary backdrop to future radon litigation. While she narrowly addressed property rental, her arguments can be extended to all realty transactions, including new construction, and perhaps to address the private owner's responsibilities toward family and guests. Nevertheless, efforts to pass regulatory legislation in these areas has languished.[22] Until such legislation succeeds, the prospects for extensive litigation that establishes case law as a defacto form of regulation may be remote.

Conclusion—Radon and Regulation

The nonregulatory approach to radon has failed to quickly advance the prevention of radon exposure that is justified by risk assessment of this hazard. Particularly telling has been the failure to advance quasi-regulatory handles on the issue, involving real estate transfer and new construction. Given the priority demanded by geologic radon as a comparatively major risk factor, the lost opportunities for relatively decentralized and low cost-to-government forms of regulation are significant indeed. It remains to be seen whether this federal regulatory gap will be filled by states, or whether the courts and the issue of liability will provide an equivalent impetus.

Notes

1. Note that radon is a regulated point source emission under the Clean Air Act regulations issued by EPA in 1989 (EPA, 1991a).

2. They further argue that remediation may be required of as many as half of U.S. schools at a cost of ten thousand dollars per school.

3. This figure is based upon estimates of $2.2 billion for measurement, $6.6 billion for remediation and $0.8 billion yearly for operation and maintenance. Nero's figures are net costs based on an annual 5 percent discount rate over a thirty-year time span. Assumed is screening of eighty million residences at fifteen dollars per charcoal monitor, long-term follow-up in 20–30 percent of homes exceeding 4 pCi/l using two alpha track detectors costing fifty dollars, and remediation of some 4.4 million single-family dwellings at a cost of $1,500 per subslab ventilation system. Annual operation and maintenance costs were estimated at $135 for energy costs ($100 for electricity and $35 dollars for lost heat) and $50 for monitoring.

4. Mossman and Sollitto (1991) also contrast a radon policy seeking reduction of radon in all homes over 4 pCi/l—estimated to cost eight hundred million dollars—versus one that targets only hot houses. While the 4 pCi/l guidance is credited with an annual savings of two hundred million dollars in medical expenses and lost productivity, the analysts conclude that this radon policy is four times as expensive as it is beneficial, a case of "regulatory unreasonableness." Instead, they favor a policy based upon the small num-

ber of homes with high levels, citing the potential for substantial individual risk reduction. Illustrating the arbitrary nature of cost-benefit analysis, these authors offer no analysis as to how the hot houses will be identified and at what cost. Their assumptions about smoking and the costs of mitigation are also questionable.

5. The one trillion dollar estimate assumes that some seventy million of the current ninety million U.S. residences would require ten to sixteen thousand dollars in total remediation costs. To achieve ambient radon levels, it is assumed that a combination of the following steps would be required in each dwelling: reduced soil gas entry to near zero (at six thousand to ten thousand dollars), filtration of indoor air (at four thousand to six thousand dollars), and water filtration and avoidance of radon-emanating building materials (both comparatively inexpensive).

6. Our discussion draws particularly upon Edelstein (1988a), Baum et al. (1981), and Couch and Kroll-Smith (1985).

7. The agency made an effort to shift resources toward the highest ranked problems. However, it isn't clear how much of an effect it had. Most EPA funding is spent on mandated programs or according to congressionally directed initiatives. The General Accounting Office concluded in 1991 that "despite a considerable growth in its responsibilities, EPA's budget has been essentially 'capped' for over a decade" (Hembra, 1991). Funding would later be even more severely limited under the Contract with America congressional program begun in the mid-1990s. Thus, the concept of a proactive EPA working on the highest risk problems, rather than responding to socially defined crises, was, at best, challenging to implement.

8. Illustrating the subjective nature of the very objective-looking risk assessment process, estimates of the cost of cigarette smoking by cigarette companies and their sympathizers have recently concluded that, given the extreme cost to society of having people age, premature death due to cigarette smoking actually saves society money. By extension, inaction on radon is certainly equally cost effective.

9. Nero et al. (1990) also suggest that other voluntary programs affecting individually controlled spaces are even less expensive than is radon. For example, they note that the cost for a death averted by smoke detector is thirty thousand dollars and for use of passive restraints in the automobile is one hundred thousand dollars. The authors note that these cost-effective lifesaving steps are not uniformly required (see also Nazaroff and Teichman, 1990).

10. The DOE scientists cast doubt as to whether the assumptions underlying these savings in life can be achieved. First, thirty-year effectiveness is assumed for mitigation, an assumption not at all justified by current data on the persistence of remedial effects. Second, the current state of radon measurement is incapable of inexpensively measuring down to outdoor (ambient) levels with precision. Third, there has not been experimental demonstration that indoor radon levels can be reduced to the levels found outdoors. Finally, there are the problems of inaccuracies in screening measurements and the noncompliance of the public in taking radon action.

11. Certainly comparative risk also supported a fourth context of radon risk assessment, that connected with the never-implemented standard of 300 pCi/l for radon in wa-

ter (see chapter 3). That standard was advanced because of radon's comparatively high risk as a water pollutant, notable because the water risk is a tiny fraction of the unregulated air risk. The radon in water standard also led to widely divergent estimates of the costs, and thus the cost-benefit ratios, of implementation that further illustrate the imprecision of this tool.

It is instructive to review the impacts of a 300 pCi/l radon in water standard in just one state, California. A study by the Association of California Water Agencies projected that abatement would be required in as many as 289 water systems in California, while EPA had predicted abatement in only 239 systems nationwide. The California study projected that between 71 percent and 98 percent of all the water system wells in the state would require treatment, necessitating abatement of as many as nearly ten thousand wells at three times the $150,000 cost predicted by EPA. Overall, the agency projected a cost of between $2.7 and $3.7 billion for capital improvements in California—with a $710 million yearly operating cost. EPA had predicted that the cost of abatement for the whole country would only be $1.6 billion. By California's figures, the resulting annual cost in California to avoid each nonsmoking lung cancer death would be between $400 and $592 million under the program (Beck, 1992). Such uncertainties contributed to the refusal of Congress to approve the regulation, as written.

12. An exception is Florida's pioneering law that became effective in 1990 and was supported by the Florida Realtor's Association. The law required that a notice of radon disclosure be included in standard sales and rental contracts (Knox, 1989). However, the program only required the dissemination of information about radon and, given a belief that there was no major radon problem in the state, the disclosure statements generated little testing for radon (GAO, 1992).

13. It is interesting to look at the converse situation, where radon is actively managed so as to avoid environmental stigma. Mayor Robert Nulman of Clinton, New Jersey, described the conscious strategy employed by his community to deal with the stigma associated with the Clinton Knolls radon hot spot as follows:

> the goal of the Town of Clinton is to get a reputation of being the most tested community in the State of New Jersey as far as radon is concerned. And then, beyond that, to be the most remediated town in the State of New Jersey. That is, when we saw we had a problem, we fixed it. We can pretty much certify, at that point, that if you move to Clinton, you are going to move into a house that has been fully checked, has been remediated, and let's get on with business (1988, pp. 430–31).

14. Concerns were also raised that radon testing would invite tampering that would skew results and would force decisions to be made on only short-term tests. The GAO survey confirmed that decisions about purchase were frequently based only on short-term screening tests.

15. Perhaps the first lender to require radon testing as a condition of mortgage approval was the First National Bank of Central Jersey, headquartered in Bridgeton, N.J.,

([Middletown] *Times-Herald Record*, October 27, 1985). The policy did not last long, however.

16. The potential for market demand to force radon resistant construction was suggested by Jennifer Keller of EPA's Residential Construction Team. Citing a recent study conducted by economists at the National Association of Home Builders, she reported that more than a quarter of surveyed home buyers wanted homes with radon resistant construction. These desires have been translated into the market in some areas designated as high in radon on EPA's national radon map. Thus, Keller (1996) observed of radon-resistant construction, "In Northern Virginia, all the builders are doing it because their competition is doing it. So they have to. In other places, they look at you like you are crazy if you suggest it. It is hit or miss."

17. Some codes are specification-based with detailed required methods, techniques, and materials, while others are performance-based, only requiring the achievement of a goal or standard of performance. Three regional code organizations—the Building Officials and Code Administrators International (BOCA) in the northeast, the International Conference of Building Officials (ICBO) in the west, and the Southern Building Code Congress International (SBCCI)—offer somewhat different general performance codes to state and local governments. These codes are amended yearly. In addition, the Council of Building Officials (CABO), an umbrella group for BOCA, ICBA, and SBCCI, issues a specification code (One and Two Family Dwelling Code) every three years, written by one of the three member groups. Some of its provisions may disagree with all three general building codes. CABO codes are used nationwide, instead of or in addition to the regional codes. About one fifth of the country is governed just by CABO codes. In many states, local government authorities have total responsibility for building codes, while in others, state-mandated codes are preemptive or can only be made more restrictive. In some states such as New Jersey, two different model codes are adopted and builders may choose either one (Osborne, 1988; Keller, 1996). In addition to these codes, there are specialized codes such as the CABO Model Energy Code or the Northwest Energy Code (NEC) (Osborne, 1988).

18. Offering both prescriptive and performance paths, The Northwest Residential Radon Standard was targeted for communities in the four Northwest states of Washington, Oregon, Idaho, and Montana. Option 1 (performance-based) requires only that the builder achieve a radon level below 4 pCi/l (to be lowered over time) based on a long-term follow-up test as defined by EPA protocols. The builder is responsible for modifying the house and retesting until this goal is achieved. Option 2 (prescriptive-based) requires certain foundation construction features, sealing, and a roughed-in subslab depressurization system, which then relieves the builder of any other responsibility.

19. The SBCI had accepted the EPA code at a preliminary hearing in 1996, but only as a nonmandatory appendix. The measure was due for a vote of the membership before the end of that year. The ICBO turned the EPA code down in 1995, before enacting a moratorium on new changes. And BOCA also was operating with a moratorium (Keller, 1996).

20. Information on the Radakovich case was drawn from the complaint (1995), press coverage of the case, including Baird (1996), Angotti (1996a, 1996b, 1996c, and 1996d), Schmitz (1996), and Abel (1996), as well as from an interview with EPA's Elizabeth Zanowiak and from a 1996 EPA fact sheet on the case.

21. A side effect of publicity about the psycho-social harm of the elevated radon was a return to the kinds of imagery associated with Colebrookdale Township. This possiblity was not lost on EPA. As Jennifer Keller of the agency's Center for Healthy Buildings commented (1996), "In a way it (the Radakovich case) is bad for us because it sounded like radon would be almost as horrible as a Superfund site. It may be that horrible if you have a hard mitigation. But commonly people put in the system all the time, and it is no big deal." The fact that the jury saw the matter so differently is instructive of just how resistant the radon issue has been to "toxic" imagery.

22. Most notable was legislation sponsored by Senator Lautenberg and Congressman Markey. The Senate readily passed Senator Lautenberg's bill, which continued existing directions in the Radon Action Program and sidestepped the question of regulation (Burham, 1992). Representative Markey's comparatively controversial "1992 Radon Awareness and Disclosure Act" did not fare so well in the House. The bill directly regulated real estate transactions by dictating disclosure of radon warnings and known radon problems and provided the buyer with a brief period for testing the property. The focus on home sales as a trigger point for radon testing led to opposition by powerful real estate interests (Locke, 1993). Opposition to the Markey bill was led by the National Association of Home Builders, arguing that radon testing should not be required in new construction because the methods were inadequate, and they feared that results would be used by bankers against builders. The EPA and Bush administration also opposed the bill. EPA's opposition was said to have been forced on the agency by the OMB (Melamud, 1992; *IAR*, June, 1992a, p. 25). By 1993, when both the Markey and Lautenberg bills were reintroduced into the 103d Congress, efforts had been made to incorporate the regulatory stance of the House version into the Senate bill (Markey, 1993; Lautenberg, 1993; Wagner, 1993). Another effort to attract support for the bill was launched in June 1995 for the 104th Congress (*Radon News Digest*, 1995). For a further discussion of the Markey and Lautenberg bills, see chapter 3. Note that proposed federal legislation even included citizen suit provisions, by which citizens would be empowered to enforce the statutes in court.

Chapter 11

The Myth of Decentralization

We've known that radon was there for a long time. Yet, we have to prove it over again in every state.
—Richard Guimond.

One of the key tenets of the Reaganomic program was embodied in Executive Order No. 12612 on "federalism," which directed that "decision making be left to state and local governments wherever possible" (Belzer, 1991, p. 2). The rationale of using the smallest unit of government was that it would be closest to the constituents. Specifically, federal practice was redefined so as to dictate that "an important alternative [to federal programs] that may often be relevant is regulation at the state or local level. . . . The smallest unit of government capable of correcting the market failure should be chosen—balanced against the possibility of higher costs because national firms would be required to comply with more than one set of regulations" (OMB, 1991a, pp. 654–55; OMB, 1991b). Jed Harrison (1991) of EPA's Radon Action Program explained in an interview that a decentralized approach would allow flexibility for states to tailor programs according to their own needs and resources: "We have tried to avoid a federal program in order to allow the states to come up with something that will suit their needs. Our perspective is to encourage responsibility for the radon issue to get people and institutions to act to require local programs. If we establish federal programs, it will be a disincentive to state programs."

However, there were clear obstacles to the success of a decentralized approach. First, states had varied levels of experience with radon and preparation for addressing it. Second, states varied dramatically in their technical, financial, and institutional capabilities (EPA, 1987b), and had different organizational styles and political makeups. The prospects for a coherent national policy through decentralization were questionable from the start. Finally, states needed to be motivated to recognize and accept radon as a hazard demanding serious response. Under decentralization, the growth of state and nongovernmental radon programs was to be facilitated by federal research, most notably the state radon surveys. By searching for new hot houses and hot areas in each state, the program was to advance through repeated rediscovery of the geologic radon issue, de novo. It is not surprising that, prior to the state funding program created by the 1989 Indoor Radon Abatement Act, decentralization had yielded only minimal program development, and that was mostly concentrated in the states connected to Colebrookdale Township through the Reading Prong (Edelstein, 1988b). However, even after more than five years of federal funding for state

263

programs under the 1989 legislation, there was still little sustainable progress evident. The magic of the Watras event was to prove a hard act to follow. In fact, the greatest prospects for success were in the states originally mobilized by the event in Colebrookdale Township.

The Reading Prong States

As we discussed in chapter 5, the Reading Prong states were thought early on to contain the greatest population at risk from radon. Instructively, significant differences were found in state programs within the prong, with Pennsylvania and New Jersey addressing radon in a more serious manner than did New York.

Pennsylvania's Radon Program

Radon had the greatest immediacy in Pennsylvania. The Watras discovery had interrupted the 1984 Christmas party of the Pennsylvania Department of Environmental Resources (DER). Disbelieving the extraordinary radon levels reported to them, the DER made the Limerick plant retest (Gerusky, 1986).[1] Spurred by confirmation of the crisis, as well as by EPA's reluctance to treat geologic radon in the Superfund framework used for properties contaminated through human activity, Pennsylvania formed the first real state radon program in the country. Initial efforts centered on Colebrookdale Township, where testing, as well as the eighteen-home remediation study, were undertaken with the assistance of EPA. Efforts soon spread to a wider area. Shortly after the Watras family moved, the DER undertook a testing program in southern Berks County, screening 2,461 homes in six months (Scheberle, 1994). To support these efforts, a substantial radon staff was organized. Funding was provided through million dollar budgets in 1985 and 1986. Political resistance was overcome by the advocacy of State Senator Michael O'Pake, the representative of the Berks County area, which included Colebrookdale Township.

In 1985, a major screening effort using alpha track detectors was undertaken by the Commonwealth, involving some twenty-six thousand homes on the Reading Prong. In fact, it was some time before Pennsylvania would accept the possibility that radon was not geographically bounded in the Reading Prong. But by 1987, Pennsylvania extended its radon advisories to thirty-five counties statewide. The Commonwealth also provided confirmatory monitoring, and a diagnostic team was sent to homes registering more than 20 pCi/l. Subsequent efforts by Senator O'Pake succeeded in funding a one million dollar demonstration program and low-interest loans to spur remediation (Gerusky, 1986; GAO, 1986; Gaertner, 1988; Granlund, 1988). A pioneer effort to certify radon mitigation and testing contractors came that same year (O'Pake, 1988; Pennsylvania

Environmental Quality Board, 1988). By 1989, the radon program in the Pennsylvania DER was staffed by twenty-one professionals, with additional support from other state agencies. Funding for the program was $1.4 million, from the state budget (EPA, 1990b).

New Jersey's Radon Program

New Jersey, already sensitized to human-caused radon exposures by the radium-contaminated soils issue, was directly influenced by events in neighboring Pennsylvania. The presence of one quarter million New Jersey homes atop the Reading Prong gave particular meaning to the view that the prong was a hot zone for radon. This myth was publicized by the May 19, 1985, *New York Times* article by Philip Shabecoff, graphically depicting the Reading Prong in New Jersey (see chapter 3). Subsequently, the DER received hundreds of phone calls from the concerned public, as well as from realtors complaining of lost real estate sales due to adverse publicity. While officials well knew from the National Uranium Resource Evaluation (NURE) study that radon was not confined to the Reading Prong, and that an estimated 1.6–1.9 million houses were potentially affected (Deieso, 1987; Nichols and Cahill, 1988), New Jersey's radon problem came to be firmly associated with the Reading Prong (Edelstein and Boyle, 1988; Edelstein, 1991).

Officials from the state's Departments of Environmental Protection (DEP) and Health (DOH), already experienced with the Essex County industrial radon problem, met quickly to develop a response. Anticipating little federal help, State Senator John Dorsey and Assemblyman Richard Zimmer collaborated to write legislation that would enable New Jersey to address its radon issues (Dorsey, 1988). New Jersey was the first state to pass significant radon legislation, initially funding a DEP-led radon program at $3.2 million dollars, about twice the funding appropriated for EPA's national radon action program. Another million dollars was subsequently added.

The New Jersey radon program offered a successful model for state action (DePierro and Cahill, 1988; Deieso, 1987 and 1988; Nichols and Stern, 1988; Rahman et al., 1988; Tuccillo et al., 1988). At the local level, county health officers were trained to assist the public. Because responsibility for testing rested with the homeowner, the program was based upon the parallel goals of informing the public about radon and developing the radon private sector. With a fortyfold increase in testing firms in the state in the first two years of the program, New Jersey moved quickly to license and regulate this private radon industry. Initial certification of testing and remediation firms was done through a voluntary program, later followed by mandatory certification. In the first three years of the program, confirmatory monitoring was provided by the state for more than 7,000 homes tested over 4 pCi/l (with confirmation of the original test results in 85 percent of the cases) and postremediation monitoring was offered to some 1,500 homes. A low-interest loan program was developed to assist with mitigation; local building inspectors were involved in the approval of remediation work. Additional legislation required radon prevention in new construction, focused on high-risk areas. Other legislative initiatives focused on radon testing at the time of home sale and the need for further research on radon mitigation. A taskforce on public buildings, schools, and workplaces offered recommendations about testing.

The New Jersey program rested upon a strong research base. Results from an initial statewide radon survey of six thousand homes led to the division of New Jersey into three tiers, each with different recommendations to the public regarding the urgency of testing. The survey was combined with data from the confirmatory testing program, as well as data on twenty-five thousand homes submitted by firms as part of the early voluntary certification program. The DEP also conducted an evaluation of the success of remediation efforts through its postremediation testing program (see chapter 7). Meanwhile, the DOH undertook an epidemiological study of nonsmoking female lung cancer victims in order to identify the link between residential radon exposure and lung cancer (see chapter 4). A voluntary registry of individuals exposed to high radon levels was developed by the DOH, with newsletters sent to registrants to advise them about their health risk. The state also funded psychological studies of radon perception and communication (see chapter 9).

The strength of this program was clearly demonstrated by New Jersey's response to the radon hot spot discovered in rural Clinton, New Jersey, in spring 1986 (chapter 3; Nulman, 1988). The Clinton Knolls development took on Colebrookdale Township for the honors as the hottest hot spot yet discovered. Of 105 homes in the development, all tested over 4 pCi/l, five were found to have more than 1,000 pCi/l, and one was measured as the highest recorded residential radon exposure. The DEP and DOH closely collaborated with town officials. New Jersey officials tested the community, keeping the identity of the affected houses confidential. Then, in conjunction with the EPA, a remediation pilot program was conducted at no cost to the homeowners on ten Clinton homes with radon concentrations between 635 and 2,254 pCi/l. Follow-up measurements in 1987 showed all the buildings to have been reduced below 16 pCi/l, although some difficulty in pushing levels below 4 pCi/l was encountered (Carvitti, 1988). Free diagnosis was provided for another twenty homes. Meanwhile, Senator Frank Lautenberg succeeded in having radon recognized as a disaster by the Federal Emergency Management Agency (FEMA) in order to bring aid to the local area. In the wake of the Clinton experience, New Jersey also commenced a cluster identification program triggered by the discovery of any home having a radon level at or above 200 pCi/l.

As of 1989, the New Jersey program employed nineteen staff, sixteen of them based in the Department of Environmental Protection, two in the DOH, and one in the Department of Community Affairs. The fiscal year 1990 budget was $1.2 million funded by the state (EPA, 1990b). Leadership in addressing radon has also come from local communities, as well as the state. For example, in fall 1989, the New Jersey Township of Parsippany-Troy Hills became the first community in the country to mandate radon testing and mitigation (*RIR*, October 1989g).

Thus, New Jersey reveals a comparatively proactive approach against the primarily reactive effort to address radon found in Pennsylvania. The radon issue was tackled head on without delay and with adequate resources. Close collaboration existed between cooperating agencies and key legislators. Active use was made of the private sector to mobilize an effective program quickly. New Jersey took a leadership role in state radon action.

New York's Radon Program

The aggressive war on radon found in New Jersey and Pennsylvania, however, did not stretch across the Reading Prong into New York, despite that state's early involvement with geologic radon. At the time of the magic Watras event, the semipublic New York State Energy Research and Development Agency had already commenced a long-term study of radon in 3,300 homes in response to utility concerns over the impacts on indoor air quality of energy conservation (see Rizzuto, 1988).[2] Also prior to the Colebrookdale Township radon discovery, the State Energy Office (SEO) included a module that addressed radon and other indoor air pollutants in its training programs entitled "Building and Remodeling for Energy Efficiency." The module was to serve as the basis for the first model radon training program sponsored by EPA. With such early attention to radon, New York State would have been positioned to create an effective radon program had not authority for radon belonged to the state's Department of Health (DOH), historically involved in issues relating to radiation protection. At the Governor's Conference on Indoor Radon in early March of 1986, DOH Commissioner David Axelrod promised an aggressive radon program, unveiling a new brochure espousing EPA's position on radon risk. However, Axelrod did not speak for a powerful segment of his staff who opposed the EPA assessment, believing instead that radon exposure at lower levels is harmless. Axelrod's support for radon was undercut by this faction and his address was even omitted from the conference proceedings (N. Cohen, 1986).

Instead of a broad search for homes exceeding 4 pCi/l, the DOH restricted its attention to three rock types in the state believed to be likely to yield high radon clusters, including the Reading Prong. However, even in the Reading Prong, DOH employees sought to minimize the threat of radon. Thus, in a July 1985 public meeting in Tuxedo, New York, which was held in response to concerns that publicity about the Reading Prong would dampen local real estate development, a DOH official, John Matuszek, played down the radon threat: "it does not look like this area has a big problem. . . . It's doubtful that we have found anything that would require further testing. . . . The samples are terribly dull from a scientific point of view" (Boice, 1985, p. 3). Beyond minimizing radon incidence, radon risk was also qualified. Slides were shown of attractive women bathing in radon waters at an Austrian spa, implying that radon is not only safe, but, perhaps even beneficial. A New York University professor then compared the risks from radon to those associated with accepted personal activities, characterizing radon as having "a very small risk" (Boice, 1985, p. 3). Publicity surrounding the meeting contributed to the perception that radon was not a problem in Orange County. That view persisted despite the efforts of a local nonprofit corporation, Orange Environment, Inc., to document the extent of the local radon problem. Buying alpha track detectors in bulk, OE conducted a voluntary measurement program for concerned residents between 1985 and 1987, showing that nearly a quarter of the more than two hundred homes tested had radon levels over 4 pCi/l. While more than a thousand residents used OE's radon hot line during this period, overall, radon has never been defined as a local problem in Orange County in the wake of the Tuxedo meeting (Edelstein and Hoodes, 1988; Makofske and Edelstein, 1988).

Continuing disharmony within the DOH was evidenced in a 1986 account of a public meeting called to discuss discoveries of high radon houses in Voorheesville, New York (see also chapter 9). Karim Rimawi, head of the DOH's Bureau of Environmental Radiation Protection, addressed a public meeting in an effort to underscore the seriousness of the high radon readings found in the area. A reporter, Ken Thurman (1986), described what happened next. "But during the presentation . . . John Matuszek, director of the Health Department's radiological sciences laboratory, who attended the meeting as a private citizen, repeatedly challenged the validity of the measurements and the procedures used to gather information" (p. C1).

The lack of commitment to a radon threat was also evident in the state legislature, where heated debate dragged on over two competing radon bills, one supported by Democrats, the other by Republicans, that together required only $200,000 in public funding. One bill sought to create a radon hot line and provide staff support, the other set up a revolving fund through which the state would provide radon detectors to the public at cost. Partisan squabbling and administrative delays prevented even these minimal programs from commencing until 1987. A radon advisory task force appointed to help spur the DOH programs never met because of bureaucratic red tape.

In the midst of this ambivalent leadership, the SEO stepped in to offer creative direction. With a $200,000 grant from the EPA, the SEO developed a model mitigation training program. Additionally, it helped the DOH to capitalize on a financial windfall for its radon program, the legislatively approved use of $2.25 million in Exxon overcharge monies. Because this funding was limited, by court mandate, to use for energy-related projects, the program that resulted had to link energy and radon. Even though the agency itself understood that energy efficiency and radon were not related, the SEO used the myth of the tight house as a rationale for the program. Two free radon detectors were provided to residents of buildings that had received a home energy audit by their utility (Reese, 1988).

The resulting New York radon program rested on the use of a hot line to provide information, and the distribution of free or low-cost radon tests through the state or county health departments. Other program elements were copied from the New Jersey program, such as the cluster evaluation program, diagnosis for houses registering over 100 pCi/l, and creation of a radon exposure registry (NYDOH, 1989). By 1989, some fifty thousand calls had been reported and another twenty thousand detectors were targeted for dispersal. Some fifteen employees were involved with the state radon program, most in the DOH. The entire program was funded over three years with $6.7 million in appropriations, of which only $200,000 per year came from the state budget.[3] Free diagnostic services were subsequently offered for residences testing over 4 pCi/l (EPA, 1990b).

However, additional radon legislation was stalled and, by January 1995, the SEO had been closed. Furthermore, the DOH commitment to radon remained questionable. Thus, in February 1996, a DOH spokesperson told a reporter not to panic over EPA numbers extrapolated from health risks faced by "coal miners" [sic] (Swanwick, 1996). "In the reality of the real world, they can't point to actual cases. It gets people unnecessarily concerned. It just shows potentially what can happen. It's not a statewide problem. The EPA gave the impression, and not rightly so, that there could be problems in everyone's homes. Our approach is a non-panic approach" (pp. 1, 3).

Comparing the Three Reading Prong States

It may be useful to contrast the three Reading Prong states in their response to radon. Despite prior awareness of geologic radon, officials in all three Reading Prong states were forced to respond to the issue only after the Watras discovery. Pennsylvania reacted in crisis to Colebrookdale Township. New Jersey, even before finding its own hot area in Clinton, realized its vulnerability given its concentration of population on the Reading Prong. New York, although pulled along into radon-crisis management as a Reading Prong state, experienced comparatively less pressure: it had less area of Reading Prong, it was furthest from Colebrookdale Township, and it never found a comparable cluster of its own hot houses.

The differing demands on these states also affected their responses. It may not be surprising that New York chose to stay with its research-oriented mode of addressing radon, while Pennsylvania was forced into fast action to help the public, and New Jersey, benefiting from a little time and distance in order to plan its response, offered the best integration of acting on and studying the problem.

An important organizational difference was also evident. In Pennsylvania and New Jersey, the environmental departments took the lead; in New York, the Department of Health was in charge. While there may be a general tendency toward comparative risk conservatism in health departments and risk advocacy in environmental organizations, such a difference is certainly evident here. New York's health department embodied risk conservatism at its core. Many of its health physicists were "threshholders," and even radon rejectionists, who believed that the radon risk was generally overstated except for hot houses. Given the revolt within its ranks, the DOH was not a firm foundation for a program that would convince the public to take a hidden hazard seriously. The involvement of the SEO and NYSERDA only made the program more confusing to the public, even if the SEO's hook into sources of nonpublic money allowed a substantial state program to be mounted while utilizing minimal public funding and commitment.

There were also important differences in the manner by which the three states invited the formation of private radon services and encouraged their use by the public. Ironically, by offering free initial tests, New York State mounted serious competition to the growth of a radon private sector in that state (see Koehler and Giardina, 1988).[4] In contrast to New York's modest radon private sector, New Jersey created the most vibrant radon private sector in the nation, followed by Pennsylvania, while at the same time developing well-funded public radon initiatives.

The myths of the Reading Prong and the hot houses were evident in each of these programs. In all three states, efforts were made to geographically bound the radon problem. Pennsylvania eventually broadened its original focus on the Reading Prong to include other counties where radon levels were high. New Jersey developed a three-tier system indicating the urgency of radon testing, with the Reading Prong indicated as the highest risk area. New York, similarly, focused its efforts on research aimed at identifying which geologically defined parts of the state have higher radon potential. In all three states, such geographic markers have proved to be misleading. Yet, all three persisted in various ways to demarcate boundaries for radon likelihood.[5]

A Further Point of Comparison—Washington State

If the Reading Prong states were compelled to action by Colebrookdale Township, how well has the radon issue developed in states far from the Reading Prong and not forced to act by undeniable evidence of a problem? Washington

State's radon program is a good point of contrast because there was a similar early awareness of the potential for geologic radon exposure.[6] In the early 1980s, the federal Bonneville Power Administration (BPA) filed an environmental impact statement for its weatherization program for electrically heated houses. When this document predicted that tightening houses would result in a substantial risk from various indoor air pollutants, including radon, the BPA modified its program to avoid houses deemed to be particularly susceptible to indoor air problems, excluding some 70 percent of the formerly eligible buildings. In the case of radon, a vented crawl space was required for participation in the weatherization program. Subsequently, the BPA conducted thirty-five thousand radon tests to evaluate the effect of the weatherization program, instituting mitigation for all homes over 3 pCi/l (BPA, 1984), although the action level was later raised to 5 pCi/l (BPA, 1987).

Washington's early involvement with geologic radon did not translate into an active state radon program, however. The fact that BPA was so actively pursuing the radon issue meant that there was little impetus for government to be overly active.[7] Furthermore, testing revealed a fairly low incidence of radon in Washington, with no extremely high readings. The state's relative "hot spot" was in the eastern Spokane area, not the populous and politically powerful western section. A final factor retarding Washington's response to radon was its organizational similarity to New York, namely in placing control of radon programs in a very skeptical health department, the Department of Social and Health Services (DSHS).

With the support of Washington's public health system, DSHS staff fomented a rebellion against the EPA's Radon Action Program reminiscent of the New York experience. DSHS staff opposed both the EPA and BPA action levels as being unnecessarily protective, questioned the health data for radon, and communicated their skepticism to the public with every opportunity. For example, a radon flyer released by DSHS highlighted in bold letters the statement **"The real risk from radon to the public of contracting lung cancer from radon in homes is unknown."** Then in 1986, EPA issued two key radon booklets, *A Citizen's Guide to Radon: What It Is and What to Do about It*, and *Radon Reduction Methods: A Homeowner's Guide*. DSHS personnel felt that EPA had disregarded their comments that risk estimates were too high. When Washington State agreed to issue these publications, DSHS staff went into full rebellion, inserting the following disclaimer onto the inside jacket of the *"Citizen's Guide"* printed for release in Washington State (Strong, 1986):

> Washington Department of Social and Health Services has agreed with EPA to distribute this pamphlet to residents of the state. However, it is the judgement of the Department's Division of Health that the lung cancer risk estimates presented in this pamphlet are excessively high. The assessment of lung cancer risks due to radon exposure was done using past epidemio-

logical studies that appear inaccurate and incomplete. Further studies are underway which may better define the actual risk of radon exposure. With the above caveat, this pamphlet provides information for the public to make informed decisions about their risk from radon.[8]

The EPA responded as though the caveat was a slap in the face (Strong, 1986). The agency, along with the BPA and the American Lung Association, successfully demanded that the altered booklets be recalled and destroyed. However, the incredulity of the state officials had already made its mark on the public acceptance of the radon risk. Newspaper articles reported at length the reasons why DSHS officials discounted the risk from radon. These reasons are all familiar: the problems of generalizing risk from miner data to the public, the adequacy of the miner data given the potential exposure of miners to other carcinogens, and the lack of epidemiological evidence of dedicated dead bodies attributable to radon. An Associated Press newspaper article in the *Olympian*, in late December 1986, reported that the state isn't doing any testing "because it doubts radon poses much of a health risk." DSHS epidemiologist Sam Milham expounded on these doubts (Associated Press, 1986). "We've evolved as a species with radon all around us. It's not like we're dumping something new into the world. . . . in some places, if you look at the EPA estimates, radon would have to be responsible for all observed lung cancer cases, which is nonsense, because smoking is responsible for probably 83 percent" (p. B1). These efforts by the DSHS lessened the likelihood that state residents and legislators would act on radon. Public confusion was evident, for example, when a family moved out of its home after 17.9 pCi/l of radon had been found. When the house was foreclosed by the mortgage company, the family sued for recovery of its losses (Carollo, 1987).

The Washington Energy Extension Service, a champion of the radon issue much as was New York's State Energy Office, held a private radon forum for regional radon professionals on May 6, 1987 in Spokane to identify areas of consensus that might allow for a coherent approach to radon. Attendance at the forum was by invitation only, and neither the media nor the general public was invited. The session, at which the first author spoke, resulted in an agreement to set aside debate about the actual risk from radon, since all parties agreed that radon was extremely hazardous. With this dispute out of the way, a concentrated effort to get people to test their homes could commence (Moody, 1988). By 1991, observers of the Washington scene were lauding the effectiveness of a serious radon program put in place with the help of the same officials who had earlier opposed the issue. Another sign of an active program was the successful development and acceptance of a regional ordinance for new construction under the leadership of the Washington Energy Extension Service. However, radon never garnered political support in Washington, and the program was supported by no state legislation, funding, or full-time staff (Washington State Energy Office, 1989).

In confirming the New York experience, Washington State may be more representative of the national issues in radon diffusion than are New Jersey and Pennsylvania. Washington illustrates the barriers to addressing radon in states lacking a dramatic radon crisis—one that forces a quick consensus leaving little room for questioning. Absent such a consensus, radon's nagging doubts emerge. The resulting dissensus was seen in the influence of the myth of the dead bodies within the agency taking a lead on radon, the health department. It was also seen in the failure of the state to provide a clear mandate and support for radon action, except when support came through the EPA grants program or, as in New York, some nonpublic source of funding. Thus, Washington points to the downside of decentralization, namely that substantial sources of resistance exist for radon program development where the urgency has not been demonstrated by high radon levels. Decentralization demands a search for the hot house, but it does not easily address lower levels of radon questioned by health physicists and local health officials.

Results of Decentralization

We have seen that substantial barriers confronted the diffusion of the radon issue across the United States. At the same time, significant differences between programs were evident, even within the mobilized Reading Prong states, where there was reasonable cross-fertilization. Finally, it is evident that a bias in favor of finding hot spots permeated the entire decentralization effort. How successful was this diffusion effort?

In 1987, the EPA categorized five states as having fully operational radon programs—New Jersey, New York, Pennsylvania, Florida, and Maine (EPA, 1987b).[9] It is instructive that states were compelled by the specifics of their history and geology to mobilize around geologic radon, not by any influence related to the federal radon program. It was not surprising that the only four states that had passed legislation mandating air radon programs as of 1987 were Pennsylvania, New York, New Jersey, and Florida and that, of the nearly $20 million spent by all the states, more than $18 million was appropriated by the same four states. Half of the total of 119 full-time equivalent employees in all state radon programs were employed in Pennsylvania, New York, and New Jersey (EPA, 1987b).

In contrast to the operational programs, EPA (1987b) noted that some fourteen other states were actively developing radon programs by carrying out an initial problem assessment involving statewide radon testing. Of the remaining states, all at least disseminated EPA information to residents and most had begun to formulate radon programs. Based on this minimal level of success, the EPA acknowledged that the decentralized model required improvements. In 1987, EPA and the Conference of Radiation Control Program Directors, Inc., convened state and federal radon officials in a two-day conference in Atlanta to discuss the effectiveness of the radon action program and to seek a consensus on further courses of action. Participants set forth a list of ways that EPA could support continued growth of state radon programs by providing information and training and by developing model legislation and testing protocols (EPA/ CRCPD, 1987).

However, when state program ratings were updated in 1989 (EPA, 1990b), the number of states with "extensive radon programs" had dropped to four (with Maine eliminated because it never extended its program beyond waterborne radon) and, of the fourteen developing programs identified in 1987, only seven were classified as having reached a "moderate program" level.[10] Overall, by 1989, EPA reported an uneven and modest diffusion of radon programs throughout the United States. While all states were distributing radon fact sheets, only nine states had established hot lines to provide radon information. The number of states participating in the EPA Radon Action Program had approached half, with twenty-three states and several Indian tribes participating in the EPA state indoor radon surveys, seventeen states participating in the HEP, and eight in the Radon Mitigation Research Program. Additionally, twelve states had passed some form of radon legislation and a smaller number had begun to regulate radon businesses (EPA, 1988a, 1990b). Radon legislation was under consideration in fifteen states (*RIR*, October 1989e). The infusion of significant federal grant monies to the states was needed to jumpstart widespread action.

Impact of the State Indoor Radon Grants

The Indoor Radon Abatement Act called for $10 million in yearly grants over three years. More than $21 million in state grants was provided by EPA from 1990 through 1993, with grants going to forty-eight states, the District of Columbia, and Guam. In line with the myth of the Reading Prong and the myth of the hot house, these grants were targeted to high-risk areas within states, and states with high-risk and heavily populated areas (EPA 1992b; GAO 1992). An evaluation of the success of these grants is difficult because EPA transferred management of state programs to the EPA regions; however, EPA radon staff believe state activity to be extensive (Wagner, 1993). Confirmation of success is further impeded because EPA did not require the states to evaluate whether their programs led to increased testing and mitigation (GAO, 1992). Information is available regarding proposed and enacted state radon legislation. For the 1992–93 legislative sessions, forty-one pieces of legislation were reported for twenty-five states and the District of Columbia, more than half dealing with realty transfer (Environmental Law Institute, 1993a). A July 1994 EPA survey on the same topic shows forty-two pieces of state radon legislation enacted. Eighteen states had adopted some form of certification, registration, or licensing for radon testers and mitigators, five had legislation addressing school testing, fifteen had required some form of real estate radon disclosure, and four had incorporated EPA model standards for new radon construction. Twenty-seven states in all had enacted some form of radon legislation (EPA, 1994). As noted previously, by 1996, twenty-eight had enacted some form of real estate disclosure law (Zanowiak, 1996).

The Nongovernmental Sector

Beginning in the late 1980s, EPA reached out to key national organizations as part of its decentralized approach. EPA's nongovernmental partners include the National Association of Counties, which has worked to further radon action by members, including an initiative in support of radon building codes. Radon programs targeted to smokers were developed by the American Lung Association and the American Public Health Association. The Consumer Federation of America developed a postcard to accompany radon test results that would facilitate requests for mitigation information and the tracking of mitigation activity. The National Safety Council created a coupon system for organizations to promote test kits through direct mailings. The National Civic League held workshops with community leaders in high-risk areas. The National Research Center of the National Association of Home Builders involved itself in the testing of radon-resistant construction approaches and, with other groups, the development of new radon codes. The National Association of Realtors, the Employee Relocation Council, the Mortgage Bankers Association, and other housing groups cooperated to address radon testing and mitigation in conjunction with real estate transactions (EPA, 1992b). The Environmental Law Institute assisted EPA in tracking state radon programs and in providing training to the states and to the real estate community. On behalf of the National Conference of State Legislatures, the institute developed a booklet entitled "State Radon Legislation—Issues and Options" designed to help states identify the legislation necessary to support a comprehensive radon program (Environmental Law Institute, 1993b). Other partners included the Parent-Teacher Association, the National Association of County Health Officers, the International City/County Management Association, the Association of State and Territorial Health Officials, the Environmental Assessment Association, the American Association of Radon Scientists and Technologists, the American College of Preventive Medicine, and the National Environmental Health Association.

These organizations provided the agency with direct access to desired target audiences. Additionally, organizations offered special expertise and credibility, as well as flexibility and effectiveness (EPA, 1993c). The organizational network was to be used primarily for education and information distribution, although it was hoped that social norms favoring radon action would form. Additionally, the partners were enlisted to help push for radon discloure and new construction legislation in the various states (Zanowiak, 1996).

With developing concerns over environmental justice and the radon program in the mid 1990s, EPA sought a new set of partners to broaden their reach. Working through its Center for Outreach and Partnerships, relationships were targeted with organizations connected to diverse sectors of the U.S. population. African Americans were approached through the National Medical Association, a physicians group whose local affiliates participate in health fairs and network to hospitals and local government, as well as through the National Council of Negro Women, another national organization that works through local affiliates. The Hispanic community was approached through COSSMHO (translated as the National Coalition of Hispanic Health and Human Services Officials). COSSMHO operates a Spanish-language radon hot line, produces Spanish-language materials, and funds six community groups working on health issues in states with large Hispanic populations. A related organization, the Self-Reliance Foundation, broadcasts call-in radio programs on indoor air issues over the Hispanic Radio Network. The Association of Asian and Pacific Community Health Organizations (AAPCHO) has helped EPA translate radon information into Chinese, Korean, and Vietnamese and has included radon among six community-based risk reduction programs for Asian populations. Native Americans have been deeply involved in radon programs, with the Navaho, Cherokee, Hopi, Omaha, and Intertribal Council of Arizona taking the lead. Tribes have qualified for the state grants program. Finally, other groups that address the needs of the poor have recently been included in EPA's radon program, including Habitat for Humanity and a group called American Neighborhoods. Additional outreach efforts are targeting the elderly (Carpentier, 1996).

By 1996 there were a total of twenty-seven partners working with EPA on radon and other indoor air issues (Zanowiak, 1996). Table 11.1 depicts the agency's concept of repetition and reinforcement of radon messages through this decentralized network, depicting some of these institutional partners. While these nongovernmental organizations have certainly helped to reinforce the EPA radon program, their primary effect is to gradually "socialize" radon, bringing it into the mainstream of thinking about health promotion. There have been noticeable strides in this direction; however, one must look to the long-term to anticipate significant effects on voluntary testing and action. These methods do not generate short-term preventative health responses commensurate with the urgency accorded to geologic radon. For that, firm government action is required.

Lessons of Radon Decentralization

Given the importance of decentralization through the states for the effectiveness of EPA's Radon Action Program, the picture that emerges from our examination of early state response is not rosy. Against one of the most risky environmental hazards, government launched an uneven and gradual effort. As a result, states have differed widely in their recognition and acceptance of the radon issue. Few allocated significant resources to the problem. Often, one or a few staff members in an overworked agency are given the radon issue as part of their workload. Inconsistencies in policy and approach are rampant. From our review, we stress four limits of decentralization.

Table 11.1   EPA's Partners Used for Reaching Targeted Segments of the Public (*Source*: Zanowiak, 1996)

PARTNER	SECTOR REACHED
Committee on Indoor Air Quality (CIAQ)	Federal Agencies
Conference of Radiation Control Program Directors (CRCPD)	State Agencies
National Conference of State Legislatures (NCSL)	Sate Legislators
Association of State and Territorial Health Officials (ASTHO)	Health Officials
National Safety Council (NSC)	Safety Officials
National Conference of States on Building Codes & Standards (NCSBCS)	Code Officials
Advertising Council (AdC)	Public Service Directors
Radon Proficiency Programs	Radon Industry
Radon Training Centers (RTC)	Industry/Trainees
National Association of Home Builders (NAHB)	Home Builders
Environmental Law Institute (ELI)	Real Estate Leaders/ Attorneys
Environmental Assessment Association (EAA)	Environmental Assessors
Science Advisory Board (SAB)	Scientists
National Academy of Sciences (NAS)	Scientists
American Medical Association (AMA)	Physicians
American College of Preventive Medicine (ACPM)	Preventive Medicine Physicians
National Medical Association (NMA)	African-American Physicians
American Lung Association (ALA)	Local Affiliates
National Environmental Health Association (NEHA)	Environmental Health Specialists
Parent-Teacher Association (PTA)	Teachers
National Civic League (NCL)	Civic Leaders
Consumer Federation of America (CFA)	Consumer Advocates

A Need for Reinventing the Wheel

In effect, the implication of the decentralized program is that the environmental policy cycle has been repeated all over again in every state, with relatively little gain from experiences elsewhere. One result of this need to reinvent the wheel in every state has been that successful efforts in one state have had minimal benefits as models for other states. In particular, New Jersey has served as an excellent potential model for effective radon programming. Along with the other Reading Prong states and Florida, key innovations have been introduced, tried, and evaluated there. Yet, these states have continued to be the only centers of advanced radon action. It would appear that the diffusion model has been slow, inefficient, and not particularly effective to date. In the absence of federal action, there is uneven and disappointing state response, even in the face of a severe environmental hazard.

Chasing the Hot Houses

For decentralized radon programs to develop, states had to be mobilized to act through the continued rediscovery of radon. As the result of EPA's state radon surveys, state radon programs would be created in response to the discovery of new "hot" areas. Using this approach, EPA hoped to foster similar levels of radon program development in states within similar regions of the country (EPA, 1987b). As we established in chapters 5 and 6, the need to motivate each state through a process of repeated rediscovery of geologic radon wedded decentralization to the search for hot houses. Screening measurements focus on identifying the highest levels present in a structure, and are useful for identifying the relatively small number of houses with high risk levels. Screening offers the opportunity to quickly profile an area in terms of hot houses at the expense of valid characterization of the radon health threat.

However, the search for hot houses was a double-edged sword for decentralization. As a tool for diffusion, screening offers the possibility of creating radon concern when hot spots are found, but in their absence, it has the opposite effect. Thus, while the Watras discovery certainly motivated New Jersey, New York, and Pennsylvania to develop the most aggressive early programs in the country to address natural radon, the myth of the Reading Prong proved to be a disincentive to action outside this area, even within the mobilized states. The approach was only successful where new radon hot spots were documented, as with the discovery of a "western Reading Prong" (EPA, 1988b). EPA was aware of the confusion inherent in its approach, but continued to embrace it. Ironically, screening, justified by its speed in locating the worst radon problems, was coupled with the glacial diffusion of radon programming, contradicting its only real justification. Not only were residents of "hot houses" not reached quickly, but also those living with less but significant risk were often not reached at all. Decentralization relies on this ineffective and misleading approach.

Inconsistency across States As an Impediment to the Radon Industry

Our case studies document major discrepancies between state programs, something to be expected given the decentralized approach. Such divergence characterized the early years of geologic radon (Edelstein, 1988b). Decentralization not only invited dramatic differences in where radon was taken seriously, but also in how it was addressed. States varied in their resources, as well as their technical and institutional capabilities (EPA, 1987b). As our comparative case studies have shown, states approached the issue in idiosyncratic ways, with variations in approach and effectiveness. The challenge facing EPA was how to introduce consistency into this varied array of programming. In response, the agency proposed guidelines covering six key program elements considered to be necessary for an effective state radon program: public information, development of clear goals and policies, creation of a strategy, efforts to characterize the problem in the state, implementation of a program response, and development of the means to administer the program (EPA, 1988c). There is little evidence that these guidelines led to much program homogenization.

Because of this decentralized federal policy and the freedom of different states and municipalities to develop their own radon programs, the emerging radon industry faced the prospect of fifty different laws in fifty different states governing radon certification. The result is confusion, expense, and frustration among radon companies (Koopersmith, 1989). This problem was recognized by the EPA Radon Action Program's Jed Harrison in a 1991 interview. "New Jersey, Florida, Pennsylvania and, somewhat, Iowa are advanced in their program development. The problem is that we have left things to themselves and all of a sudden you have so many different requirements for companies operating in all states. Even now the states are not reciprocating." Harrison cited as a positive indicator the increasing reliance of states on the Radon Measurement Proficiency (RMP) program and the emerging Radon Contractor Proficiency (RCP) program, an outcome that we earlier critiqued in chapters 6, 7, 8, and 10. As noted in chapter 8, EPA eventually issued a "Guidance to States on Radon Certification Programs" in an effort to inspire consistency.

Is Federal Money a Requisite?

With the passage of the Indoor Radon Abatement Act, significant federal funding over a three-year period became available to move states toward a common ground regarding radon. Forty-nine of fifty states applied for grants giving 25 percent matching funds. However, by 1992, EPA officials were concerned that significant state programming would not continue without federal funding. These concerns were voiced to the authors by EPA's Steve Page (1991). "States are moving. The policy question is how many will have self-sustaining programs at the end of their period of EPA support. They have money problems. Some states fear their programs will fold." The fear that diffusion would fail without federal support was taken seriously. Despite the administration's clear admonition that state radon grants would end after three years, the state grants were extended (Page, 1991). By 1996, the grants continued at a cost of eight million dollars per year.[11] Thus, decentralization's gradual success in diffusing radon programming throughout the states appears to contain a caveat. State interest in radon will continue as long as a sizable amount of the funding comes from Washington. Broad decentralization without federal support is a myth.

Conclusions

In sum, this evaluation reveals that decentralization has real promise for the slow diffusion of concern and understanding about the radon hazard that may, over time, cause radon to be a comprehensively addressed issue. However, decentralization has been an ineffective approach for quickly meeting a health threat defined by the EPA as a top priority for action. Decentralization has rested on the inappropriate and misleading foundation of screening for hot houses (see also chapters 4, 5, and 6). Additionally, decentralization has resulted in a confusing hodgepodge of state responses. Finally, the evidence suggests that sustained state action is unlikely without substantial continued federal support. Ironically, the Reaganomic principle that the buck should be passed from federal to state and local levels appears to imply that federal funding is required if an unmandated issue such as radon is to be addressed. Radon raises a new twist on the key battle cry of neo-Reaganomics over the injustice of the "unfunded mandates." Here we see the consequences of a "funded, unmandate."

Notes

1. The DER was apparently unaware that the state Department of Health had been collaborating in a radon survey with the Department of Energy's Argonne National Laboratory since the winter of 1983 (Strecklow, 1985a; see chapter 2).

2. An early NYSERDA/EPA remediation project involved houses in the Reading Prong area.

3. Of this funding, about $2.5 million came from Exxon oil overcharge litigation funds and another $4 million came from stripper-well-exemption litigation funds (EPA, 1990b).

4. At one hearing on radon called by state senators, a long line of frustrated businesspeople complained about how the competition from the New York program had made them secondary players in testing within the state. One concession to the local radon industry that resulted was that New York later contracted with an in-state private lab for its testing program.

5. For a comparison of Pennsylvania's program to Massachusetts' radon efforts, see Krimsky and Plough (1988).

6. Observations of the Washington State program were made during a visit by the first author to Spokane in May 1987 and through subsequent discussions with state radon officials and review of documents.

7. A further complication was BPA's failure to adopt the same guidance as EPA.

8. An internal DSHS memo written a few days after the brochures's release elaborated further: "Health professionals within the Division of Health believe the EPA may have overstated the risks from radon. It was forced to set an action level without any real evidence linking household radon concentrations to mortality. In most instances, we cannot measure a proportionate gain in safety for the cost necessary to reduce radon levels to the EPA's guideline of 4 pCi/l" (Strong, 1987).

9. Maine had been concerned since the 1960s with the extremely high waterborne radon levels found there; its early program grew up with a focus on water but little attention to airborne radon. In Florida, a history of phosphorus slag exposures influenced the state to focus its program on building materials and construction techniques. Recognizing that phosphate contains uranium, which gives off radon, Florida developed an extensive five-year survey to ascertain the effects of its 420,000 acres of phosphate lands. In addition, legislation passed in Florida gave the state authority to establish and enforce environmental standards, adopted 4 pCi/l as a state standard, prescribed radon-proof construction techniques for use in phosphate lands and other high-radon areas, and mandated certification (GAO, 1986).

10. While extensive programs averaged sixteen full-time staff members and mean budgets of $1.4 million in 1989, these moderate programs averaged budgets of around $200,000 and staffs of one or two people. Against an average of almost 1,400 phone inquiries per month in the extensive states, moderate state agencies handled between twenty and six hundred telephone calls about radon per month. The moderate states were actively moving to survey in-state radon, to provide radon information, and in some cases, to provide information on radon companies and to offer radon training courses—all activities offered by the mature "extensive" state programs. In contrast, forty states with only "core programs" were limited in the extent to which they provided information, were engaged in assessing the scope of their state's radon problems, and were actively responding to radon issues.

11. At the time of publication, EPA was considering converting its state radon grants into a "performance partnership." As a result, states would be able to roll all their environmental funds into one block grant, allocating the funds according to their own priority. This shift in funding mechanism might threaten use of federal funds for state radon programs given the pressure on states to pay for mandated environmental programs (Feldman, 1996).

Part IV

Radon and Risk

Chapter 12

Societal Implications of Radon Exposure

Each social arrangement elevates some risks to a high peak and depresses
others below sight.
—Douglas and Wildavsky

In this final chapter, we examine the societal implications of radon, exploring
the three themes of our subtitle—science, environmental policy, and the politics
of risk. We see that environmental policy is defined both through science, our
means of approximating reality in the face of uncertainty, and by the political
and social dynamics of risk, as fueled by that uncertainty. We learn some clear
and provocative lessons from the deadly daughters.

Radon—Myths and Science

Radon provides us with a perspective on how science is applied to the task of explaining uncertainty related to environmental risk issues. Beyond the rigorous
application of data in order to test and improve theory, what is apparent in the
radon story is the profound influence of often-shallow belief systems that serve as
heuristics or shortcuts in thinking (Kahneman et al., 1982). These myths, rather
than some empirical framework, determine the direction of policy. The radon
case demands a general effort to explore the underlying assumptions behind the
scientific—as well as sociopolitical—means of thinking about risk. In this, radon
shares the pervasive problems of most environmental hazards, including invisibility, unclear patterning, outcroppings of effects that may be the tip of the ice-
berg or may be isolated occurrences, the profound but ill understood issue of
cumulative causes and effects, and the potential for some causes to mask others.

We have set forth several myths of radon that illustrate the limits of scientific understanding. These myths cloud the only scientifically solid basis for thinking about radon risk, namely, the clear epidemiological record tying radon
exposure to lung cancer in miners. Having carefully reviewed and assessed the
evidence pertaining to radon's risk, we have come to believe that radon is indeed
a serious hazard, the major source of general exposure to radiation. However, we
have raised serious questions about the testing, mitigation, and bounding of radon, obscured by myths originating with the Colebrookdale and Clinton experiences that have misinformed radon policy. Neither have we found most critics of
EPA policy to be free of mythical thought, given their totally unrealistic demand
for a clear epidemiological record (i.e., dead bodies) as a requisite for recogniz-

285

ing the degree of risk. These various myths demonstrate that thinking about geologic radon has easily been confounded by the inherent limitations of applying "hard" science to a "soft" world. These myths have influenced not only scientists, but also politicians, bureaucrats, publicists, the media, and the public. At a deeper level, these myths reflect our social values about risk, about science, and—in the post-Watras geologic radon period—about the role of government, the marketplace, and the environment. The myths of radon thus serve as a lens for focusing on how we have understood this hazard. Let's revisit several of them.

The Myth of the Dead Bodies

The myth of the dead bodies reflects the unwillingness of some experts, officials, and others to accept the reality of risk without clear-cut proof, demanding, for example, dedicated dead bodies to account for radon's lung cancer toll. This same simplistic approach to radon risk has plagued other environmental issues, including the contemporary attack on the risk of dioxin led by CDC's Vernon Houk.

For radon, there may be no better exposition of this myth than Leonard Cole's rant against EPA policy that "because the number of annual deaths that the EPA presumes comes from radon is so high—between 7,000 and 30,000—if there is an effect, it should hit you in the eye" (1993, p. 201). But do environmental symptoms necessarily hit one in the eye? When adherents of the myth of the dead bodies seek dedicated fatalities for radon, they assume that causes of cancer leave specific markers and that a given cancer is caused by a single factor. In the world of environmental exposure, such demands are most often tantamount to a denial of the effect. Furthermore, when critics argue that smoking is so dominant a cause of lung cancer that radon's effects are comparatively trivial (see, for example, Yallow, 1988; Nazaroff and Teichman, 1990; Cole, 1993), they ignore the probable synergy between smoking and radon that means that many lung cancers are really a result of the interaction of both rather than caused by either in isolation. Clearly a better understanding of this synergy is required in order to comprehend the consequences of radon exposure. Additionally, scientific "experts" who so readily dismiss environmental factors in disease must become more open to interactive effects. Radon helps dismiss this myth of isolated cause and effect.

Myths of the Reading Prong and the Hot House

The radon issue has been overwhelmingly dominated by the perception that radon risk is concentrated in geographically bounded areas and that the focus of radon policy should be to identify the hottest radon houses. We have referred to these beliefs, respectively, as the myth of the Reading Prong and the myth of the hot houses. As discussed, the particular outline of radon boundaries took shape when the Watras case was mythologized by the media and government. Initial scientific and official hypotheses became foundational assumptions for later thinking about the radon issue. Such basic beliefs die slowly because they are partially true and are, thus, reinforced. In this instance, the Reading Prong indeed features high radon potential. The error is one of omission, stemming from the assumption that radon potential outside of identifiable "hot spots" is insignificant. Yet vast areas of the country have moderate to high radon potential. And there are many higher radon homes in regions of relatively low radon potential.

There are psychological as well as historical reasons for drawing boundaries, even when none exist in reality. Because the concept of the universal hazard is deeply threatening, we tend to bound—to literally place some boundaries or conditions—around environmental (and social) threats. Once radon came to be seen as the property of delimited hot areas or houses, the rest of us could relax. On their part, residents of the hot area or the hot house may be forced to address the threat. Conversely they may find some other boundary definition that defines them as safe; a drafty house—albeit on the Reading Prong—may be deemed (perhaps falsely) secure. Furthermore, because we understand environmental conditions according to their boundaries, the notion of a diffused threat is foreign to us. We can readily understand that there are some conditions that cause a few people to be at particularly high risk while the rest of us are safe. But the idea that everybody may be at considerable, unknown, and invisible risk is much harder for us to accept.

We have previously shown how myths of boundedness underlie EPA policy. It is interesting that key critics of EPA also espouse these myths. Thus, while complaining that EPA construes radon as an "epidemic" requiring rapid action, scientists at the DOE instead advocate a policy focused on finding the approximately seventy thousand U.S. homes with radon levels of 20 pCi/l or more—the "hot houses." Pointing out that a 75 percent occupancy of such buildings results in a cumulative radon exposure equal to the limit for underground uranium miners (4 WLM y^{-1}), at which male smokers have a 33 percent risk of lung cancer, they argue that discovery and remediation of these homes is a far greater priority than is action on homes closer to the 4 pCi/l guidance. To achieve their goal, they propose to utilize geological information, data about indoor radon concentrations in a given area, and information dissemination to local residents (Nero et al., 1990; Nazaroff and Teichman, 1990). In much the same way as the EPA policies they criticize, these recommendations assume that the radon issue is somehow bounded; if one can only identify the boundaries (the hot region, the hot neighborhood, the hot house), effort can be concentrated on addressing the highest risks.

We refuted such thinking in chapters 4 and 5. We are far from having adequate predictability of radon levels in individual buildings based upon geologic or regional survey data. The time delay before the level of predictiveness from geology and surveys is enhanced undermines the claims of urgency in finding hot houses. The argument of high individual risk is undermined by the mobility of the population, which lowers individual risk while redistributing it to a larger population. Furthermore, the emphasis on hot houses omits the fact that most of the radon risk is widely distributed among many houses and people at lower levels.

The Myth of the Quick Test

The seemingly urgent search for hot houses married radon policy to the short-term screening test. Lost in EPA's haste to encourage people to test was the test's meaning. Household characterization, the identification of a building's overall health threat, lost out to crude and inexpensive measurement (see Kerr, 1988). As demonstrated in chapter 6, errors of policy, methodology, device, measurement, analysis, and interpretation placed the validity of radon testing in question (see also Nero, 1989). Thus, a fascinating consequence of the myth of the quick test has been the sacrifice of good science to marketing considerations. Citing "consumer preference," EPA policy traded off the short-run consideration of making testing cheap and easy against long-term credibility and interpretability. In the 1992 *Citizen's Guide*, EPA rationalized the problems of false negatives and positives in a manner that we believe defied science, ethics, and the public trust. Assuming that our goal is the protection of health, rather than cost control, a screening approach to testing would only be justified if guidelines were sufficiently overprotective to balance out methodological weaknesses. This clearly has not been the case with radon.

We have seen how radon's variability on all time scales (daily, seasonally, yearly) makes suspect the determination of a yearly average radon concentration based on short-term screening measurements. A problem with the quick test has been its application to any circumstance regardless of conditions. Given that context (i.e., weather, geology, building features, lifestyle, occupant behavior) is so clearly important to understanding radon entry and prevention, the quick test implies a simplicity and consistency that defies the reality of the radon issue.

There is no reason to assume that the measurement issues reflected here are unique to radon gas. Such threats to the validity of radon testing are suggestive of problems with the larger field of environmental testing. Our analysis indicates that a careful analysis of error in policy, methodology, device, measurement, analysis, and interpretation is essential for the critique of environmental policy.

The Myth of the Tight House

The myth of the tight house involves the confusion of energy conserving buildings (i.e., low air exchange and high insulation levels) with high radon concentrations. The fear of radon may have helped discourage energy conserving activities, both because it was perceived that conservation efforts would increase danger and because it was perceived that drafty buildings must be safe. As discussed in chapter 7, insulation levels, per se, have no effect on radon levels and low air exchange does not lead to high radon levels unless a strong radon source is present. In assuming that energy-conserving houses always enhance radon exposure, the myth of the tight house forces us to ask whether lower energy bills are obtained at the cost of increased risk. This is the wrong question. The real question is how can we achieve cost-effective energy efficiency while also assuring adequate ventilation and low radon entry, thus, minimizing exposure to all forms of indoor air pollution while saving money and conserving energy? That question became surprisingly hard to ask in the post-energy-crisis period of Reaganomics, dominated as it was by a new optimism over energy resources.

The Myth of the Quick Fix

Growing from its apparent success in Clinton, New Jersey, EPA was able to conclude that the "mitigatory gap" for radon was closed. Not only could radon levels be lowered, but this could be done cheaply and quickly by trained professionals. However, the results of radon remediation efforts as outlined in chapter 7 do not support the assumption that radon is a solved problem. Rather, the variability of radon levels suggests that radon is a hazard on the prowl. The fact that mitigations may not show long-term success after promising short-term evaluations only underscores the persistence of radon gas. Given a constant source, the hazard merely awaits the deterioration of the mitigation or else finds another avenue of entry made available by changed house conditions, weather conditions, or occupant behaviors. Ironically, there are reasons to suggest that a widespread recognition of these problems would seriously undermine radon reduction efforts. Why act on radon if there are doubts about the efficacy of the remedy?[1]

Again, it can be noted that such issues are not unique to radon. Environmental problems are sometimes identified for which no solution is evident. Often there are serious questions about mitigations that are instituted under existing environmental policy (e.g., were incinerators a mitigation for the waste crisis?). And, at Superfund sites, disagreements over how clean the cleanup will be are nearly universal. Other similar questions are often asked. How long will liners under artificial replacement wetlands last and who fixes them when they go? Will removal of PCBs from the bottom of the Hudson River increase or decrease the hazard? As Bogard (1989) insightfully suggested, the mitigation is merely a restatement and acknowledgment of the hazard. Whether it is a remedy for the hazard is much more problematical. With existing hazards, one should act to remediate. But the effectiveness of the solution over time requires repeated and careful monitoring and adjustment.

The Continuing Mythical Basis for EPA Radon Policy

Perhaps the most important conclusion regarding radon's scientific myths is that key myths have persisted over time and continue to serve as underlying assumptions for radon policy despite ample evidence of invalidity. In Congress, proposed legislation focused on "priority radon areas," and quick tests that would have been mandated for real estate transactions. At EPA, an evaluation of the Radon Action Program (1992a) charted a course consistent with the myths of the Reading Prong and the hot houses, and in some ways even, with the myth of the dead bodies. The program review sought to broaden EPA's support by even more narrowly focusing on the highest risks first. This was to be done first by targeting current and former smokers, thought to comprise 90 percent of the risk.[2] Second, it was recommended that the program focus primarily upon the twelve states having average screening results above 4 pCi/l, which were said to suffer more than half of the total number of radon-caused lung cancer deaths per year despite containing only one-fifth of the U.S. housing stock. Because the likelihood of living in a high radon house would be greater there, the cost per death avoided was calculated to be less.[3] In such high-radon potential states, even the continued use of the heavily criticized motivational Ad Council campaign was deemed appropriate.

The EPA program review reflects a continued moderation of EPA efforts in order to mollify outspoken critics, moving closer to the DOE agenda focused on finding the hottest houses and, by targeting smokers, to the "dead body" critics, as well. Targeted high-radon areas involve risk levels that supersede the debates over uncertainties in health risk or over the tone of communications about radon. And a more aggressive campaign on radon might be socially tolerated in high-risk areas, while it would meet with debilitating criticism nationwide. Thus, the recommendations were inherently political, not scientific.

In fact, neither risk analysis nor programatic considerations favors targeting of high-risk areas. Although somewhat less advantageous in its cost-benefit analysis, the risk from radon in nontarget areas is still rated among the top five cancer risks addressed by EPA and average individual risk in homes above the action level is roughly the same in all areas. While the majority of people having very high radon risk might fall within the targeted areas, as much as 75 percent of the total population risk was estimated to lie outside bounded regions. Similarly, there are programatic reasons not to geographically bound radon. For example, EPA recognized that targeting high-risk areas suggested to residents of other areas that their radon problem deserved lower priority. The agency was also aware that, by defunding nontargeted states, inaction would result despite the fact that radon might still be the highest ranked risk. Similarly, bounding the program to smokers offers liabilities. Never-smokers may conclude that they are not at risk when smokers and former smokers are particularly targeted. What we are seeing here is simply the myths of the Reading Prong and hot houses embedded deeply in practice.

The Politics of Risk: Reaganomics and Neo-Reaganomics

Throughout this volume, we have noted the remarkable fit between radon risk and the Reaganomic program. This fit reflected the characteristics of radon as a natural hazard affecting the private home. Radon stood in contrast to the paradigm of environmental regulation that literally branded industry the "potentially responsible party" for the destruction of the physical environment. Such regulation resulted, in the view of some, in an unwarranted and costly attack on the bastions of economic progress and the dominant social paradigm of economic growth. Riding the social denial of the energy crises of the 1970s, Reaganomics sought to restore confidence in economic progress and to unleash market forces. Key to this objective was mounting a challenge to environmental regulation. Radon was perfect for this role. It was blameless, in the sense that neither industry nor government could be held liable for its presence. At the same time, it inspired a new area of private enterprise. Radon was the ultimate business-friendly issue. The radon issue could thus be seen as an environmental issue benefiting the public that did not penalize the societal power structure—a structure that the Reagan and Bush administrations sought to protect.

These characteristics made radon a socially acceptable risk at a time when new risk issues were actively discouraged and an effort to eliminate previously recognized environmental risk issues was underway. The success of post-Watras radon as an environmental issue relied on the way that this startling problem demanded uncommonly quick recognition and development of government policy. This rapid movement through the environmental policy cycle not only reflected radon's risk personality, but also the manner in which the issue was defined and developed so as to fit within the dogma of Reaganomics. In short, radon was not only an urgent issue but also an acceptable one.

Tenets of Reaganomics and Radon

How did the key tenets of Reaganomics affect the development and degree of success of the radon issue? Said another way, what does the degree of success of radon action tell us about the success of Reaganomics?

In defining radon as a private problem, a market solution could be envisioned that shifted responsibility for action from government to the homeowner as consumer. Radon would not be regulated. Indeed, it was argued that it could not be regulated because regulation would invade the private sanctity of the home. Rather than government deciding how much risk the family would tolerate, choice would rest with the resident, who would be educated as a consumer of a new radon industry. Needed government action would be decentralized, part of a general trend to pass the demands of government down the ladder to the states. As a result, costs to the federal government would be minimal, and growth of the federal government would be held in check.

Radon As a Private Problem

But, is radon truly a private issue of the individual? In a sense, yes. However, the definition of radon as a private problem entailed a false assumption that the individual is vigilant to environmental risks, actively controlling potential threats, and motivated by benefits of action that outweighed the costs. Perhaps, as one critic of radon policy noted, a societal basis for risk action is also needed (Nero et al., 1990).

> To an extent, the decisions about whether to measure and to mitigate are appropriately left to individual residents. However, there is a public interest in reducing indoor radon exposures. Because the U.S. population is highly mobile, a homeowner will be less likely to adopt control measures than would the society operating as a unit unless mitigation is required or unless its cost is recovered through increased property values. Furthermore, the costs of medical care are largely borne by society through insurance, rather than directly by individuals. In addition, under the current policy, remediation is unlikely in homes that are rented (p. 110).

A recognition of the societal need for radon action would, of course, demand some form of regulatory or intrusive government action in the home. The most often cited precedent for such action has been the mandated termite inspection.

Decentralization

The decentralized policy approach has led to an uncoordinated and divergent multitude of perceptions and policies, ranging from total social denial of radon to social vigilance. In one state, radon is defined as a serious threat deserving of major funding and action; in the next, it is a nonissue. Regulation has emerged at the state and even local level in a form that presents great inconsistencies. The decentralization process was so uneven that EPA had gone to Congress in the late 1980s for money to assist state radon programs. When this three-year program was up, however, there were few indications that radon responsibility had been transferred to the states. State policy was uneven. Some new states had developed stronger policies, others, notably New York, revealed program slippage from where it had previously been. It was evident to the EPA that continued funding of the state programs was needed if they were to be maintained, even though the original agreement to create the funding clearly saw it as ending afer three years. The 1992 program evaluation's recommendation for continuing state radon program funding has been followed. Clearly, decentralization required more of a sustained boost than was anticipated.

The Market Solution to Radon

The enabling force in the war on radon was to be a private sector capable of providing radon-related services not offered by government. As we have seen, a dramatic explosion in such services did indeed occur. However, the promise of high demand brought about an early industry that was ill prepared and ill supervised. Spurred by reports of abuses, inaccuracies, and ineffectiveness, state and federal regulation of the industry became increasingly necessary. Meanwhile, when the radon issue failed to stimulate anywhere near the predicted volume of demand, the expansive industry was left extended far beyond the actual market. Implementation of nonuniform state and local regulation occurred just at the point that the industry was already vulnerable due to the business slump. As a result of the combined forces of regulation and minimal demand, there was a dramatic falling out within the industry at the end of the 1980s and into the 1990s. The adversity of the business climate meant the demise of many small, local, entrepreneurial radon efforts and favored the eventual survival of large, consolidated national corporations, often diversified across environmental hazards rather than concentrating upon radon. Many interested professionals with an existing investment in gaining expertise in radon were, thus, lost from the field.

The radon issue illustrates the intimate connections between the private market and public policy, as discussed in chapter 8. DOE critics blame the EPA's focus on a "radon epidemic" for this bust in the initial radon boom (Nero et al., 1990). In contrast, we see the radon epidemic era as a response to, not a cause of, this bust. In any case, market solutions for radon illustrate the extreme volatility of such approaches. They are riskier for the public, for government, and, particularly, for the entrepreneur. The ability to grow quickly a competent private supply of radon services demands active government regulation to police the industry and, then, to create the demand needed to maintain it. In short, government market solutions demand active government intervention and regulation.

Research and Radon Action

Another marker of the Reagan years was the use of science to kill or slow up actions with undesired policy implications. While policy responses to acid rain, ozone depletion, or global warming were articulated in terms of a "need" for more research before action could be taken, a slightly different pattern occurred for radon. Perhaps reflecting the uncommonly clear and compelling miner data and the magnitude of events in Colebrookdale Township, EPA's Radon Action Program was mounted without delay. However, in order to survive review by the Office of Management and Budget, much of the Radon Action Program was disguised as research. As a result, major facets of the radon program took the positive form of "action research"—research that addresses a problem even while studying it. Action research was successfully employed with the early mitigation research programs that helped radon victims without committing agency resources.

Yet, in other instances, the research approach utilized by EPA helped to obscure rather than clarify key issues, along the lines of our radon myths. For example, EPA's reliance upon state radon surveys employed screening based upon short-term measures primarily useful for identifying hot houses. As we have shown, these data were unable to define the actual population exposure and risk, critical information for determining the magnitude and extent of the problem. Similarly, the research effort to create a national radon map reinforced myths about radon hot spots, supporting the notion that radon risk could be delineated within geographic boundaries. These activities were inconsistent with EPA's policy that everyone should test for radon. Finally, EPA action research on the issue of overcoming public apathy at times made program objectives subservient to experimentation on how to best communicate.

While EPA used research as a means of focusing its actions, the same cannot be said for the research interests evidenced by EPA's nemesis agency, the Department of Energy (DOE). The DOE has played a conservative role for radon, initially arguing that the EPA risk estimates exceed the scientific evidence. This questioning of radon risk was well rewarded in research appropriations for basic research on radon. Money spent at the DOE would not threaten the Reaganomic agenda.[4]

The Myth of Blameless Radon

Although not a scientific myth, per se, we also return here to the myth of blameless radon. The blamelessness of radon, so central to its governmental selection as a risk, illustrates the way that a risk can be configured so as to avoid trampling on whatever is culturally taboo. In this regard, there is a lesson to be learned from the dual nature of blamelessness. Thus, the very feature that made radon an acceptable societal risk—that neither government nor industry is responsible—deflates the definition of radon as a personal risk. Described as a "natural" hazard, radon contradicts the tendency to assume human hegemony, the "fundamental attribution error" according to which we assume that people—rather than "circumstances"—are responsible for what happens around us. In some sense, to ask people to control natural radon amounts to an oxymoron; it is to ask them to control that which, by its very definition, is beyond control. Radon is a feature of the ambient environment, a category that is outside of our socially oriented understanding of reality. Blameless radon, thus, falls beyond our societal paradigm of understanding and action. In contrast, human-caused radon, evidenced by the radium-contaminated soil cases, does not. In sum, blamelessness may be good politically, but socially it dampens human response. In generalizing the lessons of radon, the importance of blamelessness for the shaping of the geologic radon issue mirrors the importance of blamefullness for other types of environmental hazards (see Edelstein, 1988a).

Importantly, because radon was not compelling as a personal threat, the issue was deprived of a broad political constiuency consisting of fearful citizens. Thus, while the Watras revelation itself commanded enough momentum to allow Guimond to launch the issue through the environmental policy cycle, there was never enough pressure to bring the issue to full maturity. In this regard, Scheberle (1994, p. 84) has observed, "In the absence of abhorrent human misconduct and culpability, there was little incentive to initiate a strong governmental response. Therefore, the resulting policy was 'underwhelming' in the sense that no dramatic steps were taken to address what the EPA identified as the public's number one health risk."

As noted in prior chapters, a strong case can be made for the fact that radon exposure is not, afterall, blameless. While naturally occurring, it is drawn into buildings that generate negative pressure vis-à-vis the soil. The fact that the normative modern building concentrates radon hardly supports the blame of nature for the hazard. Rattlesnakes may be hazardous, but if our buildings were designed to serve as accessible snake dens, we would quickly change the design and probably sue the builders. Radon lacks the rattle, the venom, and the cultural and primal fear value. It is an invisible and uninteresting hazard compared to the snake, even if it accounts for many more deaths.

This analysis of radon raises the question of whether we can so easily dichotomize natural and human-caused hazards. When we consider the components of cause of the hazard and cause of the exposure, as well as the added ingredient of responsibility for helping those affected, we see that natural disasters invariably have human contributants, much as technological disasters have natural components. A much more complex way of thinking about hazards is demanded, as suggested by table 12.1. Here we see a variety of manifested hazards due to natural and/or human sources and modes of human exposure. What is unique for radon is not that exposure is caused by human actions, but rather that those actions are so easily overlooked when responsibility for addressing radon is passed from government to the individual.

Table 12.1   Factors Affecting the Blamelessness of Various Environmental
             Hazards

Hazard	Source of Hazard	Source of Exposure	Response
Geologic radon	Natural	Human	Private problem
Industrial	Human	Human	Governmental
Three Mile Island	Human	Natural/Human	Governmental
Earthquake	Natural	Natural/Human	Governmental
Flood	Natural/Human	Natural/Human	Governmental
Superfund site	Human	Natural/Human	Governmental

Radon As a Nonregulatory Problem of the Private Consumer

The nonregulatory model of environmental protection represented by radon
fit well with the attempt by the Reagan and Bush administrations to perform a
policy U-turn from prior practice. Yet, we have uncovered many reasons to question the notion that an environmental policy based upon voluntary action will
offer adequate public protection with minimal government intervention.

The first limit to the nonregulatory approach was the abject failure of the
EPA program directed at individual consumers. Able to establish widespread
recognition and concern, yet achieve only minimal action, EPA was forced increasingly to use Madison Avenue tactics to sell radon, in the end giving in to
the kind of gimmickry that one sees in modern horror/"sci fi" media. Having begun with the mature premise that people would take responsibility for evaluating
their own risks, EPA then turned to media manipulation in order to scare people
into action. Radon thus has been a reflection of the times, where the media is
manipulated so as to direct the perception of the masses. Blameless radon might
seem like an "apple pie" issue, but it was hardly "Alar." The consumer could not
be convinced to bite. A second basis for criticism of the nonregulatory approach
is that there are accessible and acceptable targets for effective regulation. Some
4 million existing homes are sold per year, with another 1.4 million new homes
achieving occupancy. Significant regulatory handles on radon have thus been
present from the onset.

But, perhaps the clearest critique of the Reaganomic approach to radon was
found in the growing recognition among key EPA staff that regulation was indeed required in order to address radon. These officials offered a convenient
clarification. Within its Reaganomic structure, EPA never opposed regulation,
per se; it just opposed federal regulation. Thus, Richard Guimond, by then promoted to the rank of deputy administrator of EPA, commented in a April 2,
1991 speech that the agency saw regulation of realtors and the construction in-

dustry as vital, but that the model for regulation was through state and local government, along the lines of termite inspections.

However, EPA officials also acknowledged that such state action had evolved only slowly during the study period. EPA's Margo Oge (1991a) reported that few states had mandated radon disclosure in realty transfer, radon-resistant construction practices, or school testing. Furthermore, she rationalized the failure of education to motivate private protective action against radon: "This is depressing. So we have gone back and looked at anti-smoking and seat belts to see what we can learn from these campaigns. They used massive media campaigns and they took ten years before they saw a change. In smoking, the first 3–4 years there was actually an increase in smoking. They used a mix of strategies, incentives, and laws."

Such models suggest that it could take several decades to develop an effective public success with radon (Maconaughey, 1991).[5] However, regulation—the unmentionable "R" word of Reaganomics—came to be viewed as a means of shortcutting this interval. Thus, EPA's Page commented in an interview (1991): "If you have 80 percent public awareness, people are thinking about the issue. They are now deciding whether to test. If the issue is like smoking or seat belts, it will take 15–20 years. However, I do not accept that radon has to take that long. There are key and pivotal things that can accelerate it, such as federal regulations." Page and his EPA colleagues were careful not to officially endorse regulation. However, in the same interview, Page acknowledged the need for federal regulation of radon: "You need a bag of tools that includes all the things that need to be institutionalized. You need to do real estate because it is your best shot. You need to do schools and hope that it spills over to residences. You need the construction code."

By this time, the agency's Science Advisory Board had endorsed precisely these steps. In its testimony before Congress on the reauthorization of the Indoor Radon Abatement Act, EPA targeted the need for tools to deal with real estate and new construction, smokers, and high-risk areas (Oge, 1991). And the 1992 EPA radon program review recommended that EPA begin long-term strategies to promote radon-resistant new construction, as well as testing and mitigation during realty transfers.[6]

Rather than a major departure from past actions, Page (1991) saw the shift toward regulation as being a natural progression within the agency's radon activities. As the original range of activities failed to bring about public action on radon, the agency continually tried new approaches. These continuing efforts effectively moved the agency along a continuum from EPA's original informational and educational programs toward a regulatory approach to radon. Figure 12.1 presents this continuum, based upon Page's analysis. When information alone had failed to bring about public radon action, efforts to motivate such action increased. Thus, the revised *Citizen's Guide* replaced an educational with a directive tone. These efforts, in turn, have been supplemented by the use of incentives aimed at encouraging compliance, managing the radon industry, and getting lower levels of government to act. As this level of governance proved inadequate, increasingly directive efforts were initiated. Finally, a new generation of actual regulatory programs were under consideration.

Informational	Motivational	Incentive	Directive	Regulatory
State surveys, pilot mitigation programs, school surveys, Employee Relations Council	1986 *Citizen's Guide*, Ad Council Campaign	Original RMP, State Grants, Standards/Model Codes, School Grants	New RMP, RCP, Institution-alization through Codes and Schools, 1992 *Citizen's Guide*	Proposed RMP, RCP, Realty and School Testing Requirements in Proposed Legislation

Fig. 12.1.   Continuum between information and regulation
(After Page 1991).

Radon As a Disconfirmation of Reaganomics

Reaganomics hardly resulted in an efficient approach to radon. The inherent irony of the EPA radon strategy was that the geologic radon issue began with the view that radon action was urgent, imperative, and demanding immediate action. Yet, a decade later, EPA rationalized that a protracted period was required for public acceptance of the hazard.[7]

Government management of the radon issue failed to distinguish between areas where regulation might quickly lead to major steps to protect health and avoid cost and areas less susceptible to a regulatory approach. Thus, there is little real excuse for the failure of government to quickly move to enforce radon-resistant construction and to regulate real estate transfer to ensure valid testing. Instead, inaction has resulted in the construction of millions of buildings, a substantial number of which may, in the future, require mitigation that is far more costly than prevention. Real estate testing has proceeded in a manner that defies rational understanding, fraught with fraud and use of invalid tests. Even as these areas of required regulation were neglected, the bulk of domestic testing has employed a screening approach that is hardly cost effective and consumer protective. As a result, of two million families with homes tested for radon, relatively few have potentially valid indications of their actual risk from the radon in their home. The problematic screening approach for determining the 4 pCi/l guidance discredits the issue and allowed many people to rationalize inaction or fraud. Because EPA's Radon Action Program sought to work creatively within the governmental boundaries erected by Reaganomics, the recognition at EPA that regulation is, after all, necessary demonstrates the failure of Reaganomics in what may have been its most fertile field. Furthermore, because of antiregulatory furvor central to the neo-Reaganomic idealogues who took over Congress in 1995, the story of radon is important to debunking the naive claims that the public interest can be served by simply sweeping government regulation aside.

Is there nothing positive to be said of the Reaganomic context based upon the radon issue? Whether it directed innovations or they occurred merely because other aproaches were shut off, it is clear that there were important developments in organizational and agency operation made through the federal radon program. These include efforts to understand the public perception of radon, to educate the public to voluntarily address risk, to encourage state and local programs, and to develop diverse partnerships. Indeed, the radon program has become a model for addressing risks that fall outside of the territory of command and control regulation. Within EPA, other programs have emulated radon, notably programs that seek to use consensus, education, and social change to address voluntary risk reduction. Among these are the areas of recycling and waste avoidance, as well as programs to reduce pollution from vehicles by encouraging the public to maintain inspections and properly operate cars. Outside EPA, radon was selected by the Council for Excellence in Government as their benchmark federal program. EPA staff subsequently helped to train some one thousand private and public sector managers in the delivery of "bottom-line, results-focused programs" (Rowson, 1996). Regardless of where the credit lies, these programatic inventions are a constructive development in environmental risk reduction.

In the next section, we examine a final characteristic of Reaganomics—namely, the reliance on the cost-benefit analysis of risk. We explore a potential ulterior motive for the fast growth of the radon issue, that the very strengths of the radon hazard showed, by comparison, the relative weaknesses of chemical and nuclear hazards central to public concern and the public's demand for governmental action. An embedded, if not entirely hidden, agenda for radon policy was, therefore, its utility in minimizing or qualifying environmental hazards that had captured the public's imagination (something radon failed to do). The radon issue, accordingly, offered a tool for questioning the paradigm of environmental regulation altogether—an excuse for "regulatory reform."

Radon and the Critique of Regulated Risk

We opened this chapter by quoting Mary Douglas and Aaron Wildavsky's observation (1982) that society selects which risks will receive attention and which will be ignored. Radon illustrates the ambivalence of this choice. During the Reagan/Bush years, one might well argue that radon gas was "the" official environmental risk of choice. However, the remarkable success of radon as a societal risk was not matched by its recognition as a personal risk. While radon demanded societal attention according to the prevalent criteria for recognizing serious hazard, it has barely been able to motivate individuals to be protective.

Radon As a Risk from the Center

Douglas and Wildavsky (1982) observe that new risks are usually introduced into social consciousness at the periphery of society, where environmental and social activists sit outside the mainstream. Radon, however, turned this process around. With minimal input from mainstream environmental groups and very little grassroot support, the definition of radon as a major threat came from government while the environmental and grassroots movements gave radon relatively little recognition. Radon has, thus, lived its brief issue life being molded from the center—by government.

It is interesting to ponder the consequences of radon being a risk from the center. After the lessons of Colebrookdale Township, where local citizen action was instrumental in broadening the governmental response, comparatively little public pressure was needed in order to attract governmental attention. Benefiting from the existence of strong data to support the issue in a cost-benefit analysis, a relative consensus among experts developed around the risk of natural radon. In a manner differing from most regulated environmental hazards, geologic radon was elevated to government action based upon its scientifically recognized risk merits rather than because of constituent mobilization and pressure. In fact, one might almost question whether the absence of such mobilization, with the attendant publicity, might have deprived the radon issue of public urgency even as it reflected scientific urgency.

As an expert's risk, radon has excited little passion in the hearts of laymen not convinced that they have already been seriously victimized. In contrast, the pollution of the "perceived to be pure" ambient environment—our water, food, soil, and air—has increasingly threatened perceptions of personal security, arousing citizen action even in the face of an official and scientific revisionism aimed at rolling back estimates of the involved risks. As a centerist risk, however, radon had revisionist implications for such peripheral risks.

Radon As a Revisionist Risk

What are the implications of radon's comparative risk with other hazards regulated by government? Ponder, first, the report of an interview with radon rejectionist Bernard Cohen (Bolch and Lyons, 1990). "Dr. Cohen told me, 'You understand, radon is the most serious risk with which the EPA is now dealing.' 'But, Dr. Cohen,' I said, 'you just got through telling me that residential radon poses no public health risk!' 'That's right,' he said" (p. 67). Those disputing Cohen might argue that radon is indeed a serious risk, but doing so still raised disturbing conclusions for regulated risks. Thus, in EPA's own internal risk comparisons, radon provided an environmental risk so strong that critics might use it to help diminish the significance placed on exposure to hazardous chemicals and human-caused radioactivity. In fact, radon could be used to devalue the environmental hazards that led to the very founding of the agency.

Radon As a Tool for De-emphasizing Chemical Risks

The geologic radon issue occurred at a time when the existing paradigm of risk was strongly under attack. Comparative risk was an important tool for the regulatory "reformers" of the political right. By the end of the 1980s, strong counterattacks were being made against the significance of environmental exposures. Even dioxin, tauted as the most hazardous substance known to humans in the 1970s and early 1980s, was being redefined as only a modest threat; pesticides and additives in food were being reclassified as less hazardous than natural food poisons, and living at Superfund sites was being redefined as comparatively safer than consuming peanut butter sandwiches (Houk, 1989; Wartenberg and Chess, 1992; Michaels, 1988). Leading this revisionist onslaught, Assistant Surgeon General Vernon Houk, who had issued the health warning on radon, argued that our society is adept at recognizing new environmental threats, but it lacks any mechanism to reclassify a recognized risk as a nonthreat (Houk, 1989). Simultaneously, the foundation of knowledge about chemical risk, based upon experimentation with animals, came under severe attack over the validity of its application to humans. So did the use of worst-case scenarios as the basis for estimating health consequences (see, for example, OMB, 1991a; Center for Risk Analysis, 1991). At the very same time, ironically, the public was defining Alar as so dangerous as to stigmatize apple crops.

This social ambiguity provided a context within which radon might be used, under the guise of comparative risk assessment, to make trivial the one per million acceptable risk level that had emerged for chemical exposures. For those wishing to curb the social aversion to chemical exposure, radon proved to be the perfect revisionist risk. In a Reaganomic sense, radon was the "white knight" of environmental hazards sent to rescue societal practices that caused comparatively less risky yet socially undesirable environmental hazards. The result was a predicament for environmentalists—to strongly champion radon left them culpable to the comparative risk argument, so many left radon alone.

Undermining the Regulation of Radon in Water

As discussed in chapter 3, the contradictions surrounding radon policy resulting from risk comparison appeared nowhere more clearly than they did with the issue of EPA's effort to develop a maximum contaminant level (MCL) for radon in water. A draft rule was published in the *Federal Register* on July 18, 1991, proposing an MCL for radon of 300 pCi/l in all but private groundwater supplies (those serving fewer than twenty-five persons). This action was projected to entail a total capital cost of $1.6 billion and annual costs of $180 million with a projected avoidance of eighty annual cancer cases. In determining its environmental regulations, EPA has historically set acceptable risk levels within the range of 10^{-4} to 10^{-6} individual lifetime risk. Significantly, compared to the costs for treating other radionuclides, the proposed radon regulation was inexpensive. Furthermore, regulation at 300 pCi/l offered a substantial benefit to public health compared to EPA's other drinking water regulations and regulatory programs.[8]

However, despite its comparative benefit, EPA now faced the dilemma of proposing a costly program to regulate radon in water, at a savings of eighty cancer cases, when unregulated airborne radon causes as many as twenty thousand annual cancer deaths. The 4 pCi/l guidance for radon in air is the equivalent of about forty thousand pCi/l of radon in water. At 300 pCi/l in water, EPA was recommending regulation of radon that was below the ambient air equivalent. EPA does not even recommend mitigating for radon in water until soil gas radon has been abated. Given this contradiction, it was not surprising that the draft MCL for radon in water confronted both a Congress loath to require communities to spend the necessary money for water treatment and scientists critical of the uncertainties in the risk analysis. Even EPA's own agency science advisor, William Raub, reacted negatively to the proposed MCL, reflecting the myth of the dead bodies in the process. "(There are) inconclusive epidemiological findings as to whether radon (either ingested or inhaled) actually presents an appreciable risk within the typical American household if none of the occupants smokes tobacco products" (Stone, 1993, p. 1514).

In lieu of the 300 pCi/l standard, Raub suggested a "relative-risk" approach comparing radon in water to that in outdoor air, with the MCL to be in the 1,500 to 2,000 pCi/l range. Subsequently, the EPA's Science Advisory Board recommended an even higher MCL of 3,000 pCi/l. On its part, Congress voted (through an amendment attached to the 1994 budget) to delay the implementation of an MCL for radon in water until October 1994 (Stone, 1993). As part of the Safe Drinking Water Amendments of 1996, the issue was finally resolved by Congress and signed by President Clinton in a manner that sought to address many of the contradictions of policy discussed above. Promulgation of a maximum contaminant level (MCL) for radon was delayed for up to four years. Proposal of a new MCL for comment will only occur after completion of a risk assessment and comparative assessment of health risk reduction benefits of mitgation alternatives to be prepared by the National Academy of Sciences or another independent science organization. Should the resulting MCL reduce radon in water to a lower concentration than found in the ambient air, then an alternative MCL would be developed to set water levels at the equivalent of ambient air concentrations. States or public water systems could seek approval of alternative programs for controlling indoor radon capable of achieving the equivalent or greater reduction in risk as achieved by implementing the MCL. The alternative MCL would be achieved through the use of "multimedia" measures for reducing indoor airborne radon, including "public education, testing, training, technical assistance, remediation grant and loan or incentive programs, or other regulatory or nonregulatory measures" (Senate 1316.13.G.ii). The alternative MCL would provide a great deal of flexibility for exploring how best to reduce aggregate risk while avoiding the awkwardness of having a water standard more stringent than the air standard (Schmidt, 1996; Senate 1316 "Safe Drinking Water Act Amendments of 1996").

Radon and the Risk from Nuclear Energy

If radon comparatively served to undermine precaution against a chemically altered biosphere, it also served to advance an agenda near and dear to the hearts of many health physicists and DOE scientists, the social restoration of nuclear energy. That industry had ground to a halt following the nuclear siting fiascos of the 1970s and 1980s, the accidents at Three Mile Island and Chernobyl, and high costs combined with reduced electrical demand growth. A symbol of the technological paradigm, nuclear power remained key to the military/industrial complex, banked within government at the DOE. Therefore, the industry never died; rather it awaited its chance for resurgence. During geologic radon's first decade, it appeared that time had arrived. The Reagan/Bush agenda sought the reinstatement of nuclear energy in America's future, with Reagan forcing the issue of nuclear waste repository siting and the Bush energy plan streamlining siting procedures for nuclear plants in an effort to circumvent public opposition. At the same time, the emergence of global warming as a meta-environmental crisis allowed proponents to tout nuclear power as an environmentally desirable alternative to greenhouse gas-forming combustion power sources. In this context, radon's naturalness was an inviting feature.

Radon As Background Radiation. Radon was uniquely suited to revise our view of acceptable radiation exposure, helpful in promoting a new period of nuclear development. Beyond its extreme risk profile and its natural geologic origins, radon is an ambient hazard. It exists as "background" radiation, establishing an unavoidable baseline of natural risk against which human-caused hazards can be compared. This ambient risk is not inconsequential. Ambient radon accounts for about 55 percent of the total average effective dose equivalent of radiation for Americans (Mossman and Sollitto, 1991).

The significance of background radon for nuclear power was not a new realization. The issue had been hotly debated during nuclear licensing hearings for many years before the Watras discovery. As noted in chapter 2, both proponents and opponents of nuclear power liberally cited radon data to back their positions. For nuclear proponents, the danger from radon in energy-conserving homes was viewed as far more serious than was the danger from nuclear power plants. For nuclear opponents, radon emitted during uranium mining and uranium processing bolstered the argument that nuclear power was dangerous (Mazur, 1987). For example, antinuclear groups cited long term radon exposure from uranium mill tailings against restarting the undamaged reactor at Three Mile Island while pronuclear activists looked to Bernard Cohen's research to prove that ambient radon levels nearby Three Mile Island posed more health risk for local people than would potential radiation releases from the plant (Johnsrud, 1987).

Radon Risk Versus Three Mile Island and Chernobyl. Aside from comparisons of radon risk to that expected from routine operations of nuclear facilities, it has also been possible to compare the radon hazard to that resulting from severe nuclear accidents. If we compare radon, for example, to the Three Mile Island and Chernobyl accidents, we are struck by the levels of extreme concern that surrounded the nuclear accidents as contrasted with the relative indifference that surrounds radon. Such perceptions of risk contradict the actual estimates for radioactive doses and resulting deaths, particularly if nuclear plant workers are excluded from the comparison (i.e., many Chernobyl workers and emergency responders received lethal doses of radiation). In this comparison, we employ data developed by Bodansky (1987). Updated figures, particularly on the severity of consequences from the Chernobyl accident, do not change the point.

Recall that rem is a measure of biological damage from radiation; a mrem is one thousandth of a rem. All sources of background radiation, excluding radon, give an average dose of 200 mrem per year per person. As a result of the Three Mile Island accident in Harrisburg, Pennsylvania, nearby residents received exposure to a maximum one-time dose of radiation estimated at 70 mrem; the average exposure to the population within a fifty-mile radius was estimated to be 2 mrem. The Chernobyl accident produced an average exposure of 110 mrem to the people of the western USSR during 1986. An additional exposure of 16 mrem per year (both external and internal) is projected for the next fifty years as the result of Chernobyl. These nuclear accident exposures can be contrasted with the Reading Prong, where the maximum dose equivalent in the highest radon home was about 400,000 mrem/yr and the average dose equivalent for 5,011 homes was about 3,000 mrem/yr. Accordingly, not only does the Reading Prong produce dramatically greater average and maximum population exposures, but the expected deaths from radon dwarf the death toll related to the two nuclear accidents.

Furthermore, the cancer fatalities caused by the Three Mile Island accident were projected to be less than one over fifty years. In contrast, Chernobyl produced serious consequences. Total projected cancer fatalities from the Chernobyl accident in the western portion of the former U.S.S.R. (specifically, the Ukraine, Russia, and Belorussia) were estimated to be about ten thousand in a population of 74.5 million people. In comparison, assuming that U.S. radon deaths per year were constant in the five thousand to twenty thousand range, there will be between a quarter of a million and one million lung cancer deaths attributable to radon over the next fifty years in the United States alone. In other words, according to this analysis, naturally occurring radon is as much as one hundred times worse than the worst nuclear accidents (Bodansky, 1987).

Radon As a Test of Linear Versus Threshold Theories. Beyond the issue of radon's use as a comparative radioactive risk to nuclear power, radon has served as a potential means for testing the threshold and linear theories, which are so central to the debate over nuclear safety. Pronuclear radon skeptics have made use of the absence of dead bodies easily attributable to radon in order to question the danger of low levels of radiation. Showing slides of women bathing in radon-emanating waters, they go so far as to imply that in small doses, radon may even be healthful, a finding that appears in Cohen's crude correlational studies between county lung cancer and radon levels.

Radon Versus Energy Conservation

A final energy implication for radon has been in the area of energy conservation. Signaling the end to a publicly recognized energy crisis, the Reagan/Bush administrations acted quickly to stem a growing social movement that sought to limit dependence upon imported oil in favor of conservation and renewable energy. Radon, itself, became a force working against energy conservation, given the myth of the tight house and the attendant concerns over whether conservation was dangerous.

Conclusion—Comparative Risk As a Distorting Formulation

The geologic radon issue was an exemplar for the regressive social transformation from a preventative perspective about risk back toward the acceptance of environmental risk as the cost of progress. However, in our view, the use of comparative risk in the case of radon represents a confusion of policy. Risk comparison cannot serve as the guiding principle behind environmental policy. It is merely a limited tool that has been embued with ever-greater powers (see Shrader-Frechette, 1991).

Our objections to risk comparison include its dependence upon risk assessments that are highly variable, subject to bias, and merely subjective assessments made to look like objective facts. Risk comparisons can easily be used to contrast nonparallel cases as though they were comparable. For example, should the fact that people may be more likely to be injured in falls at home or in automobile accidents necessarily diminish their desire to avoid the less-likely threat of chemical hazards in their water, soil, or air? One has little to do with the other! And, should an environmentally induced cancer be manifested in a person, of what regard is their success at having avoided home and automobile accidents? These are independent factors that become confounding when they are used in risk comparisons.

Furthermore, the lines between what is voluntary and involuntary are often fuzzy. Often the "voluntary" risks cited by those seeking to make environmental hazards appear mundane are not so voluntary after all. Once hooked, do people make a choice to smoke? Is driving in a world offering few alternative means of mobility really voluntary? Is there much of a choice about whether to take baths, climb steps, or carry out other daily activities that comprise the considerable risks of living at home? And, one of the intriguing questions of radon is that, in a parallel vein to choosing to live on the San Andreas Fault, when one fails to test or remediate, does this natural hazard then become a "voluntary" risk, as well?

At the same time as it compares apples and oranges, risk comparison selectively ignores synergy, as in the case of smoking and radon. There are myriad interacting elements of the environment. Thus, we are exposed to hundreds if not thousands of hazardous chemicals in the course of daily life. Even if the risk from each is comparatively small, the interaction may be what harms us. Yet, none of these contributing environmental exposures may violate existing environmental standards.

One can understand the effort by agencies, pioneered at EPA, to create a comparative calculus of risk for use in prioritizing policy goals. Yet, these comparisons can never be free of bias (see Shrader-Frechette, 1991). Thus, we have seen that, by comparison to other risks, radon can be molded to many ends. Because radon overshadowed the risks of radioactive exposure associated with nuclear power use as well as hazardous chemical exposure, much as natural aflatoxin in peanuts overshadowed contaminated drinking water (Ames et al., 1987), then the natural radon hazard could be used as a tool for resurrecting a technological society based upon chemicals and nuclear power. In this way, radon emerged as a tool to revise definitions of acceptable risk, an environmental hazard that worked against the major assumptions of environmental protection.

Meanwhile, as often perceptive DOE radon critic Anthony Nero (1989, p. 39) observes, from a comparative risk perspective, it is possible to dismiss the risk from radon, itself, as comparable to that from daily activities. On the other hand, EPA compares this risk to that from its regulated chemicals, and concludes that the risk is tremendous. Nero concludes of both comparisons that "Neither view makes sense in the real world." Rather, a general societal perspective on risk is required before the issue of radon risk can be sorted out. Unfortunately, risk comparison, along with its root technologies of cost-benefit analysis and risk assessment, has emerged as a simplistic surrogate for a true consensus about acceptable risk. This development is evident in the shift from Reaganomic thought to neo-Reaganomics, moving further and further from the policy consensus around environmental protection that characterized the first Earth Day.

Radon and the Clinton Presidency

Under President Bill Clinton, governmental power shifted decidedly toward the legislative branch, controlled as of January 1995 by a conservative-leaning Republican party. Clinton's centerist administration embraced the view that the federal government should be streamlined. Under the new EPA administrator, Carol Browner, radon programs no longer continued to grow. However, in a period of sharply limited resources for the agency, overall, radon held its own and the program did not lose ground.[9] In this sense, the special attention to the issue continued and the consensus that radon is one of the bigger risks faced by the agency broadened even further (Smith, 1995; Feldman, 1996; Rowson, 1996).

Risk and the Arrival of Neo-Reaganomics

In the early 1990s, EPA officials were careful to blame the regulatory drift of the radon program on "the mood of Congress" (Maconaughey, 1991). However, by the end of geologic radon's first decade, that mood had decidedly changed. Not only had federal radon regulation failed to arrive, but a Congress hell-bent on reducing all federal environmental regulation had done so. Their toolbox was filled with the techniques of cost-benefit analysis and risk assessment. The 104th Congress was sworn in with the new year of 1995. Immediately in the House, implementation of Republican campaign promises called "The Contract with America" commenced. With terms such as "fiscal responsibility," "job creation and wage enhancement," "regulatory flexibility," "unfunded mandate reform," and "common sense legal reform," this neo-Reaganomic program embodied the fundamental precepts of the early Reaganomic revolution, combining the rhetoric with a method for rapid implementation. Within one hundred days, a package of bills had been sent to the Senate that sought to undermine the existing program of environmental protection in myriad ways. While the promised fast revolution hardly materialized in the intended fashion, we can look at the neo-Reaganomic thrust as a social commentary on the paradigm of risk, much as was the Reaganomic revolution before it. What did the revolution attempt to achieve (see Republican National Committee, 1994; Barbour, 1996)?

Neo-Reaganomics was based upon the ideology of "regulatory reform," whereby the corporate world would be freed from "the burden" of new and existing federal regulation. Corporations would also face considerably diminished liability through civil court proceedings demanding damages for environmental and consumer harms. Key to neo-Reaganomics was the reestablishment of the preeminence of private property rights in the face of gains in public and communal rights over the past twenty-five years, such as the right to clean water, clean air, safe food, and a diverse biota. Public lands would more freely be exploited for private gain. Efforts to regulate would undergo cost-benefit analysis and, if there was more than minimal economic impact, only programs where benefits could be shown to exceed costs would be approved. Rather than the "Delaney Clause" as a precautionary basis for protection from environmental and consumer harm, only provable and sizable threats—where monetary harm exceeded the costs of regulation—would now win regulatory approval. Efforts to eradicate the national debt while cutting taxes promised severe triage of government programs, passed down from the federal to the state and local levels. Environmental programs that survived the direct frontal assault might easily be made ineffectual or defunct in this manner. While the contract's success was moderated by the 1996 election, significant shifts had already become evident in the national political discourse and the Republicans retained control of Congress. What might this effort to redraw the environmental map of the United States, were it to be inacted, mean for the evolving radon issue?

Radon and Takings

Under the Private Property Protection Act of 1995, the House sought to obligate the federal government to compensate property owners for takings, where property use was limited by agency action, resulting in at least a 20 percent loss of fair market value. This provision could dissuade government from designating areas as having a high radon potential or more directly requiring radon testing, mitigation, or prevention. Particularly for properties resistent to remediation or other stigmatizing occurrences, scenarios requiring compensation under the act might be contemplated. The likely outcome is the avoidance of any new regulations or other agency actions that might be construed as constraining property use or diminishing property values.

Regulatory Reform

Under the Regulatory Reform and Relief Act of 1995, the House sought to make it easier for small businesses to challenge the "Regulatory Flexibility Analysis" issued by an agency to justify a new regulation. It further decreased the trigger requiring a "Regulatory Impact Analysis" for intended government rules, giving the Office of Management and Budget greater authority in determining the adequacy of the analysis. The net effect of this act would be to make new environmental regulations exceedingly more difficult to issue and much more likely to be challenged. These challenges would be faced by radon regulations aimed at realty or new construction and open to challenge by those industries. The delay and then weakening of the radon in water regulation reflects the influence of regulatory reform.

Risk Assessment and Cost-Benefit Analysis

Under the Risk Assessment and Cost/Benefit Act of 1995, comparative risk analysis and cost-benefit analysis would become the basis for evaluating all federal risk reduction and prevention strategies. Agencies would be required to use these techniques to justify new rules, the OMB would employ these techniques to provide a common calculus for comparing all federal programs, and outside scientific auditors would overlook every agency and program.

While, again, the intent of these provisions is to make it exceedingly difficult to introduce new or reauthorize existing regulations addressing environment, health, and safety, it will be interesting to see whether radon fares better than other issues given its strong comparative risk profile. This advantage does not mean that radon will be regulated, however. Despite rhetoric about scientific review, cost-benefit analysis is so inherently judgmental that the overall antiregulatory mood may simply predominate. In short, despite radon's comparative riskiness, it is unlikely that the period of neo-Reaganomics will allow much growth in environmental protection. Despite our conclusions about the ineffectuality of the nonregulatory radon program and the regulatory drift evidenced in the early 1990s, the time for new regulation became even less ripe in the mid-1990s than it was under President Reagan. However, we do expect the continued use of radon in comparative risk assessment in order to diminish the standing of other less-risky environmental hazards—and as a tool for potential deregulation.

Conclusion—The Impact of Neo-Reaganomics

The use of presidential vetoes combined with the retraction of the mandate for neo-Reaganomics at the polls in late 1996 are likely to limit the full impact of the Contract with America on legislation. But this period certainly channeled environmental policy into an ever-more conservative frame. Furthermore, under President Clinton, there has been an evident shift of the left toward (and some might argue past) the center. These trends checked the regulatory drift of the federal radon program and may additionally limit state regulatory programs and quasi-regulatory practices. In the midst of this period of questioning of the role of government and demonstration of "business friendly" environmentalism, blameless geologic radon continues to appear a politically safe environmental hazard—a model, in fact. Here the rights of the citizen are not set against the rights of corporations. The assumptions underlying society that Reaganomics and neo-Reaganomics were intended to protect are upheld, rather than challenged, by geologic radon.

Radon As an Anomalous Anomaly

What are the paradigmatic implications of the radon issue—our hidden most basic assumptions about our relationship to the world. The emergent "dominant social paradigm" in the period after World War II has at its roots the social values of economic growth and of scientific and technological progress (see Olsen et al., 1992; Milbrath, 1989). These social values are furthered by defining the individual rather than the community as the basic social unit, by linking individual self-interest to the marketplace, by making the person separate and above nature, by valuing economics over environment, by imbuing corporations with the rights but not the responsibilities of the individual, and by accepting the virtue of technological progress regardless of resulting costs or risks to some individuals.

Beginning in the 1960s, this paradigm has been repeatedly challenged by anomalous discoveries that link human well-being to the well-being of nature and that show that our actions have degraded our natural surround. From concerns such as over surfacewater and groundwater, air pollution, toxic contamination, pesticide use, food additives, ozone depletion, and global warming, there has begun a broad understanding of the failings of the dominant paradigm in its unsustainable use of resources, its destruction of species diversity, and its poisoning of the biosphere. While the dominant paradigm has attempted to explain away many of these anomalies, concern over environmental risk represents a serious challenge to the paradigm of economic growth. However, by the 1980s and 1990s, a competing ecological paradigm had not sufficiently evolved to allow for a societal shift. Instead, the ideological vacuum was filled by Reaganomic and, later, neo-Reaganomic platforms that undertook an active defense of the old paradigm.

Thus, the issue of geologic radon arrived during a period of paradigmatic crisis, characterized by doubt, ambiguity, and contradiction. When the Carter administration reacted to the energy crisis of the 1970s as an indication of a need for fundamental change, Ronald Reagan ran for president as the champion of the paradigm of economic growth. Reaganomics under the Reagan and Bush administrations represented an effort to allow an unfettered marketplace to resolve the challenging anomalies. Despite the election of a Democratic president in 1992, the era of reaffirmation of the dominant social paradigm continued, being boldly reasserted beginning with the "Contract with America" in the congressional elections of 1994, as we have seen.

Our concern is the social ambivalence over risk that characterized this period. Through the 1970s, the preponderant social direction was risk aversion, in contradiction of the dominant social paradigm, wherein risks are accepted as an necessary cost of progress. German social commentator Ulrich Beck (1992) characterizes this change as a shift of paradigm to a "Risk Society," focused on how "the risks and hazards systematically produced as part of modernization can be prevented, minimized, dramatized or channeled" (p. 19). In the risk society, threats demanding mobilization are not external to society; rather they are the direct outcomes of its organization and production. Accordingly, in an era of wealth and overconsumption, where social action is no longer driven by the fear of hunger and the need for survival, it is instead movitated by anxiety over safety due to the risks we have ourselves unleashed.

Beck's analysis is descriptive of the human-caused, technological hazards that have victimized millions of people, and it may even extend to those who view themselves as radon victims. However, for most people, geologic radon is less the "dangerous intruder" of EPA's characterization than a natural, blameless, managable, and perhaps even negligible hazard—clearly not a self-induced threat of modernization. It is not a risk that necessarily excites, panics, or even inspires vigilant search for information. Moreover, given the vigilance of modern citizens to human-caused threats, when it comes to radon, most people may just be looking the other way. Thus, even in the midst of a society focused on environmental risk, the focus is elsewhere. To the extent that people have been easily aroused by some risks, they have noticeably not been aroused by geologic radon. We merely underscore here our prior conclusion that, within the context of modern life, radon risk will be most broadly addressed if there is a pragmatic reason for people to do so; it will be avoided if there is not. The lesson of radon is that the effectiveness of a voluntary risk reduction program, excluding a regulatory or punative framework, must rest on pragmatics. In sum, then, radon suggests the contours of a risk society—indeed focused upon the risks caused by humans, but, absent proof of disaster, not compelled by blameless natural threat.

Reaganomics represented a counterattack of the establishment against the antigrowth and antiprogressive onslaught, an effort at denying the risk society. The question was how to protect the dominant interests of capitalism while appeasing those concerned over environmental risk—balancing the demands of both the victimizers and the victims. The means were simple. The standards could be weakened and the words altered, so that the language of risk could be appropriated while the meaning was inverted. New risks—the costs of regulation and government action—offset the health and environmental risks to victims. Environmental "cleanup" signalled the least costly means of containing the damage from remaining pollution. As the excesses of the Reaganomic period (the savings and loan crisis, military overspending, etc.) sapped the financial wealth of the United States, even those willing to trade off some economic growth in favor of environmental protection were forced to consider compromising on acceptable risk. The resources to clean up the environment were scarce. Now the mitigation of contaminated urban areas, newly termed "brownfields," could employ weaker standards for clean up, trading off health and safety as an incentive for private investment. Any negative consequences from the reappraisal were merely shunted to the future. Neo-Reaganomics merely renewed this trend.

The timing of the geologic radon issue during this paradigmatic upheaval has, in our view, been crucial. While all risk issues can be plumbed for contradiction and complexity, perhaps none offers a greater dose than radon. In the search for tools for narrowing and redefining risk, geologic radon was a special case. Within the context of environmental anomalies that challenged the dominant paradigm, radon was itself anomalous. Here was a hazard that could be used to buttress the dominant paradigm because its risk profile contradicted basic assumptions of the emergent new environmental paradigm. If nature was so much more dangerous than many of the human-caused conditions that had come to be reviled, then how could one justify a major regulatory effort to wipe out the comparatively less important hazards? It was almost as if Reagan's mistruth that trees cause pollution had come true.

Contemporary to the geologic radon issue, demand/control environmental regulation came under increasing fire, environmental standards were reviewed, state and federal agencies prioritized—and thus traded off—environmental protections, and the sanitizing of environmental risk was solidified as a goal of the establishment. While heated debate over where to draw the line of protection has occurred for radon, such controversy is not nearly as important as the role of radon itself in the larger effort of society to discern acceptable levels of safety. In concluding, we reexamine this notion of acceptable risk.

Conclusion—Accepting Radon in Context

What then does radon tell us about our societal choice of risks and how we address them? The case of radon demonstrates, with uncommon clarity, the political, social, and cultural contributions to the shaping of an environmental risk issue. The risk becomes particularly open for disagreement and discussion when the risk involves some hazard that is invisible in its occurrence and its near-term consequences. Risks are "selected" by the social forces that discover, define, and divulge hazards. They take meaning in light of the social and cultural context. Despite efforts to disguise the issues within mathematical formulae, the perception of risk remains a psychosocial phenomenon. Radon looms large as a risk when compared to most environmental health and safety issues. It shrinks back when we contrast it to other life risks or to smoking. How we frame the comparison and what assumptions we build it upon determines the outcome. The distinction between risk perception and risk assessment, intended to somehow separate out the public's view of risk from that of the experts, falls apart when we realize that both involve judgments based upon chosen assumptions and prej-udices. Unless we understand the cause and consequence of these various frames of bias, we cannot really comprehend the significance of the hazard. In short, there is no culturally unbiased method of comparing risk.

Radon and the Cumulative Context of Risk

Our social tendency to use reductionistic and deductive modes of thought is no more apparent than in our examination of the radon issue. Much as we have dissected the human body into its smallest parts, but ill understand the health of the whole body, we have defined the environment as a collection of measurable conditions that can be discovered and addressed in isolation. But we don't dwell in a fractionated environment. Rather than treating radon as though it were an isolated phenomenon, in the end, we must learn to see radon in context.

The case of radon illustrates the manner by which issues become context isolated. Thus, policies and programs for radon have emerged generally outside the larger set of issues within which radon research naturally belongs, namely, the question of indoor air quality, life in a synthetic environment, and the result-ing cumulative exposure to environmental hazards. What would an integrative approach to environmental hazards look like? Could such an approach be used to define healthy environments?

EPA began experimenting with the study of cumulative hazard exposure in the Total Exposure Assessment Methodology, or "TEAM," study done in the mid-1980s, involving four hundred residents of New Jersey, North Carolina, and North Dakota. Although this study did not include radon, it is relevant because it crossed important boundaries. First, it included different pollutants—twenty different volatile organic chemicals—not normally assayed simultaneously in the same population. Additionally, it also employed measures of different expo-sure contexts, including indoor air, outdoor air, drinking water, and air actually breathed. Among the many provocative findings was the discovery that all of the organic chemicals studied are as much as ten times as prevalent in indoor air as in the outside air (Wallace et al., 1987). The notion of cumulative multiple expo-sure, documented in the TEAM study, is inherently integral to the radon issue, where smoking synergy is a major factor in discussing radon's effects. The con-cept of cumulative response puts in perspective the narrow arguments that there are no dedicated corpses accountable to radon. We cannot assume single cause and effect in the real world.

Likewise, while evidence of radon's effect beyond lung cancer (see chapter 4) requires more substantiation, our cultural obsession with simple cause and ef-fect relationships is equally applicable to the consequences of radon exposure. The cultural bias has been particularly noticeable with regard to cancer as an effect, to the frequent exclusion of teratogenic, mutagenic, somatogenic, and neurotoxic consequences. The implications of this narrow perspective are seen, for example, with the emerging study of chemicals that mimic or block hormonal functioning (Colborn et al., 1996). In sum, radon must be placed back within the context of the multiple exposures to environmental hazards that people suffer. Rather than seeking dead bodies associated with a given risk factor, there is a need to recognize that the cumulative legacy of dishealth itself reflects an unhealthy environment.

The Holistic House

A requirement for placing radon back into the overall indoor air context is a holistic view of the building. The ecological or holistic view of buildings predates the geological radon issue, and can be associated with the same groups of builders who were concerned about the effects of energy conservation activities on ventilation rates and other health side effects of construction. Such "quality home" builders as Terry Brennan of Camroden Associates have greatly influenced thought about radon transfer and mitigation. They recognize that there are synergisms between building construction, change in the building over time, and use of the building.

The holistic approach to the building demands a very different direction in radon testing. Multiple aspects of environmental quality could be addressed simultaneously during a testing program in the home, a practice that does sometimes occur during the postcontract phase of home purchase. One would examine multiple separate indicators of environmental quality, as well as the interaction and cumulative picture suggested by the data. Mitigation is likewise potentially interactive in at least two ways. First, more than one problem might be solved by a common remediation effort appropriate to multiple indoor air problems (e.g., the use of ventilation to reduce other indoor contaminants simultaneously with radon). Second, care must be taken so that a given mitigation that works for one problem does not make another indoor air problem worse (e.g., where subslab ventilation might cause downdrafting from a combustion device, where sealing to prevent radon entry might drop ventilation rates so low that exposure to other indoor pollutants increases or that a moisture problem develops that creates a mold habitat, or where a charcoal filter placed on a water supply that was unknown to have high radon becomes a radioactive hazard).

From the perspective of efficiency and impact on residents, it would be a major step forward to employ a cumulative building assessment to provide an overall environmental profile and remediation program, complementing an ecological understanding of buildings and their use. Thus, an ecological program would supplant the notion that radon is merely a "problem" that can be fixed technologically, without the need to question either the basic construction of the home or the impacts of the American lifestyle on health. It is instructive that organizational changes at EPA discussed below reflect this new emphasis, offering hope of new policy shifts in how risks are defined and addressed.

The Need for an Integrative Approach

In its failure to address these larger concerns, the mythology of radon embodies many of the shadows or ambiguities built into our way of seeing and doing. With our tendency to focus specifically on how risk factors can be bounded and isolated, many real questions about environmental risks, including radon, are easily lost. Thus, in the real world, environmental risk involves the cumulative and synergetic issues involved in living in an environment where we are subjected to multiple and interacting sources of risk. Hazards are faced in all facets of life, from pesticides and other food impurities, groundwater contamination, contamination of the outdoor air, soil contamination, and the pollution of indoor air. While a bounded perspective focuses on the isolated effects of each of these factors, *the real question* involves the consequences of the mix of hazards faced in the reality of life. Ecological theory tells us that we are not subject to bounded conditions. A preventative view toward health, based on environmental vigilance, will similarly need to understand risk in a cumulative, interactive fashion. Our total lack of preparation for looking at cumulative, interactive conditions is readily evident in the limits to our understanding of homes. The focus on the whole house, rather than just specialized and isolated issues such as radon, mirrors the larger need to examine the whole earth, rather than just localized and immediately visible environmental degradation.

The effort to simplify and regiment the response to radon further reveals the disjunctive tendencies of modern society. In this instance, radon was packaged as an isolated hazard, deserving of its own government programs and staff, demanding its own industry, receiving its own educational and promotional efforts. Thus, despite the fact that a whole host of indoor air pollutants relate to ventilation rates and building operation, radon mitigation has tended to focus on remedial actions aimed at minimizing only radon. Evident is the absence of interdisciplinary and ecologically focused science necessary to understand the big picture—the cumulative threat from interacting forms of pollution. Integrative thinking about buildings is still rare. There is scant attention to the home as an ecological system. This is in marked contrast to other areas of science, particularly global change science, where there is now a recognized need for interdisciplinary approaches to understand the earth system.

Some positive steps have been taken by EPA to move in these directions. The 1992 *Citizen's Guide* had begun to address the synergistic relationships between smoking and radon. More importantly, in the long run, were organizational changes (Smith, 1995; Rowson, 1996; Feldman, 1996). The Indoor Air Program was brought into the Office of Radiation so that some of the new approaches and relationships that had been successful for radon could be capitalized upon for the whole area of indoor air, which shares elements of its risk profile with radon and has similarly limited resources. In this regard, the radon partnerships have been expanded to include other indoor air pollution issues, principally environmental tobacco smoke, the new division's second-ranking issue. But radon had something to gain from indoor air, as well. The indoor air group already had a comprehensive and integrated approach that could offer a more holistic perspective to the radon program.

In September 1995, EPA founded a new Indoor Air Division out of the radon, indoor air, and electromagnetic programs. Four "centers" were created within the division, the Center for Analysis and Study, the Center for Pollution and Source Guidance, the Center for Outreach and Partnerships, and the Center for Healthy Buildings.[10] Staff from these centers were organized in interdisciplinary teams around specific tasks. The entire structure was interdisciplinary, task oriented, and tightly cross-networked.

These changes were also reflected in the radon private sector. *Radon Industry Review* was merged into *Indoor Air Review*. And by the end of the period of study, testing and mitigation was increasingly being done by home inspection services that take responsibility during building transfers for assessing a wide range of environmental hazards. Despite these indications of a shift toward integration, there is still a long way to go before an ecological approach to radon is evident—one that recognizes that nothing occurs in isolation.

Acceptable Risk Is the Avoidance of Preventable Risk

Significant exposure to geologic radon is preventable, therefore its social and health costs are avoidable. However, lacking a culture focused on the prevention of health or environmental problems, we rely on symptom identification of problems already manifest. We allow the problem to occur and then, maybe, we try to fix it. Radon will be tested and remediated when required by a sales contract, but long-term avoidance is outside of our consciousness. Thus, with radon, the continued sale and construction of radon-prone buildings assures that hazardous exposure will continue unabated. Here we have a dissonance between the short-term orientation of growth-economics and the long-term perspective of environmental sustainability. No matter how cost-benefit analysis is computed, ours is a costly way to do things. And, because of our nonpreventative approach, the cost of solving environmental problems is so extraordinarily high that it forces decision makers to think Reaganomically.

Thus, Reaganomics and neo-Reaganomics have asked whether it is worth the costs to fix the problems caused by a prior era, even while protection of the future is denied. If there is anything constructive to come from this denial, it is the forced creation of alternative approaches to environmental action. The result has been both a search for a broader consensus and partnerships, and other ways to get the job done. Despite our criticisms, we see in the federal radon program the seeds for governmental innovation. But to the extent that such compromise merely keeps alive the social source of problems, it fails to recognize that we have to change the way we do things. This same error characterizes much of the environmental field, encompassing notions of environmental "management" and sustainable "development." One can become adept at confronting and even fixing discrete problems within the current system but never learn how to change the system so that the same problems are not manifest again. In this sense, even if we interpret the Reaganomic context as progressive rather than regressive, we must conclude that it does not go far enough to prove that society—its individuals and corporations—are mature enough to be self-regulating.

Our Isolation from Nature

In large part, these issues reflect the fact that humans have never sorted out their place in the environment. Indeed, radon reflects the tendency of modern people to take their natural surroundings for granted—neither valuing them nor fearing them. By focusing on isolated issues, such as radon, we reinforce the basic perception of people that they somehow live outside of an environmental envelope, except for certain discrete problems or anomalies that need to be addressed. How then do we broach the larger picture, whereby radon would have a context, rather than dealing with radon as an anomaly?

Clearly, a much more informed understanding of the ambient environment is demanded. People need to be placed into an environmental surround the integrity of which they protect as if it were a second skin (see von Uxekull, 1984). Rather than viewing the person as a separate entity from the environment, both must be viewed as an integral whole. Such a perspective cannot be merely social, it must be personal as well.

When individuals were not moved to take responsibility for radon, they simply mirrored government's own aversion to owning the issue. Thus, geologic radon was elevated to the status of a societal risk precisely because nobody really wanted responsibility. While there is a strong likelihood that the issue will become institutionalized over time, there is also a chance that it could disappear from the screen—a fad risk whose novelty had worn off. But it does not appear likely that geologic radon will ever become a popular risk. Meanwhile, radon will continue to decay to bismuth, polonium, and lead in an endless chain of radioactive transmutation, indifferent to what humans think and do.

Notes

1. In fact, someone contemplating mobility might well conclude that, given the chance that a quick fix might deteriorate prior to the time of sale, it is prudent to wait until then to undertake remediation. Whether the mitigation works over time will then be unimportant. Rather, mitigation just needs to work long enough to consumate the realty transfer.

2. For example, the EPA evaluation panel calculated that smokers (30 percent of the population or seventy-five million Americans) suffer 9,400 deaths due to radon exposure, comprising 70 percent of the risk. Mitigation of homes over 4 pCi/l would prevent 1,600 of these deaths. An additional 23 percent of the population (or fifty-eight million people) consists of former smokers, who bear about 34 percent of the total radon risk (accounting for some 3,200 lung cancer deaths per year). Mitigation of homes over 4 pCi/l would save some five hundred of these.

3. Although all action to avoid deaths from radon falls below the range of cost per life saved found for the entire EPA regulatory program (roughly between $2.5 million and $7.5 million), the cost per life saved is particularly low in the targeted area (about $0.5 million in the target area against $1.5 million outside the targeted area—with the nationwide average just under $1 million per avoided death and the cost in California, the state having the lowest radon levels, falling just shy of $3 million per avoided death).

4. It is instructive that, by 1990, with relatively little new health research completed, DOE health estimates seemed little different from EPA's original estimates (Nero et al., 1990).

5. However, citing the delay in regulating smoking or seat belts may not be good analogies to radon, reflecting, as they do, the resistance of strong vested interests with political clout—the tobacco companies and auto manufacturers. There is no parallel opposition to radon in its nonregulatory form, although realtors and home builders have promised to fight efforts at regulating their turf.

6. The agency used the following justification for its recommendations. Regarding radon resistance in new construction, between thirty and fifty lives per year would be saved in the most radon-intense areas of the nation depending upon whether passive or active radon removal systems were used, respectively. The saved lives would increase exponentially, doubling yearly, so that as many as three thousand lives would be saved over a decade. As with new construction, an effort to implement radon reductions during real estate transfer would show an exponential savings of life over time. Testing and necessary mitigation in all homes sold nationwide would save 110 lung cancer deaths in one year; by the tenth year, one thousand deaths would be avoided, but the cumulative

savings in life would be six to seven thousand. While the savings in lives is less if the program focuses only on the high-risk areas, the cost per life saved would be nearly halved ($700,000 for the entire country and $400,000 for just the targeted areas) (EPA 1992d).

7. Public health objectives for the year 2000 were set in 1991 at the testing of 40 percent of all U.S. residences including 50 percent of residences housing smokers, former smokers, or children (DHHS, 1991).

8. Of some fifty standards currently in place, only ethylene dibromide, at an avoidance of an estimated seventy-two cancer cases per year, exceeds the benefit of regulating radon in water as originally proposed. The next most effective regulation, of vinyl chloride, avoiding twenty-seven annual cancer cases, is comparatively less beneficial.

9. David Rowson, who had succeeded Margo Oge as head of the radon division before its merger with the indoor air program, noted that radon had shared in the general agency downsizing, losing about 10 percent of its resources in the Clinton government reduction effort (Rowson, 1996). An interesting additional note on the evolution of the radon program under Clinton was the proposed step back from regulation being considered for proficiency programs under consideration in 1996 (Feldman, 1996). In an effort to get the federal government out of the proficiency business while still meeting the statutory responsibility to have proficiency monitored, EPA was considering privatizing the RMP and RCP programs, divesting the federal government from the role it plays in monitoring industry performance.

10. Before publication, a number of staff in this new integrated division were interviewed. They included Mary Smith, the director of the Division of Indoor Air; Elissa Feldman, the assistant director; David Rowson, the director of the Center for Healthy Buildings; Elizabeth Zanowiak of the Center for Outreach and Partners; Jennifer Keller of the Center for Healthy Buildings Residential Construction Team; Anita Schmidt, in the process of shifting from the Center for Analysis and Study to the Center for Healthy Buildings; and Marcia Carpentier, a staff health physicist given the role of coordinating environmental justice issues. It was interesting to see how completely the radon staff group had turned over since the beginning of the issue. Rich Guimond, the guiding figure for the early radon issue, was not even at EPA, having moved to, of all places, the Department of Energy which had long been as his nemesis. Steve Page and Margo Oge had moved upward and laterally within EPA. David Rowson was the only former head of the program still on staff there.

Bibliography

Abel, Scott. "Pete Radakovich Is Taking Some Pretty Big Names to Court in this Landmark Radon Lawsuit." *Radon News Digest* 8, no. 3 (1995): 14–20.

Abelson, Philip. "Uncertainties about Health Effects of Radon." *Science* 250, 4979 (October 1990): 353.

_____. "Mineral Dusts and Radon in Uranium Mines." *Science* 254, 5033 (November 1991): 777.

_____. Editorial response to Oge and Farland. *Science* 255 (March 6, 1992): 1194–95.

ACS (American Cancer Society). *Cancer Facts and Figures*. Atlanta, Ga.: ACS, 1996a.

_____. *The Great American Smokeout Media and Promotion Guide*. Atlanta, Ga.: ACS, 1996b.

Agard, S. S., and L. C. S. Gunderson. "The Geology and Geochemistry of Soils in Boyertown and Easton, Pennsylvania." In *Field Studies of Radon in Rocks, Soils and Water*, ed. L. C. S. Gunderson and R. B. Wanty. U.S. Geological Survey Bulletin 1971. Washington, D.C.: U.S. Government Printing Office, 1991.

Alavanja, M. C. R., R. C. Brownson, J. H. Lubin, E. Berger, J. Chang, and J. D. Boice, Jr. "Residential Radon Exposure and Lung Cancer among Nonsmoking Women." *Journal of the National Cancer Institute* 86, no. 24 (1994): 1829–37.

Alter, H. W., and R. A. Oswald. "Nationwide Distribution of Indoor Radon Measurements." In *Proceedings of the 1988 EPA International Symposium on Radon and Radon Reduction Technology*. Denver, Colo.: October 1988.

Ames, B. N., R. Magaw, and L. S. Gold. "Ranking Possible Carcinogenic Hazards." *Science* 236 (1987): 271–80.

Angotti, Rose. "Franklin Park Couple's Radon Suit under Way." *Pittsburgh Tribune-Review*, April 30, 1996a, C2.

_____. "Radon Trial Questions Disclosure of Test Results." *Pittsburgh Tribune-Review*. May 2, 1996b, B1, B8.

_____. "Radon Lawsuit: Tampering with Test Results Called Easy." *Pittsburgh Tribune-Review*. May 3, 1996c, 4.

_____. "Franklin Park: Testimony Details Radon-Venting Woes." *Pittsburgh Tribune-Review*. May 4, 1996d.

_____. "Radon Case: Jurors Deliberate Home Test Disclosure Liability." *Pittsburgh Tribune-Review*. May 10, 1996e, A1, A5.

Associated Press. "Radon Hazards Unclear." *The Olympian*, December 26, 1986, B1.

_____. "Radon Pioneer Safe at Home?" *Philadelphia Daily News*, September 19, 1988a, 18.

_____. "Scientist Combats Radon Hysteria." *(Middletown, New York) Times-Herald Record*, October 14, 1988b, 6.

_____. "Unhealthy Radon Levels Found in Nation's Schools, EPA Reports." *(Middletown, New York) Times-Herald Record*, April 21, 1989a, 23.

_____. "State Officials Advise Restraint over Testing." *(Middletown, New York) Times-Herald Record*, April 21, 1989b, 23.

_____. "Radon in Jersey Called a Grave Risk." *New York Times,* October 1, 1989c.

_____. "Study Calls Radon Big Risk." *(Middletown, New York) Times-Herald Record,* June 6, 1995, 8.

Auvinen, A., I. Makelainen, M. Hakama, O. Castren, E. Pukkala, H. Reishacka, and T. Rytomaa. "Indoor Radon Exposure and Risk of Lung Cancer: A Nested Case-Control Study in Finland." *Journal of the National Cancer Institute* 88, no. 14 (1996): 966–72.

Baird, Robert. "Couple Sues over Radon in New Home." *Pittsburgh Tribune-Review,* April 29, 1996, A5, AA.

Baker, Russell. "Man Here Gets Free Gas." *New York Times,* 1986, A23.

Barnes, A. James. Interview with author. Washington, D.C., August 4, 1988.

Barron, Teddi. "EPA's Regional Training Centers Observe Second Anniversary." *Indoor Air Review,* October 1991, 25.

_____. "Revised RMP Gets Mixed Reviews from Participants." *Indoor Air Review,* February 1992, 25–26.

Baum, Andrew, Raymond Fleming, and Jerome Singer. "Coping with Victimization by Technological Disaster." *Journal of Social Issues* 37 (1981): 4–35.

Beck, James. "EPA's Efforts to Regulate Radon in Drinking Water Spotlight Cost, Benefit, and Risk." *Indoor Air Review,* May 1992, 21–22.

Beck, Ulrich. *Risk Society: Toward a New Modernity.* London: Sage Publications, 1992.

BEIR IV, National Academy of Sciences/National Research Council. *Health Risks of Radon and Other Internally Deposited Alpha-Emitters: 1988, Report of the Committee on the Biological Effects of Ionizing Radiation* (BEIR IV). Washington, D.C.: National Academy Press, 1988.

Belkin, Lisa. "Warning: Home Energy Conservation May Be Dangerous to Your Health." *National Journal,* August 2, 1980, 1274–76.

Belzer, Richard. "Regulating Risk: An OMB Perspective." Paper presented at the National Safety Council Conference "Regulating Risk: The Science and Politics of Risk," Washington, D.C., June 24, 1991.

Berman, Steven, and Abraham Wandersman. "Fear of Cancer and Knowledge of Cancer: A Review and Proposed Relevance to Hazardous Waste Sites." *Social Science and Medicine* 31, no. 1 (1990): 81–90.

Berreby, David. "The Radon Raiders: Turning Peril into Profits." *New York Times,* July 26, 1987.

Bierma, T. J., K. G. Croke, and D. Swartzman. "Accuracy and Precision of Home Radon Monitoring and the Effectiveness of EPA Monitoring Guidelines." *Journal of the American Air Pollution Control Association* 39 (1989): 953–59.

Bodansky, D., K. L Jackson, and J. P. Geraci "Comparisons of Indoor Radon to Other Radiation Hazards." In *Indoor Radon,* ed. D. Bodansky, M. A. Robkin, and D. R. Stadler. Seattle: Environmental Radiation Studies Committee, University of Washington, February 1987.

Bogard, William. *The Bhopal Tragedy: Language, Logic, and Politics in the Production of a Hazard.* Boulder: Westview Press, 1989.

Boice, Ruth. "Scientists Discount Radon Risk." *(Middletown, New York) Times-Herald Record,* July 10, 1985, 3.

Bolch, Ben, and Harold Lyons. "A Multibillion-dollar Radon Scare." *Public Interest* 99 (Spring 1990): 61–67.

Bowden, Mark. "Your House Could Be Killing You." *Today: The Inquirer Magazine,* November 21, 1982, 18–21, 31.

Boxall, Bettina. "Radon-plagued Families Waiting for the Fallout." *The Sunday Record,* December 8, 1985, A1, A24.

BPA (Bonneville Power Administration). *Final Environmental Impact Statement: The Expanded Residential Weatherization Program,* vol. 1, app. N. Portland, Ore., 1984.

_____. Division of Residential Programs. "Indoor Air Quality Monitoring and Mitigation Procedures." April 1987.

Brennan, T., and M. Osborne. "Overview of Radon-Resistant New Construction." In *Proceedings of the 1988 EPA International Symposium on Radon and Radon Reduction Technology,* Denver, Colo., October 1988.

Brennan, Terry. "The Impact of Radon Gas Concern upon the Construction Trades and Codes." In *Radon and the Environment,* ed. William Makofske and Michael Edelstein. Park Ridge, N.J.: Noyes Publications, 1988.

_____. Interview by author. Philadelphia, Pa., April 5, 1991.

Brenner, David J. *Radon: Risk and Remedy.* New York: W. H. Freeman and Co., 1989.

Brookes, Warren. "Radon Terrorism Unleashed by EPA?" *Washington Times,* June 29, 1989, F1.

Brookins, D. G. *The Indoor Radon Problem.* New York: Columbia University Press, 1990.

Burham, Lynne. "Senate Passes Radon Reauthorization Legislation by 82–6 Vote." *Indoor Air Review,* April 1992, 21.

Burkhart, J. F., and D. L. Kladder. "A Comparison of Indoor Radon Concentrations between Pre-Construction and Post-Construction Mitigated Single Family Dwellings." In *Proceedings of the 1991 EPA International Symposium on Radon and Radon Reduction Technology.* Philadelphia, Pa., April 1991.

Camroden Associates. Private communication from T. Brennen, 1989.

Carlisle, D., and H. Azzouz. "Geological Parameters in Radon Risk Assessment—A Case History of Deliberate Exploration." In *Proceedings of the 1991 EPA International Symposium on Radon and Radon Reduction Technology.* Philadelphia, Pa., April 1991.

Carollo, Russell. "Radon: Living with Poison." *(Spokane, Washington) Spokesman Review,* 1987, 1, 8.

Carpentier, Marcia. Interview with author. Washington, D.C., October 1, 1996.

Carvitti, Joseph. "Project Summary: Clinton, New Jersey, Radon Mitigation Follow-up and Long-term Monitoring." EPA/600/S7-88/005, May 1988.

Cattafe, J. S., C. A. Ranney, K. E. Miller, and R. H. Andolsek. "Regional NURE, Geology and Soils Data as Predictors for Indoor Radon." In *Proceedings of the 1988 EPA International Symposium on Radon and Radon Reduction Technology.* Denver, Colo., October 1988.

CDC (Centers for Disease Control). "Cigarette Smoking among Adults, U.S." *Morbidity and Mortality Weekly Report,* 1994, 43, 59, 925.

Center for Risk Analysis. "OMB vs. the Agencies: The Future of Cancer Risk Assessment." Harvard School of Public Health, June 1991.

_____. "A Historical Perspective on Risk Assessment in the Federal Government." Harvard School of Public Health, March 1994.

Chafee, John. S 744. Radon Program Development Act. *Congressional Record—Senate*, July 8, 1987, S9427–9433.

Chicago Tribune. "Radon Threat Reduced: Study Can't Link Gas, Cancer." *(Middletown, New York) Times-Herald Record*, December 21, 1994, 8.

Clarkin, M., and T. Brennan. *Radon-Resistant Construction Techniques for New Residential Construction.* U.S. Environmental Protection Agency, EPA/625/2-91/032, February 1991.

Cohen, Bernard. "A National Survey of ^{222}Rn in U.S. Homes and Correlating Factors." *Health Physics* 51 (1986): 175–83.

———. "Correlation between Mean Radon Levels and Lung Cancer Rates in U.S. Counties: A Test of the Linear No Threshold Theory." In *Proceedings of the 1988 EPA International Symposium on Radon and Radon Reduction Technology.* Denver, Colo., Report EPA-600/9-89-006a, 1989a.

———. "Expected Indoor Rn-222 Levels in Counties with Very High and Very Low Lung Cancer Rates." *Health Physics* 57 (1989b): 897–907.

———. "Reply to Oge." *Health Physics* 59 (1990): 354.

Cohen, Bernard, and the Editors of Consumer's Reports Books. *Radon: A Homeowner's Guide to Detection and Control.* Mount Vernon, N.Y.: Consumers Union of United States, Inc., 1987.

Cohen, Bernard, and Nickifor Gromicko. "Adequacy of Time Averaging with Diffusion Barrier Charcoal Absorption Collectors for Rn-222 Measurements in Homes." *Health Physics* 54 (1988): 195.

Cohen, Norman, ed. *Governor's Conference on Indoor Radon.* Tuxedo: New York University Medical Center, 1986.

Colborn, Theo, Dianne Dumanoski, and John P. Myers. *Our Stolen Future: Are We Threatening Our Fertility, Intelligence and Survival? A Scientific Detective Story.* New York: Dutton, 1996.

Cole, Leonard. *Element of Risk: The Politics of Radon.* Washington, D.C.: AAAS Press, 1993.

Committee on Indoor Air Quality Radon Work Group. "Federal Radon Activities Inventory: 1988–1989." U.S. Department of Energy and U.S. Environmental Protection Agency, DOE/ER-0409, 1989.

Cook, J. E., and D. J. Egan, Jr. "Mitigation." In *Environmental Radon,* ed. C. Richard Cothern and James E. Smith, Jr. New York: Plenum Press, 1987.

Cothern, C. Richard. "History and Uses." In *Environmental Radon,* ed. C. Richard Cothern and James E. Smith, Jr. New York: Plenum Press, 1987.

Couch, Stephen, and J. Stephen Kroll-Smith. "The Chronic Technical Disaster: Toward a Social Scientific Perspective." *Social Science Quarterly* 66 (1985) 564–75.

Coyle, Marcia. "Unless Law Changes, Superfund Won't Clean Up Radon." *(Allentown, Pa.) Morning Call,* September 8, 1986, B4–5.

Coyle, Marcia. "Superfund Can't Finance Most Cleanups." *(Allentown, Pa.) Morning Call,* October 28, 1986, 4.

Coyle, Marcia, and Stephen Drachler. "Officials Tread Lightly in Radon Minefield." *(Allentown, Pa.) Morning Call,* October 28, 1986, 1.

Crawford-Brown, Douglas J. "Dosimetry." In *Environmental Radon,* ed. C. Richard Cothern and James E. Smith, Jr. New York: Plenum Press, 1987.

Cross, F. T. "Health Effects." In *Environmental Radon,* ed. C. Richard Cothern and James E. Smith, Jr. New York: Plenum Press, 1987.

_____. "Invited Commentary: Residential Radon Risks from the Perspective of Experimental Animal Studies." *American Journal of Epidemiology* 140, no. 4 (1994): 333–39.

Cross, F. T., N. H. Harley, and W. Hofmann. "Health Effects and Risks from Radon-222 in Drinking Water." *Health Physics* 48 (1985): 649–670.

Daggott, Christopher. "The Radon Problem: A Federal Perspective." In *Radon and the Environment,* ed. William Makofske and Michael Edelstein. Park Ridge, N.J.: Noyes Publications, 1988.

Danysh, Terrence. "Radon: A Legal Perspective." Paper presented at the Radon Forum sponsored by the Washington State Energy Extension Service, Spokane, Wash., May 6, 1987.

Deieso, Donald. "Opening Remarks." In *Proceedings of the CRCPD/EPA Radon Workshop.* Atlanta, Ga., 1987.

_____. "An Overview of the Radon Issue in New Jersey." In *Radon and the Environment,* ed. William Makofske and Michael Edelstein. Park Ridge, N.J.: Noyes Publications, 1988.

DePierro, N., and M. Cahill. "Radon Reduction Efforts in New Jersey." *Proceedings of the 1988 EPA International Symposium on Radon and Radon Reduction Technology* Denver, Colo., 1988.

DePierro, N., T. Key, and J. Moon. "The Effectiveness of Radon Reduction in New Jersey." *Proceedings of the 1990 EPA Symposium on Radon and Radon Reduction Technology* Atlanta, Ga., 1990.

Dingell, James. 1988. "Indoor Radon Abatement." Report 100-1047 accompanying H.R. 2837, October 4, 1988.

Doll, R., and R. Petro. *The Causes of Cancer.* New York: Oxford University Press, 1981.

Dorsey, John. "The New Jersey Radon Program: A Legislative Perspective." In *Radon and the Environment,* ed. William Makofske and Michael Edelstein. Park Ridge, N.J.: Noyes Publications, 1988.

Douglas, Mary, and Aaron Wildavsky. *Myth and Culture: An Essay on the Selection of Technological and Environmental Dangers.* Berkeley: University of California Press, 1982.

Doyle, James, Gary McClelland, William Schultz, Paul Locke, Steven Elliott, Glenn Russell, and Andrew Moyad. "An Evaluation of Strategies for Promoting Effective Radon Mitigation." U.S Environmental Protection Agency, Office of Policy, Planning, and Evaluation, EPA 230-02-90-075, March 1990.

Drachler, Stephen. "Warnings of Radon Ignored: Officials Told of Threat 4 Years before Incident." *(Allentown, Pa.) Morning Call,* September 22, 1985, A1, A4–6.

Dudley, C. S., and A. R. Hawthorne. "Seasonal and Annual Average Radon Levels in 70 Houses." In *Proceedings of the 1988 EPA International Symposium on Radon and Radon Reduction Technology,* Volume 1-Symposium Oral Papers. EPA-600/9-89-006a, Air and Energy Engineering Research Laboratory, Research Triangle Park, N.C. March 1989.

Dunlap, R .E., M. E. Kraft, and E. A. Rosa, eds. *Public Reactions to Nuclear Waste: Citizens' Views of Repository Siting.* Durham, N.C.: Duke University Press, 1993.

Eason, Charles. "Developing a Health and Safety Program for the Radon Mitigator." *Radon Industry Review* 1 (October 1989): 21.

Eaton, R. S. "Radon Reduction." *Science* 241 (August 19, 1988): 990.

Eatough, J. P., and D. L. Henshaw. "Radon and Prostate Cancer." *Lancet* 335 (1990): 1292.

Eckholm, Eric. "Radon: Threat Is Real, but Scientists Argue over Its Severity." *New York Times,* September 2, 1986, C1, C7.

Edelstein, Michael R. "The Social and Psychological Impacts of Groundwater Contamination in the Legler Section of Jackson, New Jersey." Report to the Law Firm of Kriendler and Kreindler, 1982.

————. *Contaminated Communities: The Social and Psychological Impacts of Residential Toxic Exposure.* Boulder, Colo.: Westview Press, 1988a.

————. "The State Radon Survey." In *Radon and the Environment,* ed. William Makofske and Michael Edelstein. Park Ridge, N.J.: Noyes Publications, 1988b.

————. "Ecological Threat and Spoiled Identities: Radon Gas and Environmental Stigma." In *Communities at Risk: Community Responses to Technological Hazards,* ed. Stephen R. Couch and J. Stephen Kroll-Smith. Worcester: Peter Lang Publishing, 1991.

Edelstein, Michael R., and Valerie Boyle. "Media and the Perception of Radon Risk." In *Radon and the Environment,* ed. William Makofske and Michael Edelstein. Park Ridge, N.J.: Noyes Publications, 1988.

Edelstein, Michael R., Margaret Gibbs, and Susan Belford. "Psychosocial Issues in the Perception of Radon Gas Exposure." In *Proceedings of the 1988 EPA International Symposium on Radon and Radon Reduction Technology.* Denver, Colo., October, 1988. 600-B. Washington, D.C.: Government Printing Office, 1989.

Edelstein, Michael R., and Liana Hoodes. "A Grass Roots Model for Radon Response." In *Radon and the Environment,* ed. William Makofske and Michael Edelstein. Park Ridge, N.J.: Noyes Publications, 1988.

Egan, Daniel. "The EPA Radon Action Program." In *Radon and the Environment,* ed. William Makofske and Michael Edelstein. Park Ridge, N.J.: Noyes Publications, 1988.

Eheman, Christie. "Overview of Federal Radon Planning and Guidance." In *Radon and the Environment,* ed. William Makofske and Michael Edelstein. Park Ridge, N.J.: Noyes Publications, 1988.

Eichholz, G. G. "Human Exposure." In *Environmental Radon,* ed. C. Richard Cothern and James E. Smith, Jr. New York: Plenum Press, 1987.

Environmental Law Institute. "Proposed and Enacted Radon Legislation, 1992–93 Legislative Sessions." July 23, 1993a.

————. "State Radon Legislation—Issues and Options." Draft of document prepared for the Radon Working Group of the National Conference of State Legislatures. 1993b.

"EPA: 20% of U.S. Schools Have High Levels of Radioactive Radon." Knight-Ridder Newspapers. *Chicago Tribune,* March 22, 1993, 7.

EPA (Environmental Protection Agency). Office of Air and Radiation, and Centers for Disease Control. *A Citizen's Guide to Radon: What It Is and What To Do about It.* OPA-86-004. Washington, D.C.: U.S. Government Printing Office, 1986.

_____. Office of Policy Analysis. "Unfinished Business: A Comparative Assessment of Environmental Problems: Overview Report." February 1987a.

_____. "Summary of State Radon Programs." 1987b.

_____. "EPA Finds Radon Problems in 10-State Survey." EPA News Release and Fact Sheets. August 4, 1987c.

_____. Office of Radiation Programs. *Radon Reduction Methods: A Homeowner's Guide*, 2d ed. OPA-87-010. Washington, D.C.: U.S. Government Printing Office, 1987d.

_____. *Radon Reference Manual.* EPA 520/1-87-20. Washington, D.C.: U.S. Government Printing Office, September 1987e.

_____. "Radon Facts." Agency publication, 1988a.

_____. "EPA and Assistant Surgeon General Call for Radon Home Testing." EPA Press Release of September 12, 1988b.

_____. Office of Radiation Programs. "Key Elements of a State Radon Program." May 1988c.

_____. Office of Radiation Programs. "The National Radon Measurement Proficiency (RMP) Program, Cumulative Proficiency Report." September 1988d.

_____. Office of Policy, Planning, and Evaluation. "Region 3/OPPE/State of Maryland Radon Risk Communication Project: An Evaluation of Radon Risk Communication Projects." November 1988e.

_____. Office of Radiation Programs. "Indoor Radon and Radon Decay Product Measurement Protocols." EPA-520/1-89-006. Washington, D.C.: U.S. Government Printing Office, February 1989a.

_____. Office of Radiation Programs. "Radon Measurements in Schools: An Interim Report." EPA 520/1-89-010. Washington, D.C.: U.S. Government Printing Office, March 1989b.

_____. "Radon Contractor Proficiency Program Radon Mitigation Guidelines." October 1989c.

_____. Office of Policy Planning and Evaluation. "Comparing Risks and Setting Environmental Priorities: Overview of Three Regional Projects." August 1989d.

_____. "Model Standards and Techniques for Controlling Radon within New Buildings." (Draft Copy). 1989e.

_____. Science Advisory Board. "Reducing Risk: Setting Priorities and Strategies for Environmental Protection." SAB-EC-90-021. Washington, D.C.: U.S. Government Printing Office, September 1990a.

_____. Office of Air and Radiation. "1989 Summary of State Radon Programs." ANR-464, EPA 520/1-91-015. Washington, D.C.: U.S. Government Printing Office, September 1990b.

_____. Office of Policy, Planning, and Evaluation. "An Evaluation of Strategies for Promoting Effective Radon Mitigation." Risk Communication and Economic Research Series. EPA 230-02-90-075. Washington, D.C.: U.S. Government Printing Office, March 1990c.

_____. *Radon Mitigation Update.* EPA/600/9-90/048. Washington, D.C.: U.S. Government Printing Office, December 1990d.

_____. "Part II. 40 CFR Parts 141 and 142: National Primary Drinking Water Regulations; Radionuclides; Proposed Rule." *Federal Register* 56, 138 (July 18, 1991a,): pp. 33049–43573.

_____. Office of Radiation Programs. "The State Indoor Radon Grant Program: Progress and Future Directions." August 1991b.

_____. *Radon Mitigation Research Update.* EPA/600/9-91/038. Washington, D.C.: U.S. Government Printing Office, November 1991c.

_____. Program Evaluation Division. "Radon Program Review." May 1992a.

_____. Radon Division. "Implementation of OPPE Panel Recommendations." July 1992b.

_____. *National Residential Radon Survey: Summary Report.* EPA 402-R-92-011. Washington, D.C.: U.S. Government Printing Office, October 1992c.

_____. Radon Division, Office of Radiation Programs. "Technical Support Document for the 1992 Citizen's Guide to Radon." May 20, 1992d.

_____. *Consumer's Guide to Radon Reduction: How to Reduce Radon Levels in Your Home.* EPA 402-K92-003. Washington, D.C.: U.S. Government Printing Office, August 1992e.

_____. *A Citizen's Guide to Radon: The Guide to Protecting Yourself and Your Family from Radon* 2d ed. ANR-464, 402-K92-000. Washington, D.C.: U.S. Government Printing Office, May 1992f.

_____. Fact Sheet on School Survey, April 29, 1993a.

_____. Fact Sheet on Mitigation Costs, April 29, 1993b.

_____. Office of Air and Radiation. "EPA Strategy to Reduce Risk of Radon." June 1993c.

_____. *EPA Map of Radon Zones (Draft).* Environmental Protection Agency, dated April 22, 1993d.

_____. Fact Sheet on the RMP and RCP, April 29, 1993e.

_____. *Home Buyer's and Seller's Guide to Radon.* 402-R-93-003. Washington, D.C.: U.S. Government Printing Office, March 1993f.

_____. Fact Sheet Summarizing the CRCPD "Radon Risk Communication and Results Study" April 29, 1993g.

_____. *Legislating Lower Health Risks: Radon.* 402-F-94-006. Washington, D.C.: U.S. Government Printing Office, July 1994a.

_____. *Model Standards and Techniques for Control of Radon in New Residential Buildings.* 402-R-94-009. Washington, D.C.: U.S. Government Printing Office, 1994b.

_____. "Landmark Radon Case." Undated fact sheet, 1996.

EPA/CRCPD. "State Radon Workshop, Atlanta Georgia, October 1987." *Proceedings of the CRCPD/EPA Radon Workshop.* Atlanta, Ga., October 1987.

Erdman, Richard. Interview with author. Washington, D.C., June 14, 1988.

Ethier, William. "Builders, Buyers, Agents and Lenders: A Sensible Approach to Radon." National Association of Home Builders, 1988.

Evdokimoff, V., and D. Ozonoff. "Compliance with EPA Guidelines for Follow-Up Testing and Mitigation after Radon Screening Measurements." *Health Physics* 63 (1992): 215–17.

Feldman, Elissa. Interview with author. Washington, D.C., August 29, 1996.

Field, R. W., and B. C. Kross. "Field Comparison of Several Commercially Available Radon Detectors." *American Journal of Public Health* 80 (1990): 926–30.

Findlay, W. O., A. Robertson, and A. G. Scott. "Follow-up Durability Measurements and Mitigation Performance Improvement Tests in 38 Eastern Pennsylvania Houses

Having Indoor Radon Reduction Systems" EPA Project Summary, EPA/600/S8-91-010, May 1991.

Fischoff, Baruch, and Ola Svenson. "Levels of Environmental Decisions." *Journal of Environmental Psychology* 5 (1985): 55–67.

Fisher, Ann. Interview with author. Washington, D.C., June 14, 1988.

――――. "Facing Up to High Radon Levels." *EPA Journal*, November/December 1989, 19–20.

Fisher, Ann, and Lennart Sjoberg. "Radon Risks: People's Perceptions and Reactions." In *Environmental Radon: Occurrence, Control and Health Hazards*, ed. Shyamal Majumdar, Robert Schmalz, and E. Willard Miller. Philadelphia: Pennsylvania Academy of Science, 1987.

Fleisher, R. L., A. Mogro-Campero, and L. G. Turner. "Indoor Radon Levels in the Northeastern U.S.: Effects of Energy-Efficiency in Homes." *Health Physics* 45 (1983): 407–12.

Ford, D. F., T. C. Hollocher, H. W. Kendall, J. J. MacKenzie, L. Scheinman, and A. S. Schurgin. *The Nuclear Fuel Cycle.* San Francisco: Friends of the Earth, 1974.

Ford, Earl, Christie Ehman, Paul Siegel, and Paul Garbe. "Radon Awareness and Testing Behavior: Findings from the Behavioral Risk Factor Surveillance System, 1989–1992." *Health Physics* 70 (March 1996): 363–6.

Freudenberg, William. "Perceived Risk, Real Risk: Social Science and the Art of Probabilistic Risk Assessment." *Science* 242 (October 7, 1988): 42–49.

Gaertner, Jason. "Commonwealth of Pennsylvania Radon Monitoring Program." In *Radon and the Environment,* ed. William Makofske and Michael Edelstein. Park Ridge, N.J.: Noyes Publications, 1988.

Galant, Debbie. "Living with a Radium Nightmare." *New York Times,* September 29, 1996, 13.

Galbraith, Susan. "1989—The Radon Year in Review." *Radon Industry Review* 2 (February 1990): 3.

Galen, Michele. "Nowhere to Run from Radon." *The Nation,* 244, February 14, 1987, 180–83.

GAO (General Accounting Office). "Indoor Air Pollution: An Emerging Health Problem." CED-80-111, September 1980.

――――. "Air Pollution: Hazards of Indoor Radon Could Pose a National Health Problem." Report to the Pennsylvania Congressional Delegation, June 30, 1986.

――――. "Indoor Radon: Limited Federal Response to Reduce Contamination in Housing." Report to Senator Frank Lautenberg, April 6, 1988.

――――. "Radon Testing: Uncertainty Exists in Radon Measurements." Report to the Chairman, Committee on Science, Space, and Technology, House of Representatives. RCED-90-25, October 1989.

――――. "Air Pollution: Changes Needed in EPA's Program that Assesses Radon Measurement Firms." Report to the Chairman of the Committee on Science, Space, and Technology, House of Representatives, RCED-90-209, August 1990.

――――. "Air Pollution: Actions to Promote Radon Testing." Report to the Committee on Science, Space, and Technology, House of Representatives. December 1992.

Gaylord, Clarice, and Elizabeth Bell. "Environmental Justice: A National Priority." In *Faces of Environmental Racism,* ed. Laura Westra and Peter Wenz. Lanham, Md.: Rowman & Littlefield, 1995.

Gearo, Joseph. Interview with author. Washington, D.C., June 13–14, 1988.

George, A. C. "Instruments and Methods for Measuring Indoor Radon and Radon Progeny Concentrations." In *Radon and the Environment*, ed. William Makofske and Michael R. Edelstein. Park Ridge, N.J.: Noyes Publications, 1988.

George, A. C., and L .E. Hinchliffe. "Measurements of Radon Concentrations in Residential Building in the Eastern United States." *Radon and Its Decay Products: Occurrences, Properties, and Health Effects*. American Chemical Society Symposium No. 331, April 1986.

George, A. C., E. O. Knutson, and H. Franklin. "Radon and Radon Daughter Measurements in Solar Buildings." *Health Physics* 45 (1983): 413–20.

Gerusky, Thomas. "Pennsylvania's Radon Program." In *Governor's Conference on Indoor Radon, March 4 and 5, 1986, Albany New York*, ed. Norman Cohen. Tuxedo, N.Y.: New York University Medical Center, 1986.

————. Interview with author. Denver, Colo., October 1988.

Gesell, T. F. "Background Atmospheric Rn-222 Concentrations Outdoors and Indoors: A Review." *Health Physics* 45 (1983): 289–302.

Gofman, J. W. *Radiation-Induced Cancer from Low-Dose Exposure: An Independent Analysis*. San Francisco: C.N.R. Book Division, 1990.

Goldstein, Bernard. "Risk Assessment and the Interface between Science and the Law." *Columbia Journal of Environmental Law* 14, no. 2 (1989).

Goldstein, Steve. "Radon Seeps into Home Sales Concern over Real Estate Deals, Rather Than Health, Seems to Be Driving Radon Issue Now." *Philadelphia Inquirer*, July 28, 1991, M01.

Gordon, Michael. "Brief and Appendix for Respondent Dorothy Tascoe and Cross Appellants, Township of Montclair and Harriette Nash." *Township of Vernon and Others vs. Department of Environmental Protection and Others*. Superior Court of New Jersey Appellate Division Docket No. A-531-85T5, September 30, 1986.

Gosink, T. A., M. Baskaran, and D. F. Holleman. "Radon in the Human Body from Drinking Water." *Health Physics* 59 (1990): 919–24.

Granlund, C. "Pennsylvania's Radon Certification Program." In *Proceedings of the 1988 EPA International Symposium on Radon and Radon Reduction Technology*. Denver, Colo., October, 1988.

Granlund, C., and M. Kaufman. "Comparison of Three Month Screening Measurements with Yearlong Measurements Using Track Etch Detectors in the Reading Prong." *Proceedings of the Technical Exchange Meeting on Passive Radon Monitoring*. CONF-8709187, U.S. DOE, Technical Measurements Center, Grand Junction, Colo., September 1987, Section M.

Greenberg, Harvey. Interview with author. Philadelphia, Pa., April 4, 1991a.

————. "NJDEP's Newly Adopted 'Certification of Radon Testers and Mitigators' and its Impact on the Home Inspection Industry." Unpublished paper and attached documents circulated by Radon Engineering, Mahwah, N.J., 1991b.

Greer, William. "Radioactive Gas Alters Lives of Pennsylvanians." *The New York Times*, October 28, 1985.

Grisham, C. M. "Radon Prevention in Residential New Construction: Passive Designs That Work." In *Proceedings of the 1991 EPA International Symposium on Radon and Radon Reduction Technology*. Philadelphia, Pa., 1991.

Guimond, Richard. "Opening Remarks." In *Proceedings of the CRCPD/EPA Radon Workshop*. Atlanta, Ga., October 1987.

_____. Interview with author. Washington, D.C., June 13, 1988a.

_____. "The History of the Radon Issue: A National and International Perspective." In *Radon and the Environment*, ed. William Makofske and Michael Edelstein. Park Ridge, N.J.: Noyes Publications, 1988b.

_____. Interview with author. Philadelphia, Pa., April 3, 1991.

Gunderson, L. C. S. Interview with author. Goshen, N.Y., June 1990.

Gunderson, L. C. S., G. M. Reimer, and S. F. Agard. "Correlation between Geology, Radon in Soil Gas, and Indoor Radon in the Reading Prong," In *Geologic Causes of Natural Radionuclide Anomalies*, ed. M. A. Marikos and R. H. Hansman. Proceedings of the GEORAD Conference, St. Louis, Mo. Special Publication, No. 4, April 21–22. Rolla: Missouri Department of Natural Resources, Division of Geology and Land Survey, 1987.

Gunderson, L. C. S., G. M. Reimer, C. R. Wiggs, and C. A. Rice. "Map Showing Radon Potential of Rocks and Soils in Montgomery County, Maryland." Miscellaneous Field Studies Map (MF-2043). U.S. Geological Survey, 1988.

Gunderson, L. C. S., R. R. Schumann, J. K. Otton, R. F. Dubiel, D. E. Owen, K. A. Dickinson, R. T. Peake, and S. J. Wirth. "Preliminary Radon Potential Map of the United States." *Proceedings of the 1991 EPA International Symposium on Radon and Radon Reduction Technology*, Philadelphia, Pa, April 1991.

Gunderson, L. C. S., and R. B. Wanty, eds. *Field Studies of Radon in Rocks, Soils, and Water*. U.S. Geological Survey Bulletin 1971, Washington, D.C.: U.S. Government Printing Office, 1991.

Gutin, JoAnn. "At Our Peril: The False Promise of Risk Assessment." *Greenpeace Magazine*, March/April, 1991, 13–18.

Hall, F. R. "Geologic Controls on Radon Gas in Ground Water." In *Radon and the Environment*, ed. William J. Makofske and Michael R. Edelstein. Park Ridge, N.J.: Noyes Publications, 1988.

Harbuck, Stan. "Professionalism in the Wake of Tampering." *Radon Industry Review* 1 (November 1989): 24–25.

Hardert, R. A. "Public Trust and Governmental Trustworthiness: Nuclear Deception at the Fernald, Ohio, Weapons Plant." In *Research in Social Problems and Public Policy*, vol. 5, ed. W. R. Freudenburg and T. I. K. Young. Greenwich, Conn.: JAI Press, Inc., 1993.

Harley, N. H. "Does 4 Equal 2? Decisions Based on Radon Measurements." *American Journal of Public Health* 80 (August 1990): 905–6.

Harley, N. H., and T. B. Terelli. "Predicting Annual Average Indoor Rn-222 Exposure." Paper presented at the Health Physics Annual Meeting, 1987.

Harris, J. "Radon and Formaldehyde Concentrations as a Function of Ventilation Rates in Residential Buildings in the Northwest." Proceedings of the Air Pollution Control Association Annual Meeting, 1987.

Harrison, Jed. Interview with author. Philadelphia, Pa. April 4, 1991.

Harrison, Kathryn, and George Hoberg. "Setting the Environmental Agenda in Canada and the United States: The Cases of Dioxin and Radon." *Canadian Journal of Political Science* 24 (March 1991): 3–27.

Heine, Kurt. "A New Danger Unearthed Radon Poses a Cancer Threat." *Philadelphia Daily News*, November 12, 1985, 8.

Hembra, Richard L. "Observations on the Environmental Protection Agency's Budget Request for Fiscal Year 1992." Testimony of the General Accounting Office before the Committee on Environment and Public Works, United States Senate, March 7, 1991.

Henschel, D. Bruce. *Radon Reduction Techniques for Detached Houses: Technical Guidance,* 2d ed. EPA/625/5-87/019. Washington, D.C.: U.S. Government Printing Office. Revised January 1988.

Henshaw, D. L., J. P. Eatough, and R. B. Richardson. "Radon as a Causative Factor in Induction of Myeloid Leukemia and Other Cancers." *Lancet* 335 (1990): 1008–12.

Hess, Charles, C. V. Weiffenback, and S. A. Norton. "Environmental Radon and Cancer Correlations in Maine." *Health Physics* 45 (1983): 339–48.

Hess, C. T., J. Michel, T. R. Horton, H. M. Prichard, and W. A. Coniglio. "The Occurrence of Radioactivity in Public Water Supplies in the United States." *Health Physics* 48 (1985): 553–86.

Hickey, R. J., E. J. Bowers, and R. C. Clelland. "Radiation Hormesis, Public Health and Public Policy: A Commentary." *Health Physics* 44 (1983) 207–19.

Higham, Scott, and Jeffrey Fleishman. "Many Fear Lawsuits Will Increase." *(Allentown, Pa.) Morning Call,* October 28, 1986, 6.

Hoornbeck, John, and Barbara Zakheim. "Draft Guidance to States on Radon Certification Programs." Paper presented at the 1991 EPA International Symposium on Radon and Radon Reduction Technology, Philadelphia, Pa., April 1991.

Hopper, R. "National Ambient Radon Study." In *Proceedings of the 1991 EPA International Symposium on Radon and Radon Reduction Technology,* Philadelphia, Pa., U.S. Environmental Protection Agency, April 1991.

Horton, T. R. *Nationwide Occurrence of Radon and Other Natural Radioactivity in Public Water Supplies.* EPA Report 520/5-85-008, U.S. Environmental Protection Agency, Eastern Environmental Radiation Facility, Montgomery, Ala., 1985.

Houk, Vernon, Interview with author. Washington, D.C., June 22, 1989.

Hurwitz, H. "The Indoor Radiological Problem in Perspective." Uncited publication, 1981.

IAR (Indoor Air Review). "Chances for Federal Radon Legislation Uncertain at Best, Proposals Back away from Real Estate Disclosures." June, 1992a, 25.

———. "Radon in Water Proposal by EPA Draws Fire from New Jersey Health Officials." June 1992b, 27.

———. "Radon Bill Dies in Congress." November, 1992, 22.

———. "Indoor Air Quality, Lead-Based Paint Seen as Strong Markets in 1990's, Radon in Need of Greater Public Interest if Industry Is to Grow." December 1992, 4, 27.

Jackson, K. L., J. P. Geraci, and D. Bodansky. "Observations of Lung Cancer: Evidence Relating Lung Cancer to Radon Exposure." In *Indoor Radon,* ed. D. Bodansky, M. A. Robkins, and D. R. Stadler. Environmental Radiation Studies Committee, University of Washington, 1987.

Jalbert, Philip, John Hoornbeck, and Jed Harrison. "National Radon Measurement Proficiency (RMP) Program." Paper presented at the 1991 International Symposium on Radon and Radon Reduction Technology, Philadelphia, Pa., April 1991.

James, A. C. "Lung Dosimetry." In *Radon and Its Decay Products in Indoor Air,* ed. W. W. Nazaroff and A. V. Nero, Jr. New York: John Wiley and Sons, 1988.

Johnson, Dan B. Interview with author. Spokane, Washington, September 24, 1996.

Johnson, F. Reed, and Ralph Luken. "Radon Risk Information and Voluntary Protection: Evidence from a Natural Experiment." *Risk Analysis* 7, no. 1 (1987).

Johnsrud, Judith. Interview with author. Mahwah, N.J., September 18, 1987.

Johnston, Barbara, and Susan Dawson. "Resource Use and Abuse on Native American Land: Uranium Mining in the American Southwest." In *Who Pays the Price? The Sociocultural Context of Environmental Crisis*, ed. Barabra Rose Johnston. Washington, D.C.: Island Press, 1994.

Johnstown Tribune-Democrat. "About Face on Radon Study," January 12, 1989.

Jonassen, N., and J. P. McLaughlin. "Removal of Radon and Radon Progeny from Indoor Air." In *Radon and Its Decay Products in Indoor Air*, ed. W. W. Nazaroff and A. V. Nero, Jr. New York: John Wiley and Sons, 1988.

Jones, Kay (and family). Interview with author. Colebrookdale Township, Pa., June 29, 1986; also August 7, 1987.

Jordan, Richard. "Radon Service Agreement Corporation Announces Home Protection Plan." *Radon News Digest*, September 1988, 4.

Kahneman, Daniel, Paul Slovic, and Amos Tversky. *Judgment under Uncertainty: Heuristics and Biases.* New York: Cambridge University Press, 1982.

Kaku, M., and J. Trainer, eds., *Nuclear Power: Both Sides.* New York: W.W. Norton, 1982.

Kass, Stephen, and Michael Gerrard. "Real Estate Transactions and Radon." *New York Law Journal*, July 15, 1987, 289–93.

Keller, Jennifer. Interview with author. Washington, D.C., September 13, 1996.

Kerr, Richard. *Science* 242 (September 23, 1988): 1594–95.

Koehler, Laraine, and Paul Giardina. "State Radon Program Development in Region II." Paper presented at the 1988 EPA International Symposium on Radon and Radon Reduction Technology, Denver, Colo., October 1988.

Knox, Carol S. Testimony before the Senate Minority Task Force on Radon, Newburgh, N.Y. March 2, 1989 (see also appended New Jersey Association of Realtors, "Summary of Radon Survey").

Koopersmith, Jeffrey. "Reading between the Lines." *Radon Industry Review*, December 1989, 6–7.

Kotrappa, P., and W. H. Jester. "Electret Ion Chamber Radon Monitors Measure Dissolved Rn-222 in Water." *Health Physics* 64 (1993): 397–405.

Kotrappa, P., J. C. Dempsey, J. R. Hickey, and L. R. Stieff. "An Electret Passive Environmental Rn-222 Monitor Based on Ionization Measurement." *Health Physics* 54 (1988), 47–56.

Krimsky, Sheldon, and Alonzo Plough. *Environmental Hazards: Communicating Risks as a Social Process.* New York: Auburn House, 1988.

Kunz, C., "Radon Reduction in New Construction: Double Barrier Approach." Paper presented at the 1991 EPA International Symposium on Radon and Radon Reduction Technology, U.S. Environmental Protection Agency, Philadelphia, Penn., April 1991.

Kunz, C., C. A. Laymon, and C. Parker. "Gravelly Soils and Indoor Radon." In *Proceedings of the 1988 EPA International Symposium on Radon and Radon Reduction Technology.* Denver, Colo., October 1988.

LaDuke, Wiwona, and Ward Churchill. "Native America: The Political Economy of Radioactive Contamination." *Journal of Ethnic Studies* 13, no. 3 (1985): 107–32.

Lautenberg, Frank. Radon Task Force, Report of February 11, 1986.

_____. "Radon—The Federal Response." In *Radon and the Environment*, ed. William Makofske and Michael Edelstein. Park Ridge, N.J.: Noyes Publications, 1988.

_____. S. 657, 103d Congress. "Indoor Radon Abatement Reauthorization Act of 1993."

Letourmeau, E. G., D. Krewski, N. W. Choi, M. J. Goddard, R. G. McGregor, J. M. Zielinski, and J. Du. "Case-Control Study of Residential Radon and Lung Cancer in Winnipeg, Manitoba, Canada." *American Journal of Epidemiology* 140, no. 4 (1994) 310–22.

Levine, Adeline. *Love Canal: Science, Politics and People.* Boston: Lexington Books, 1982.

Lewis, Larry. "Gloom and Anger Hang Heavy in 'Radon Hills.'" *Philadelphia Inquirer*, May 26, 1985, B01.

Locke, Paul A. "Promoting Radon Testing, Disclosure, and Remediation: Protecting Public Health through the Home Mortgage Market." *Environmental Law Reporter* 20 (November 1990) 10475–82.

_____. Interview with author. Washington, D.C., July 13, 1993.

Lowry, Jerry. "Radon Progeny Accumulation in Field GAC Units." Final Report to the Maine Department of Human Services, Division of Health Engineering, March 1988.

Lowry, Jerry, and Sylvia Lowry. "Techniques and Economics of Radon Removal from Water Supplies." In *Radon and the Environment,* ed. William Makofske and Michael Edelstein. Park Ridge, N.J.: Noyes Publications, 1988.

Lowry, Tom. "Trying to See a Colorless Gas." *(Allentown, Pa.) Morning Call*, October 28, 1986a, 9.

_____. "They Mix Casseroles with Visits to the Hill." *(Allentown, Pa.) Morning Call*, October 28, 1986b, 12.

Lubin, J. H. "Invited Commentary: Lung Cancer and Exposure to Residential Radon." *American Journal of Epidemiology* 140, no. 4 (1994): 323–32.

Lubin, J. H., and J. D. Boice, Jr. "Estimating Rn-Induced Lung Cancer in the United States." *Health Physics* 57 (1989): 417–27.

Lubin, J. H, J. M. Samet, and C. Weinberg. "Design Issues in Epidemiologic Studies of Indoor Exposure to Rn and Risk of Lung Cancer." *Health Physics* 59 (1990): 807–17.

Luckey, T. D. *Radiation Hormesis.* Boca Raton, Fla.: CRC Press, 1991.

MacMullin, Susan. Interview with author. Washington, D.C., June 13, 1988.

Maconaughey, Kirk. Interview with author. Washington, D.C., June 13, 1988; also Philadelphia, Pa., April 2 and 4, 1991.

Makofske, William, and Michael Edelstein, eds. *Radon and the Environment.* Park Ridge, N.J.: Noyes Publications, 1988.

_____. "Results of the Orange Environment, Inc. Radon Testing Program." In *Proceedings of the 1988 EPA International Radon Symposium.* Denver, Colo., October 1988, EPA/ORP, 600-B, 1989.

Manegold, C. S. "Hot House for a Family in Berks, It Was Home, Sweet Radioactive Home." *Philadelphia Inquirer*, January 14, 1985, A01.

Marcinowski, F., R. M. Lucas, and W. M. Yeager. "Airborne Radon Concentrations in U.S. Homes." *Health Physics* 66 (1994): 699–706.

Mardis, Michael. Interview with author. Washington, D.C., June 13 1988.

Markey, Edward. H.R. 2448 103d Congress. Radon Awareness and Disclosure Act of 1993.

Martin, William. Letter to A. James Barnes, September 24, 1987; cosigned September 29, 1987.

Martz, D. E., A. S. Rood, J. L. George, M. D. Pearson, and G. H. Langner, Jr. "Year-to-Year Variations in Annual Average Indoor Rn-222 Concentrations." *Health Physics* 61 (1991b): 409–13.

Martz, D. E., J. L. George, and G. H. Langner, Jr. "Comparative Performance of Short-Term Diffusion Barrier Charcoal Canisters and Long-Term Alpha-Track Monitors for Indoor Rn-222 Measurements." *Health Physics* 60 (1991a) 497–505.

Mazur, Allan. *The Dynamics of Technical Controversy.* Washington, D.C.: Communications Press, 1981.

———. "Putting Radon on the Public's Risk Agenda." *Science, Technology and Human Values* 12 (summer/fall 1987): 86–93.

———. "Putting Radon and Love Canal on the Public Agenda." In *Communities at Risk: Community Responses to Technological Hazards,* ed. Stephen Couch and J. Stephen Kroll-Smith. Worster, Mass.: Peter Lang, 1990a.

Mazur, Allan, and Glenn Hall, "Effects of Social Influence and Measured Exposure Level Response to Radon." *Sociological Inquiry* 60 (August 1990): 274–84.

Melamed, Dennis. "New Jersey Municipalities Question Radon Rankings, State Changes Calculations: Local Officials Fear Real Estate Effects." *Indoor Air Review,* June 1992, 27.

Michaels, L., T. Brennen, and M. Osborne. "Development and Demonstration of Indoor Radon Reduction Measures for 10 Homes in Clinton, New Jersey." EPA-600/8-87/027 (NTIS PB87-215356), U.S. Environmental Protection Agency, July 1987.

Michaels, Robert. "Health Risk Assessment: WRE vs. Peanut Butter." *Solid Waste and Power,* October 1988, 22–27.

Michel, Jacqueline. "Sources." In *Environmental Radon,* ed. C. Richard Cothern and James E. Smith, Jr. New York: Plenum Press, 1987.

Middletown (New York) Times-Herald Record. "Senator Says White House Suppressed Radon Report." October 11, 1985a, 3, 11.

Middletown (New York) Times-Herald Record. "Jersey Mortgagers Demand Radon Test." October 27, 1985b, 16.

Milbrath, Lester. *Envisioning a Sustainable Society.* Albany: State University of New York Press, 1989.

Miller, Kristy. "National Radon Action Week." Paper presented at the 1991 EPA International Symposium on Radon and Radon Reduction Technology, Philadelphia, Pa., April 1991.

Moody, Thomas. Interview with author. Denver, Colo., October 1988.

Moreau, Dan and Adrienne Blum. "Change Agents." *Changing Times* 43, no. 2 (February 1989): 104 (1).

Mose, D. G., G. W. Mushrush, and S. Kline. "Realistic Uncertainties for Charcoal and Alpha-Track Radon Monitors." In *Proceedings of the 1988 EPA International Symposium on Radon and Radon Reduction Technology.* Denver, Colo., October 1988.

Mossman, Kenneth, and Marissa Sollitto. "Regulatory Control of Indoor Radon." *Health Physics* 60 (1991): 169–76.

Moynahan, Patrick. *Congressional Record—Senate.* July 8, 1987, S9432.

Muessig, K. W. "Correlation of Airborne Radiometric Data and Geologic Sources with Elevated Indoor Radon in New Jersey." In *Proceedings of the 1988 EPA International Symposium on Radon and Radon Reduction Technology*. Denver, Colo., October 1988.

Mullen, R. M., and A. E. Nevissi. "Home Weatherization and Its Effects on Indoor Rn-222 Levels." *Health Physics* 59 (1990): 211–15.

Murane, D. M. "New House Evaluation Program (NEWHEP)." In *Proceedings of 1988 EPA International Symposium on Radon and Radon Reduction Technology*. Denver, Colo., 1988.

Nazaroff, W. W., and A. V. Nero, Jr. "Transport of Radon from Soil into Residences." Lawrence Berkeley Laboratory Report (LBL-18374), University of California, Berkeley, 1984.

Nazaroff, W. W., and K. Teichman. "Indoor Radon." *Environmental Science and Technology* 24 (1990): 774–82.

Nazaroff, W. W., S. M. Doyle, A. V. Nero Jr., and R. G. Sextro. "Radon Entry Via Potable Water." In *Radon and Its Decay Products in Indoor Air*, ed. W. W. Nazaroff and A. V. Nero, Jr. New York: John Wiley & Sons, 1988a.

Nazaroff, W. W., B. A. Moed, and R. G. Sextro. "Soil as a Source of Indoor Radon: Generation, Mitigation, and Entry." In *Radon and Its Decay Products in Indoor Air*, ed. W. W. Nazaroff and A. V. Nero, Jr. New York: John Wiley & Sons, 1988b.

NCRP (National Council on Radiation Protection and Measurements). *Evaluation of Occupational and Environmental Exposures to Radon and Radon Daughters in the United States*. NCRP Report No. 78. Bethesda, Md.: 1984.

Nero, A. V. "Indoor Radiation Exposures from Rn-222 and Its Daughters: A View of the Issue." *Health Physics* 45 (1983a): 277–88.

————. "Airborne Radionuclides and Radiation in Buildings: A Review." *Health Physics* 45 (1983b): 303–22.

Nero, A. V., Jr. "Radon and Its Decay Products in Indoor Air: An Overview." In *Radon and Its Decay Products in Indoor Air*, ed. W. W. Nazaroff and A. V. Nero, Jr. New York: John Wiley & Sons, 1988.

Nero, A. V., A. J. Gadgil, W. W. Nazaroff, and K. L. Revzan. "*Indoor Radon and Decay Products: Concentrations, Causes and Control Strategies*." Technical Report Series, U.S. DOE, Offices of Energy Research and Health and Environmental Research: DOE/ER-0480P, November 1990.

Nero, A. V., C. D. Hollowell, J. G. Ingersoll, and W. W. Nazaroff. "Radon Concentrations and Infiltration Rates Measured in Conventional and Energy-Efficient Houses." *Health Physics* 45 (1983c): 401–5.

Nero, A. V., M. B. Schwehr, W. W. Nazaroff, and K. L Revzan. "Distribution of Airborne Radon-222 Concentrations in U.S. Homes." *Science* 234 (1986): 992.

Nero, Anthony. "Earth, Air, Radon and Home." *Physics Today*, April 1989, 32–39.

Neuberger, J. "Residential Radon Exposure and Lung Cancer: An Overview of Ongoing Studies." *Health Physics* 63 (1992): 503–9.

New Jersey Department of Health. "A Case-Control Study of Radon and Lung Cancer Among New Jersey Women." Technical Report—Phase I. Trenton, N.J.: 1989.

New Jersey Register. (21 N.J.R. 3696–698), Division of Housing and Development, Uniform Construction Code, Radon Mitigation Subcode, December 4, 1989.

New Jersey Register. "Subchapter 27. Certification of Radon Testers and Mitigators." 22 (November 1990): 3533–45.

New York Times News Service. "Radon Specialists Swamped by Calls after U.S. Report." *(Middletown, New York) Times-Herald Record*, September 14, 1988, 37.

Nicholls, Gerald, and Mary Cahill. "Radon in New Jersey: Preliminary Characterization and Strategy." In *Radon and the Environment*, ed. William Makofske and Michael Edelstein. Park Ridge, N.J.: Noyes Publications, 1988.

Nicholls, Gerald, and Robert Stern. "Status of the New Jersey Radon Program." Paper presented at the 1988 EPA International Symposium on Radon and Radon Reduction Technology, Denver, Colo., October 1988.

Nitschke, I., M. Clarkin, T. Brennan, J. Rizzuto, and M. Osborne. "Preliminary Results from the New York State Radon-Reduction Demonstration Program." In *Proceedings of the 1988 EPA International Symposium on Radon and Radon Reduction Technology* Denver, Colo., October 1988.

Nitschke, I. A. "Project Summary: Radon Reduction and Radon Resistant Construction Demonstrations in New York." EPA/600/58-89/001; U.S. Government Printing Office 1989/748-012/07188, December 1989.

Norton, Joseph. Interview with author. Goshen, N.Y., July 11, 1989.

NRC (National Research Council). *Comparative Dosimetry of Radon in Mines and Homes*. Panel on Dosimetric Assumptions Affecting the Application of Radon Risk Estimates. Washington, D.C.: National Academy Press, 1991.

Nuess, Michael. Northwest Residential Radon Standard, Volume I: Project Report. Washington State Energy Office, Prepared for Bonneville Power Administration (U.S. DOE), September 1989.

Nuess, Michael. Interview with author. Philadelphia, Pa., April 4, 1991.

Nuess, R. M., and R. J. Prill. "Radon Control—Toward a Systems Approach." Paper presented at the 1991 EPA International Symposium on Radon and Radon Reduction Technology, Philadelphia, Pa., April 1991.

Nulman, Robert. "Discussion: The Role of Government—The New Jersey Response." In *Radon and the Environment*, ed. William Makofske and Michael Edelstein. Park Ridge, N.J.: Noyes Publications, 1988.

NYDOH (New York State Department of Health). *Radon Update* 2 (March 1989): 1.

NYSEO (New York State Energy Office). *Reducing Indoor Radon*. Albany, N.Y.: New York State Energy Office, 1989.

Oge, Margo. "Response to 'Expected Indoor Rn-222 Levels in Counties with Very High and Very Low Lung Cancer Rates.'" *Health Physics* 59 (1990): 353.

_____. Address to the 1991 EPA International Symposium on Radon and Radon Reduction Technology, Philadelphia, Pa., April 2, 1991a.

_____. Interview with author. Philadelphia, Pa., April 2, 1991b.

Oge, Margo, and William Farland. "Radon Risk in the Home" (letter to the editor). *Science* 255 (March 6, 1992): 1194.

Olsen, Marvin, Dora Lodwick, and Riley Dunlap. *Viewing the World Ecologically*. Boulder, Colo.: Westview Press, 1992.

OMB (Office of Management and Budget). "Regulatory Program of the United States Government: April 1, 1990–March 31, 1991." 1991a.

OMB (Office of Management and Budget). "Budget of the U.S. Government, Fiscal 1992." 1991b.

O'Pake, Michael. "Pennsylvania: A Legislative Perspective on Radon." In *Radon and the Environment*, ed. William Makofske and Michael Edelstein. Park Ridge, N.J.: Noyes Publications, 1988.

338   *Bibliography*

Osborn, David. "A Suburban Life that Changed Forever." *(Allentown, Pa.) Morning Call,* October 28, 1986, 11.
Osborne, M. C. *Radon-Resistant Residential New Construction.* Washington, D.C.: U.S. Government Printing Office. EPA/600/8-88/087, July 1988.
Overby, Peter. "Radon: Overlooked Peril." *The (Bergen) Record,* May 2, 1986, A8.
Page, Steven. Interview with author. Washington, D.C., June 8, 13, and 14, 1988; also Philadelphia, Pa., April 4, 1991.
Paigen, Beverly. "The Ethical Dimensions of Scientific Conflict: Controversy at Love Canal." *Hastings Center Report,* June 1982, 29–37.
Pearson, Jessica. "Hazard Visibility and Occupational Health Problem Solving: The Case of the Uranium Industry." *Journal of Community Health* 6, no. 2 (1980): 136–47.
Pearson, M. D., D. E. Martz, J. L. George, and G. H. Langner, Jr. "A Multiyear Quality Control Study of Alpha-Track Radon Monitors." *Health Physics* 62 (1992): 87–90.
Pennsylvania Environmental Quality Board. "Proposed Radon Certification Program." *Pennsylvania Bulletin* 18, no. 30 (1988).
Pershagen, G., Z-H Liang, Z. Hrubec, C. Svensson, and J. D. Boice, Jr. "Residential Radon Exposure and Lung Cancer in Swedish Women." *Health Physics* 63 (1992): 179–86.
Philips, J. L., and F. Marcinowski. "Comparing the State/EPA and National Residential Radon Surveys." Undated report received from EPA in May 1993.
Phillips, Jeffrey, Jane Bergsten, and S. B. White. "A Cumulative Examination of the State/EPA Radon Survey." Paper presented at the 1991 EPA International Symposium on Radon and Radon Reduction Technology, Philadelphia, Pa., April 1991.
Pohl, Robert O. "Will It Stay Put." In *Nuclear Power: Both Sides,* ed. M. Kaku and J. Trainer. New York: W.W. Norton and Co., 1982.
Pollack, Robert. "Personnel Radon Monitoring." *Radon Industry Review* 1, no. 3 (1989): 18.
Pratt, Lawrence. "Policy and Technical Considerations for the Development of Environmental Protection Agency Guidance on Radon and Real Estate." Paper presented at the 1991 EPA International Symposium on Radon and Radon Control Technology, Philadelphia, Pa., April 1991.
Prill, R. J., W. J. Fisk, and B. H. Turk, "Monitoring and Evaluation of Radon Mitigation Systems over a Two-Year Period." Paper presented at the 1988 EPA International Symposium on Radon and Radon Control Technology, Denver, Colo., October 1988.
PR Newswire, "Senator Arlen Spector Forms Task Force to Study Health Risks of Exposure to Radon." December 6, 1985.
Prussman, Jeanne. "The Radon Riddle: Landlord Liability for a Natural Hazard." *Environmental Affairs* 18 (1991) 714–50.
Public Citizen, News Release, January 4, 1989, 2.
Pugh, T. D. "Project Summary: Interim Radon-Resistant Construction Guidelines for Use in Florida—1989." EPA/600/S8-90/062, September 1990.
Radakovich v. Filia et al. Second Amended Complaint, February 15, 1995.
Radon Industry Directory, 1989. Alexandria, Va.: Radon Press, Inc., 1988.
Radon News Digest. "Markey Seeks Co-Sponsors for Radon Awareness Act." 8, no. 3 (1995): 1.

Rahman, Mohammed, William Hoyle, and Karen Tuccillo. "Radon Measurements in New Jersey." Paper presented at the 1988 EPA International Symposium on Radon and Radon Control Technology, Denver, Colo., October 1988.

Reese, John Paul. "New York State Energy Office Radon Update." In *Radon and the Environment*, ed. William Makofske and Michael Edelstein. Park Ridge, N.J.: Noyes Publications, 1988.

Reimer, G. M., et al. "Reconnaissance Approach to Using Geology and Soil-Gas Radon Concentrations for Making Rapid and Preliminary Estimates of Indoor Radon Potential." In *Field Studies of Radon in Rocks, Soils and Water*, ed. L. C. S. Gunderson and R. B. Wanty. U.S. Geological Survey Bulletin 1971. Washington, D.C.: U.S. Government. Printing Office, 1991.

Repace, J. L., and A. H. Lowrey. "A Quantitative Estimate on Non-Smoker's Lung Cancer Risk from Passive Smoking." *Environmental International* 11 (1985): 3–22.

Republican National Committee. *The Contract with America.* New York: Random House, 1994.

RIR. "The North American Radon Association (NARA) Creates Umbrella Association." *Radon Industry Review* 1 (August 1989a): 5.

_____. "Key Technology Streamlines Operations." *Radon Industry Review* 1 (August 1989b): 2.

_____. "EPA Selects Regional Training Centers." *Radon Industry Review* 1 (August 1989c): 1.

_____. "Employee Relations Council Recommends Radon Tests." *Radon Industry Review* 1 (August 1989d): 4.

_____. "Leading Home Builder Takes Lead on Radon Precaution." *Radon Industry Review* 1 (August 1989e): 13, 21.

_____. "NAHB Offers Glimpse of Position on Radon." *Radon Industry Review* 1 (August 1989f): 3.

_____. "Key Policy and Market Drivers in the Radon Industry." *Radon Industry Review* 1 (August 1989g): 1, 14.

_____. "Radon Industry Hunkers Down during the Summer." *Radon Industry Review* 1 (September 1989a): 22.

_____. "What about RMP Seven?" *Radon Industry Review* 1 (September 1989b): 10.

_____. "Radon Resistant Building Subcode Circulated in New Jersey." *Radon Industry Review* 1 (September 1989c): 3.

_____. "The Home Loan Board Looks at Environmental Package." *Radon Industry Review* 1 (September 1989d): 1, 14.

_____. "Florida Radon Industry Bristles." *Radon Industry Review* 1 (September 1989e).

_____. "Radon Industry Political Action Committee Working Capitol Hill." *Radon Industry Review* 1 (October 1989a): 1–6.

_____. "Sears Bows out of Mitigation—For Now." *Radon Industry Review* 1 (October 1989b): 19.

_____. "Florida Turns to Private Trainers." *Radon Industry Review* 1 (October 1989c): 23.

_____. "Indiana Enacts Radon Certification Program." *Radon Industry Review* 1 (October 1989d): 2.

_____. "Proposed State Radon Legislation for 1989." *Radon Industry Review* 1 (October 1989e): 3.

_____. "How Will the Radon Industry Tackle Public Apathy?" *Radon Industry Review* 1 (October 1989f): 1, 14.

_____. "New Jersey Town Mandates Testing and Mitigation." *Radon Industry Review* 1 (October 1989g): 1, 4.

_____. "Ad Council Campaign for Radon Awareness." *Radon Industry Review* 1 (November 1989a): 7.

_____. "Tech/Ops Files Patent Suit." *Radon Industry Review* 1 (November 1989b): 2.

_____. "Radon Political Action Committee Underwritten." *Radon Industry Review* 1 (November 1989c): 18.

_____. "EPA Announces Ad Council Campaign." *Radon Industry Review* 1 (November 1989d): 1, 6.

_____. "Kudos for Les Salmon and the RCPP." *Radon Industry Review* 1 (November 1989e): 4.

_____. "Tort Law Forming Radon Policy." *Radon Industry Review* 1 (November 1989f): 3, 13.

_____. "RMP Round Six Results out to Radon Detection Firms." *Radon Industry Review* 1 (December 1989a): 1.

_____. "Realtors and Radon Policy." *Radon Industry Review* 1 (December 1989b): 1, 19.

_____. "The Future Role of Property Insurance Industry in Radon." *Radon Industry Review* 1 (December 1989c): 22.

_____. "Ad Council Threatens to Pull Spots in Response to Industry Pressure." *Radon Industry Review* 2 (January 1990a): 1.

_____. "Tech/Ops Landauer and REM Working to Settle Dispute." *Radon Industry Review* 2 (January 1990b): 5.

_____. "EPA Published RMP 6 Report." *Radon Industry Review* 2 (February 1990a) .

_____. "Correction Notice." *Radon Industry Review* 2 (February 1990b): 3.

_____. "Ad Council's Radon Campaign Begins Shift into High Gear," *Radon Industry Review* 2 (February 1990c): 3.

Rizzuto, Joseph. "New York State Energy Research and Development Authority Program." In *Radon and the Environment*, ed. William Makofske and Michael Edelstein. Park Ridge, N.J.: Noyes Publications, 1988.

Roberts, Leslie. "Counting on Science at EPA." *Science* 249 (August 10 1990): 616–18.

Robkin, M. A., "Dosimetry." In *Indoor Radon*, ed. D. Bodanksy, M. A. Robkin, and D. R. Stadler. Seattle, Wash.: Radiation Studies Committee, 1987.

Rose, Susan. Interview with author. Denver, Colo., October 1988; also Philadelphia, Pa., April, 4, 1991.

Rowson, David. Interview with author. Washington, D.C., September 27, 1996.

Sachs, Harvey. Letters to Margaret Riley, Pennsylvania DER, July 6, 1982, November 12, 1982, and February 14, 1983.

Sachs, Harvey. "Fraud-Resistant Radon Measurements for Real Estate Transactions." In *Radon and the Environment*, ed. William Makofske and Michael Edelstein. Park Ridge, N.J.: Noyes Publications, 1988.

Salmon, G. L., John MacKinney, John Hooenbeek, and Jed Harrison. "EPA's National Radon Contractor Proficiency Program." Paper presented at the 1991 EPA International Symposium on Radon and Radon Reduction Technology, Philadelphia, Pa., April 1991.

Samet, J. M. "Comparative Dosimetry of Radon in Mines and Homes: An Overview of the NAS Report." In *Proceedings of the 1991 EPA International Symposium on Radon and Radon Reduction Technology.* Philadelphia, Pa., 1991.

Samet, J. M., J. Stolwijk, and S. L. Rose. "Summary: International Workshop on Residential Rn Epidemiology." *Health Physics* 60 (1991): 223–27.

Sandman, Peter. "Communicating Radon Risk: Alerting the Apathetic and Reassuring the Hysterical." In *Radon and the Environment*, ed. William Makofske and Michael Edelstein. Park Ridge, N.J.: Noyes Publications, 1988.

Sandman, Peter, Neil Weinstein, and M. L. Klotz. "Public Response to the Risk from Geological Radon." *Journal of Communication* 37, no. 3 (summer 1987): 93–108.

Saum, D. W. "Mini Fan for SSD Radon Mitigation in New Construction." In *Proceedings of the 1991 EPA International Symposium on Radon and Radon Reduction Technology.* Philadelphia, Pa., April 1991b.

Saum, D. W. and M. C. Osborne. "Radon Mitigation Performance of Passive Stacks in Residential New Construction." In *Proceedings of the 1990 EPA International Symposium on Radon and Radon Reduction Technology.* Atlanta, Ga., 1990.

Saum, David. "EPA Radon Policy and Its Effects on the Radon Industry." In *Proceedings of the 1991 EPA International Symposium on Radon and Radon Reduction Technology.* Philadelphia, Pa., April 1991a.

Scheberle, Denise. "Radon and Asbestos: A Study of Agenda Setting and Causal Stories." *Policy Studies Journal* 22, no. 1 (Spring 1994): 74–86.

Schmidt, Anita. Interview with author. Washington, D.C., September 11, 1996.

Schmitz, Jon. "Pair Suing over Radon Asked Why They Stayed." *Pittsburgh Post-Gazette.* May 7, 1996, A7, A8.

Schneider, Keith. "Uranium Miners Inherit Dispute's Sad Legacy." *New York Times*, January 9, 1990, A 11.

_____. "New View Calls Environmental Policy Misguided." *New York Times*, March 21, 1993a, 1 ,30.

_____. "EPA Proposes Costly Rules to Curb Radon Threat in New Houses." *New York Times*, April 7, 1993b.

Schutz, Donald. "AARST Commitment." *Radon Industry Review* 1 (August 1989): 7.

Scott, Arthur G. "Preventing Radon Entry." In *Radon and Its Decay Products in Indoor Air*, ed. W. W. Nazaroff and A. V. Nero. New York: John Wiley and Sons, 1988a.

_____. "Effect of Indoor Radon Variability on the Duration and Interpretation of Radon Measurements." Paper presented at the 1988 EPA Symposium on Radon and Radon Reduction Technology, Denver, Colo., October 1988b.

Scott, Arthur G. "Site Characterization for Radon Supply Potential: A Progress Review." *Health Physics* 62 (1992): 422–28.

Scott, Arthur G., and A. Robertson. "Precision of Alpha-Track Radon Exposure Estimates Determined from Field Measurements." *Health Physics* 61 (1991): 267–69.

Scripps Howard News Service. "Radon Threat Forgotten, but Not Gone." *(Middletown, New York) Times Herald Record*, December 17, 1991, 29.

Sextro, R. G. "Radon in Dwellings." In *Radon and the Environment*, ed. William Makofske and Michael Edelstein. Park Ridge, N.J.: Noyes Publications, 1988a.

Sextro, R. G. "Soil Permeability and Radon Concentration Measurements and a Technique for Predicting the Radon Source Potential of Soils." In *Proceedings of the*

1988 EPA International Symposium on Radon and Radon Reduction Technology. Denver, Colo., October 1988b.

Sextro, R. G. "Issues in the Use of Short-term Radon Concentration Measurements for Estimating Long-term Exposures." In *Proceedings of the 1990 EPA Symposium on Radon and Radon Reduction Technology.* Atlanta, Ga., February 1990.

————. Interview with author. (*Philadelphia, Pa.*) April 4, 1991.

Shabecoff, Philip. "Radioactive Gas in Soil Raises Concern in Three-State Area." *New York Times,* May 19, 1985, 1, 4.

————. "Issue of Radon: New Focus on Ecology." *New York Times,* September 10, 1986, A24.

————. "E.P.A. Report Says Agency Is Focusing on the Wrong Problems." *New York Times,* February 18, 1988a, B1, B6.

————. "Radon Alert: The EPA Goes after the Carcinogen that Nature Made." *New York Times,* September 18, 1988b, 1, 4.

Shrader-Frechette, K. S. *Risk and Rationality: Philosophical Formations for Populist Reforms.* Berkeley: University of California Press, 1991.

Silverman, Jennifer. "Radon Industry Calls New Citizen's Guide Pretty, but Dissatisfied with EPA Approach." *Indoor Air Review,* September 1992a, 29.

————. "Most Georgia Water Systems Thought to Exceed Proposed EPA Radon Limit." *Indoor Air Review,* December 1992b, 22, 24.

————. "EPA Focuses on Contractor Qualifications, Handling Radon Reducation Systems in New Guide." *Indoor Air Review,* December 1992c, 21–22.

————. "EPA Delists Major Alpha Track Device Maker, Move Provokes Anxiety over RMP Program." *Indoor Air Review,* September 1992d, 1, 32.

————. "EPA Proposes Model Standards, Techniques to Create Radon Resistant Environments in New Buildings." *Indoor Air Review,* May 1993, 23–24.

Slovic, Paul. "Perception of Risk." *Science* 236 (April 17, 1987): 280–85.

Slovic, Paul, Baruch Fischhoff, and Sarah Lichtenstein. "Rating the Risks: The Structure of Expert and Lay Perceptions." In *Radon and the Environment,* ed. William Makofske and Michael Edelstein. Park Ridge, N.J.: Noyes Publications, 1988.

Smay, V. E. "Radon Exclusive—How Dangerous? How Widespread? How You Can Test for It in Your Home—What to Do about It." *Popular Science* 227 (November 1985): 76–81.

Smith, B. M., W. N. Grune, F. B. Higgins, Jr., and J. G. Terrill, Jr. "Natural Radioactivity in Ground Water Supplies in Maine and New Hampshire." *Journal of the American Water Works Association* 53 (1961): 75.

Smith, Mary. Interview with author. Washington, D.C., November 6, 1995.

Smith, V. Kerry, and F. Reed Johnson. "How Do Risk Perceptions Respond to Information? The Case of Radon." *Review of Economics and Statistics* 70, no. 1 (1988): 1–8.

Smith, V. Kerry, William Desvousges, F. Reed Johnson, and Ann Fisher. "Can Public Information Programs Affect Risk Perception?" *Journal of Policy Analysis and Management* 9, no. 1 (1990): 41–59.

Spears, J. W., and M. S. Novak. "Radon Mitigation in New Construction: Four Case Studies." In *Proceedings of the 1988 EPA International Symposium on Radon and Radon Reduction Technology,* Denver, Colo., October 1988.

Steck, D. J. "Statewide Screening Surveys; Screening vs. Long Term Measurements." In *Proceedings of the 1988 EPA International Symposium on Radon and Radon Reduction Technology*. Denver, Colo., October 1988.

——. "A Comparison of EPA Screening Measurements and Annual Rn-222 Concentrations in Statewide Surveys." *Health Physics* 58 (1990): 523–30.

——. "Spatial and Temporal Indoor Radon Variations." *Health Physics* 62 (1992): 351–55.

Steinhausler, F. "Epidemiological Evidence of Radon-Induced Health Risks." In *Radon and Its Decay Products in Indoor Air*, ed. W. W. Nazaroff and A. V. Nero, Jr. New York: John Wiley and Sons, 1988.

Stevens, William. "Big Increase Expected in Radon Pollution Suits." *New York Times*, September 28, 1986, 54.

——. "What Really Threatens the Environment?" *New York Times*, January 29, 1991a, C4.

——. "EPA Moves to Change Environment Priorities." *New York Times*, January 26, 1991b, L11.

Stone, Richard. "EPA Analysis of Radon in Water Is Hard to Swallow." *Science* 261 (September 17, 1993): 1514–16.

Strecklow, Steve. "As Radon Levels Soar in Pa. Homes, Action Lags." *Philadelphia Inquirer*, March 20, 1985b, A01.

——. "PE Donates $40,000 to Study Radon in Home." *Philadelphia Inquirer*, April 17, 1985b, B03.

——. "Record Level of Radon Is Found in Pa. House." *Philadelphia Inquirer*, October 23, 1985c, B01.

——. "Penna. to Aid Families Hurt by Radon Leak." *Philadelphia Inquirer*, October 24, 1985d, U04.

——. "Pa. Aid May Not Clear Homes of Radon." *Philadelphia Inquirer*, November 6, 1985e, A01.

——. "A Family That Is Living with Fear Radon Still an Unwanted Guest in Pa. Home." *Philadelphia Inquirer*, November 21, 1985f, B01.

——. "No Stranger to Radon, and Now a Dabbler in Its Detection." *Philadelphia Inquirer*, September 15, 1988, B01.

Strong, Terry. "Radon Status Report No. 1." State of Washington Department of Social and Health Services, December 31, 1986.

——. Letter to Bob Rolfs, State of Washington Department of Social and Health Services, January 7, 1987.

Sullivan, Joseph. "House Sale Affected by Radon." *New York Times*. October 7, 1990, 13.

Suomela, M., and H. Kahlos. "Radiative Exposure Following Ingestion of Radon-222 Rich Water." *Health Physics* 23 (1972): 641–52.

Swanwick, Kathy. "How Real Is Radon Risk?" *(Middletown) Times Herald Record*, February 25, 1986, 1, 3.

Swift, Robert B. "Pennsylvania Steps up Battle with Radon." *(Middletown) Times Herald Record*, March 27, 1987, 22.

Tanner, A. B. "Measurement of Radon Availability from Soil." In *Geologic Causes of Natural Radionuclide Anomalies, Proceedings of the GEORAD Conference, St.*

Louis, Mo, ed. M.A. Marikos and R.H. Hansman. Missouri Department of Natural Resources, Division of Geology and Land Survey Speculative Publication No. 4, April 21–22, 1987, 139–46.

Thomas, Lee M. "Environmental Regulation: Challenges We Face." *EPA Journal* 14 (March 1988): 2–3.

Thurman, Ken. "State Scientists Debate Radon Threat in Voorheesville." *(Albany) Sunday Times Union,* December 7, 1986, c1.

Tomasek, L., S. C. Darby, A. J. Swerdlow, V. Placek, and E. Kunz. "Radiation Exposure and Cancers Other Than Lung Cancer among Uranium Miners in West Bohemia." *Lancet* 341 (1993): 919–23.

Toomey, David, and David Sykes. "The Legal Aspect of Radon." In *Radon and the Environment,* ed. William Makofske and Michael Edelstein. Park Ridge, N.J.: Noyes Publications, 1988.

Tuccillo, Karen, Elaine Makatura, and William Hoyle. "The New Jersey Radon Outreach Program." Paper presented at the 1988 EPA International Symposium on Radon and Radon Reduction Technology, Denver, Colo., October 1988.

Turk, B. H., R. J. Prill, W. J. Fisk, D. T. Grimsrud, B. A. Moed, and R. G. Sextro. "Radon and Remedial Action in Spokane River Valley Residences." Report LBL-21399, Lawrence Berkeley Laboratory, Berkeley, Calif., 1986.

VanLaningham, Robert. "How the National Concrete Masonry Association Views Radon." *Radon News Digest,* September 1988, 8.

Varady, Kathy (and family). Interview with author. Colebrookdale Township, Pa., June 29, 1986; also September 21, 1996.

Vermont Agency of Natural Resources. "Environment 1991: Risks to Vermont and Vermonters, A Report of the Public Advisory Committee, the Strategy for Vermont's Third Century." Agency of Natural Resources, 103 South Main St., Center Building, Waterbury, Vt. 05676. July, 1991.

von Uxekull, Thure. "Ambient and Environment—or Which Is the Correct Perspective on Nature." Paper presented at the International Association for the Study of People and Their Physical Surroundings, West Berlin, West Germany, July 25–29, 1984.

Vroman, Barbara. "The Original Radon House." *San Jose Mercury News,* September 14, 1988, 10B.

Vyner, Henry. *Invisible Trauma: The Psychosocial Effects of the Invisible Environmental Contaminants.* Boston: Lexington Books, 1988.

Wagner, Dennis. Interview with author. Washington, D.C., July 11, 26, 1993.

Wagner, Dennis, and Mark Dickson. "Radon Media Campaign." Paper presented at the 1991 EPA International Symposium on Radon and Radon Reduction Technology, Philadelphia, Pa., April 1991.

Wallace, Lance, Edo Pellizzari, Tyler Hartwell, Charles Sparacino, Roy Whitmore, Linda Sheldon, Harvy Zelon, and Rebecca Perritt. "The TEAM Study: Personal Exposures to Toxic Substances in Air, Drinking Water, and Breath of 400 Residents of New Jersey, North Carolina and North Dakota." *Environmental Research* 43 (1987): 290–307.

Wartenberg, Daniel, and Caron Chess. "Risky Business: The Inexact Art of Hazard Assessment." *The Sciences,* March/April 1992, 17–21.

Washington State Energy Office. "Proposed Northwest Residential Radon Code: Draft No. 2." March 30, 1989.

Watras, Stanley (and family). Interview with author. Colebrookdale Township, Pa., August 7, 1987; also September 22, 1996, and January 31, 1997.

Weart, Spencer. *Nuclear Fear: A History of Images*. Cambridge: Harvard University Press, 1988.

Weinstein, Neil. "Response of the New Jersey Public to the Risk from Radon." In *Radon and the Environment*, ed. William Makofske and Michael Edelstein. Park Ridge, N.J.: Noyes Publications, 1988.

Weinstein, Neil, Peter Sandman, and M. L. Klotz. "Public Response to the Risk from Radon, 1986." Final Report, January 1987a.

_____. "Public Response to the Risk from Geologic Radon." *Journal of Communication* 37, no. 3 (1987b): 93–108.

Weinstein, Neil, Peter Sandman, and Nancy Roberts. "Communicating Effectively about Risk Magnitudes." Report to the U.S. Environmental Protection Agency, September 12, 1989a.

_____. "Public Response to the Risk from Radon, 1988–89." Final Report of Research Contract C29418, NJDEP, November 1989b.

_____. "Determinants of Self-Protective Behavior: Home Radon Testing." *Journal of Applied Social Psychology* 20, no. 10 (1990): 783–801.

Wilson, Frank, et al. v. Marshall Koval et al. Amended Summons 88201958-9 filed before the Superior Court, State of Washington, County of Spokane, May 30, 1989.

Wing, M. A. and H. M. Mardis. "The Radon/Radon Progeny Measurement Proficiency Program: A Voluntary, Quality Assurance Program." Supplement to Proceedings of the Second APCA International Specialty Conference: Indoor Radon II, Cherry Hill, N.J., April 1987.

Wyckoff, P. L. "Inaction, Mistakes Prolong Crisis in 3 Towns." *(Newark) Sunday Star-Ledger*, March 29, 1987, 1, 30, 31.

Yallow, Rosalee. Testimony presented to the New York State Minority Committee on Radon, New York City, November 22, 1988.

Yeager, W. M., R. M. Lucas, K. A. Daum, E. Sensintaffar, S. Poppell, L. Feldt, and M. Clarkin. "A Performance Evaluation Study of Three Types of Alpha-Track Detector Radon Monitors." *Health Physics* 60, (1991): 507–15.

Wlazelek, Ann. "If You're a Worrier, Radon Can Make Stress Worse." *(Allentown, Pa.) Morning Call,* September 9. 1986, B5, B8.

Zanowiak, Elizabeth. Interview with author. Washington, D.C, September 24, 1996.

Index

Abelson, Philip, 64, 76n7, 235
Ad Council, 182, 206–7, 209–11, 225, 277, 290
AEC (Atomic Energy Commission), 38
Agricola, 35
Air Chek, 176, 183–84
air exchange. *See* energy conservation and radon
Alar, 204, 210, 231n3, 296, 301
alpha track detectors. *See* radon testing devices
alum-shale bedrock. *See* Sweden
American Association of Radon Scientists and Technologists (AARST), 178–79, 183, 190, 275
American Atcom, 22
American Cancer Society, 83, 204
American College of Preventive Medicine, 275, 277
American Lung Association (ALA), 57, 202, 204, 206, 215, 272, 275, 277
American Medical Association (AMA), 57, 202, 206, 277
American Neighborhoods, 276
American Public Health Association, 275
American Radon Association (ARA), 178
American Society of Testing and Materials (ASTM), 163, 251
Argonne National Laboratory, 45, 280n1
ARIX, 20, 26–7
asbestos, 71
ASHRAE (American Society of Heating, Refrigeration, and Air Conditioning Engineers), 75n6
Associated Press, 76n8, 272

Association of Asian and Pacific Community Health Organizations (AAPCHO), 219, 276
Association of State and Territorial Health Officials (ASTHO), 277
Atomic Energy Act, 75n5
Auburn University, 57, 183
Axelrod, David, 267

Barnes, James, 49, 59, 66, 70, 73–74
Beck, Ulrich, 311
BEIR IV, 87
BEIR VI, 84
Belanger, William, 15, 45
Belgium, 75n6
Belzer, Richard, 233–34
Bergen Record, 212
bergkrankheit (mountain sickness). *See* lung cancer
Bhophal, 236
Bloomsburg, Pa., 45
BOCA (Building Officials and Code Administrators International), 260n17, n19
Boyertown, Pa., 3, 20–22
Boyertown Area Times, 100
Boyle, Valerie, 219
BPA (Bonneville Power Authority), 44, 75n6, 160, 250, 254, 271–72, 281n7
Brafford v. Susquehanna Corp., 253
Brennan, Terry, 48, 145, 159, 166, 314
Broadhead, Bill, 229, 255
Browner, Carol, 217, 307
building codes, 42, 162–64
Bush administration. *See* Reagan, President Ronald, and Reagan/Bush administrations
Butte, Mont., 39, 44

About the Authors

Michael R. Edelstein is professor of environmental psychology at Ramapo College of New Jersey. Since 1979, his research has focused on psycho-social impacts of contamination and environmental hazard issues. His publications in this area include *Contaminated Communities: The Social and Psychological Impacts of Residential Toxic Exposure* (Westview, 1988). Current work focuses on environmental impacts on indigenous peoples and more broadly on issues of ecological literacy, sustainable societies, and ecopsychology. Edelstein is additionally president of a nonprofit environmental organization, Orange Environment, Inc., based in Orange County, New York.

William J. Makofske is professor of environmental physics at Ramapo College of New Jersey. After a decade of nuclear physics research, since 1974 his attention has focused broadly on the impacts of energy production and the development of renewable energy sources. His books include *Radon and the Environment* (coauthored with Michael Edelstein; Noyes Publications, 1988) and *Technology and Global Environmental Issues* (coauthored with E. Karlin; HarperCollins, 1995). Makofske was a coauthor of the New York State Energy Office (NYSEO) manual *Reducing Indoor Radon* (1989), and for several years he taught radon mitigation training and laboratory testing courses offered through the NYSEO. His current work focuses on the issues of energy and climate change.